PURCHASING & SUPPLY CHAIN MANAGEMENT

Analysis, Strategy, Planning and Practice

For Ineke, Vivianne and Marijn,
who represent the most lovely and
most skillful negotiators I know ...

FOURTH EDITION

PURCHASING & SUPPLY CHAIN MANAGEMENT

Analysis, Strategy, Planning and Practice

ARJAN J. VAN WEELE Eindhoven University of Technology, The Netherlands

THOMSON

Australia • Canada • Mexico • Singapore • Spain • United Kingdom • United States

Purchasing & Supply Chain Management: Analysis, Strategy, Planning and Practice

Copyright © Thomson Learning 2005

The Thomson logo is a registered trademark used herein under licence.

For more information, contact Thomson Learning, High Holborn House, 50-51 Bedford Row, London WC1R 4LR or visit us on the World Wide Web at:
http://www.thomsonlearning.co.uk

British Library Cataloguing-in-Publication Data
A catalogue record for this book is available from the British Library

ISBN-13: 978-1-84480-024-7
ISBN-10: 1-84480-024-5

First edition published by Chapman & Hall 1996
Second edition published 2000 by Thomson Learning
Third edition published 2002 by Thomson Learning
Reprinted in 2002 by Thomson Learning
This edition published by Thomson Learning 2005
Reprinted 2005 by Thomson Learning

Typeset by Photoprint, Torquay, Devon

Printed in Croatia by Zrinski d.d.

BRIEF CONTENTS

CONTENTS

LIST OF MEMOS

ACKNOWLEDGEMENTS

The author and publishers would like to thank the following reviewers who provided invaluable commentary to the author before preparing his manuscript for this new edition:

Dr N.D. Caldwell, Research Officer CRiSPS, School of Management, University of Bath.

Mr Gino Franco, Senior Lecturer in Purchasing and Supply Chain Management, Derbyshire Business School, University of Derby.

Dr Steve New, Säid Business School, University of Oxford.

Mr Simon Snowden, Program Director, e-Business Division, University of Liverpool Management School.

PREFACE TO THE 4TH EDITION

I t is almost impossible to monitor the developments which are going on in most management disciplines nowadays. This is certainly true for the area of purchasing and supply management and was the main reason to review the text of this book.

Over the past few years purchasing and supply management has met an ever-increasing interest. Not only from professional purchasing managers: the interest from general managers, functional managers and business consultants is stronger than ever before. Many professionals have become aware that purchasing in general and supplier relationships in particular represent a fantastic area for improvement. More recently, the number of articles on purchasing management issues has increased as has the acceptance of purchasing and supply management as a key area for improving competitive power.

The business chain is as strong as its weakest link and one of the important links in the business chain is the purchasing and supply function. Many top managers are becoming increasingly aware of how much money is involved in purchasing decisions. In general, only the money related to the purchase of production materials is considered. However, in practice, large sums are also spent on investment goods, and we must not forget the purchase of all kinds of services. In many industrial companies the purchasing share takes up more than half of the cost of goods sold and in most trading companies this figure is even higher! This implies that purchasing decision making has a great influence on the company result: one dollar saved in purchasing costs contributes directly to the company's bottom line. However, the reverse is also true. A non-professional, amateur approach to purchasing decisions can readily lead to overlooking cost-savings opportunities, which in the end may lead to a significant financial loss.

In their efforts to arrive at a sustainable competitive advantage managers increasingly differentiate between core and non-core activities. Companies try to focus on those core activities which provide them with a competitive edge in their end-user markets. Activities which have been defined as non-core are subcontracted to suppliers. As a consequence of this development the effect of purchasing decisions on the company's financial results is growing in many sectors.

When dealing with suppliers suboptimization must be prevented because it is very tempting to make price the central issue in negotiations. Strategic purchasing and supply management is more than just negotiating a deal with suppliers. It is about managing supplier relationships in such a way that suppliers actively support the company's overall business strategy and value proposition. It is about fostering a climate where suppliers are challenged to continuously improve their performance and value added contribution. It is about integrating suppliers into the company's overall business processes to boost productivity. It is about developing the physical and information infrastructure to enable these new ways of working.

This book attempts to introduce the reader to some important principles underlying purchasing and supply management. The ideas are derived from my experience as a management consultant, trainer and academic, obtained from working with a large number of companies in Europe. Regarding its structure and presentation, the underlying idea is that this book should be both balanced, easy to read and easy to teach.

The idea of writing this book dates back a number of years. The success of the original version which appeared in Dutch in 1988, together with the many positive reactions which

I received, convinced me that a translation would be worthwhile. This version, in English, based on the many reactions I have received since the book was published, appeals to a large audience. It is used at universities and business schools as a leading textbook in many countries. Hence, I decided to make the investment and to review it carefully. I hope you will find even more value in using it.

Those who are familiar with its contents will soon find that this fourth edition cannot be used next to the third edition. Too many topics needed to be rewritten and updated. This is true for Chapter 1 where more space is given to the changes going on in the business context of organizations and on how these impact on the role and position of purchasing and supply management. It is also true for Chapter 6, where we have included new material on the value of the Internet for purchasing market research. Chapter 7 is completely new and covers the important topic of outsourcing and risk management. New material on developing leveraged purchasing strategies and portfolio-management has been included in Chapter 8. Chapter 12 is devoted to material on supply chain management, some of which was covered by other chapters in the first edition. The supply chain perspective, and the role purchasing plays in it, is reinforced in this chapter. Chapter 13 has been significantly updated and brought in line with how large companies organize for purchasing today. In particular, the topic of how to create advantage through fostering purchasing synergies in a multinational company is elaborated. Chapter 17, 'Buying for retail companies' has been completely rewritten and now contains discussions on modern retail concepts such as efficient consumer response, collaborative planning, forecasting and replenishment, vendor managed inventory and radio frequency identification. Chapter 18 also contains a new text on purchasing and facilities management and the buying of services. The latter has developed rapidly into a key area of concern to most purchasing managers. Chapter 19 on public procurement is updated to reflect the latest changes in the EC Directives. Throughout the text, some introductory cases have been replaced and updated as have the memos and other illustrations. Teaching materials and background reading materials can be found on our website www.thomsonlearning.co.uk/businessand management/vanweele4

Writing a book can be compared to choosing from a restaurant menu in that it is often more difficult to decide what *not* to include. In this sense the book displays several personal choices and some subjects may not have received sufficient attention. In due course we would appreciate hearing from you, the reader, as to whether you agree with the selection we have made.

Realization of this book has been made possible thanks to the enthusiastic support of several people, and its contents have been enriched as a result of their critical and constructive comments. Thanks to the diligence of Thomson Learning, this book can be presented to you in its present form. Jennifer Pegg and Jim Collins encouraged and supported me in reviewing the book again and worked on the fourth edition. Thanks to them this edition is published in its present form: a new layout which provides for better and more colorful reading. Through her meticulous work and sharp eye for detail, Claire Martin prevented me from making unnecessary errors in the text. She put a lot of work into making this a flawless book. I am grateful to the professional staff for the meticulous examination of the text, for the many improvements that have been made and for the valuable suggestions concerning the layout and design.

I thank the many practitioners I have met over the years and for whom I was happy to work as a consultant. Without exception, this work gave me the feeling that purchasing and supply management is a challenging area to work in and that it represents a business area of still unknown potential for companies. Many thanks also to my students, who always prove to be a challenging and rewarding audience to work for. Special thanks to Martin Kampinga who provided useful material on outsourcing for the new Chapter 7. I would also like to thank my colleagues at the Institute for Purchasing and Supply Development at Eindhoven University of Technology for their support, endeavor and superb working climate. Especially, I would like to thank the Dutch Association of Purchasing Management (NEVI) in The Netherlands, who for so many years have consistently supported me in my academic teaching activities and research projects.

Finally, my wife Ineke encouraged me to rewrite this book. She knew, as no other, the sacrifices which this personal project would entail for my beloved family. Ineke, Vivianne and Marijn accepted these and gave me constant moral support. It is thanks to them that I found the time and the inspiration necessary to complete this task. It is undoubtedly their book too.

Prof dr Arjan van Weele
NEVI Chair Purchasing and Supply Management
Eindhoven University of Technology

Maarssen, The Netherlands
February, 2004

GUIDED TOUR

THE ROLE OF PURCHASING IN THE SUPPLY CHAIN

Learning objectives

Bullet points at the start of each chapter focus on the main ideas that need to be understood in each chapter. ——————

LEARNING OBJECTIVES

After studying this chapter you should understand the following:

- How changes in the business context affect business strategy and the supply strategies of organizations.
- The role and importance of the purchasing and supply function in business.
- The difference between concepts such as ordering, buying, purchasing, procurement, supply chain management and value chain management and how these are interrelated.
- The most important tasks and responsibilities related to the purchasing and supply function.
- The different products which may be sourced from suppliers.

Case studies

These appear at the start of each chapter to foreground the main concepts of the chapter in a real-world situation. ——————

CASE STUDY   BRITISH AIRWAYS FLIES TOWARDS $996 SAVINGS GOAL

Suffering from heavy international competition and a growing field of small European and US-based competitors offering no frills service and cheap fares, British Airways in October 2001 decided to review its operations. The company needed to improve its operating margin dramatically to an unprecedented 10 per cent. To get to that margin at existing revenue rates, the company determined that it would have to cut costs by $996 million.

Headcount was targeted for more than two-thirds of the cost cuts and BA unveiled plans to cut 13 000 people or 20 per cent of its staff, including members of its purchasing operations. Another area of cost reduction focused on how BA captures customers. Rather than paying high fees to travel agents and other services to book customers on BA flights, the company designed a new pricing strategy to push traffic to a self-serve web model for booking flights.

But cutting costs alone was not enough. 'We realized that rather than just go through a cost-cutting exercise, we needed to fundamentally rethink the business model,' says Jonathan Counsell, head of strategy and performance at BA. Standardized procurement processes were seen as one way to transform BA's newly trimmed procurement staff of 200 to become more strategic in sourcing the airline's $6 billion annual buy, which is largely made up of fuel, user charges, in-flight products such as catering and engineering, and airport services. The purchasing operations at BA are centralized; its procurement director reports directly to the CFO.

BA outlined its major goals in its procurement overhaul. First, it wanted to reduce total costs by more than $250 million. Second, it wanted to increase its online ordering to 80 per cent of all materials and services. Next it wanted to reduce procurement transaction costs to $15 each. Also,

3

Memo

Provide interesting insights into the key issues that are being discussed in terms of a theory/concept or a practical example.

- Environmental issues and business integrity. Environmental problems in many European countries become more and more prevalent. National governments have become more strict in their regulations on this point. In Germany, for instance, strict regulations on industrial and consumer packaging recently came into force. In due course all superfluous packaging needs to be avoided (e.g. blister packaging and the box-packaging of toothpaste); aluminium cans are charged and need to be recollected. Manufacturers of packaging will increasingly be held responsible for its disposal after use. This is one reason why Volkswagen constructed its latest Golf (America: Rabbit) in such a way that the different parts and components can be easily disassembled and reprocessed at the end of the car's lifespan. Volkswagen has even founded its own rework facilities for this purpose. Apart from environmental issues there is a growing pressure from the public that products should be clean, and come from countries with free trade. Child labor has become an issue of particular concern, implying that buyers should ensure that the products they buy come from sources of high integrity. These issues pose new and important challenges to purchasing.

Memo 1.3 provides an illustration of some of the challenges that lie ahead for buyers and purchasing and supply chain managers.

It can be appreciated from this discussion that purchasing and supply represents a business area which is being confronted with many changes and challenges. Most of the problems, however, require intensive interaction, communication and cooperation with other disciplines in the organization. Purchasing and supply is developing increasingly as a business function which cuts across other disciplines. Managing the purchasing and supply function requires a thorough understanding of the purchasing processes that take place within the organization. Only then can these challenges be dealt with effectively

MEMO 1.3   WHAT'S AHEAD?

As supply chain strategies mature, a major part of a business will involve managing the external value supply chain. Important will be the need to manage costs strategically at all levels of the supply chain. Supply managers will find they are doing more business with outside suppliers than inside ones. They will be working much more with Tier 1 and Tier 2 suppliers to take costs out of products. They will require ongoing development, cost reduction, and innovation on a collaborative basis among all participants in the supply chain.

Many supply chain managers will be deeply involved in building e-sourcing and supply portfolios. Many will be forced to make more informed decisions about whether to use industry-sponsored consortia, build private exchanges, or use markets. Many will need sophisticated assortments of e-sourcing, supply, and collaboration tools. They will need to do more in the way of building value-chain models to understand both product and logistics costs as well as technology. They will need to decide where research, development and design will occur in the value chain.

Supply chain leaders over the next five years will also need to decide the extent to which their companies create unique designs or standardize, and at what levels in the product or service they do these things. Creating entirely unique designs risks creation of production difficulties and/or features that don't mean anything to customers. The ideal will be to standardize – at the right level – and make unique only what is important to the customer. Most companies have a long way to go in making this work on a consistent basis.

Source: Monczka and Morgan, Purchasing, 6 June, 2002, pp. 26–28.

To be able to outsource, excellent suppliers are needed, referred to by some companies as world-class suppliers, or best-in-class suppliers. More and more suppliers are professional enough to deliver complete functional units or subsystems with the required quality, flexibility and innovativeness. The key to strategic success for many firms in the future will be their coalition with the world's best suppliers, product designers, advertising agencies, distribution channels, financial houses, or other outside sources. Nike has served for some time as a nice example, since this highly successful company concentrates on design, marketing, and distribution, while virtually all production of its sporting goods lines is made through co-manufacturing arrangements with suppliers. However, over the past years other companies, like Dell and Cisco, have followed Nike's example.

Given the pressure that consumers and some industrial manufacturers exert on their suppliers, companies increasingly are organizing their activities around processes which are relevant for their customers, rather than functions. The functional organization gradually is being replaced by the process organization. By process we mean a set of activities that, taken together, produce a value to a customer. Hammer and Champy (1993) suggest that by adopting a process orientation we need to look at the entire process beyond organizational boundaries. In these companies staff actually may work for several managers, making the traditional one-line-of-command obsolete. More and more work is being done in cross-functional teams or cross-departmental project teams or even joint customer-supplier teams. Employees are encouraged to take the initiative and to collaborate with their peers to solve problems rather than to await instructions from their departmental managers. Later in this book we will see that the process orientation and cross functional teams are very powerful concepts in the area of purchasing and supply management.

THE ROLE OF PURCHASING IN THE VALUE CHAIN

In many business strategies the concept of value chain management plays a central role, therefore this subject is elaborated on in this section. There will be an explanation of what value chain management is. When describing the role and position of the purchasing and supply function in industrial companies, the value chain of Porter (1985) is taken as a term of reference (see Figure 1.1).

The value chain in Figure 1.1 is composed of value activities and a margin which is achieved by these activities. Value activities can be divided into physically and technically different groups of activities. Porter differentiates between primary activities and support activities. Primary activities are those which are directed at the physical transformation and handling of the final products which the company delivers to its customers. As can be seen from Figure 1.1, distribution to the customer and providing services are parts of these primary activities.

Support activities enable and support the primary activities. They can be directed at supporting one of the primary activities as well as supporting the whole primary process. Porter differentiates between five generic categories of primary activities (1985, pp. 39–40).

- Inbound logistics. These activities are related to receiving, storing and disseminating inputs to the product, such as materials handling, warehousing, inventory control, vehicle scheduling and returns to suppliers.
- Operations. Activities associated with transforming inputs into the final product, such as machining, packaging, assembly, equipment maintenance, testing, printing and facility operations.

ONLINE TEACHING AND LEARNING RESOURCES:

Visit the companion website for *Purchasing and Supply Chain Management: Analysis, Strategy, Practice and Planning* 4th edition to find valuable further teaching and learning material for both students and lecturers:

www.thomsonlearning.co.uk/businessandmanagement/vanweele4

For students:

- Further reading and literature references to help you develop your understanding of each topic in the text
- Web links to all case companies and other relevant sources of information
- Learning objectives for each chapter to support your progress and understanding

For lecturers:

- A password protected site
- Instructor's Manual with teaching notes containing helpful tips and hints for answering questions that appear in the text.
- PowerPoint™ slides of the key ideas and illustrations in the textbook.

SUPPLEMENTARY RESOURCES:

Online Courses:

All of the web material is available in a format that is compatible with virtual learning environments such as Blackboard and WebCT. This version of the product is only available from your Thomson sales representative.

INTRODUCTION

PURCHASING AND SUPPLY MANAGEMENT ON THE MOVE

During the past years purchasing and supply management as a discipline has changed considerably in many companies. This is reflected in the increased attention this discipline is receiving from business managers and practitioners. Considering the amount of money generally involved in the preparation and execution of purchasing and supply decisions, this is not a surprise. An effective and efficient purchasing and supply function can make an important contribution to company results. However, there is more. As a result of the implementation of improvement programs in engineering, manufacturing and logistics management, many companies feel the need to improve relationships with suppliers. These relationships necessarily should result in lead time reduction in new product development, and just-in-time delivery and zero defects on components. More than that these relationships should result in a better value proposition on the company's end user markets. Traditionally, the purchasing department acts as the intermediary which records the agreements with suppliers on these issues and supervises their fulfillment. This traditional role, however, is changing rapidly as can be seen from the purchasing practices in some major, leading edge companies. Moving away from their traditional, operational roles, purchasing and supply managers are assuming more strategic roles in their organizations, focusing on getting better performance from suppliers and the active management of supplier relationships.

These are a few important reasons why management is becoming increasingly interested in purchasing and supply management as a business discipline.

WHY THIS BOOK?

Compared with other management, relatively little academic research has been undertaken in the area of purchasing and supply management. This explains why there is quite a gap in the development of a solid body of knowledge compared with other disciplines in business administration. As a result, it is far from simple to disseminate knowledge across organizations concerning this discipline. Most handbooks on purchasing are of American origin and date back to the 1950s. Fortunately, some new textbooks covering modern purchasing practices have become available during the last decade. Most of these, however, have been written from a truly academic background and insufficiently cover the developments which are at present taking place in the purchasing and supply practices of leading edge companies. Practical descriptions of purchasing situations, which can serve as a learning vehicle and study material for students, are few. This contrasts with disciplines such as marketing, financing, organizational behavior and other management disciplines, where many pragmatic textbooks exist.

It is gratifying that several business schools, polytechnics and academic institutions have decided to include purchasing and supply management in their curriculum. This initiative has no chance of success, however, if there is no effective and up-to-date supportive material. This book aims to fill that need.

INTENDED AUDIENCE

This book is intended for those who are interested in purchasing and supply management in the broadest sense. Its contents aim to provide an in-depth discussion of purchasing and supply issues, both from a strategic and managerial perspective. Reading this book will not make you a buyer nor a purchasing manager. In this the text differs from the more practitioner-oriented literature.

In particular this book is intended for:

- Polytechnic and academic students in business administration and industrial engineering who want to specialize in business strategy, manufacturing strategy and/or supply chain management.

- Professional managers in trade and industry, active in purchasing and/or supply chain management, who are interested in opportunities for improving the effectiveness and efficiency of the purchasing and supply function in their companies.

- Participants in management development programs in the area of strategic management, manufacturing and supply chain management.

- Account managers and industrial sales representatives who in their professional capacity regularly meet with professional buyers, and who are interested in the way these buyers execute their tasks.

- Those who supervise purchasing staff directly or indirectly, and who come from a non-purchasing background and are interested in the latest developments in the area of purchasing.

FRAMEWORK

The book has been developed using the following principles.

- Strategic management perspective. In this book the subject of purchasing and supply management is presented as an essential link of the business system. This business system is only as strong as its weakest link. The way purchasing and supply management is executed or should be executed is presented from a strategic management perspective. This implies, for example, that attention is given to subjects such as how company objectives may influence purchasing and supply strategies and policies; how purchasing and supply strategies should support overall business strategy; how to develop these strategies; how to execute them; how to manage the purchasing process; and how to monitor and manage purchasing performance.

- Practical orientation. Business administration and industrial engineering are concerned with analysing and solving practical business problems. For this reason, the various subjects are discussed from a practical point of view. This book does not aim to transform the reader into a professional buyer. The intention is to introduce the reader to the discipline and familiarize him/her with the key concepts.

- Scientific basis. In discussing the subject matter, repeated reference is made to existing management literature. In this way the individual reader can broaden his/her orientation if he or she so desires. When possible, views on purchasing issues are illustrated with research results from national and international specialist literature.

- Identical structure of each chapter. Every chapter is alike in structure and encompasses:
  - learning objectives;
  - introductory case study to illustrate the practical relevance of the subject;
  - introduction which provides a survey of the most important subjects which will be discussed in the chapter;
  - body text explaining the core concepts and techniques;
  - practical illustrations and memos to emphasize certain subjects in a chapter;
  - summary at the end of each chapter;
  - assignments for classroom discussion, if desired.

STRUCTURE

The book is divided into three sections, each containing a number of chapters. The overall structure is presented in Figure 0.1.

Section i: Analysis is aimed at getting acquainted with the discipline. The key concepts and terms are presented here.

Chapter 1 focuses on the role and significance of the purchasing function for industrial companies. This is done by describing the purchasing role in the company's value chain. Further, definitions of some important terms and concepts are provided. In the remainder of the book a clear distinction will be made between the activities of the purchasing department and the purchasing function. The second term, as we will see, has a broader meaning than the first. An active, market-oriented purchasing policy can make a large contribution to innovation and quality improvement. This chapter also discusses the differences in the purchasing function of industrial companies, trade and retail companies and government institutions and provides a framework for the rest of the book.

Chapter 2 addresses the buying behavior of organizations. The major differences between the buying behavior of consumers and organizations are discussed. Several stages may be distinguished in the decision-making process regarding organizational buying behavior. These are illustrated by presenting a purchasing process model, in which each of the steps is briefly described. Various models of organizational buying behavior, developed in the (industrial) marketing literature, are also presented. In this way the reader will gain insight into the complexity which characterizes many purchasing decisions in organizations.

The purchasing process model is elaborated in Chapter 3. First, we discuss how to arrive at a consistent purchasing order specification, which serves as the basis for requesting a quotation. Next, we describe all activities required in order to arrive at a systematic supplier selection. Major aspects of contracting are then examined. Various subjects which should be considered in making a contractual agreement with suppliers are discussed in depth. Finally we pay attention to how to order and expedite. All these subjects are dealt with from the buyer's point of view.

Chapter 4 deals with the subject of markets and products. First, we focus on the different types of markets that buyers encounter. Second, several specific characteristics are described, related to the purchase of materials, components, supplies for maintenance, repair and operating supplies, investment goods and services.

Chapter 5 covers the purchasing management process. Purchasing practices vary in different organizations, depending not only on the strategic importance of purchasing, but also on management's view of purchasing. In order to manage purchasing effectively, management must pay attention and give substance to every element in the purchasing management process. This chapter concludes with a discussion on how purchasing and supply management develops within organizations over time.

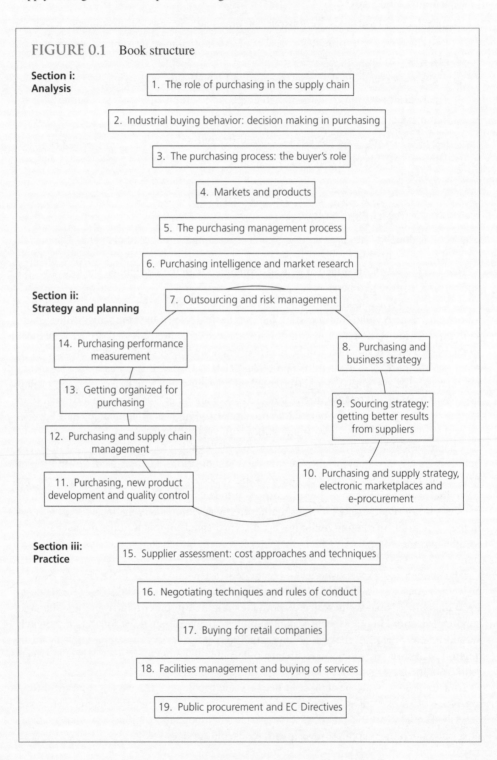

FIGURE 0.1   Book structure

Section i:
Analysis

1. The role of purchasing in the supply chain

2. Industrial buying behavior: decision making in purchasing

3. The purchasing process: the buyer's role

4. Markets and products

5. The purchasing management process

6. Purchasing intelligence and market research

Section ii:
Strategy and planning

7. Outsourcing and risk management

14. Purchasing performance measurement

8. Purchasing and business strategy

13. Getting organized for purchasing

9. Sourcing strategy: getting better results from suppliers

12. Purchasing and supply chain management

11. Purchasing, new product development and quality control

10. Purchasing and supply strategy, electronic marketplaces and e-procurement

Section iii:
Practice

15. Supplier assessment: cost approaches and techniques

16. Negotiating techniques and rules of conduct

17. Buying for retail companies

18. Facilities management and buying of services

19. Public procurement and EC Directives

Chapter 6 deals with purchasing intelligence and market research. The purchasing department is an important observation post for the company on its supply markets. In particular, this chapter discusses ways to organize purchasing intelligence. How to conduct purchasing market research will become clear in this chapter. Extensive attention is given to how the Internet can be used to generate purchasing market information.

Section ii: Strategy and planning discusses in detail the elements of the purchasing management process.

Purchasing's strategic role is discussed in Chapter 7. Outsourcing and risk assessment are the prime topics of this chapter. Attention is given to the growing trend towards outsourcing. Many companies decide nowadays to focus on what they can do best and those activities that provide them with a competitive edge in their end-user markets. Non-core activities are increasingly outsourced to specialist suppliers. This is, however, not without risk, as companies can become too dependent on their suppliers. This chapter deals with the issue of how outsourcing may be structured in a company, the underlying change processes that are required and how companies can reduce their risk profile *vis-à-vis* their suppliers.

Chapter 8 focuses on how to design effective purchasing strategies. Attention is given to the issue of how purchasing strategies can be linked to the overall business strategy of the company. Mirroring some strategic concepts that have been developed in marketing, a purchasing portfolio approach is presented on which four basic, differentiated supplier strategies are based.

In Chapter 9 the central issue is how to get better results from suppliers. Major changes which are occurring in the relationship between industrial companies and their suppliers are described. It will become clear from this chapter that suppliers do not always act in the interest of their customers. Hence, an active approach to the management of supplier relationships is required. This chapter explains how companies may develop such an approach.

Modern supply strategies need to be grounded in a sound information structure. During the past few years a number of new IT-supported solutions have become available to purchasing managers. Among them are reverse auctions, electronic catalogs, ordering and payment solutions and electronic marketplaces. Chapter 10 discusses the functionality of these solutions to buyers and also points out what organizational conditions should be in place to implement them successfully. Compared to the previous edition new material on e-auctions can be found here.

The purchasing function has a complex network of relations in the company because it maintains relationships with nearly all departments within a company. Chapter 11 presents the possible problems and opportunities in the relationships between purchasing and engineering, and purchasing and quality management. Special attention is given to how to improve supplier quality. Here, supplier quality assurance and supplier certification are presented as techniques which can be used in this respect.

Chapter 12 describes the role of purchasing within supply chain management. After providing some important definitions, the basics of supply chain management are presented. This is achieved by providing a logistics reference model, which differentiates between several manufacturing situations (assembly type of operations versus job shop). This model explains why purchasing situations within different companies and industries may be vastly different. Next, it covers a detailed discussion on materials requirements planning, just-in-time management and the required information technology.

The subject of how to organize for efficient purchasing is covered in Chapter 13. In practice a large variety of organizational structures are observed and the most important of these are discussed. There is no one best way to organize for purchasing. Specific attention is given to the issue of centralized versus decentralized purchasing in a multi-plant environment. Here different coordination structures are discussed through which companies try to capture purchasing synergies. Next, the issue of how to organize for efficient purchasing at the business unit level is presented.

Chapter 14 concludes Section ii with a discussion on purchasing performance measurement and evaluation. The central issue here is how to measure and assess the performance of the purchasing department. Several important methods and benchmarking techniques are presented.

Section iii: Practice presents a number of operational purchasing methods and techniques. This section also gives specific attention to the purchasing policies of retail and service companies and those of governmental bodies.

All purchasing decisions, and decisions concerning supplier selection, must be based on sound business analyses. In Chapter 15 some methods and techniques which can be used to support the decisions involved are discussed. Among other things, special attention will be given to the learning curve and cost modelling.

In industrial and trade practice intensive negotiations often precede signing the purchasing contract. Chapter 16 describes how to conduct purchasing negotiations. It focuses on the tactics used in purchasing negotiations and the rules of conduct when considering relationships with suppliers.

Chapter 17 deals with buying for retail. The most important differences with the industrial purchasing function are discussed. Some modern retail concepts such as efficient consumer response (ECR), collaborative planning, forecasting and replenishment (CPFR), vendor managed inventory (VMI) and radio frequency identification (RFID) and its implications for supplier relationships are presented.

Chapter 18 shows how to deal with the purchasing function in service-oriented companies. Here, the purchasing cost relative to total sales turnover is much lower than for industrial and trade companies. The role of the purchasing function and its perceived importance to management therefore differs widely, and purchasing practices obtained from industrial and trade companies have only limited value. The chapter deals elaborately with purchasing in a facilities environment and the buying of services, an area of increasing importance to most buyers in a facility environment.

Finally, Chapter 19 describes the specific characteristics of buying for governmental institutions. From this chapter it will become clear that large differences exist between buying for the government versus buying for private enterprise. Governmental bodies are not free in choosing their purchasing procedures. Therefore, this chapter gives elaborate attention to the most important EC Directives on Public Procurement, its purchasing procedures, and how to work with these.

ANALYSIS

CASE STUDY   BRITISH AIRWAYS FLIES TOWARDS $996 SAVINGS GOAL

Suffering from heavy international competition and a growing field of small European and US-based competitors offering no frills service and cheap fares, British Airways in October 2001 decided to review its operations. The company needed to improve its operating margin dramatically to an unprecedented 10 per cent. To get to that margin at existing revenue rates, the company determined that it would have to cut costs by $996 million.

Headcount was targeted for more than two-thirds of the cost cuts and BA unveiled plans to cut 13 000 people or 20 per cent of its staff, including members of its purchasing operations. Another area of cost reduction focused on how BA captures customers. Rather than paying high fees to travel agents and other services to book customers on BA flights, the company designed a new pricing strategy to push traffic to a self-serve web model for booking flights.

But cutting costs alone was not enough. 'We realized that rather than just go through a cost-cutting exercise, we needed to fundamentally rethink the business model,' says Jonathan Counsell, head of strategy and performance at BA. Standardized procurement processes were seen as one way to transform BA's newly trimmed procurement staff of 200 to become more strategic in sourcing the airline's $6 billion annual buy, which is largely made up of fuel, user charges, in-flight products such as catering and engineering, and airport services. The purchasing operations at BA are centralized; its procurement director reports directly to the CFO.

BA outlined its major goals in its procurement overhaul. First, it wanted to reduce total costs by more than $250 million. Second, it wanted to increase its online ordering to 80 per cent of all materials and services. Next it wanted to reduce procurement transaction costs to $15 each. Also, the company's number of suppliers would be reduced to 2000 and key relationships would be built with existing suppliers.

Benchmarking played an important role in inspiring BA's move to a more process-led organization. BA used several vehicles to talk with other airlines and OEMs about procurement best-practices. It used its participation in the One World alliance to share best-purchasing practices with other airlines. Some years ago, BA established a strategic procurement forum for blue chip UK-based companies that meets monthly to share these practices.

'We saw a big difference between the best-practices companies and our practices, especially in the absence of consistent processes,' says Gavin Boswell, technology and performance manager at BA. 'We wanted to get people in our organization to agree on the processes because they had too many ways of doing things.'

In order to foster standardization in its purchasing processes, process leaders were nominated, who would report to the procurement director and who are responsible for ensuring BA has set up best-practice processes.

Currently, there are five process leaders in place to identify and implement best-practices in five areas: supplier relationships, strategy and performance, supplier negotiations, transactional procurement and supply chain development.

The overhaul of the procurement department at BA is getting a lot of attention throughout the company from the executive level down and across. So far, apart from significant cost savings, 40 per cent of UK-based purchase orders are online and the supply base has been cut in half to 7000, well on its way to the goal of 2000 . . .

Source: adapted from *Purchasing*, 8 August, 2002

INTRODUCTION

As business is becoming more and more competitive, purchasing and supply chain management are increasingly recognized as key business drivers by top managers. Again and again it appears that buyers and supply managers can contribute significantly to the company's bottom line. Since most companies today spend more than half of their sales turnover on purchased parts and services, efficient and constructive relationships with suppliers are key to the company's short term financial position and long term competitive power.

Many companies cannot escape from exploiting the huge potential that purchasing and supply chain management represents to them today. The Case Study of British Airways above illustrates how companies can bring this potential to fruition. Given their need to improve their overall operating margin, BA's purchasing staff needed to generate significant cost savings. Several high level cross functional teams were set up in the company to deal with this issue. Apart from price, these teams looked into possibilities of how to reduce supplier leadtime, reduce inventory and increase quality levels. Next, they looked into opportunities to reduce the number of suppliers dramatically to a mere 2000, leading to more business per supplier and hence increasing the value of BA as a customer to them. More collaborative relationships needed to be established. Given the huge number of purchasing transactions, purchase orders, delivery documents and invoices, BA also targetted reducing its transaction costs in relationships with suppliers. New solutions, based upon web-enabled information technology, are available now to companies. In order to be able to implement these new systems company-wide, BA needed to standardize its administrative and procurement processes.

The Case Study shows the new role that purchasing and supply professionals now play in organizations. First, they play a strategic role in terms of analyzing the purchasing spend of the company, identifying the core and non-core suppliers and, based upon this data, developing differentiated supplier strategies. Next, their activities are tactical in character: based upon the selected supplier strategy, purchasing professionals need to be able to standardize business processes, establish effective information links with their suppliers and strive for continuous improvement of supplier performance. Finally, these professionals need to secure efficient material supply from their suppliers in time, at the right quality and quantity and at the lowest overall cost.

In this chapter we discuss the role and importance of the purchasing function. We will take Porter's value chain as a point of departure to show that we need to differentiate between direct and indirect purchasing. Some time is spent in defining important terms and concepts and we elaborate on the role which buyers may play in cost reduction, and product and process innovation. The chapter concludes by describing some important trends and developments which may be perceived in the purchasing strategies of companies who are leading edge in purchasing and supply chain management. In this way Chapter 1 sets the stage for the remaining chapters in Section i.

CHANGES IN THE BUSINESS CONTEXT

The business context of many companies is nowadays radically changing. Most changes are not mere trends but the result of large, unruly forces which have a lasting effect on the world economy. Examples are the increasing globalization of customer markets, the rapid development of information technology and computer networks, the increasing importance of services in our economies, and the ongoing changes in customer demands and preferences. All these changes happen to businesses at the same time . . . and they are happening fast. These changes are causing a revolution in business, as has been shown by Wal-Mart, Dell, and Cisco,[1] and are changing the nature of competition dramatically.

The message is clear: business is changing, but to what extent? In what way? What are the consequences? What are the challenges large companies are confronted with? And how will they impact purchasing and supply strategies? Let's have a closer look at some of the most important changes. They can be grouped under three headings: globalization of trade, the information society and changing consumer patterns.

Globalization of trade

Competition in many industries has intensified all over the world in just a few years. The emerging position of China and some other low cost countries as attractive sources of supply has not gone unnoticed. The reasons why this has happened are many and relate to:

- deregulation, which is going on in many industries (ranging from energy supply to the airline industry);
- intercultural homogenization and the resulting homogenization of consumer preferences around the world;
- forming of trade regions (GATT, NAFTA, EEC) in major parts of the world;
- improved transportation facilities and opportunities to track and trace shipments through advanced information technology;
- more sophisticated information and communications technology which has become available and which has facilitated international business transactions.

The latter especially enables people and organizations to overcome the barriers of physical distance. It is assumed that modern information technology will challenge and redefine commonly accepted notions of geographic nations, companies, industries and commun-

---

1 See among others Margretta (1998, 1998a)

ities. Modern information technology has made traditional borders obsolete, not only between nations but especially between organizations and nations. Thanks to the new information technologies, companies in some industries are reallocating and reconfiguring their activities into global value chains (see Memo 1.1).

Adopting these value chain concepts seems most appropriate for products with a high value-to-weight ratio, such as semiconductors, microchips and some consumer electronic products. However, also in service industries (like transportation and logistics) we see a rapid development of global supply networks (for example: DHL, Federal Express, UPS) which are enabled through advanced computer and Internet technologies.

Next, changes in the international trade-blocs have affected global trade flows. Post-war tariffs under GATT have gone down to a historically all-time low level. Some developed countries have established free-trade zones. Examples here are the EEC (Europe), NAFTA (US, Canada, Mexico) and the 'Yen bloc', that includes the Asian nations. It is expected that these three trade zones will greatly affect the world economy in the early years of the twenty-first century. It will be clear that as a consequence of these developments opportunities for global sourcing have increased. By the early twenty-first century it is expected that there will be five Asian countries among the top ten economies of the world.

The information society

Information technologies are the core of today's economy. The economic value from generating, using, and selling information is growing fast. Examples can be found in modern retail, where companies apply database marketing to monitor changes in consumer buying behavior and preferences. Detailed information about buying patterns and consumer profiles is readily available, enabling retail buyers (or category managers, see Chapter 17) to quickly adapt their product assortments and services. Moreover, advanced retail information systems enable an efficient tracing and tracking of goods flows and a detailed monitoring of supplier performance. Through EDI interlinkages manufacturers of fast moving consumer goods are requested to schedule their deliveries based on continuous replenishment and to take care of logistics activities which traditionally used to be done by the retailer.

This is not only becoming common practice in modern retail. Similar trends can also be perceived in some leading-edge industrial manufacturing companies. The Xerox Corporation has adopted the concept of 'pay for production' in many of its manufacturing plants. In this concept suppliers of major (and costly) components are paid by Xerox only for the products that actually have been consumed in the production of a specific day. Suppliers have been made totally responsible for materials planning, managing pipeline inventory and efficient replenishment. Advanced electronic linkages lie at the heart of these modern manufacturing and logistics concepts.

Electronic networks will be in many industries one of the key success factors for the years to come. This is nowhere more evident than in the automotive industry. The elec-

---

MEMO 1.1   TOWARDS THE GLOBAL VALUE CHAIN

Some Japanese companies have already become 'global' in that their R&D is networked, involving American and Asian scientists. Their design concepts are detailed by low-cost Indian engineers in Bangalore or Bombay and then switched over to Singapore. Their components are produced in Taiwan and shipped to Tianjin for final assembly and inspection. And then final products are sold in Europe and North America (Ohmae, 1994).

tronic capabilities of suppliers increasingly will determine whether they will be able to survive in a specific customer relationship. It is expected that manufacturers will increasingly exclude suppliers from future business who do not offer electronic linkages, or who have incompatible information systems. This development is fostered and facilitated by the emergence of electronic marketplaces, which are available today for many industries and products. Examples are Covisint for the automotive industry, the WorldWide Retail Exchange for the retail sector and Chemdex for the chemical and similar industries.

Changing consumer patterns

Of course we cannot underestimate the importance of changes in consumer patterns nowadays. In the past consumers would value a product or service on the basis of some combination of quality and price. Today's consumers, by contrast, use an expanded concept of value that includes convenience of purchase, after-sales service, dependability, uniqueness and so on. This idea is also reflected by some leading authors on business marketing where value is defined as: 'the worth in monetary terms of the economic, technical, service and social benefits a customer firm receives in exchange for the price it pays for a marketing offering' (Anderson and Narus, 1998, p. 5).

Increasingly, customers are demanding quality products which are tailored to individual needs and tastes. During the 1990s, the well-informed and highly-educated consumers became more aware of their purchasing power, and showed more critical buying behavior. We see the empowerment of the consumers against remote and irresponsible organizations (as can be illustrated by the reaction of some action groups against global trade and child labor). In essence, people will no longer settle for whatever companies are offering. Instead, they will seek out and command their first choices in products and services. Consumers take charge: they now tell manufacturers what they want, when they want it, how they want it and what they are willing to pay. They demand products and services designed for their unique and particular needs.

As a result many manufacturers of consumer products (ranging from fast moving consumer goods to cars and furniture) need constantly to look for opportunities to reduce costs and improve efficiency. At the same time, however, they need to constantly innovate and renew their product and service offerings. In more and more industries services are becoming an integrated part of the value proposition. In many cases companies simply do not have the knowledge and resources to develop all the solutions in-house. This is one reason (as we will see in more detail in Chapter 7) why outsourcing has become so widespread a phenomenon. In order to be able to confront these challenges companies need to work together with suppliers more closely in the areas of manufacturing, logistics, services and product development.

This poses new demands on the purchasing and supply function of those companies. Let's identify how these changes affect purchasing and supply strategies.

IMPACT ON BUSINESS STRATEGIES AND STRUCTURES

As a result of the new unruly forces imposed on them, companies need to rethink their position in the value chain. Doing so effectively requires a clear view on what they consider to be their core versus non-core activities. In order to improve their competitive position companies need to focus their core activities on the needs and requirements of their customers. Non-core activities are increasingly outsourced to specialist suppliers, which explains why supplier management is becoming a key issue in corporate strategies. In dealing with their supplier relationships companies increasingly adopt a process and value orientation. These subjects are now discussed in more detail.

The term value chain is used to describe the various steps a good or service goes through from raw material to final consumption. Michael Porter considers every firm basically as a collection of primary and supporting value activities that are performed to design, produce, market, deliver and support products that are valuable for customers. As he argues, a firm's value chain and the way in which it performs individual value-activities are a reflection of its history, its strategy, its approach to implementing its strategy and the underlying economics of the activities themselves (Porter, 1985). This explains why there can be explicit differences between organizations with regard to structure, operations management, ways of planning, style of management, and sometimes notable differences in competitive position between organizations operating within the same sector.

Seen from this perspective, competitive advantage depends primarily on the art of positioning a company in the right place on the value chain. According to Quinn (1992) each company should focus on just a few core activities, where it thinks it can achieve and maintain a long-term competitive advantage. All other activities in which it cannot achieve world-class status should be outsourced. Contracting out non-core activities to specialized suppliers can contribute to cost reduction, quality improvement, lead time reduction and innovation at the same time. This explains the high and rising purchasing to sales ratio which can be observed in many companies.

Quinn (1992) has suggested the following ideas for developing a sustainable competitive advantage through core competencies:

■ Companies need to focus their internal resources on those core sources of intellectual or service capabilities which presently create a meaningful distinctiveness in their customers' minds.

■ The next step to competitive advantage is to consider the company's remaining capabilities as a group of service activities that could be either 'made' internally or 'bought' externally from a wide variety of suppliers specializing or functionally competing in that activity.

■ For continued success companies need to actively command, dominate, and build barriers to entry around those selected activities critical to their particular strategic concept. Concentrating more power than anyone else in the world on these core competencies as they affect customers is crucial to strategic success

■ Managers need to plan and control their outsourced activities so that their company never becomes overly dependent on, or later is dominated by, their partners. This means consciously developing and monitoring multiple competitive sources and strategically controlling certain critical steps in the process.

Using this approach to core competencies, companies, according to Quinn, can develop a much higher level of focus, and hence a higher leverage, for their business strategies than through traditional product-focused strategies. Quinn's ideas, which have been refined by Hamel and Prahalad (1994), have been adopted by a score of companies worldwide. It is fair to say that these ideas have set the stage for the emergence and widespread acceptance of advanced purchasing and supply strategies.

Outsourcing is, as has already been argued, becoming more and more a strategic issue in many industries, with great importance for the survival of the company. Often specialist suppliers can perform the outsourced activities at lower cost and with higher value-added than the buying company.

To be able to outsource, excellent suppliers are needed, referred to by some companies as world-class suppliers, or best-in-class suppliers. More and more suppliers are professional enough to deliver complete functional units or subsystems with the required quality, flexibility and innovativeness. The key to strategic success for many firms in the future will be their coalition with the world's best suppliers, product designers, advertising agencies, distribution channels, financial houses, or other outside sources. Nike has served for some time as a nice example, since this highly successful company concentrates on design, marketing, and distribution, while virtually all production of its sporting goods lines is made through co-manufacturing arrangements with suppliers. However, over the past years other companies, like Dell and Cisco, have followed Nike's example.

Given the pressure that consumers and some industrial manufacturers exert on their suppliers, companies increasingly are organizing their activities around processes which are relevant for their customers, rather than functions. The functional organization gradually is being replaced by the process organization. By process we mean a set of activities that, taken together, produce a value to a customer. Hammer and Champy (1993) suggest that by adopting a process orientation we need to look at the entire process beyond organizational boundaries. In these companies staff actually may work for several managers, making the traditional one-line-of-command obsolete. More and more work is being done in cross-functional teams or cross-departmental project teams or even joint customer-supplier teams. Employees are encouraged to take the initiative and to collaborate with their peers to solve problems rather than to await instructions from their departmental managers. Later in this book we will see that the process orientation and cross functional teams are very powerful concepts in the area of purchasing and supply management.

THE ROLE OF PURCHASING IN THE VALUE CHAIN

In many business strategies the concept of value chain management plays a central role, therefore this subject is elaborated on in this section. There will be an explanation of what value chain management is. When describing the role and position of the purchasing and supply function in industrial companies, the value chain of Porter (1985) is taken as a term of reference (see Figure 1.1).

The value chain in Figure 1.1 is composed of value activities and a margin which is achieved by these activities. Value activities can be divided into physically and technically different groups of activities. Porter differentiates between primary activities and support activities. Primary activities are those which are directed at the physical transformation and handling of the final products which the company delivers to its customers. As can be seen from Figure 1.1, distribution to the customer and providing services are parts of these primary activities.

Support activities enable and support the primary activities. They can be directed at supporting one of the primary activities as well as supporting the whole primary process.

Porter differentiates between five generic categories of primary activities (1985, pp. 39–40).

- Inbound logistics. These activities are related to receiving, storing and disseminating inputs to the product, such as materials handling, warehousing, inventory control, vehicle scheduling and returns to suppliers.

- Operations. Activities associated with transforming inputs into the final product, such as machining, packaging, assembly, equipment maintenance, testing, printing and facility operations.

- Outbound logistics. These are activities associated with collecting, storing, and physically distributing the product to buyers, such as finished goods warehousing, materials handling, delivery vehicle operations, order processing and scheduling.

- Marketing and sales. These activities relate to advertising, promotion, sales, distribution channel selection, the management of channel relations and pricing.

- Services. Activities associated with providing services to enhance or maintain the value of the product, such as installation, repair and maintenance, training, parts supply and product adjustment.

Support activities are grouped into four categories.

- Procurement. Procurement relates to the function of purchasing inputs used in the firm's value chain. These may include raw materials, supplies, and other consumable items as well as assets such as machinery, laboratory equipment, office equipment and buildings. These examples illustrate that purchased inputs may be related to primary activities as well as support activities. This is one reason why Porter classifies procurement as a support activity and not as a primary activity.

- Technology development. 'Technology' has a very broad meaning in this context, since in Porter's view every activity embodies technology, be it know-how, procedures or technology embodied in process or product design. Most value activities use a technology that combines a number of different subtechnologies involving different scientific disciplines.

- Human resources management. These are all the activities directed at recruiting, hiring, training, developing and compensation of all types of personnel, active in both primary and support activities.

- Firm infrastructure. The whole company is customer of these activities. They don't support one or more primary activities – rather, they support whole company processes. Examples of these activities are management, planning, finance, accounting, legal, government affairs, quality management and facilities management. In larger companies, which often consist of different operating units, one sees these activities divided among headquarters and the operating companies. This division is often the subject of discussion which is why it changes so frequently.

FIGURE 1.1   Purchasing and the value chain.

Source: redrawn from Porter (1985)

All activities need to be performed in such a way that the total value generated by the company is more than the sum of its costs. In Porter's terms, the total value of the company is determined by the whole of its sales value. The margin reflects the reward for the risks run by the company. Porter regards procurement as a support activity. He uses the term procurement rather than purchasing since, as he argues, the usual connotation of purchasing is too narrow among managers (1985, p. 41). 'The dispersion of the procurement function often obscures the magnitude of total purchases and means that many purchases receive little scrutiny.' Although this statement was made many years ago, it is still true for many organizations today.

Based on these observations the conclusion is that procurement should provide support to the following business activities.

- Primary activities. The procurement function should be able to meet the material requirements related to inbound and outbound logistics, and, often more importantly, related to operations. Operations may have a different structure among manufacturing companies. Usually manufacturing processes can be characterized according to the following categories.
  - Make (and distribute) to stock (MTS). Standard products are manufactured and stocked, customers are serviced from an end product inventory. Production is on dedicated machinery, often in large batches. Materials requirements planning (and therefore also planning of purchased products) is based on sales forecasts. Examples are steelplate and most maintenance, repair and operating supplies.
  - Make to order (MTO). Products are manufactured from raw material or the purchased components inventory after a customer order has been received and accepted. This is common in situations with very large or customer-specific product ranges (e.g. packaging materials) or bulk products that are very expensive to stock (e.g. insulation materials).
  - Engineer to order (ETO). All manufacturing activities from design to assembly and even purchasing of the required materials are related to a specific customer order. Production is usually on multipurpose machinery, requiring highly skilled operators, for example large customer-specific equipment and machines, vessels.

These contrasting manufacturing situations explain why procurement activities may be radically different between companies and industries. Procurement operations for a manufacturer producing cars in large batches, controlled by a materials requirements planning system, may differ largely from those in a job-shop environment, like a shipyard, where every project may be new to the organization and where materials are obtained from a vast, frequently changing, supplier base! Buying for primary activities will be referred to throughout this book as 'production buying', 'buying of production items' or 'purchasing direct materials'. Usually this area gets most of the attention from management.

- Support activities. Procurement activities may also be related to supplying products and services for the other support functions. Some examples are the buying of:
  - laboratory equipment for research and development;
  - computer hardware and software for the central computer department;
  - lease-cars for the sales force and senior management
  - office equipment for accounting;
  - food and beverages for the catering department;
  - cleaning materials for housekeeping, etc

Again we see that the procurement function aimed at providing supplies and services for the support activities may be very different in character. Some of the purchases to be made are routine purchases, maintenance, repair and operating supplies (MRO-supplies), and may be repetitive and low in value. Other purchases may have a 'project character' and may be unique and high valued (investment goods, capital equipment, buildings).

In general this type of purchase will be referred to as 'non production buying', 'purchasing indirect materials' or 'general expenses'. They may be classified into MRO-supplies, investment goods and services. The high variety of these types of purchases makes them extremely difficult to support by one uniform computer information system and/or buying procedure. The character of these types of purchases also explains why professionalism in purchasing is usually low. This is one reason why some international companies, which have set up special programs in this area (such as IBM, Shell, Lucent and Philips Electronics) have reported high savings. Table 1.1 summarizes the most important differences between buying for primary and for support activities.

DEFINITION OF CONCEPTS

The purchasing function traditionally encompasses the process of buying. It involves determining the need, selecting the supplier, arriving at a proper price, specifying terms and conditions, issuing the contract or order, and following up to ensure proper delivery. In the old days it was argued that the purchasing function should obtain the proper equipment, material, supplies and services of the right quality, in the right quantity, at the right price and from the right source (Aljian, 1984, p. 3). In this description, the purchasing function is regarded predominantly as an operational activity.

In practice, as well as in the literature, many terms and concepts nowadays are used in the area of purchasing. However, no agreement exists about the definition of these terms. Terms like procurement, purchasing, supply and logistics management are used interchangeably.

Throughout this book the definition of *purchasing* is:

The management of the company's external resources in such a way that the supply of all goods, services, capabilities and knowledge which are necessary for running, maintaining and managing the company's primary and support activities is secured at the most favorable conditions.

TABLE 1.1 Main differences between buying for primary activities and buying for support activities

Aspects	Buying for primary activities	Buying for support activities
Product assortment	Limited to large	Very large
Number of suppliers	Limited, transparent	Very large
Purchasing turnover	Very large, considerable	Limited
Number of purchase orders	Considerable	Very large
Average order size	High	Small
Control	Depends on type of production planning	Limited, forecast-related or project-related planning
Decision-making unit	Engineering, manufacturing specialists dominant	Fragmented, varies with product or service.

The *purchasing function* in this definition covers specifically activities aimed at:

- determining the specification (in terms of required quality and quantities) of the goods and services that need to be bought;
- selecting the most suitable supplier and developing procedures and routines to select the best supplier;
- preparing and conducting negotiations with the supplier in order to establish an agreement and to write up the contract;
- placing the order with the selected supplier and/or to develop efficient purchase order and handling systems;
- monitoring and control of the order to secure supply (expediting);
- follow up and evaluation (settling claims, keeping product and supplier files up-to-date, supplier rating and supplier ranking).

Figure 1.2 schematically illustrates the main activities within the purchasing function. It shows that these activities are closely interrelated. This picture is referred to as the purchasing process model.

The purchasing function does not include the responsibility for materials requirements planning, materials scheduling, inventory management, incoming inspection and quality control. However, in order to be effective, purchasing operations should be closely linked and interrelated to these materials activities. In the author's opinion a purchasing manager should support each of the six activities mentioned above. However, this does not necessarily imply that all these activities should be conducted by the purchasing department, as illustrated in the following example.

A buyer who is responsible for maintenance, repair and operating supplies, is often confronted with the 'small-order problem'. Many requisitions which he receives from internal departments concern simple products of low expense. Handling these requisitions, however, is often a laborious task if the buyer is to issue a purchase order for every requisition. An alternative may be to arrange for a so-called 'catalog' agreement with a specific

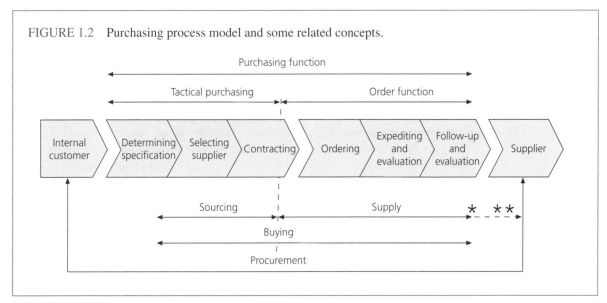

FIGURE 1.2 Purchasing process model and some related concepts.

Note: * = USA; ** = UK

supplier for e.g. the delivery of hand-tooling. In this arrangement he may establish the product range, which will be bought from that supplier, including the price per product. He may agree with the supplier that the latter will provide a web-enabled catalog to his company, enabling employees and technical staff to order directly from the supplier. Furthermore he may negotiate a bonus from that supplier tied to the total purchasing turnover over 12 months. Next he may communicate terms and conditions of this contract to the staff of Technical Services. Through the on-line catalog employees of this company can order directly from the supplier, without involving the purchasing department. In this example it is the task of the buyer to develop an overall commercial agreement with the supplier and to establish an electronic catalog and an (electronic) order routine with that supplier on the one hand, and the internal customer on the other hand. In fact, what happens is that the ordering function is delegated, in a rather controlled way, to the internal customer. In this manner it is possible to combine the purchasing power of the organization with optimal flexibility and efficiency for Technical Services.

From the definition of *purchasing* it may be derived that this covers all activities for which the company receives an invoice from outside parties. Hence the playing ground of purchasing includes inter company business, counter trade arrangements, hiring of temporary personnel from outside agencies, contracting for advertising, etc.. However, many of the activities for which the company may receive invoices from suppliers may be arranged without interference from the purchasing department (this will be discussed later). Therefore the scope of the purchasing function is usually much broader than that of the purchasing department.

The term *ordering* refers to the placing of purchase orders at a supplier against previously arranged conditions. Furthermore, this term will be used when purchase orders are placed directly, without questioning the supplier's conditions and without sufficient supplier market testing. Call-off orders fall into this category as telephone orders for products bought from a supplier catalog. Ordering is considered to be a part of the purchasing process. In fact it relates to the last three steps of the purchasing process. The use of the term 'tactical purchasing' refers to the first three steps.

Purchasing differs from buying and ordering in two ways: while specifications may be a given in the situation of ordering and buying, these are challenged when it comes to purchasing. In that case discussion may start about the degree to which the specifications are really fit for purpose. Features which are not necessary for meeting the function which the product needs to fulfill are skipped. This often leads to a situation where an (expensive) supplier branded product is replaced by an identical product from a less known supplier. Another difference is that purchasing relates to finding the best possible supplier, based upon a broad supplier market definition.

As seen from Figure 1.2 *procurement* is a somewhat broader term. It includes all activities required in order to get the product from the supplier to its final destination. It encompasses the purchasing function, stores, traffic and transportation, incoming inspection, and quality control and assurance. Some firms also consider salvage and environmental issues, as they are related to materials, as a part of procurement (see also Memo 1.2). This task is expected to become more important in future years, with the increasing impact of environmental issues.

It is difficult to find a description of *buying* in management literature. It differs from purchasing in the sense that it does not encompass the first step of the purchasing process. This is in line with the practice of trading and retail companies (e.g. department stores), where this term is most often referred to. Here, discussions about the specifications of products to be purchased are more limited compared to industrial companies, since in many cases these are decided by the supplier.

Another term often used in the materials area is *supply*. This is somewhat more difficult to grasp, because it appears that there are differences in connotation between North

America and Europe. In America 'supply' covers the stores function of internally consumed items such as office supplies, cleaning materials, etc. However, in Europe the term
supply seems to have a broader meaning which includes at least purchasing, stores and
receiving. The governmental sector also uses this broader interpretation.

A term which has become increasingly popular in the materials area is *sourcing*. This
activity relates to developing the most appropriate supplier strategy for a certain commodity or product category. A sourcing strategy describes how many suppliers the company
favors for that commodity or category, what type of relationship to pursue (arm's length or
partnership) and what type of contract to negotiate (one year or multi year).

Purchasing management refers to all activities necessary to manage supplier relationships. It is focused on structuring and continuously improving purchasing processes within
the organization and between the organization and its suppliers. Purchasing management,
hence, has an internal aspect and an external aspect. The idea behind purchasing management is that if suppliers are not managed by their customers, customer relationships will
be managed by the suppliers. Given the widespread acceptance of marketing management,
customer relationship and account management in business, suppliers usually are in a favorable position. Given the cross-functional nature of purchasing management and its wider
playing ground it is also referred to in this text as *supplier resource management.*

Purchasing management is related to *supply chain management*. The latter concept can
be described as the management of all activities, information, knowledge and financial
resources associated with the flow and transformation of goods and services from the raw
materials suppliers, component suppliers and other suppliers in such a way that the expectations of the end users of the company are being met or surpassed. Supply chain management differs from purchasing in that it also encompasses all logistics activities.

MEMO 1.2   THE VISION OF SHELL INTERNATIONAL OIL COMPANY ON PROCUREMENT

In October 1991, in the Introduction to the Procurement Business Strategy, I wrote: 'It is simply no longer
acceptable to treat the supply of goods and services as an administrative issue – it can and should be a potent
force to make competitive gains and generate significant financial benefit'.

In 1994 the Shell Group's spend on goods and services was $30 billion and a target to reduce this by
7 per cent was set for the Group. Although good results have been achieved, in some areas we have fallen
short of our targets.

The Shell Group urgently needs to improve its performance and do so more quickly. In December 1998
I set a target for reducing our overall costs by $2.5 billion a year in 2001. We cannot afford to fail; we must
deliver more than we promise, not less. It is vital that all staff working in positions where they influence the
costs we incur with our third parties acquire the portfolio of skills they need to manage these costs in a
professional manner.

New terms such as supply chain management and value chain management have become commonplace
in the procurement world. In areas where these ideas have been applied they have been consistently successful. Yet, while this experience exists within the Group, it is clear that so far we have not succeeded in achieving the transformation we need in people's commercial behavior across all of our organizations.

To achieve this change, we need to improve our commercial skills to a level that is commensurate with
our best technical skills and we must work together to obtain the combined benefits that excellence in these
two areas will bring ...

(Mark Moody Stuart, Chairman of the Committee of Managing Directors, Shell Group)

Source: quoted with permission from the Introduction to Shell's Commercial Learning Guide (1998)

Moreover it entails the management of relationships not only with first tier suppliers but also with lower tier suppliers. An example is Ford which urges its suppliers of exhaust-systems to use one steel contract. Both Ford and suppliers are buying steel; by combining the contract value all parties involved can benefit from better conditions.

Value chain management, finally, builds on the former concept. Here the idea is that suppliers are challenged by the larger customer organization to improve value proposition to their customers. Usually the suppliers work closely together with the customer's technical and marketing staff to reduce the product's overall costs, and add new designs or features to the product which are attractive for the end customer. An example here is Microsoft's X-Box, which was originally developed by Microsoft, but which actually is produced by Flextronics. Flextronics is crucial for the success of the X-Box in that it is determining the X-Box's cost price and hence, the consumer price of the product.[2]

IMPORTANCE OF PURCHASING TO BUSINESS

An analysis of the cost structure of manufacturing companies immediately shows the importance of purchasing to organizations. In general the largest part of the cost of goods sold (COGS) appears to be taken up by purchased materials and services. Figure 1.3 shows that the purchasing value in relation to cost of goods sold is approximately 50 per cent. If the other business costs, which have an important purchasing component, are added to the purchasing value, the total amounts to approximately 68 per cent.

Through the DuPont chart (Figure 1.4), the effects of purchasing savings on the company's return on investment can be illustrated. Figure 1.4 shows how a 2 per cent saving on purchasing-related expenditure for a company (in this case Heineken) may lead to an improvement of the return on net assets (RONA) of 9 per cent. Of course, the reverse is valid also: due to a lack of a well defined purchasing policy and a lack of structure in the purchasing (decision-making) process, the resulting lack of control on purchasing costs may lead to an unforeseen financial loss.

The Du Pont analysis shows that purchasing contributes to improving the company's RONA in two ways:

- Through reduction of all direct materials costs: this will immediately lead to an improvement of the company's sales margin, which in turn will affect RONA in a positive manner. A number of measures may lead to lower direct materials costs such as introducing new suppliers, competitive tendering, looking for substitute materials, etc

- Through a reduction of the net capital employed by the company: this will work out positively on the company's capital turnover ratio. Measures which will lead to lower capital being employed are many. Examples are longer payment terms, reduction of (pipeline) inventories of base materials through just-in-time (JIT) agreements with suppliers, supplier quality improvement (which will lead to less buffer stock required) and leasing instead of buying equipment.

It can be concluded that purchasing policies fundamentally contribute to business success in several ways. First, purchasing policies can significantly improve sales margins through realizing substantial cost savings. A dollar saved in purchasing is a dollar added to the bottom line. Second, through better quality and logistics arrangements with suppliers, purchasing can contribute to a higher capital turnover ratio. Third, suppliers may contribute, when addressed properly, significantly to the company's innovation processes. However, as companies become more dependent on their suppliers the strategic value of purchasing

---

2 See 'Outsourcing the X-Box', *Purchasing*, 15 August, 2002.

FIGURE 1.3 Purchased goods and services as a percentage of cost of goods sold.

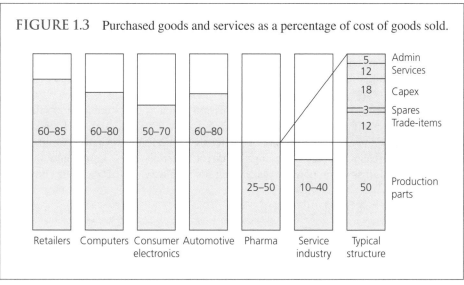

Source: adapted from Kluge (1996)

FIGURE 1.4 DuPont analysis Heineken (2002): a 2% saving on purchased materials and services leads to a 9.2% improvement of return on capital employed (ROCE).

lies in developing a world class supplier base which is more competitive than that of the company's main competitors. Looking for the most competitive suppliers worldwide and developing effective relationships with them should therefore be one of the most important concerns of any purchasing manager. As has been demonstrated even small improvements in the relationship with suppliers may have a significant impact on the company's return on net assets.

The conclusion we can draw from this discussion is that as the purchasing to sales ratio increases for a specific company, purchasing decisions will have a more profound impact on the company's net results. The same goes for the capital turnover ratio. A higher ratio will lead to a greater leverage of savings on direct materials costs. Let us now turn to a more detailed discussion on how the purchasing function may contribute to the company's profitability.

PURCHASING, COST REDUCTION AND TECHNOLOGICAL INNOVATION

Apart from immediate savings on purchasing prices, the purchasing function can also contribute to the improvement of the company's competitive position in a more indirect manner. This indirect contribution can take the shape of standardization of the product assortment, reduction of stocks, product and process innovation, reduction of quality costs (costs related to inspection, rejection, repairs), and cutting down on production lead times. In practice, these indirect contributions often turn out to be more substantial than the amounts of money which are saved directly (i.e. exclusively by purchasing).

To give an idea of the way in which purchasing can contribute indirectly to corporate performance, consider the following examples.

- Reduction of quality costs. It was mentioned earlier that purchasing can contribute to a reduction of quality costs. When products are delivered by suppliers, many companies conduct both an incoming and a quality inspection. Part of purchasing's task is to minimize quality costs in the enterprise, as far as they are related to purchased materials. The costs of incoming and quality inspection of purchased goods can be reduced by selecting suppliers who have their production well under control, and who possess a sound quality organization. However, this often is not enough, since many companies' experience is that most of the causes of bad quality are related to a lack of internal procedures and organization. Therefore quality improvement should be given first priority.

- Product standardization. Purchasing can contribute to cost-price reduction by striving for a reduction in product variety. This can be arrived at through standardization of specific products (instead of supplier-specific brands) and/or reduction of the number of suppliers. This may lead to less dependence on certain suppliers, better use of competitive bidding and a lower number of items to be kept in stock.

- Contribution to product design and innovation. Today most innovations in industry do not come from large manufacturers but from their suppliers. Academic research, e.g. Wijnstra (1998) and Van Echtelt (2004), shows that successful industrial innovations often follow from an intensive interaction between suppliers and buyers. To actively pursue this kind of interaction is a task for purchasing. In this way, purchasing can actively contribute to a continuous innovation and improvement of products, which may result in a stronger competitive position of the company in its end-user markets.

- Stock reduction. In the Western interpretation of management, stocks are seen as insurance against scheduling problems. These problems can result from the difficulty in predicting the outgoing materials flow (sales forecasts are hard to give, or are not made). On the other hand, they may be due to irregularities in the delivery of purchased materials. Traditionally, this kind of scheduling problem used to be absorbed by the use of buffer stocks. Through imposing a solid discipline on suppliers and enforcing it, through careful scheduling of deliveries and/or through special stock arrangements with suppliers (e.g. consigned stock agreements), purchasing can significantly contribute to a reduction of stock and hence the capital employed.

- Increasing flexibility. Forced by international competition, more and more companies have implemented flexible manufacturing systems or Enterprise Resource Planning systems (ERP systems).[3] These systems are geared towards improving the company's market responsiveness to ever changing customer requirements. Here, integration between the buyer's ERP systems and those of the supplier is of utmost importance in order to secure short leadtimes and to keep inventory in the entire supply chain to the minimum whilst reducing transaction cost to the lowest level possible. Implementation of this kind of system (also known as manufacturing resources planning, *kanban*[4] and just-in-time scheduling) demands a high and consistent performance level from suppliers. Purchasing will have to impose these demands on carefully selected suppliers. A purchasing policy which aims at improving supplier performance will definitely benefit the company's competitiveness in its end-user markets.

- Fostering purchasing synergy. Over the years many companies have adopted a business unit structure, where operating companies have a fairly large autonomy. In such a structure every business unit manager needs to report on the profit and loss account for which he/she is fully responsible. Hence, business unit managers are responsible both for revenues and for costs, including materials costs. In such cases the company as a group can benefit significantly from coordinated contracting of common materials requirements from a smaller supplier base.

The list of examples cannot be complete within the scope of this chapter. It is obvious that companies can benefit significantly from effective purchasing and supply strategies and that opportunities for improvement are many. In general, however, these improvement measures require a better collaboration and harmonization between the different functional domains within the company. This explains why there is often such a large potential for improvement.

CLASSIFICATION OF PURCHASING GOODS

The purchasing process may concern a large variety of goods and, of course, services. In general, purchased materials and services can be grouped into the following categories.

- Raw materials. Raw materials are materials which have undergone no transformation or a minimal transformation, and they serve as the basic materials for a production process. We may differentiate between physical raw materials, such as iron ore, copper ore, coal, and natural raw materials, such as grains, soya and coffee.

- Supplementary materials. These are materials which are not absorbed physically into the end product; they are used or consumed during the production process. Examples of this type of product are lubricating oil, cooling water, polishing materials, welding electrodes and industrial gases.

---

3 Examples of providers of ERP systems are: SAP, JD Edwards, Peoplesoft.
4 *Kanban* is a pull system in which production orders for components are generated on small cards (*kanban*s) indicating the volume of products that need to be produced based on actual consumption.

- Semi-manufactured products. These products have already been processed once or more, and they will be processed further at a later stage. They are physically present in the end product. Examples are steelplate, rolled wire and plastic foils.

- Components. Components are manufactured goods which will not undergo additional physical changes, but will be incorporated in a system with which there is a functional relationship by joining it with other components. They are built into an end product. Examples are headlight units, lamps, batteries, engine parts, electronic parts and transmissions. A distinction can be made between specific, customized components and standard components. Specific, customized components are produced according to design or specification of the customer, whereas standard components are produced according to specification of the supplier or an industry norm.

- Finished or trade products. These encompass all products which are purchased to be sold, after negligible added value, either together with other finished products and/or manufactured products. Examples of this product category are accessories which are supplied by car manufacturers, such as stripings, car radios and ornamental wheel rims. The manufacturer does not produce these products, but obtains them from specialized suppliers. Commercial products and articles sold by department stores are also in this category.

- Investment goods or capital equipment. These are the products which are not consumed immediately, but whose purchasing value is depreciated over a period of time. In general the book value is stated on the balance sheet annually. Investment goods can be machines used in production, but also include computers and buildings. These examples illustrate the varied character of this category of goods.

- Maintenance, repair and operating materials (MRO items). hese products, sometimes referred to as indirect materials or consumable items, represent materials which are necessary for keeping the organization running in general, and for the support activities in particular. These products are often supplied from stock; examples are office supplies, cleaning materials and copy paper, but also maintenance materials and spare parts.

- Services. Services are activities which are executed by third parties (suppliers, contractors, engineering firms) on a contract basis. Services can range from providing cleaning services and hiring temporary labor to having a new production facility for a chemical company designed by a specialized engineering firm (a contractor).

Having defined the most important categories of purchased goods and services we now turn to a short description of major new developments going on in the area of purchasing and supply management.

NEW DEVELOPMENTS IN PURCHASING

Many companies are now confronted with diminishing growth opportunities, which results in a situation where an increase in turnover can only be realized at the expense of the competition and only with a great deal of effort. This leads to increased pressure on sales prices and consequently on cost prices and margins, which causes two developments. On the one hand it has resulted in shifts of power between purchasing and selling parties in many markets. Due to the fact that in many cases the market has changed from a seller's market to a buyer's market, the role of the buyer is now more dominant than a number of years ago. On the other hand the increasing pressure on sales prices and margins has resulted in increased pressure on direct materials-related costs. Because the purchasing prices determine the sales prices in the industrial sector to a large extent, the company will be constantly on the look-out for opportunities to keep these prices as low as possible. As a result of both developments, the purchasing and supply strategies of industrial companies have undergone major changes. Several examples of these changes are presented below.

- Building leveraged purchasing and supply strategies. In companies with several manufacturing plants, important purchasing advantages can be realized by combining joint purchasing requirements. A trend towards leveraged or coordinated purchasing strategies is apparent in many large European companies, even across national borders. Traditionally this was already common for raw materials, which most of the time were contracted at a corporate level; at present however, a similar approach is used for the purchase of computer hardware and software, capital goods and components. Good examples of companies with an active policy towards benefiting from leveraged purchasing strategies are, apart from the automotive and computer industry, Shell, Philips Electronics Ltd and Alcatel.

- Global sourcing. As a company's competitive position is directly related to the competitiveness of its supply base, companies have adopted a global scope towards sourcing issues. Components are increasingly sourced from foreign, low cost countries, and are the reason why large manufacturing organizations have set up International Purchasing Offices (IPOs) in different regions of the world. Hence, buyers are forced to adopt an international scope towards their supply markets. Supplier benchmarking, being able to deal with different cultures effectively, and being able to negotiate in different languages have become prerequisites for today's professional buyer.

- Supplier integration. Modern information technology enables companies to improve their materials planning and supply systems internally, but also in their relationships with suppliers. Information technology significantly improves productivity within materials activities. An integrated approach of materials management requires close co peration between production planning, inventory control, quality inspection and purchasing. To achieve successful integration, system standardization is a prerequisite. Next, suppliers should be seamlessly integrated within these applications. Hence, the capability of a supplier to link up to the buyer's manufacturing and planning systems becomes of much higher concern in order to be able to apply concepts like total quality control, quick response logistics and just-in-time scheduling successfully.

- Early supplier involvement in new product development. As more and more innovations in industry come from suppliers, getting them involved early in the new product development process becomes an issue of prime concern. In many industries, both the rapid development of technology and the cost related to developing new products, force large organizations to work more closely with their suppliers. In doing so buyers need to alter their traditional ways of working and relationships with suppliers. It should be decided at an early stage what part of the development process will be done in-house and what part will be delegated to suppliers. Being able to work in cross functional development teams and a sound technical background also become important prerequisites. Buyers should be able to solve the issue of how to reward innovative suppliers for their contributions and ideas to new product development. Gain and risk sharing agreements replace the traditional price negotiations and agreements, enabling a more intensive and long term relationship with these suppliers.

- Reciprocity agreements and compensation obligations. Companies operating in international markets are often obliged to compensate part of their sales turnover by counter-purchase obligations. The opening up of the Eastern European bloc and some South-east Asian countries has made countertrade an actual issue. Buying from these countries may even open up interesting sales opportunities. Purchasing becomes increasingly involved in fulfilling such obligations.

■ Environmental issues and business integrity. Environmental problems in many European countries become more and more prevalent. National governments have become more strict in their regulations on this point. In Germany, for instance, strict regulations on industrial and consumer packaging recently came into force. In due course all superfluous packaging needs to be avoided (e.g. blister packaging and the box-packaging of toothpaste); aluminium cans are charged and need to be recollected. Manufacturers of packaging will increasingly be held responsible for its disposal after use. This is one reason why Volkswagen constructed its latest Golf (America: Rabbit) in such a way that the different parts and components can be easily disassembled and reprocessed at the end of the car's lifespan. Volkswagen has even founded its own rework facilities for this purpose. Apart from environmental issues there is a growing pressure from the public that products should be clean, and come from countries with free trade. Child labor has become an issue of particular concern, implying that buyers should ensure that the products they buy come from sources of high integrity. These issues pose new and important challenges to purchasing.

Memo 1.3 provides an illustration of some of the challenges that lie ahead for buyers and purchasing and supply chain managers.

It can be appreciated from this discussion that purchasing and supply represents a business area which is being confronted with many changes and challenges. Most of the problems, however, require intensive interaction, communication and cooperation with other disciplines in the organization. Purchasing and supply is developing increasingly as a business function which cuts across other disciplines. Managing the purchasing and supply function requires a thorough understanding of the purchasing processes that take place within the organization. Only then can these challenges be dealt with effectively.

MEMO 1.3   WHAT'S AHEAD?

As supply chain strategies mature, a major part of a business will involve managing the external value supply chain. Important will be the need to manage costs strategically at all levels of the supply chain. Supply managers will find they are doing more business with outside suppliers than inside ones. They will be working much more with Tier 1 and Tier 2 suppliers to take costs out of products. They will require ongoing development, cost reduction, and innovation on a collaborative basis among all participants in the supply chain.

Many supply chain managers will be deeply involved in building e-sourcing and supply portfolios. Many will be forced to make more informed decisions about whether to use industry-sponsored consortia, build private exchanges, or use markets. Many will need sophisticated assortments of e-sourcing, supply, and collaboration tools. They will need to do more in the way of building value-chain models to understand both product and logistics costs as well as technology. They will need to decide where research, development and design will occur in the value chain.

Supply chain leaders over the next five years will also need to decide the extent to which their companies create unique designs or standardize, and at what levels in the product or service they do these things. Creating entirely unique designs risks creation of production difficulties and/or features that don't mean anything to customers. The ideal will be to standardize – at the right level – and make unique only what is important to the customer. Most companies have a long way to go in making this work on a consistent basis.

Source: Monczka and Morgan, *Purchasing*, 6 June, 2002, pp. 26–28.

SUMMARY

Globalization of trade, the fast development of information technology and ever changing consumer demands are changing the international competitive landscape. As a result companies are changing their business processes. Positioning the company at the right place within the value chain has become a prime concern of top managers; as a result companies start to rethink their core and non-core activities. With their core activities companies try to realize a distinctive value proposition in the relationship with their prime customers. Non-core activities are increasingly outsourced to specialist suppliers. This has put purchasing and supply management in the spotlight. Given the high purchasing to sales turnover ratio which can be perceived nowadays in many companies, purchasing and supply chain management has developed into one of the key business drivers in business. Its main purpose is to develop a competitive, world class supply base for the company. In order to be able to do so companies need to adopt a process orientation rather than a functional orientation towards purchasing issues.

Purchasing encompasses everything the company receives an invoice for. Based upon this broad scope of purchasing we have differentiated between direct and indirect purchasing. Both are important activity domains within purchasing, though each has a different logic due to their different characteristics. Traditionally direct purchasing has received the most attention. However, this picture is changing.

Although developed some years ago, Porter's Value Chain is still a useful concept for explaining the role which the purchasing function has for many companies. Contrary to his opinion however, we have stressed the strategic importance of purchasing to organizations. We have explained our view by using the DuPont model. This enables the purchasing manager to demonstrate the sensitivity of his company's financial results to purchasing savings. As we have seen, the leverage effect of purchasing can be enormous, depending on: (a) the purchasing-to-sales ratio and (b) the capital turnover ratio.

Purchasing and supply chain management can contribute in several ways, both quantitative and qualitative, to improve the company's bottom line.

In shaping their purchasing and supply chain strategies, companies can use different connotations and definitions related to the scope of purchasing, ranging from ordering, buying, purchasing to procurement, sourcing, supply (chain) management and value chain management. As the activity goes through each of these definitions the scope of purchasing broadens its impact to the business. New challenges lying ahead will change the scope and role of purchasing within organizations. The most important ones are the need to develop leveraged purchasing and supply strategies, global sourcing, integration of suppliers in both materials and new product development processes, reciprocal and countertrade arrangements, environmental and business integrity issues. Without doubt these challenges will put purchasing and supply chain management more in the spotlight in business.

ASSIGNMENTS

1.1 Take the annual report of an industrial company. Calculate the purchasing value in relation to the turnover. Calculate the effect of a 2 per cent and 5 per cent saving on the purchasing value.

(a) Do the same for a 2 per cent and 5 per cent increase in the purchasing value *ceteris paribus*.

(b) Describe the elements in the Du Pont chart (Figure 1.4) that are affected by purchasing policy directly or indirectly.

1.2 What would you consider to be purchasing's added value to a company? What would you consider to be purchasing's core and non-core activities?

1.3 What are the major differences between purchasing, supply, sourcing and supply management? Would you consider the purchasing function to be part of supply chain management or would you favor the reverse? Discuss.

1.4 What are the major differences between the activities of the purchasing function and the activities conducted by the purchasing department? Do you think it is important to differentiate between these two concepts? Why?

1.5 The chapter describes a number of new developments in purchasing and also addresses the aim for total quality control in companies. Describe the major consequences of total quality control on the purchasing policy in general and on the relationships with suppliers in particular.

CASE STUDY   BUYING COMPUTER SYSTEMS IN A CAR LEASING COMPANY

The management of a car leasing company has requested its business systems manager to prepare a proposal for further automation of all activities related to customer order handling. This management decision is in line with the intention to increase the efficiency of the sales back office: in the future, more administrative work must be done with fewer people. The management already has its eye on a particular system: contact has been made with a software supplier, who has references from the automobile branch. Documentation has been requested and the systems manager is asked to give his opinion.

The systems manager thinks that the management's ideas on further computerization of administrative sales tasks is best elaborated in close co-operation with the future users of the system. A project group is installed, consisting of employees from the internal sales department, the field sales organization, the internal control department and an external consultant. The working group's course is plotted. It immediately becomes clear during the first meetings that there is no apparent fit between the intended software system and the organization's present ways of working. When asked, the supplier states that this is usually the case: the current operating procedures will have to be adjusted here and there. However, before going ahead, the systems manager decides to get information from other suppliers. It appears that adjustments in the sales organizations are necessary no matter what software system management decides to implement. There is no system readily available on the market that corresponds exactly with the organization's present needs. The working group decides to invite another software company to help determine

25

whether the organization will have to develop its own system. The question is: what type of software will qualify? The systems department at headquarters is asked about their experience with software companies. Several names are provided, and it is decided to approach four companies. After talking to these four suppliers, the group decides to go ahead with one selected supplier for the time being.

The supplier in question proposes to start with a thorough analysis of the information needs of the company. Only then can the system requirements be defined. Supervision of these first steps will cost money, of course! A €150 000 quote is submitted and accepted. All this has taken three months.

The activities turn out to be more complex than expected. They also turn out to take much more time than anticipated: it has taken four months to describe the system requirements. Analysis of available software systems is then commenced. This reveals that one system will do, but that a considerable amount of 'application engineering' will be necessary. The software company can be of help in this too. A quotation is solicited: it amounts to €650 000. The systems manager has the strong impression that this price is far too high and again wants to invite competitive quotations from other software companies. However, the management is opposed: the current supplier is well-informed about the organization's problems. A new supplier would have to start all over, and that would cost too much money and time . . .

INTRODUCTION

The situation described above outlines one part of a complex decision-making process related to an important purchase. Decision-making processes concerning the purchase of products or services that are still to be developed, are generally characterized by a high degree of complexity and uncertainty. For this reason the decision making in such situations usually involves many disciplines and departments in the organization. In this car-lease company it involved the management, the systems manager, the marketing department, the sales department, and the internal controlling department. In addition, the external consultant and the suppliers involved exerted considerable influence on the decisions that were made. So various disciplines and stakeholders are involved, with varying interests and different views and opinions about what should be done! Circumstances such as these often make the purchasing decision making process complex and obscure. When ill structured, these processes can easily end up in frustration, considerable loss of time and budget overruns. Hence, a major question is how decision-making processes in purchasing can be structured in such a way that all parties involved arrive at solutions which are satisfactory to them.

In this chapter different models that are available to answer this question will be explained, starting with the main differences between organizational and consumer buying behavior. Next, the purchasing process will be described in more detail. Finally, some sources from business marketing theory on how organizational buying behavior can be modeled and analyzed are described.

ORGANIZATIONAL BUYING BEHAVIOR: BASIC CHARACTERISTICS

It is tempting to take the literature on consumer buying behavior as a frame of reference for studying buying processes in organizations. However, it soon becomes clear that these theories have only limited value in this regard. There appear to be major differences between consumer marketing on the one hand and industrial or business-to-business marketing on the other. The industrial marketer has to deal with companies, governmental organizations or institutions, who need the purchased product to feed, support and maintain their primary and supporting processes. In consumer marketing, however, the marketer faces individuals who strive for an immediate satisfaction of their needs. Table 2.1 summarizes the major differences between both types of marketing.

The following are a few important characteristics of industrial markets.

- Professional purchasing. Usually, professional buyers are involved in purchasing, decision-making and purchase operations. Because of their education, experience and responsibilities, they are usually experienced discussion partners for industrial salesmen and account managers.

- Derived demand. Most companies sell to other companies. Few manufacturing companies deliver directly to the end user. For this reason developments in industrial markets are often related to changes which occur in the end-user markets.

- Inelastic, fluctuating demand. Due to the complex decision making, the price-elasticity in industrial markets is frequently lower than for consumer products.

- Geographical concentration. Many industrial markets are geographically concentrated (unlike consumer markets, which are geographically dispersed). The European chemical industry, for example, is concentrated in the Ruhr area in Germany, the automobile industry in southern Germany, France and northern Italy (as the microchip industry is concentrated in Silicon Valley in the United States).

- Large order quantities and large amounts of money involved. Business-to-business transactions often involve large quantities of goods and services and, therefore, large sums of money.

TABLE 2.1 Main differences between industrial and consumer markets

Aspect	Industrial market	Consumer market
Buying objective	Enable production	Personal need satisfaction
Buying motive	Mainly rational	Also emotional
Purchasing function	Professional buying, predominantly men	Consumers, mainly women
Decision making	Many persons involved, much discussion	Often impulsive, without consulting others
Characteristics	Negotiations, intense interaction	Often without negotiation, little interaction
Product and market knowledge	Large	Limited
Order size	Often large	Mostly small
Demand	Derived demand, may fluctuate strongly	Autonomous demand, relatively stable
Price elasticity	Rather inelastic	Rather elastic
Number of customers	Mostly limited	Very large
Spread of customers	Sometimes large geographic concentration	Large geographical spread

Source: adapted from Matthijssens and Rijcke (1982)

- Limited number of customers. The customer market of industrial suppliers often consists of only a few companies. In Europe, the automotive industry – if limited to the producers – is made up of approximately six major independent manufacturers! Manufacturers of fast moving consumer products are confronted with only a handful of supermarket chains in most European countries. Therefore, only a limited number of buyers in fact determine the success of a new product.

A major difference between the consumer sector and the industrial sector is related to the interaction and (mutual) interdependency between buyer and seller. Unlike the consumer sector, business-to-business markets are often characterized by long-lasting relationships between the buying and the selling parties. As a consequence, business-to-business marketers must regard their markets as a network of relationships. Their marketing strategies are aimed at extending, investing in and continuously maintaining these networks. In other words, business-to-business marketing, and professional purchasing, require active management of relationships within complex organizational networks (see Figure 2.1).

THE PURCHASING PROCESS

In Chapter 1 some purchasing terms and definitions were given. In this chapter the purchasing process model described there will be elaborated on, based on Figure 2.2. The purchasing process model shows how the different purchasing activities are interrelated. Some of the important aspects of this model are now emphasized and explained.

- Process approach. Throughout this book purchasing and supply issues will be considered from a process approach. The various steps in the process model are closely connected. The quality of the output of the preceding steps determines to a large extent the quality of the output of the subsequent steps. Deficiencies in one step will lead to problems in the next steps. As an example, quality problems related to purchased materials often become visible at the end of the purchasing process in terms of rejected deliveries (step 5). In practice, however, bad quality of incoming materials can frequently be traced to incorrect or incomplete specifications (step 1), or to an incorrect sourcing decision in that a supplier has been selected who cannot deliver against required specifications (step 2). Also the contract that has been drawn up may have been incomplete in that it did not provide for any penalty clauses when delivering bad quality (step 3).

- Defining the interfaces. The purchasing process model implies that in order to get a full grip on buying operations, the output of each phase is clearly defined. Preferably it should be possible to trace and track every activity that has been done in the purchas-

FIGURE 2.1   Purchasing management requires management of supplier relationships within organizational networks.

ing process. Every consecutive step should only be started when the previous step has been concluded by a decision. Therefore, it is recommended that the result of each step is documented in the form of a 'go-no-go' document. This will help to structure the purchasing process and to formalize it. The way this is done is usually explained in the company's purchasing procedures, which are laid down in a purchasing manual. When such procedures are absent, this usually results in highly unstructured purchasing decision-making processes and operational problems.

■ Determining responsibilities. The author considers purchasing to be a cross-functional responsibility. As indicated before, the purchasing process is not limited to the purchasing department only. Many echelons in the organization are usually involved. This demands adequate communication and cooperation among the disciplines involved. The tasks, responsibilities and authority of each department should be indicated in each phase, to prevent misunderstandings and role conflicts. For example: when deciding on specifications of technical components, engineering departments often have the sole authority to do this. Engineering departments, however, are in most cases not responsible for the supply of base materials in the manufacturing stage. What often happens is that engineers, after careful selection, decide to integrate supplier and brand-specific components in their final designs leaving the buyer with a monopolist supplier. The author suggests that deciding on specifications of purchased materials and supplier selection are considered as a joint activity between engineers and buyers. Wijnstra (1998) has presented an interesting framework which may serve as a terms of reference to structure collaboration on product development between engineering, purchasing and suppliers.

■ Combining different skills, different types of knowledge and expertise. The first three steps, called the initial or tactical purchasing function, are primarily of a technical–commercial nature. The remaining three steps, referred to as the ordering function, are of a more logistics–administrative nature. A key problem in many companies is how to

FIGURE 2.2   Purchasing process approach: managing interfaces.

	Define specification	Select supplier	Contract agreement	Ordering	Expediting	Evaluation
P&S Role	• Get specification	• Assure adequate supplier selection	• Prepare contract	•Establish order routine	• Establish expediting routine	• Assess supplier
Elements	• Functional specification • Technical changes • Bring supplier-knowledge to engineering	• Prequalification of suppliers • Request for quotation	• Contracting expertise • Negotiating expertise	• Develop order routines • Order handling	• Expediting • 'Trouble-shooting'	• Supplier evaluation • Supplier rating
Documents	• Functional specification • Norm/spec control	• Supplier selection proposal	• Contract	• Order	• Exception report • Due date listings • Invoices	• Preferred supplier list • Supplier ranking scheme

Source: redrawn from van Weele (1994)

combine the different types of knowledge, skills and expertise in such a way that all parties involved arrive at an optimal solution for the company. It would be almost impossible to combine all these elements in one person, which is why we see an increasing tendency towards specialization in purchasing jobs, while at the same time cross-functional cooperation between different disciplines is growing.

The added value of the professional buyer primarily lies in his ability to act as a facilitator for the entire purchasing and supply cycle. This includes, among other things:

- Being involved in new product development projects and investment projects at an early stage, based on proven expertise.

- Preparing a list of approved suppliers in cooperation with the internal customer, and after that drawing up requests for quotations and preparing their evaluation together with the user, as well as selecting a supplier by mutual agreement.

- Preparing and carrying out the contract negotiations as well as drawing up and reviewing the terms and conditions of the contract.

- Setting up requisitioning and ordering routines in such a way that the users (if possible and so desired) can place orders themselves, within the terms and conditions established with the suppliers.

- In case orders cannot be placed by users themselves, take care of order handling i.e. handling internal requisitions; place orders at suppliers and maintain and monitor order and supplier files.

- Expediting (arranging) or follow-up of outstanding orders and monitoring outstanding financial obligations.

- Follow up and evaluation in terms of settling claims, evaluating supplier performance and maintaining and keeping up to date the relevant supplier documentation.

The cause of delivery problems of purchased materials is often related to late requisitioning by other departments, often due to time pressure. In practice this leads not only to a higher price being paid (as a result of extra work, speed delivery, buying from stock-keeping wholesaler), but also in many cases to higher organizational costs and operational problems (the delivered materials do not comply with the specifications, many partial deliveries, postponed delivery of critical parts, etc.). The presented purchasing model may help managers to structure their purchasing decision-making processes and the operational processes involved. The results will not only pay off in terms of lower prices paid for materials and services, but certainly also in lower organizational costs and a higher productivity.

There are relatively few situations in which all of the steps in the purchasing process are passed through. This only happens in the case of a first-time purchase of a product and/or service. In practice, most purchasing transactions involve more or less straight rebuys. In general, three types of purchasing situations are distinguished (Robinson *et al.*, 1967; see for the first studies on this subject Brand (1968)).

- The new-task situation. This situation occurs when the organization decides to buy a completely new product, supplied by an unknown supplier. This type of transaction is characterized by a high degree of uncertainty and high risk in that the specifications of the product still have to be mapped. The decision-making process is characterized by extensive problem solving and becomes protracted because various disciplines, distributed across various hierarchical levels in the organization, will probably assert their influence. The new-task situation occurs, for example, in the acquisition of capital goods and the purchase of new components which must be produced to the organization's specifications (see Figure 2.3). The Case Study of the car-lease company at the beginning of this chapter also falls into this category.

- The modified rebuy. This is when the organization wants to purchase a new product from a known supplier, or an existing product from a new supplier, and usually occurs when there is some dissatisfaction about the current supplier, or when better alternatives for existing products have become available. This situation is less uncertain than the new-task situation because the relevant criteria on how to value the functionality of the product or service or how to select the supplier are more or less known. The purchasing process focuses in particular on the last four steps of the model and decision making is characterized by limited problem solving.

- The straight rebuy. This is the most common situation and entails the acquisition of a known product from a known supplier. Uncertainty regarding the outcome of the transaction is low because the terms and conditions of the contract are known and are periodically re-established in negotiations with the supplier. In the case of regularly recurring (repetitive) deliveries of identical goods, blanket orders or annual agreements are used that cover the main terms and conditions. Ordering takes place through call-off orders, often placed directly by the user department through advanced e-procurement solutions. This benefits both the speed and efficiency of the transaction (for buyer as well as supplier). In this situation the purchasing process only covers the final three steps of the model. Straight rebuy situations relate to all kinds of consumable items, such as office supplies, fixing materials, cleaning materials, catering products. After negotiations with distributors about the contract, orders should be placed directly by the users without interference from the purchasing department. As will be explained later, Internet technology and especially e-commerce provide interesting solutions for efficient order handling in this area (see also Chapter 10).

This typology of buying situations explains that the degree of uncertainty and risk that buyers may deal with, strongly depends on the type of purchasing situation. This is reflected in the way the decision-making process evolves. The higher the sums of money involved and the higher the technical complexity, the higher the perceived risk will be, and more functions and persons will become involved in the decision making. The involvement of these persons as well as their role will vary in each step of the purchasing process model. They are sometimes referred to as the Decision-Making Unit (DMU) (Webster and Wind, 1972). In light of the interdisciplinary nature of many purchasing decisions, it is essential that the decision-making process is well organized. Many problems with supply and suppliers are caused by a lack of organization within the DMU.

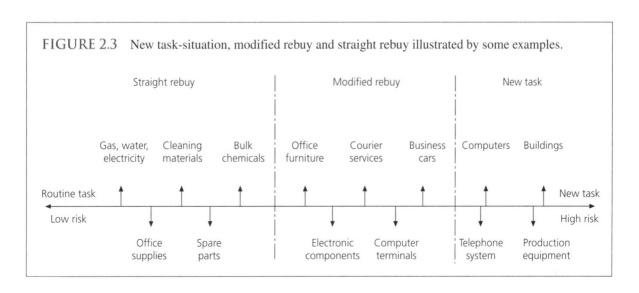

FIGURE 2.3   New task-situation, modified rebuy and straight rebuy illustrated by some examples.

MAJOR BOTTLENECKS AND PROBLEMS

The purchasing process model is a construct, an abstraction from reality, and in the real world organizational purchasing processes deviate from this model. Observation of numerous companies and institutions over many years has demonstrated that the purchasing process can be obstructed by the following situations.

- Supplier or brand specifications. With the exception of some leading-edge companies in the automotive, computer and consumer electronics industry, most buyers are involved only to a minor extent in the specification phase. Product specifications are usually determined unilaterally by the user, which means that they are often defined 'towards' a particular (approved) supplier. The use of a particular brand or supplier specification seriously limits the buyer's commercial latitude (in terms of negotiations) with the supplier – who in most cases is well aware of the selection of his product. Moreover, it may lead to situations where the supplier selected cannot meet the capacity and logistics requirements of the company.

- Inadequate supplier selection. Selecting a supplier is one of the most important decisions in the purchasing process, particularly if the products delivered require many years of maintenance and service, as in the case of many investment goods. Failure to check the supplier's bank references, can produce very unpleasant surprises in the shape of unexpected bankruptcy, inability to meet quality requirements, unwillingness to keep to warranty obligations, etc. It may become clear that the supplier, in order to land the contract, has made promises about delivery times he cannot keep.

- Insufficient contracting expertise. If there are problems during or after delivery, the contract's fine print comes into play. It can turn out that things thought to be handled by the supplier have to be paid for separately by the customer. Misunderstandings about the handling of problems can be prevented by means of a solid contract. Prevention is better than cure and editing of the contract is better left to the buyer.

MEMO 2.1   HOW INEFFICIENT ADMINISTRATIVE PURCHASING PROCEDURES CAN PAY OFF HANDSOMELY

The Profit Recovery Group (today known as PRG-Schulz), a specialist in audit recovery services, is a successful US-based consultancy firm which has reported considerable growth and profit. Founded in the early 1970s, the company went through a fast growth stage from 1991 on. In 1999 the company reported a sales turnover of US$40 million; at that time 1800 people were employed. From 1996 on this firm also set foot in Europe. What is the basis for its success?

Profit Recovery Group works on the basis of no cure-no pay. It targets its activities on large retailers and manufacturing firms. Based on the annual report of its prospective clients the company presents a proposal to investigate the invoices that have been paid for goods and services (including transport) by that client during a certain period. This investigation consists of checking whether the quantities invoiced and the price paid match the company's purchase orders and whether these data comply with the contract that has been negotiated with that supplier. If any variances are found (unfair prices being charged or delivered quantities lower than those invoiced) these are reported. Savings will be shared on a 50:50 basis with the client. The activities of Profit Recovery Group are also successful in Europe.

This illustrates how a consulting firm, operating in a niche market, may benefit from apparent deficiencies in the information and financial flows between buyers and suppliers.

- Too much emphasis on price. Especially when buying capital equipment, buying decisions need to be based upon total-cost-of-ownership (TCO) rather than price only. Many equipment manufacturers have adopted a sales strategy where they charge a fairly low price for their equipment. However, their warranties and service contracts require the customer to source spare parts and all maintenance services from the original equipment manufacturer. If not done so by the customer, the supplier will not guarantee the functioning of the equipment. Examples of this type of sales 'tactics' are many: copying machine manufacturers, manufacturers of computer mainframes, manufacturers of earth-moving equipment and trucks, systems packaging suppliers, all exert this kind of practice. In order to handle this type of purchase effectively, buyers need to base their decisions on TCO models where the initial purchase of the equipment is balanced against the life-of-type costs of the equipment.

- Administrative organization. Placing orders can also cause big problems. Sometimes there are no clear procedures with regard to procurement or authorization of orders, which can lead to random ordering by everybody in the organization. The result is lots of extra work in the inspection of deliveries (who is this product for?) and in making invoices payable (to what order or delivery does this invoice refer?). Inadequate administrative procedures could result in payment of invoices without any kind of check (see Memo 2.1).

THE ROLE OF THE PURCHASING DEPARTMENT IN THE PURCHASING PROCESS

In general the scope of the purchasing function is far wider than the activities of the purchasing department. In many companies, various goods and services are bought without intervention of the purchasing department (see Table 2.2). Apart from buyers, therefore,

TABLE 2.2 Examples of items purchased outside the purchasing department

Type of purchasing item	Purchased by
Key raw materials	Management
Computers and software	Accounting, computer department
Lease contracts	Accounting
Insurance	Management, accounting
Accounting services, legal and management consulting services	Management
Advertising, sales brochures, business gifts	Sales, marketing, sales promotions
Catering	Catering manager, facilities manager
Travel	Administration (or separate department)
Licences and development contracts	Research and development manager
Books and magazines	Library
Sales promotion items	Sales, marketing
Temporary labor and training	Personnel department, human resources
Cleaning materials	Facilities manager
Maintenance, repair and operating supplies	Technical maintenance

many other disciplines within the company are actively engaged in buying products and services. This is one reason why such large savings usually can be realized and is especially true for the facilities area where a growing number of management consultants have found interesting prospects.

Limiting this discussion to the role of the purchasing department in the purchasing process, it can be seen that this role varies from company to company and from situation to situation.

Table 2.3 shows the involvement of purchasing departments in the acquisition of:

■ production-related items such as raw materials, catalysts and semi-manufactured products;

■ indirect materials, such as spare parts, office supplies, cleaning materials and work-clothes;

■ investment goods, such as buildings, manufacturing equipment and computers, trucks, cars, etc.

Although this survey was conducted some time ago, the picture with regard to the role of purchasing within many manufacturing companies, apart from some leading-edge companies, is still valid. However, due to the interest that can be observed in purchasing and

TABLE 2.3 Involvement of the purchasing department in the acquisition of production-related items, indirect goods and investment goods. Numbers represent average scores

	Purchasing fully responsible		Shared responsibility		Purchasing not responsible	
	100% (5)		75% (4) 50% (3) 25% (2)		0% (1)	
	Production-related goods		Indirect materials		Investment goods	
	PM	GM	PM	GM	PM	GM
Determining purchasing requirements (quality)	1.6	1.5	1.8	2.0	1.3	1.1
Determining purchasing requirements (quantity)	2.4	2.2	2.0	1.8	1.1	1.0
Market research and supplier selection	4.3	4.0	4.1	4.0	2.8	2.7
Requests for quotation	4.6	4.5	4.5	4.8	3.7	4.0
Evaluating requests for quotation	4.1	4.2	4.2	4.3	3.0	3.1
Negotiations with suppliers	4.4	4.5	4.4	4.5	3.3	3.6
Final supplier selection	3.9	4.0	4.1	4.2	2.7	2.8
Preparing contract	4.6	4.9	4.8	4.9	4.1	4.4
Order handing and expediting	4.4	4.4	4.4	4.4	3.9	3.9
Invoice handling	2.7	3.0	2.5	2.8	2.4	2.5

Notes: PM = Purchasing manager; GM = General manager
Source: van Weele and van Hespen (1987)

supply issues from some large multinational companies and leading management consultancies, this picture will rapidly change in the years to come.

Table 2.3 shows that in general the purchasing department's involvement is highest in the purchase of indirect materials, referred to in many companies as consumable items, or maintenance, repair and operating (MRO) supplies.

Considering the various purchasing activities, it can be seen that the involvement of the purchasing department is limited during the first stages of the purchasing process. Purchasing's role becomes more important when quotations must be solicited; however, when these quotations are evaluated, involvement decreases. Involvement is at its highest in the last stage of the purchasing process, i.e. when the purchase contract is drawn up and when orders need to be placed. This seems to be true for all three types of purchasing goods. Apparently checking invoices is usually a responsibility that purchasing shares with the accounting discipline.

It can be concluded from this survey that the involvement of the purchasing department in the initial stage is rather low. Purchasing appears to be most involved in the operational activities of the purchasing process, which explains the administrative orientation of most purchasing departments. There is some risk involved when this situation applies to a particular company. In the first place the administrative work may prevent buyers from spending sufficient time on their tactical and more strategic purchasing tasks. Second, the administrative orientation may prevent a more strategic vision on purchasing and supply management to develop. Both are underlying reasons why purchasing and supply management in many organizations represent a business area with such great improvement potential!

Figure 2.4 shows that purchasing and supply activities in general have four different dimensions:

- a technical dimension, which concerns the functionality, specifications and quality of the purchased products;
- a commercial dimension, related to managing the relationship with the suppliers and the contractual conditions which must be negotiated and arranged;

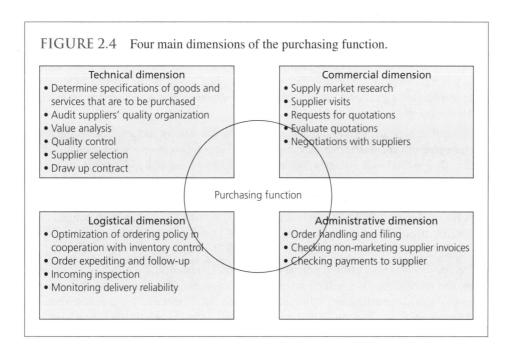

FIGURE 2.4   Four main dimensions of the purchasing function.

Technical dimension
- Determine specifications of goods and services that are to be purchased
- Audit suppliers' quality organization
- Value analysis
- Quality control
- Supplier selection
- Draw up contract

Commercial dimension
- Supply market research
- Supplier visits
- Requests for quotations
- Evaluate quotations
- Negotiations with suppliers

Purchasing function

Logistical dimension
- Optimization of ordering policy in cooperation with inventory control
- Order expediting and follow-up
- Incoming inspection
- Monitoring delivery reliability

Administrative dimension
- Order handling and filing
- Checking non-marketing supplier invoices
- Checking payments to supplier

- a logistics dimension, which concerns all activities related to optimizing the incoming materials flow from the supplier up to the point where the materials are needed and actually consumed;

- an administrative dimension, relating to the efficient order handling, expediting and follow-up and handling of invoices.

MODELS OF INDUSTRIAL BUYING BEHAVIOR

In the previous section the stages of the purchasing process were identified. The variables that affect the course and/or the outcomes of this process will now be addressed, distinguishing between (1) variables that affect the buying process; (2) variables that affect buying behavior.

Variables that affect the buying process

- Characteristics of the product. Decisions about the purchase of raw materials differ from, for example, those for the purchase of spare parts. The differences stem from the financial importance (and therefore the influence on the cost price of the end product) of both types of goods, their technical complexity and the supply risk involved. In practice, many differences in the way the buying process develops can be traced to specific product characteristics. Decisions about the purchase of technically complex products are usually made by technical specialists (designers, engineers, technical/maintenance department, etc.). Decisions concerning the purchase of standard-grade, high-volume products (such as raw materials and commodities) are made primarily by financial managers and/or top management. Purchase decisions about routine products in general are left to the lower echelons of the organization.

- Strategic importance of the purchase. The higher the importance of the purchase to the company, the more involved management will be in the purchase decision. The strategic importance is not merely determined by the amounts of money or the investment involved in the purchase. For example, low-cost bottleneck items can sometimes show significant risk in terms of availability and supply, and often turn out to be a direct threat to the continuity of production. For this reason they are of prime interest to top management. Other examples of key purchase decisions are contracting for licenses or development contracts.

- Sums of money involved in the purchases. As the amounts of money involved increase, management's role in the purchase decision will grow. This is why management is often directly involved in negotiations about important raw materials and investment goods.

- Characteristics of the purchasing market. The approach towards suppliers varies depending on the organization's freedom of choice in terms of purchasing. In a monopolist or oligopolist market, negotiations with suppliers will be far more complex and difficult than in markets characterized by free competition. The management of the company will therefore be more interested in the former.

- Degree of risk related to the purchase. As the risk related to the purchase decision is higher, more disciplines will be involved in the process. The Case Study at the beginning of this chapter illustrates this situation. The risk attached to the purchase decision decreases and the lead time of the process diminishes as the organization has more experience with the purchase of a particular product or a particular supplier.

■ Role of the purchasing department in the organization. The tasks, responsibilities and competence of the purchasing department vary between organizations. Purchasing departments in large companies usually operate more professionally than those in smaller ones, and very small companies usually dispense with having a specialist explicitly in charge of the purchasing task. The internal structure of the organization generally governs the way in which the purchasing decisions are made.

■ Degree to which the purchase product affects existing routines in the organization. The decision making will be more complex, take more time and require the involvement of more disciplines as the products that are to be purchased require adjustments in the internal organization or necessitate education and training. This situation occurs, for example, when implementing new computer and new manufacturing technology.

Lehmann and O'Shaughnessy (1974) provide an interesting elaboration of the second last aspect. These authors distinguish four categories of products, based on the potential post-purchase problems: (1) routine products; (2) products that require instruction; (3) products whose adequate technical functioning in the organization is uncertain; (4) products that can result in problems in the internal organization. As more adaptation within the organization is required, more disciplines will be involved in the buying decision, and the decision-making process will be more complex.

According to Fisher (1970) the purchasing decision-making process is primarily determined by two aspects, product complexity and commercial uncertainty. If these two aspects are combined, statements can be made about what disciplines will be involved in the decision-making process (see Figure 2.5).

Variables that affect the buying decision

Here the ideas developed by Webster and Wind (1972) are adopted. These authors distinguish between 'task' variables and 'non-task' variables. They define task variables as those variables that are related to the tasks, responsibilities and competences assigned by the organization to the person involved in the purchase decision. The engineer's main focus will be on the design, construction and quality aspects of the purchase product. A materials planner will focus mainly on logistic aspects, such as minimum order quantities, packing requirements, delivery times, etc. Every specialist will want a say in the discussion from his/her own perspective and interests.

The non-task variables are related to the professional's personality. People differ in terms of personality, for example the degree to which the person involved either accepts or avoids risks, his/her ambitions, the degree to which he/she avoids or confronts personal conflicts with suppliers, etc.

According to Webster and Wind (1972), task and non-task variables can be identified not only at the level of the individual, but also at a departmental level, at the level of the organization, and the level of the company and its environment. For example, the group culture in a purchasing department may focus on strengthening its own position within the organization, which may lead to boundary problems with other disciplines and suboptimal decisions. Another example: when the culture in an organization is highly informal, this will prevent a successful introduction of formal purchasing procedures. As an illustration of how the relationships between a company and its environment may affect relationships with suppliers, the organization's implicit objective might be to avoid introducing environmentally sensitive products to the market. As a result this company may impose requirements on its suppliers to formally comply with environmental legislation. Figure 2.6 depicts Webster and Wind's model.

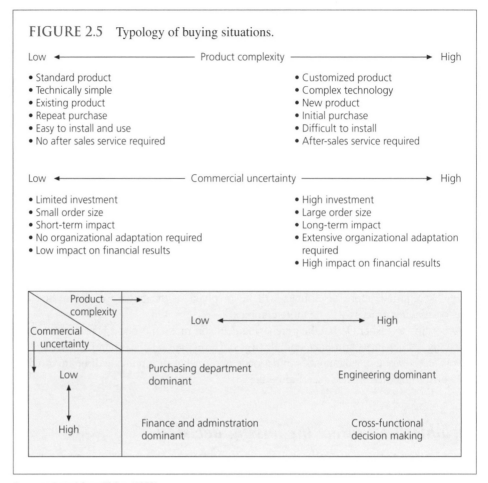

FIGURE 2.5 Typology of buying situations.

Source: adapted from Fisher (1970)

This description clearly shows that the authors attach a great significance to the influence of psychological, social, organizational and environmental factors on the buying process. They place purchasing decision processes in a larger context, suggesting that purchasing processes can only be understood if the researcher takes these factors into consideration. This perspective is also shared by Sheth (1973) and provides an understanding of the large differences which exist between organizations in the field of organizational buying behavior.

Based upon observations from a number of purchasing practices the author feels that the importance of social, psychological and emotional factors on purchasing decision making can hardly be overstated. There have been many examples where rational purchasing decision making was blurred and obstructed by the fact that deeply felt emotions and personal preferences were insufficiently recognized. Remarkably, these aspects of purchasing decision making have attracted only little interest from researchers up to now.

Collectively, the relevant literature makes it clear that organizational purchasing processes are very complex, always involving more than one person, i.e. group decision making. The literature refers to this group as the 'decision-making unit' (DMU). Webster and Wind (1972) speak of the 'buying center', which they define as 'all those individuals and groups who participate in the purchasing decision-making process, who share some common goals and the risks arising from the decisions'. Within the DMU various roles can be distinguished.

■ Users. These are the people who will work with the product, either on an individual basis or in a group context. It is obvious that the user has an important say when it concerns the specification and selection of the product.

■ Influencers. The influencers are able to affect the outcome of the purchasing process by means of solicited or unsolicited advice. In the construction business, for example, architects have an important say in the choice of materials. Software specialists can exert influence on the selection of the hardware supplier (and vice versa).

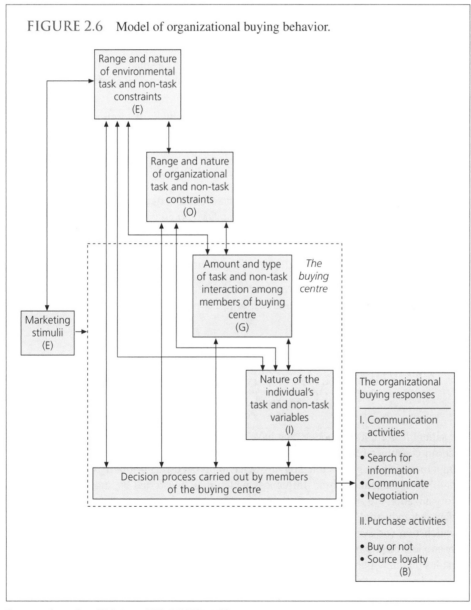

FIGURE 2.6   Model of organizational buying behavior.

Source: redrawn from Webster and Wind (1972), p. 30

TABLE 2.4 Decision stages and roles in the decision-making unit

	User	Influencer	Buyer	Decider	Gatekeeper
Identification of need	x	x			
Establishing specifications and scheduling the purchase	x	x	x	x	
Identifying buying alternatives	x	x	x		x
Evaluating alternative buying actions	x	x	x		
Selecting the suppliers	x	x	x	x	

Source: Webster and Wind (1972)

- Buyers. Buyers are not necessarily the same individuals as the users. In large organizations it is often the buyer who negotiates with the supplier about the terms and conditions of the contract and who places the order.
- Decision makers. These are the professionals who actually determine the selection of the supplier. Sometimes the decision maker is a designer who writes his specifications 'towards' a specific supplier because of positive experiences with this supplier's products in the past. In other cases the decision maker is the person who controls the budget.
- Gatekeepers. Gatekeepers are the people who control the flow of information from the supplier towards the other members of the DMU (and vice versa). In some cases the gatekeeper may be the technical director's secretary who screens contacts with particular suppliers. In other cases the buyer is the gatekeeper, when he has the power to decide whether or not to circulate specific supplier documentation within the organization.

Table 2.4 relates these roles to the various phases of the purchasing process. It can be seen that the importance of individual roles can differ, depending on which phase the purchasing process is in.

BUYING BEHAVIOR CONSIDERED AS AN INTERACTIVE PROCESS

One salient feature of the models that have been discussed so far, is that they are typically based on consumer research. In line with the consumer marketing models, these models attempt to describe organizational buying behavior as occurring primarily within the boundaries of the organization itself. Influences which may be exerted by stakeholders outside the organization are not reflected in these models. A major drawback is that they ignore the fact that industrial buying behavior actually should be studied as an interactive process in which two (or even more) organizations participate simultaneously. Although these early models on organizational buying behavior provide a systematic account of all the variables that may play a role in the purchase decision, it is unlikely that the effect of customer behavior on the industrial market will be totally independent from the supplier. Industrial markets have a far higher degree of mutual interdependency, and it is therefore essential that buying behavior is analyzed as an interactive process. This proposition is supported by literature in the field of industrial buying behavior, e.g. Hakansson *et al.* (1977); Hakansson and Wootz (1979); Hakansson (1982); and Ford (1980).

The approach of Hakansson, Johansson and Wootz

These authors describe the interaction process between buyers and sellers in terms of the following physical characteristics:

- the number of times the parties make contact;
- the properties of the object of exchange: the product;
- the degree in which the process is formalized (written record, rules and regulations);
- characteristics of the parties involved.

Based on these elements, the transaction process in terms of the physical exchange can be described.

The interaction process can, however, also be studied from a 'social exchange' perspective: in what way does the process take place, how do organizations achieve a particular interaction, under what conditions can this social process evolve? In terms of time, the interaction process will proceed faster as the parties get to know each other better and develop more trust in their mutual relationship.

A third aspect of this model is the mutual adaptation of the parties involved. During the interaction, the understanding of the mutual positions grows and the parties get closer. This is expressed in, among other things, the adjustment of the supplier's commercial and manufacturing organization to the client organization. It is of major importance for any organization to maximize the chances of a successful interaction process. Seen from the other side, the supplier will try to increase its chances for a successful interaction process by limiting its activities as much as possible to those transactions where the fit between the supplier's marketing policy and production system on the one hand, and the customer's requirements on the other hand, is optimal. The supplier can furthermore attempt to change the customer's preferences and perceptions by influencing three different types of uncertainties:

- Uncertainty with regard to the definition of the requirements ('requirements uncertainty'). The supplier responds to the question: 'Are we buying the right product for our problem/our needs?'
- Uncertainty with regard to the outcome of the transaction ('transaction uncertainty'). The question anticipated here is: 'Will the supplier actually perform in accordance with the agreement (i.e. regarding delivery times and quality)?'
- Uncertainty with regard to the right choice of supplier ('market uncertainty'). This type of insecurity is reflected in the question: 'Are we selecting the right supplier from the group of potential suppliers?'

These three types of uncertainty will ultimately determine the characteristics of the buyer–seller relationship and how it will develop over time. We will see that understanding these kinds of uncertainties and risks is important when dealing with complex purchasing decisions such as outsourcing (see Chapter 6).

Buying situations can now be characterized with the aid of these three types of uncertainty. Figure 2.7 provides an illustration.

The supplier is therefore well-advised to limit himself as much as possible to interactions in which the fit between his and the customer's organizations is optimal. As will be clear from this approach, the supplier can influence the intensity of the interaction by

FIGURE 2.7   Characteristics of buying situations: 1, buying a standard product from an existing supplier; 2, buying a standard commodity from a new supplier; 3, buying a reactor for a new nuclear power plant.

Source: Hakansson et al. (1977)

reducing, maintaining or increasing the uncertainty about requirements, transaction uncertainty and market uncertainty.

The approach of Ford

Ford (1980) emphasizes that the crucial element of industrial marketing is viewing the market as a network of relationships between organizations. Marketing policy should not employ a strategy of broad market segmentation only, it should strive to maintain and expand a particular portfolio of concrete relationships with organizations. This underlines the long-lasting nature of the relations between supplier and customer in industrial markets. This view implies that the mutual dependency between the two parties increases as the permanence of the relationship increases. These lasting relationships also form a barrier against the supplier's competitors getting into contact with the customer. One will have to 'break into' the existing relationships. Ford describes the development of relationships between organizations as a process in three stages. It starts with the first contact between the organizations, develops into an ever closer relationship, and gradually becomes more and more institutionalized. Chapter 9 describes how companies may be able to foster partnership-relationships with their suppliers.

Management of the portfolio of relationships is not only a matter of operational importance (short term), it is primarily a strategic policy issue (long term). Based on this reasoning Ford suggests that relationship managers be appointed, who coordinate all aspects for each relationship in time. Ford proved at the time of writing to have good foresight: account management in business-to-business marketing has since then been widely adopted. The account manager is more than an industrial sales representative, since apart from direct sales he is responsible for developing the relationships with his key accounts in the long term.

Ford's ideas are interesting and although initially intended for business-to-business marketing and sales organizations, are also very valuable for purchasing and supply management.

The network approach

The network approach goes beyond the interaction approach. Supporters of this approach (for example Hakansson (1982) and Wijnstra (1998)) are convinced that the dyadic relationship between supplier and manufacturer is not only influenced by the characteristics of the product and the involved organizations, but also by the relationship between these organizations and other organizations which are part of the supplier network (see Memo 2.2). Effective purchasing and effective management of supplier relationships requires a thorough understanding of the cost structures and the balance of power in the entire buyer-supplier network. The value of this approach is confirmed by the experiences of some leading manufacturers such as Honda and Chrysler-Daimler in the United States. These automotive manufacturers have focused their supplier strategies upon developing intensive relationships with relatively few selected suppliers of parts and subassemblies. Business is done based on detailed cost breakdowns, showing the high level of knowledge of the producer concerning the supplier's cost position. Components are divided into the individual sub-parts. The cost-price of these individual parts is analyzed in detail in terms of direct and indirect costs of labor, overhead, depreciation and materials. Also the operational costs as incurred by the manufacturer are analyzed relative to incoming inspection,

---

MEMO 2.2   CASE EXAMPLE OF HOW BUYER–SELLER NETWORKS INTERACT

In recent years many industries in Europe, such as the Japanese industries, have developed a tiered supplier structure. Often, this structure resembles a pyramid. The original equipment manufacturers (OEMs), producers of end-products, such as truck manufacturers, manufacturers of PCs, are at the top of this pyramid. They often buy their products (mostly subassemblies) from first-tier suppliers (main suppliers). The main suppliers purchase their subassemblies and components from second-tier suppliers (jobbers). Jobbers are companies which specialize in electro-mechanical activities (such as drilling, cutting, milling, grinding, etc.) on base materials (steel, steelplate, plastics). The base materials, however, are supplied by big international (process) manufacturers like DuPont, Dow Chemical Hoechst and Akzo Nobel. Examples of other manufacturers of base materials are steelmills and manufacturers of basic foodstuffs.

Usually these process-manufacturers target their marketing and sales strategies towards two different market segments. First, through their account managers and technical specialists they focus on getting a favored status in the relationship with the OEMs. It is important for them to have their brands and/or materials described in the specifications of new products. Therefore, sales efforts are primarily targeted at the OEM's research and development departments and engineering people. Once the OEM has decided to integrate the base supplier's materials into its components (for example to use DSM-plastics for a new bumper), the supplier of the component is limited to this sole source of supply. These suppliers often do not have any other choice but to accept the terms and conditions of these base materials suppliers.

Nowadays some leading-edge OEMs, through value chain analysis, have identified this problem and now try to integrate the first-tier suppliers into their development and operations processes. Often this leads to a situation where the OEM will actually support its first-tier suppliers in their negotiations with their second-tier suppliers and base materials suppliers. Contracts for base materials may be negotiated by the much more powerful OEM; the first-tier supplier, however, is entitled to use this contract to call off deliveries.

materials handling, storage, etc. Based upon this information both buyer and seller develop a common understanding of the cost drivers and the opportunities for cost reduction and improving business processes. As a rule ideas are developed on how to take advantage of these opportunities leading to detailed improvement plans being implemented on both sides.

As both organizations go through this process over time, relationships will become more intensive and cooperative and supply chain integration will be the result.

In practice, many organizations take the developments within the supplier's market into account when defining their own purchasing policy. For example, a take-over of a supplier by a direct competitor can result in the end of the relationship with this supplier, as happened when a major supplier of bottles to the Heineken organization was taken over in the early 1990s by Saint Gobain. Saint Gobain owns Kronenbourg, which is one of the main competitors of Heineken in France. When Saint Gobain became the owner of this bottle supplier, Heineken decided to look for another supplier. This example illustrates that changes in the supplier network actually influence individual relationships between buyers and sellers. The network approach, therefore, provides a useful and valuable concept to study the dynamics in relationships between manufacturers and their suppliers.

The network perspective is complementary to the other models and approaches which have been described in this chapter. What model to be used in a specific situation will depend, of course, on the object of study.

SUMMARY

This chapter describes how organizational buying behavior can be studied and analyzed. The conclusion is that the buying behavior of organizations differs significantly from consumer buying behavior. Industrial companies, governmental organizations and institutions buy their goods and services to feed, support and maintain their primary and supportive processes, while consumers purchase products to immediately satisfy their needs. The value of the models which have been developed for explaining consumer buying behavior is therefore, in the author's opinion, limited when studying industrial buying processes.

Although organizational purchasing processes may vary to a great extent, clear stages are still recognized. In this chapter the purchasing process model has been elaborated. The essence of this outlook is that effective purchasing decision making requires a cross-functional approach. The key issue is to direct and guide the efforts of the various organizational parties involved in such a way that an optimal result is achieved for the organization. The professional buyer can make a major contribution here. Not all phases of the purchasing process are passed through in all cases. Three types of buying situations can roughly be distinguished, i.e. the new-task situation, the modified rebuy and the straight rebuy. The composition of the decision-making unit (DMU) will be different for each of these situations.

In this chapter the position of the purchasing department was discussed. In general, the purchasing department's involvement is highest when it concerns the purchase of indirect goods or consumable items. Its role is more limited when it concerns investment goods. It has furthermore been demonstrated that purchasing's involvement is highest during the operational stages of the purchasing process; purchasing's involvement is relatively low in the early stages of product development when specifications are determined and materials selected. Theory runs ahead of practice here.

Finally, this chapter discussed several theoretical models in the field of industrial buying behavior. A distinction can be made between the models that view the purchasing process exclusively from an organizational perspective, and the models that regard the buying process as an interaction between two or more parties. Both types of models have their value: they explain why it is sometimes so difficult for an outsider to fathom organizational purchasing processes and why they are often so hard to organize.

ASSIGNMENTS

2.1   In paragraph two of this chapter it is stated that industrial markets, unlike consumer markets, are often inelastic. Do you agree with this statement? Please explain why and provide some examples.

2.2   As the strategic importance of a product increases, management's involvement in the purchase decision will also grow. Which criteria determine the strategic importance of a particular good that is to be purchased for the organization? Give examples of products that, in your opinion, can be earmarked as strategic (a) for an automobile manufacturer and (b) for an academic hospital.

2.3a The management of a medium-sized metal working company is considering buying a CNC-milling machine. This is a completely new type of machine for the company in question. Describe:

(a) the purchasing process phases that this company will go through;

(b) which disciplines will probably be involved in each phase of the buying process.

2.3b One production plant, where numerical milling machines have been in use for a number of years, is considering the purchase of an additional one. Describe how the purchasing process in this production company differs from the purchasing process described above.

2.4   What are the differences between buying standard-grade raw materials and buying customized electrical components? Discuss the differences in market structure, required expertise, product characteristics, etc. in your analysis, using Fisher's typology as a framework.

2.5   According to the interaction approach of Johansson, Hakansson and Wootz, the industrial seller can influence the course of the purchasing process by anticipating three kinds of uncertainty. First, describe these three types of uncertainty. Then indicate what arguments a seller of copying equipment can use to either (a) enlarge or (b) reduce each of these uncertainties in his relationship with a potential customer.

2.6   In this chapter the purchasing process model has been discussed. Discuss how the three different purchasing situations as identified by Robinson, Faris and Wind can be related to this model.

After studying this chapter you should understand the following:

- The most important elements of a purchase order specification.
- The various methods of contracting out, their advantages and disadvantages.
- The most important activities that precede the supplier selection decision.
- The main elements of a purchase contract.
- The way in which order follow-up and expediting can take place.

CASE STUDY   PURCHASE OF NEW CARRIAGES BY A NATIONAL
RAILWAY COMPANY

Some years ago in one European country the following story was published in various newspapers. It revealed the problems related to the purchase of new carriages by the national railway company which suffered a major financial setback because the new two-deck carriages turned out to be 30 cm wider than the railway could accommodate. The new carriages could not pass each other in at least 16 places in the country and on these (mainly curved) sections the distance between the tracks needed to be widened by at least 16 cm. The rail-way company was also compelled to replace or shift overhead wires, signals, signs, platform covering and tiling in many additional places throughout the country. The unforeseen costs involved were estimated to be at least €57 million.

These problems were caused by the design of the new trains which had five seats across the width of the carriages instead of the usual four. More passengers on a train means greater revenue; however, due to the new design the carriages had become 30 cm wider.

INTRODUCTION

This Case Study demonstrates that a lot can go wrong in the process of buying capital equipment. Several aspects in connection with the use of the carriages were obviously overlooked and, as a result, expensive adjustments in the railway infrastructure had to be made. This type of problem is not uncommon in the purchase of capital goods because the decision-making process usually focuses on the purchase of the equipment itself. Aspects such as the infrastructure required, technical maintenance, the supply and availability of spare parts, after sales service and training and education often receive attention only after the machine has been put into operation. It then becomes clear that the supplier, who was so keen to deliver the machinery, is not very service oriented and that spare parts are extremely costly. A good illustration of this is the supplier of small office printers: the acquisition cost of the printer is usually minimal, however the manufacturer makes up for his low prices through his high rates for toner cartridges. The acquisition cost of these cartridges during the lifetime of the printer is many times the acquisition cost of the printer.

This chapter further elaborates on the purchasing process model presented in Chapter 2; each of the stages distinguished there will be addressed in detail. The description will be based on the purchasing procedure for capital equipment, starting with the question of how to achieve a sound purchase specification, to be followed by a description of the main activities preceding the supplier selection. The purchasing contract is then discussed, including several special terms and conditions. Finally, several expediting methods are described.

The different stages will be illustrated by a project concerning the purchase of body carriers by an automotive manufacturer, used to transport car bodies inside the plant.

FIRST STEP IN THE BUYING PROCESS: DETERMINING THE PURCHASE ORDER SPECIFICATIONS

During this initial stage of the purchasing process, the purchasing requirements are determined and the company is also faced with the 'make-or-buy' question. It has to determine which products or activities will be produced i.e. performed by the company itself, and which products or activities will be contracted out. In what follows only the contracting-out issue will be discussed (see also Chapter 7 on this topic). The process of assessing 'make' versus 'buy' starts by drawing up the specifications of those items that will be purchased which may have a different level of detail. In general it is possible to differentiate between:

■ A functional specification. This describes the functionality which the product must have for the user. (In this chapter, the term 'user' is employed in a broader sense. It can refer to the person who actually uses the product that is to be bought, but it can also refer to the person who has to make the financial decision about the purchase, who allocates the budget). An example: when outsourcing greenkeeping a buyer may state in his contract with the gardener that he is expected to mow a lawn once every week, using personnel with a specific educational background and using a Honda low-noise, high-performance mower. However, he also may state in his contract that the gardener will keep the grass at a maximum of one inch, whilst keeping noise below a certain number of decibels during execution. The difference will be clear: in the first situation the gardener will probably mow the lawn every week (also during wintertime), since that is what has been agreed with the customer. In the second situation the gardener will only mow the grass when needed.

The advantages of working with functional specifications will be clear:

– potential suppliers are given the best possible opportunity to contribute their expertise;

– new technologies can be used, technologies that the buyer is not familiar with;

– creates one standard, against which all concepts can be evaluated.

- A detailed technical specification. This describes the technical properties and characteristics of the product as well as the activities to be performed by the supplier. Usually these technical specifications are laid down in detailed technical drawings and activity schedules which can be used to monitor the supplier's activities in detail. This way of working by the contractor can easily lead to overspecification, where the user imposes requirements on both product and supplier which easily lead to higher cost but no better functionality.

Both a functional and a technical specification are part of a wider concept, which is referred to as the purchase order specification. This document (usually a set of documents) comprises the following:

- quality specifications, describing how the product should be delivered (with or without a quality certificate) and what technical norms and standards the product should meet;
- the logistics specifications, indicating the quantities needed and the delivery time to be respected;
- a maintenance specification, describing how the product will be maintained and serviced by the supplier (and whether or not spare parts need to be supplied in the future);
- legal and environmental requirements, determining that both product and production process should be in compliance with health, safety and environmental legislation;
- a target budget, which indicates within what financial constraints the solution to be provided by the prospective supplier should be found.

In the purchase of construction work and civil projects, the purchase order specifications are usually recorded in a scope-of-work description.

The user or budget holder is responsible for specifying the purchasing order requirements and the buyer's task is to ensure that the specification is drawn up in objective, supplier-neutral terms. Several manufacturing companies have regulated this responsibility in so-called sign-off procedures. Before a specification is released to a supplier, it must have the formal approval of purchasing and/or the (potential) supplier(s). The purpose of this procedure is to prevent misunderstandings in the consecutive stages of the purchasing process. In this way the costs of so-called 'problem-solving changes' are reduced. Experience has shown that this type of preparation will result in a considerable reduction of the project's total engineering lead time.

Technical changes that occur during the project must be dealt with in accordance with the change order procedures. The buyer's job is to ensure that the supplier's work is conducted according to the last specifications sent to him. Suppliers should ideally confirm each approved change, preferably in writing. Sound configuration management can prevent many problems! In summary, the added value of the buyer during the specification stage is:

- ensuring unambiguous functional, technical, logistics and maintenance specifications;
- preventing the use of supplier or product brand specifications – to keep the possibility of alternative sources of supply open;
- recording clear procedures regarding approval of specification changes;
- ensuring a clear sample inspection procedure;
- ensuring clear descriptions of the methods to be used by both buyer and supplier for testing the quality of the product;
- ensuring a general cost breakdown and/or calculation (if possible) to help assessment of quotations at a later stage.

Memo 3.1 illustrates this first stage of the purchasing process, for the purchase of car-body carriers by a large automotive manufacturer.

SECOND STEP IN THE BUYING PROCESS: SUPPLIER SELECTION

After the purchasing requirements have been defined and described in the specifications, the buyer can start his market exploration. In practice these steps are interwoven. When drawing up the technical specifications, the practical feasibility and the costs are estimated. The selection of basic technologies – through which the product design will have to be realized – is frequently made with the names of a few suppliers in mind. In practice, the step of 'selection' contains a number of separate steps:

- determining the method of subcontracting;
- preliminary qualification of suppliers and drawing up the 'bidders list';
- preparation of the request for quotation and analysis of the bids received;
- selection of the supplier.

The first issue to be dealt with in supplier selection is whether to opt for turnkey or partial subcontracting.[1] In the case of turnkey subcontracting the responsibility for the execution of the entire assignment (often including design activities) is placed with the supplier. In the case of partial subcontracting the assignment is divided into parts which are contracted out separately, often to various suppliers. Coordination rests with the principal. Partial subcontracting usually results in savings, but obviously has some important drawbacks. Table 3.1 lists the advantages and disadvantages of both types of subcontracting.

MEMO 3.1   DECIDING ON THE SPECIFICATION OF THE BODY CARRIERS

The department of 'advanced engineering' has been requested by the technical director of the assembly plant to investigate the way in which car bodies can be transported more efficiently through the plant. For this project an advanced engineering team is created, consisting of experts from both the engineering and the assembly organization. Some preliminary investigations led to the conclusion that transportation basically can take place in three fundamentally different ways: through carriers, conveyors or chains. The carrier concept is chosen for reasons of flexibility. The assignment is then passed on to the technical operations department. Headed by a project engineer, a project team is formed, consisting of representatives from various technical disciplines (manufacturing engineering, process-control and automation, and human engineering) and purchasing. Disciplines such as cost engineering and finance and controling are involved on an *ad hoc* basis. The project group first focuses on defining the scope of the project – what is it we want? These discussions result in a technical specification, which does not express any preference for a particular supplier. The major guiding principles are that the project should, whenever possible, use 'proven technologies' and suppliers with 'proven abilities', since the car manufacturer has no wish to serve as a 'guinea pig' for suppliers in this type of project. It is decided to choose potential suppliers, who may be contacted for the next step

---

1 The term subcontracting is used here. Alternative terms used in literature for the same activity are 'outsourcing' (see Chapter 7) and 'contracting out'.

A major point against partial subcontracting is that the principal must be sure the separate contracts are attuned to one another. In this case, full responsibility for the continuity of the whole of the project activities rests with the principal. If he fails, it is clear that the expected cost advantage will not materialize, and considerable additional costs will result.

A second issue to be considered at this stage is whether the work will be awarded on a fixed-price, lump-sum or a cost-reimbursable basis.

When work is executed based on a fixed-price contract, the principal orders the supplier to perform the required activities at a fixed price, and to have the work completed by a predetermined date. The advantages of this method are:

- the principal knows exactly where he stands financially;
- after completion of the work there is no need for settlements because all risks are carried by the supplier;
- a firm completion date.

As the price is fixed, it is in the supplier's interest to execute the work as efficiently as possible. The fixed price is an incentive to complete the work, or deliver the goods, as quickly as possible within the agreed term. Disadvantages of this method are:

- it is difficult to get insight into the supplier's cost breakdown if the principal lacks expertise; this problem can be avoided by requesting quotations from more than one supplier;.
- preparation requires time – the question is whether there is enough time to prepare a detailed specification and have a formal bidding procedure;
- one does not know in advance which supplier will turn out to be the best.

In the case of a cost-reimbursable contract the nature and scope of the activities to be performed are not established in advance. The principal orders the supplier to perform the required activities at a predetermined hourly rate, sometimes in combination with a pre-arranged percentage to cover the overhead costs. Settlement follows after completion of

TABLE 3.1 Advantages and disadvantages of turnkey and partial subcontracting

	Advantages	Disadvantages
Turnkey subcontracting	Limited interference by principal during project execution	No insight in cost/price structure of project
	No experience in similar projects required from principal	Limited influence only on materials used (quality and quantities)
	Limited efforts from principal required	
Partial subcontracting	Better insight in cost/price structure of project by principal	In-depth knowledge and experience from principal required
	Better grip on suppliers and materials used	Much time and effort required for project coordination and monitoring
	Lower overall project costs in general	Risk that communications problems may delay project activities

the activities based on the supplier's day reports, stating the man hours worked, and (if relevant) the materials which have been consumed. The advantages of this method are:

- the principal obtains an exact picture of the cost structure of the work;
- the principal is free in his choice of suppliers; it is known in advance what supplier he will be dealing with.

Naturally, there are also some disadvantages:

- there is no predetermined fixed price, so the buyer is not quite sure about the financial consequences;
- there is no incentive to work faster, as the supplier is reimbursed for every hour he works; every setback is charged to the principal;
- there is no certainty about completion date.

An additional disadvantage of this method is that the principal is not forced to specify exactly what it is he wants. Frequently the specification is left to the supplier for the sake of convenience. Due to the uncertainty of the final cost, many buyers avoid working with cost-reimbursable contracts. Some only use them in the case of specific, minor maintenance/repair activities, for which the financial risks are relatively clear. Cost-reimbursable contracts are not without problems and several points have to be discussed with the supplier in advance (see Figure 3.1). The decision in favor of either fixed-price or cost-reimbursable contracts is determined by a number of factors, such as:

- Comprehensiveness of the specification. The availability of extensive specifications is a crucial prerequisite of lump-sum contracting. Absence of specifications makes a fair comparison of the various quotations impossible.
- Available time. Does the principal have enough time for a tender procedure and price negotiations or should the work be started immediately?
- Technical expertise. If the work requires specialized knowledge and skills, a cost-reimbursable contract is often preferred.
- Knowledge of the industry. The degree to which the principal knows the methods and price arrangements operating in that particular industry.

FIGURE 3.1 Aspects to be considered when contracting on a cost-reimbursable basis.

- Wages and salaries
- Percentage for general expense
- Profit percentage/mark-up
- Reporting procedures for hours worked and consumption of materials
- Costs of tooling and special equipment
- Costs related to coordinating the work of third parties
- Agreement on cost estimates for extra work
- Agreement on what to be supplied by principal
- Agreement on what facilities (telephone, electricity, housing) to be provided by principal/contractor
- Key personnel to be assigned on the job by contractor
- Arrangement of required licences and permits from local authorities
- Selection of sub-suppliers of contractors

In summary, the first step in the stage of supplier selection consists of determining whether to opt for partial or turnkey contracting out. Second, it should be decided whether execution will take place by means of fixed-price or a cost-reimbursable agreement.

A third type of contract which is often used in the subcontracting world and which should be mentioned here is the unit-rate contract. These contracts determine the cost per activity for standardized and routine work. Petrochemical companies, for example, annually negotiate unit-rates for simple installation and maintenance activities which are subcontracted to suppliers (for instance unit-rate per metre of piping that is installed, or unit rate per square metre of groundfloor which is cleaned). Unit-rate contracts are used for activities which are standardized but which are difficult to estimate in terms of volume and time.

The selected contracting method determines to a great extent how the next steps of the buying process will evolve. For that reason, these decisions must be made together with the user and/or budget holder. However, the buyer presents the different contracting methods which he thinks are possible and outlines the considerations that may influence the decision.

The selection of a supplier is one of the most important steps in the purchasing process and several activities precede this decision. Activities include:

- Summarizing the prequalification requirements, based on the purchase order specification, that the suppliers who are going to be approached for a quotation will have to meet.
- Assembling the initial bidders list (so-called bidders' long list) that indicates which suppliers may probably do the job.
- Sending out the request for information (RFI). Next, these suppliers are contacted to provide references and information about their qualifications. At this stage it may be necessary to conduct a supplier visit or audit in order to get a precise idea of their capabilities. Large companies generally work with 'approved vendors lists' in order to select the suppliers for the long list.
- Decide on the supplier short list. Based upon the information that was gathered, the most promising suppliers are selected. These short listed suppliers will be contacted through a request for quotation.
- Sending out the request for quotation (RFQ). At this stage suppliers are invited to submit a bid which meets the requirements as laid down in the request for quotation. The idea behind this is that suppliers should submit their bids in such a way that they can be compared by the buyer.

These activities are commonly referred to as the tendering process. Tenders can be formal or informal and can be open or closed. An open tender is a tender without prequalification of suppliers. A closed tender is limited to a small number of suppliers who have been carefully preselected.

Sometimes there is not a sufficient number of approved suppliers available. When this happens, new suppliers need to be found through a thorough supply market survey (see Chapter 6). For important contracts these are first scrutinized and screened before any bids will be solicited from them. It is common practice to identify three to five prospective suppliers, from whom quotations will be solicited. These suppliers make up the bidders' short list. If circumstances give cause to revise the invitation to bid, then all of the competing suppliers should be given the opportunity to respond to this revision.

After receipt of the quotations, the purchasing department will make a preliminary technical and commercial evaluation, during which all relevant aspects are acknowledged. The technical, logistic, quality, financial and legal aspects need to be weighed. Ranking schemes may be used with a different degree of sophistication in order to facilitate the process of evaluating the supplier bids. These schemes are used jointly between the users and buyers involved. Usually this step ends with a supplier selection proposal, which consists of (a) a decision to select a certain supplier, (b) the underlying ranking schemes and (c) the underlying quotations which have been considered.

The next step is to carry out a risk analysis for critical suppliers and purchase parts. During this step potential risks related to a particular choice of supplier are investigated. An example is presented in Memo 3.2.

Ultimately one supplier will be selected with whom the delivery of the product (or service) will have to be negotiated. In some cases the assignment may be given to two or more suppliers (when dual or multiple sourcing is the preferred sourcing strategy).) The suppliers who are not selected are informed about the reasons for rejecting their proposals.

Summarizing this section, the added value of the buyer's role in the selection phase is in:

- determining (or having others determine) the most adequate way of subcontracting (turnkey versus partial subcontracting and deciding on fixed-cost, cost-reimbursable or unit rate contract);
- identifying reliable supplier-partners by means of an adequate procedure of prequalification; preliminary selection of the most suitable suppliers by means of a tender and ranking procedure;
- drawing up the request for quotation in such a way that comparison of the quotations, which are received at a later stage, is possible;
- handling requests for information from suppliers in a similar manner; channelling the information between project team and supplier;

MEMO 3.2   RISK ANALYSIS BY THE MINISTRY OF DEFENCE

If a supplier does not fulfill his obligations in the realization of complex and extensive projects, this can lead to considerable damages or loss for a military organization. To limit the risk of problems as much as possible, the Ministries of Defence of several European countries sometimes carry out an analysis of the risks related to doing business with suppliers for strategic projects. In general three categories of risks are distinguished:

1 Technical risk regarding the suitability/professionalism of the management, the means of production, the skills, tools and testing equipment of the company in question for the manufacture of the required goods and services, which must meet the agreed requirements and must be delivered within the agreed term.

2 Quality risk with regard to the quality management of the company in general and the quality control system of the project in question in particular.

3 Financial risk related to the degree in which the company is considered to function soundly and effectively for the duration of the project. Of importance in this respect are: financial condition, investment elasticity and a solid financial condition in the near future.

In large and technologically complex projects the risks can be so large that additional measures and arrangements are required. These measures should consist of at least periodical preventive audits aimed at assessing the technical capacity and quality control (the so-called 'pre-award survey'), to be conducted by the military; and the financial status of the company in question, to be conducted by the accounting department. This latter analysis concerns the actual and the anticipated results of the company activities (such as turnover and company results) and ratio analysis of several financial parameters (such as liquidity and solvency).

■ conducting a balanced analysis of quotations in close cooperation with the user, making a clear distinction between the technical evaluation and the commercial evaluation.

Memo 3.3 illustrates the course of this phase in the case example.

The objective of this stage of the buying process is to arrive at a balanced selection of the most suitable supplier-partner based upon total cost of ownership. Statements that would result in premature obligations towards particular suppliers must be avoided at this stage.

THIRD STEP IN THE BUYING PROCESS: THE PURCHASING CONTRACT

After the supplier has been selected, a contract will have to be drawn up. Depending on the industry, the contract may refer to specific additional terms and conditions. The technical contents of the purchase agreement naturally depend on the product or project that is to be purchased. Specific commercial and legal terms and conditions will vary per contract, differences being caused by purchasing policy, company culture, market situation, product characteristics, etc. This limits the use of standard purchase contracts. The next section discusses several important aspects of the purchase agreement.

Prices and terms of delivery

In general the buyer should insist on a fixed price, arrived at through competitive bidding or negotiation, which is acceptable to both principal and supplier. Financial obligations should be defined unequivocally. Ideally the supplier should be willing to accept all risks, in so far as these are not excluded contractually. A fixed price is definitely preferred from the perspective of cost control or budget management.

In practice, different price arrangements are used in purchase agreements.

■ Fixed price plus incentive fee. This type of contract is designed to motivate suppliers, by means of rewards, to execute the work above the agreed standard. The incentives do not have to relate to immediately visible cost reductions, which are realized by the supplier. They can also relate to earlier delivery, a better delivery reliability and/or a better quality performance than agreed.

■ Cost-plus contract. This type of contract may have different forms: cost-plus with a percentage fee, cost-reimbursable plus a fixed fee, and cost-plus with a guaranteed maximum. In practice this type of contract often turns out to be more expensive for the

---

MEMO 3.3   PREPARATION OF SUPPLIER SELECTION

Based on the technical specifications, the project team of the car manufacturer submitted an 'internal request for quotation' to the investment buying section of the purchasing department. This request included a preselection of suppliers, the desired delivery time and an estimate of the required budget. With the aid of this information the purchasing department designed a request for quotation accompanied by purchasing conditions, etc., which was then sent to six suppliers. After a number of consultation rounds with these suppliers, the project team eventually received three quotations. These were evaluated by the team through a detailed, multi-page quotation analysis form. The three suppliers presented their proposals to the board of directors, following which one supplier finally was selected.

buyer than other types of contracts. Cost-plus contracts are used in situations where the work cannot be specified adequately, or when a fixed price constitutes too big a risk for both the supplier and the buyer.

- Cost-reimbursable contracts. This type of contract is usually based on fixed hourly rates for labor and equipment. However, without a bonus or penalty clause these contracts provide little incentive to minimize labor hours or costs. The buyer should therefore always make sure that
  - the supplier keeps a sound cost administration, so that inspection is possible;
  - a maximum price is recorded in the contract;
  - this amount may only be exceeded after written agreement has been obtained from the buyer;
  - the costs which are to be reimbursed are made payable to the supplier on a well-specified invoice.
- Agreement with price-adjustment (escalation clauses). This type of contract is used mainly for agreements with a long-term delivery, or when very specific, market-sensitive materials are processed. The price is linked to a price adjustment formula, which is based on external factors such as material costs or changes in labor costs.

It is recommended to record optional prices for future deliveries of spare parts, and, when appropriate, service rates. Finally, when buying from foreign suppliers, currency risks need to be dealt with. Although working with currency exchange clauses is an acceptable approach, it is recommended that such clauses are excluded from the purchase agreement because the supplier can cover this type of risk fairly simply by applying financial hedging techniques.

Terms of payment

When capital goods or installations are purchased, it is common practice that payment takes place in several stages, partly because the supplier will have to make large investments to be able to produce the desired product. If this method of payment is used, account should be taken of the influence of the payment terms on the final price. Attention should also be paid to covering the currency risk related to paying for goods that have not yet been delivered.

In general, the preferred method of payment is based on the supplier's performance (performance bond). For instance: payment of 20 per cent of the total sum when 25 per cent of the work is completed. The last 5 or 10 per cent of the payment is held back until the client is absolutely sure that the equipment operates exactly as it should or in the case of a service, that the supplier's work has been to the customer's satisfaction.

Advance payments should preferably be covered by a bank guarantee in which the supplier agrees to fulfill his obligations. Such a bank guarantee completely covers the prepaid sum and is valid for the period of delivery of the part that the bank guarantee relates to. If appropriate, a concern guarantee from the holding company (which is often less expensive) will suffice.

Subsequently, attention should be paid to drawing up an agreement providing specifically for the transfer of ownership.

Penalty clauses and warranty conditions

According to the general purchase conditions of several large companies, suppliers must guarantee with respect to the delivered goods that:

- they are of good quality and completely in accordance with the agreed requirements, specifications, conditions, drawings, samples, etc. and that they are suitable for their intended purpose;
- the goods will be completely new and free of defects, that new materials of good and suitable quality will be used for the manufacture of these goods and that first-rate technical and expert personnel will be used;
- the legal and government regulations of the country where the supplier is domiciled have been met and that the goods, or the use of them, do not contain any risk regarding the health or security of persons, property and environment.

Agreements will also have to be made with the supplier about the performance of the goods to be delivered. In the case of acquisition of investment goods, a performance guarantee can be agreed upon, for example by agreeing that a particular production unit will produce 10 tons of end product of a certain quality per day. If the agreed performance is not met, one should first discuss corrective measures. If these also turn out to be inadequate then the resulting costs are to be recovered from the supplier. This procedure must be agreed upon in the terms and conditions of the contract. Penalty clauses do not, therefore, provide a solution for problems occurring at the stage of execution or delivery; at most they can limit the resulting damages afterwards.

In some circumstances, a penalty clause is unacceptable. If, for example, performance is found to be more than 5 per cent under the agreed standard, or if the legal environmental regulations are not complied with, the client must have the right to refuse the product or installation in question.

It is also important that the period during which the supplier is liable for the reliability and adequate functioning of the delivered goods in the specified circumstances, is recorded in the contract. In general a period of 12 months is included as the warranty period in the terms and conditions of the agreement. The agreement should also state when the warranty comes into effect; this can be the date that the goods are put into service, or it can be the delivery date.

One special aspect in the case of investment goods is the systems responsibility; it is common to demand from the supplier that he takes measures to maintain the delivered product during the life-of-type. Maintenance and spare parts must be available during this life-of-type. In this context manufacturers of trucks are required to be able to maintain their products, sometimes for a period of more than 20 years!

Other arrangements

In many companies the issues described above will be recorded in the general purchase conditions. Other subjects that can be addressed in these regulations include:

- insurance and safety regulations;
- transfer of rights and obligations;
- contracting out to third parties;
- terms of delivery.

In general, buyers should strive for a situation in which they can prescribe the company's terms of purchase. In practice, however, a supplier will frequently accept an order only on his own terms of sale. If the supplier does not explicitly reject the terms of purchase in his order confirmation, the terms of purchase are still valid (from a legal point of view). If he does reject them, however, then there is basically no consensus and therefore no purchase agreement. In this type of situation, additional negotiations will be necessary. This tug-of-war about terms of sale and purchase is sometimes referred to as the 'battle of forms'.

Naturally, attempts have been made in international trade to standardize much-used trade terms. The Incoterms are an example. The main standard terms and conditions are discussed in Memo 3.4, whereas Memo 3.5 describes the course of the contractual stage for the carriers.

In summary, the main tasks of the buyer in the contracting stage are considered to be the following:

- supplying the required contracting expertise in the form of modular purchase contracts and general terms of purchase, in which all aspects are taken into account;
- determining what price and other commercial conditions will be negotiated;
- preparing specific contractual arrangements to minimize risks and liabilities which are related to the purchase;
- preparing and conducting the negotiations about all terms and conditions of the contract with the supplier;
- editing the purchase agreement.

STEPS FOUR AND FIVE: ORDERING AND EXPEDITING

After the terms and conditions of the contract have been agreed and recorded, the order can be placed. In some cases the contract in fact is the purchase order. In other cases, for example a routine buying situation, buyers will negotiate a call-off agreement, covering the materials needed for a longer period (one year or even longer). Next, purchase orders are placed against this agreement. In these cases contracting and ordering are separate activities.

A purchase order usually is initiated (electronically) through a purchase order requisition or a materials requisition. For production and inventory items this requisition is generated through the materials requirements planning systems through the matching of the materials volume needed for production for a given period and the available (pipeline) inventories. When inventories seem to get lower than their minimum acceptable levels, the MRP-system generates a signal to the purchasing department by means of a detailed materials or purchase order requisition. Most advanced (integrated) materials planning software packages enable the transfer of this requisition to a purchase order electronically.

When ordering from a supplier, it is very important to be specific about the information and instructions to the supplier. Generally, a purchase order will include the following entities: an order number, a concise description of the product, unit price, number of units required, expected delivery time or date, delivery address and invoicing address. All of these data need to be reflected on the delivery documents and invoice, sent by the supplier in order to facilitate (electronic) matching.

Usually the supplier is requested to send in an order confirmation for each purchase order received. Together, the purchase order, the supplier's delivery documents and invoices form the basis for the buyer's vendor rating system (see Chapter 15 for a more detailed discussion of this subject). If all of these preparatory activities have been executed adequately, there will be less work in the ordering and order handling stages. In practice, however, things often work out differently, and considerable efforts are required from the buyer during the phase of ordering and expediting. Expediting demands a lot of attention and is often conducted based on an overdue list, which records all deliveries that are late. There are several types of expediting:

MEMO 3.4   THE INCOTERMS 1990

Incoterms' is short for international commerce terms (see van Weele and Gelderman, 1998). These terms relate to several important standard conditions in connection with the delivery and transportation of, and risk attached to, goods. The Incoterms have been carefully defined: it has been established how each condition must be interpreted. Using the Incoterms may prevent misunderstandings between supplier and buyer.

The Incoterms were first published in 1936 and they have been adapted regularly since. The newest version, Incoterms 2000, distinguishes the following standard conditions:

EXW	Ex Works
FCA	Free Carrier
FAS	Free Alongside Ship
FOB	Free On Board
CPT	Carriage Paid To
CIP	Carriage and Insurance Paid to
CFR	Cost and Freight
CIF	Cost, Insurance, Freight
DAF	Delivered at Frontier
DES	Delivered Ex Ship
DEQ	Delivered Ex Quay
DDU	Delivered Duty Unpaid
DDP	Delivered Duty Paid

Each Incoterm arranges the distribution of the costs (transportation, insurance) and the risk (in case of loss and damage) of the physical delivery. In addition the Incoterms regulate which documents should be provided by the supplier, or that the supplier must help the buyer in this, and who is to pay the costs of these documents. Incoterms do not regulate the legal delivery, the legal transfer of title. This is arranged in the legal system that applies to the purchase agreement.

An Incoterm only applies if both parties have reached an agreement about it and the contract will then refer to the Incoterm in question. Incoterms are not part of permissive or imperative law and parties are free to agree to deviations from an Incoterm. This is risky, however, because adding a word or even a single letter to an Incoterm may lead a judge (especially a foreign judge) to a different interpretation than was intended by the buyer.

The 13 Incoterms 2000 can be organized according to:

- type of transportation
- type of agreement.

Table 3.2 reflects the resulting classification of Incoterms. This classification, as well as their meaning, will be briefly explained, but for a complete explanation see the *Guide to Incoterms*, 2000 edition, published by the International Chamber of Commerce.

The first classification is a very rough one: sea carriage versus 'other' methods of transportation; traditionally, the Incoterms have played an important role in sea carriage. The classification into types of contract determine to a high degree where the physical delivery from supplier to buyer takes place. Four types of contracts can be distinguished:

- departure
- main carriage unpaid
- main carriage paid
- arrival.

TABLE 3.2 Incoterms 2000 classification

Transportation method	Type of contract			
	Departure	Main carriage unpaid	Main carriage paid	Arrival
Sea carriage	EXW	FOB	CIF	DES
		FAS	CFR	DEQ
Other transportation	EXW	FCA	CPT	DAF
			CIP	DDU
				DDP

The first group consists exclusively of the Incoterm EXW (Ex Works). In the case of EXW the buyer is responsible for arranging and settling everything. The supplier only makes the goods available for the buyer, who has to collect these from the factory or warehouse.

In the second group of Incoterms the buyer arranges most of the physical delivery. In the case of sea carriage, the supplier delivers the goods to the quay (FAS) or on board (FOB). Then the ship can leave at the expense and risk of the buyer. The Incoterm FCA rests on the same principle: the supplier has met his obligations as soon as the goods have been transferred to a transporter at the agreed location. In this situation also the supplier carries the costs and responsibility up until the moment that the goods are delivered.

Characteristic of the third group is that the supplier takes responsibility for most of the transport. In the case of sea carriage the supplier will bring the goods into a harbor in the buyer's country. In the case of CIF the supplier pays the costs of loading, transportation and the transport insurance. The risk is transferred to the buyer (as it is in the case of FOB) when the goods have passed the ship's rail. Incoterm CFR is a variation on CIF in which the buyer carries the risk of transportation. It is of course wise to cover this risk by means of transport insurance. The same difference (who carries the risk?) applies to CIP and CPT. In the case of CIP the supplier carries the risk and pays for transportation to the agreed location of transfer; in the case of CPT the buyer carries the transportation risk. Within the fourth group of Incoterms, arrival, the most extreme Incoterms are DDU and DDP. DDP is the exact opposite of EXW in that the supplier brings the goods to the buyer's 'front door'. The same goes for DDU, except that the buyer pays the import duties. Less extreme is delivery to a ship (DES), to the quay (DEQ) or to the border (DAF). There are now two versions of the Incoterm DEQ: duty paid and duty unpaid. This difference is important in view of import duties. Figure 3.2 shows where the supplier is supposed to deliver under the various Incoterms.

FIGURE 3.2 Delivery under Incoterms.

- Exception expediting. In many organizations this method is referred to as the 'beep system' which means that the buyer only undertakes action when the organization sends out signals of (impending) material shortages. Late deliveries from suppliers usually disrupt production. It is therefore important that deliveries are monitored closely by the buyer or materials planner in order to prevent materials shortages. Therefore this method is not recommended.

- Routine status check. This method of expediting aims at preventing materials supply and quality problems. A particular number of days before the promised delivery date, the buyer will contact the supplier with the request to confirm the delivery date again in order to secure delivery.

- Advanced status check. This method is used for critical purchase parts and critical suppliers. Critical may refer here to supplies which are on the critical path of a materials planning. Critical may, however, also refer to materials with tight quality tolerances and/or problematic suppliers. In these cases it is recommended to negotiate in the contracting stage with the supplier that a detailed production plan, which lists the various steps of the production ('milestones'), will be handed over to the buyer before production starts. Monitoring production progress is done by means of periodical checks against the established production program. At critical moments during the production process, the buyer will carry out inspections. In the case of very large purchase contracts (e.g. orders for heavy equipment from the petrochemical industry) the buyer may want to have a specialist permanently based at the supplier's premises (field expediting).

MEMO 3.5   PREPARATION OF THE PURCHASING AGREEMENT

The project team started negotiations with the selected supplier. Eventually these negotiations resulted in a contract acceptable to both parties. Based on the invitation to bid, the engineers in the project team evaluated the technical aspects of the contract while purchasing negotiated the commercial terms. As the company initially needed only 100 carriers, and more would definitely be required at a later stage, a price adjustment formula was included in the contract. This formula reads:

$$V_1 = \frac{V_0}{100} \left(A + B_1 \times \frac{M_1}{M_{10}} + B_2 \times \frac{M_2}{M_{20}} + C \times \frac{S_1}{S_{10}} \right)$$

in which:

V_1	=	Final order value
V_0	=	Total order value (in a base month)
A	=	Constant (0,10)
B_1	=	0.30 × the price increase of mechanical components
B_2	=	0.25 × the price increase of electronic components
C	=	0.30 × the average wage increase
M_1, M_{10}	=	CBS indices (in supplier's country)
M_2, M_{20}	=	CBS indices (in supplier's country)
S_1, S_{10}	=	CBS indices (in supplier's country)

The value of such a formula would be that in the future no negotiations on price would be required when ordering extra car body carriers from the supplier.

When the products or equipment are delivered they will have to be checked to ensure that they meet the specified requirements. Acceptance of equipment often consists of a number of steps:

- acceptance test at the supplier's site before shipment;
- acceptance test at the user's site after delivery;
- acceptance test when the equipment is put into operation for the first time.

Depending on the size and technical complexity there may be more than one acceptance test at the supplier's site during installation of the equipment.

The business world is far from ideal. Notwithstanding good contracts and purchase orders, things may go wrong at delivery. Delivery times may not be respected by the supplier, quality problems may occur with purchased materials, suppliers may charge more for their products than allowed, etc. Therefore it is very important that the company has a reporting system for all the problems which may occur. Quality and delivery problems should be reported daily to the buyer (electronically) through a supplier complaint reporting procedure. These problems should be immediately communicated to the supplier in order to prevent a recurrence in the future. In other chapters in this book this matter will be discussed in more detail (see Chapters 11 and 12).

Memo 3.6 describes the main activities to be executed for the car manufacturer during the stage of ordering and expediting.

In summary, the added value of the buyer during the ordering and expediting phase lies predominantly in:

- developing efficient ordering routines between the buying company and supplier; checking that all purchase orders are confirmed by the supplier;
- developing and executing a computer-supported, differentiated method of expediting and inspection;
- maintaining a computer-supported database with regard to critical purchasing and supplier information (preferably arranged according to key technologies);
- developing a sound procedure for order handling;
- applying effective 'trouble shooting' when necessary.

MEMO 3.6 ORDER HANDLING

Now that the actual negotiations with the supplier have been concluded, the car manufacturer can proceed to order the desired equipment. During these phases of the purchasing process, the purchasing department will carry co-responsibility for:

- follow-up of the order at the supplier's plant;
- negotiations about the consequences of requested engineering changes;
- expediting the orders up to the agreed delivery times;
- settlement of all financial matters;
- all commercial correspondence with the supplier;
- handling possible warranty claims.

STEP SIX: FOLLOW UP AND EVALUATION OF THE BUYING PROCESS

The buyer's role continues even after the new product has been taken into production, or the new installation has been put into operation. Things which can go wrong in the relationship with the supplier and which have to be taken care of at this stage are:

- settling warranty claims and penalty clauses;
- settling the results of work in excess of, or work less than, that stated in the specification;
- organizing the purchase and supplier documentation;
- recording project evaluations, etc.

With regard to excess work, it is important to establish that this must be reported to the principal in advance, and that the principal must first give permission. Extra work must always be reported to the purchasing manager so that the purchase costs remain clear. Furthermore, it stimulates an adequate administrative processing of the invoices that are submitted later on.

In the case of investment goods, maintenance activities will become necessary after a while. At that time it becomes clear whether the supplier can substantiate his promises about service, maintenance and the supply of spare parts.

Experiences with individual suppliers should be documented carefully. It is recommended that buyers keep track of the supplier's quality and delivery record, his competitiveness and innovativeness, since these data can lead to an adjustment of the so-called vendor rating (Chapter 15). It is important to have a thorough and up-to-date record of the actual capabilities of each supplier. Reporting this kind of information, both to management and the supplier's management, is one major source of added value contributed by the buyer. That concludes the cycle, because this information can be used in a subsequent purchasing cycle to assemble the 'bidders short list' for future projects and contracts. In this way the company learns to work with suppliers with proven capabilities and usually results in a reduction of the supplier base. Companies, then, will gradually concentrate their business among fewer but more capable suppliers.

During the after-sales phase, the buyer's added value is primarily related to:

- settling claims, with regard to work not covered in the specification;
- recording the user's experience with specific products and suppliers by means of a detailed vendor rating system;
- recording maintenance experience;
- supervising compliance with agreements concerning the supply of spare parts and maintenance.

SUMMARY

This chapter has described the purchasing process in detail. The starting point was to discuss a new-task buying situation, i.e. a situation where every step of the buying process model needed to be prepared and conducted. Each step was illustrated through a practical example relating to the purchase of a new piece of equipment (car body carriers). For many other products the purchasing process is, fortunately, much simpler.

The starting point of the purchasing process is the purchase order specification which describes the whole of the user requirements in detail. In addition to technical requirements, the purchase specifications also reflect maintenance requirements and the logistic requirements the contract or order must meet. The purchase specification becomes in turn the basis for the supplier selection process. During this step choices need to be made about the method of contracting out (partial or integral) and the type of contract (fixed-price or cost-reimbursable). Only after this has been done can the bidder's list be assembled and the request for quotation be designed. For the evaluation and appraisal of quotations a distinction should preferably be made between the technical evaluation and the commercial evaluation. These evaluations will result in a clear and unambiguous selection of a supplier, and the selection phase concludes with the preparation of the contract negotiations.

Contracting is an art in itself. The terms and conditions which have to be included in the contract are numerous and varied. This chapter has discussed prices and terms of delivery, terms of payment, penalty regulations and warranty regulations and other, more general, terms and conditions including the much-used Incoterms.

After the agreement has been signed, the order must be placed. The order indicates quantities, product description and unit price, as well as the desired delivery date and other information necessary for effective logistic and administrative processing. The purchasing process is concluded with the follow up and evaluation phase.

This description of the purchasing process clarifies once again that a buyer must be an all-rounder with sufficient technical knowledge, a feeling for the commercial side of the process, and be familiar with the basics of logistics and administration. Every step in the buying process must be executed carefully and systematically in order to provide the internal customer with what he needs: a product which is fit for its use, on time, in the required quantity and at a reasonable cost.

ASSIGNMENTS

3.1   As a buyer you are involved in a decision to replace the copying machine in your office (30 people employed) for a new one. You decide to include, apart from your current supplier, also other, new suppliers in your tender. The first thing you need to do is to work out a functional specification of the new copier. How would such a functional specification look? What would it describe? What would a technical specification look like? Search for examples from the Internet.

3.2   Large companies want to carry out a preliminary qualification of suppliers before they place an order. What does prequalification mean? When selecting a supplier for packaging materials (e.g. corrugated board) what kind of information would you require in order to put the supplier on your shortlist?

3.3   In this chapter fixed-price contracting and cost-reimbursable contracting were distinguished. What are the most important advantages and disadvantages of both types of contract? Suppose that you as a buyer, working for a petrol company, are requested to contract a supplier for a major paintwork of one of your service stations: what kind of contract would you go for?

3.4   General terms and conditions sometimes include a penalty clause for late delivery, delivery of products that do not comply with the specification, etc. What advantages and disadvantages do you see in the application of penalty clauses?

3.5   This chapter describes three different methods of expediting. In which circumstances do you think each of these methods is useful? Explain your answer.

LEARNING OBJECTIVES

After studying this chapter you should understand:

- The various types of supply market structures.
- The influence of market structures on purchasing policy.
- The specific characteristics related to the buying of raw materials, components, maintenance, repair and operating supplies, investment goods and services.

CASE STUDY   HOW UNEXPECTED FROST LED TO AN UNPRECEDENTED BULL'S MARKET FOR COFFEE . . .

Thursday, 16 July, 1975. The market is slow this morning. The assistant buyer of a medium-sized coffee roasting factory somewhere in North-west Europe is slightly ticked off. Of all the times when he could have taken a vacation, his boss decided to leave during the frosty season in Brazil, the world's largest producer of coffee. He left a telephone number and a somewhat odd instruction: in case of frost, call immediately! And that is exactly what makes the assistant buyer so nervous. Yes, he knows the stories, but how do you judge such a situation?

It is four in the morning of that same day when Joao gets out of bed again. The weather forecast said there could be early morning frost in the area around Campinas in Parana, which is where his coffee plantation is located. Nothing serious, but it has been cold for a couple of days, and frost has already been reported in Rio Grande to the south. As he goes outside an icy wind sweeps the land. The thermometer indicates minus 28°C. He calls his broker in Rio who was still asleep, but who is instantly wide awake when Joao tells him it is freezing. 'Buy London futures'. It is midday over there, so he can make the transaction before lunch-

close. 'Buy at the market, i.e. the price is irrelevant. Buy at market price'.

In London the special weather correspondent of one of the major traders in the market also checks the thermometer and sees to his alarm that it reads minus 48°C. And at this early hour! This is going to be a major frost! So his boss is called out of bed at a quarter past four, and he succeeds in getting through to his London branch office ten minutes later, just before the noon close of the London futures exchange. £375 per ton, little trade, a single order from an unknown source. The comment from London is: 'no real excitement. Rumors about frost? Haven't heard a thing.' The message from New York is: 'OK we buy. Buy anything you can get your hands on'. First the futures, then the effective trade. In a few minutes £390 is reached, at which price the market closes for lunch. What is going on? Frost? Nobody knows exactly. Now the assistant buyer really starts to worry, and with good cause. These signals from a futures market must not be missed. If there is any purpose to the futures exchange at all, it is to pick up this type of signal. At two o'clock in the afternoon the senior buyer's siesta is rudely interrupted by a puzzled waiter who states, while it is 30°C outside: 'Il gèle au Brésil'. The senior buyer's reaction to this message is even more incomprehensible to the waiter: he races to the nearest telephone and won't move from there. Not until half past five, after the London close, when he rejoins his wife and states that he is going to take the eight o'clock plane home. It is only frost, but his wife knows this is the end of her vacation. 'Why don't you stay on?', her husband tries, but one hour later the suitcases are packed and the taxi is waiting. The next morning, 17 July, eleven o'clock. Reuter reports that although there has been some frost, the damage to the crops is minimal. The market has been open for half an hour and immediately opened $100 (25 per cent) higher because of the news. This market climbed up to £4200 in March 1977. The futures market gave the industrial buyer the opportunity to cover part of his purchasing needs at an early stage.

Source: Vanhorick (1986) pp. 17–8

INTRODUCTION

The number of sales transactions equals the number of purchasing transactions, for in each buy/sell transaction there is a buyer and a seller. Both operate in a market. The seller has various market segments or target groups and, based on a number of criteria, he will attempt to segment his market in such a way that the market opportunities are optimally aligned with his company's technical and commercial possibilities.

The buyer also has a choice. Based on his experience or on a deliberate purchasing strategy, he can decide to place his purchasing orders with a particular group of suppliers. In this decision he will be guided on the one hand by the assortment carried by the suppliers. On the other hand his choice will depend on the quality of the service these suppliers provide. And, like the seller, the buyer will also strive for an optimal fit between the product and quality of service offered by suppliers and the needs of his internal customers.

Depending on the commercial choices that sellers and buyers make in their commercial policy, different types of markets emerge. Every type of market leads to a specific type of purchasing and selling behavior. The objective of this chapter is to describe a few of the most common types of supply market structures. The introductory case indicates that purchasing raw materials is often a complex undertaking: knowledge of the market and experience, in combination with a sound analytical attitude, are indispensable properties for the raw materials buyer. Apart from supply market structures, this chapter examines the following issues: the specific problems in connection with the purchase of raw materials, the purchase of specific and standard components, the purchase of MRO goods and investment (capital) goods. The chapter concludes with a discussion of the purchase of services.

MARKETS AND MARKET STRUCTURES

The patterns of relationships between supplier and buyer are primarily determined by the underlying pattern of the goods and services deliveries, the external structure (Figure 4.1). The external structure consists of a number of links (companies, institutions) that are connected via markets. Within the external structure, industrial branches and industry columns can be distinguished.

An industrial branch is defined as the horizontal relationship of organizations that experience each other as effective competitors (for example: the leather and footwear industry, the electronics industry).

An industry column is defined as a series of companies (links) in which the consecutive stages of production of an economic product take place – from primary producer to consumer. A more popular term to denote this phenomenon is supply chain. We will use both terms here interchangeably.

Depending on the number of stages one can speak of a short or a long industry column i.e. supply chain. Depending on the location of the link in the industry column, the materials-flow between successive links can take the following forms (see Figure 4.2).

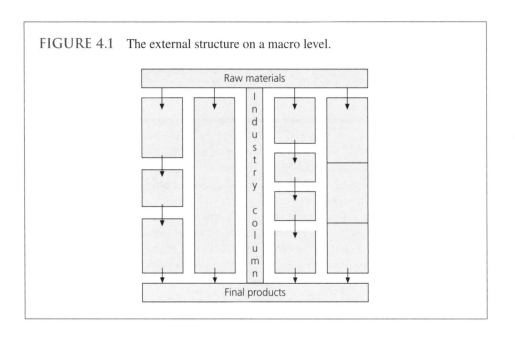

FIGURE 4.1   The external structure on a macro level.

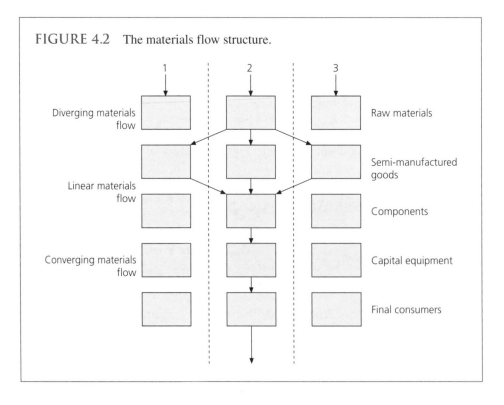

FIGURE 4.2   The materials flow structure.

- Diverging materials flow. The finished product of one link is the main or sole input for the next production stages of various other industry columns. This applies to industries which process raw materials.

- Linear materials flow. The finished product of one link is the main or sole input for the subsequent link.

- Converging materials flow. Various finished products of links of various industry columns are the input for the next link. This situation is found in companies with assembly-oriented production.

Diverging materials flows are usually found at the beginning of an industry column. Converging materials flows are found at the end of an industry column. External factors are those which determine the degree of availability of a certain product and which cannot be influenced by individual companies. Examples are:

- the number of customers or buyers in a market;

- the number of suppliers;

- the market structure (transparency, pricing method);

- the stock situation of the product in question;

- speed of technological innovation.

External factors are relevant because they determine the market structure. Market structure is defined in this book as the total set of conditions in which a company sells its products, with special attention to the number of parties in the market and the nature of the product being traded. Central to this definition are, therefore:

- the number of suppliers;

- the number of buyers;

- the degree of product differentiation.

The market is the total of supply and demand. Sometimes this refers to a physical market, where buyers and sellers actually meet, but in general abstract markets are dealt with. Economic theory uses a number of constructs to explain the relationship between the variables mentioned and market price. It distinguishes various market structures both on the supply side and the demand side, which in reality do not exist in their pure form.

Supply side

Four types of market structures are usually distinguished on the supply side.

- Pure competition. Characteristic of this market structure is that neither the supplier nor the buyer can influence the price of the product. Thus, the price is a given one for all parties involved. Furthermore it is assumed that in this market structure complete information is available. In other words, there is a high degree of market transparency. In addition, the product is homogeneous and fully replaceable by substitutes. Examples of this market type are commodities markets for natural products such as wheat, cocoa, coffee, and for metals such as iron, copper and aluminum. Most auctions (flowers, vegetables) resemble this situation.

- Monopolistic competition. This market structure is similar to many actual markets and is characterized by a high degree of product differentiation. Each supplier tries to make his product stand out in order to create a monopoly situation for himself. This situation is favorable for the supplier because it provides him with some room to manipulate his prices, within a given bandwidth. There is no direct pressure on his prices from competitors' offers. Examples are the markets for cigarettes, detergents, hi-fi equipment and other durable consumer goods.

■ Oligopoly. An oligopoly is a market type characterized by a limited number of suppliers and a limited product differentiation. Moreover, it is very difficult to get a foothold in the market, due to some important entry barriers. The suppliers are familiar with each other's market behavior. An oligopoly can have various forms (see Figure 4.3). Depending on the situation the market price can be set by a market- or price-leader, or arranged through some form of price arrangements (cartels). Also, it may happen that the players in the market cannot combine to pursue cut-throat competition.

When there are few suppliers, but a differentiated or heterogeneous product, it is referred to as a heterogeneous oligopoly. As soon as there are more suppliers in such a situation, the preferred term is monopolistic competition. Examples are found primarily in the industrial sector: the markets for forklift trucks, chemical semi-manufactured goods, flavorings, etc.

■ Monopoly. A monopoly is characterized by the presence of only one supplier of the product in question. Substitutes are virtually absent. This enables the monopolist to pursue his own pricing policy. Natural monopolies exist when the entire supply of raw materials or a particular manufacturing process is owned by just one producer or manufacturer, excluding others by means of contracts or patents (e.g. oil concessions, diamonds). Government monopolies exist when based on special licences which are required from the government or when based on state law. Examples are postal services, railways and some public utilities (gas, etc.).

The big advantage of a monopoly for the supplier is that it enables him to dictate the price and other contractual conditions to the market. Naturally this dictate has its limits in so far as the buyer is not obliged to purchase the product. Purchasing practice shows many situations which resemble monopolies:

■ an original equipment manufacturer's (OEM) clause in the service contract that only original spare parts are to be used under penalty of lapse of the warranty conditions;

■ purchase requisitions on which the applicant merely indicates brand name and a specific supplier's name;

■ strict guidelines from an engineering department to use only one particular technology for some component that needs to be purchased.

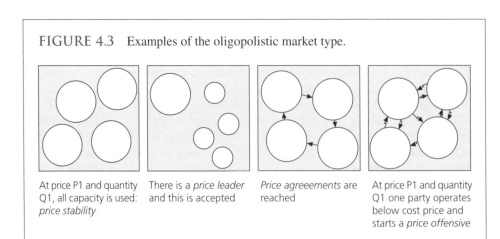

FIGURE 4.3   Examples of the oligopolistic market type.

At price P1 and quantity Q1, all capacity is used: *price stability*

There is a *price leader* and this is accepted

Price agreeements are reached

At price P1 and quantity Q1 one party operates below cost price and starts a *price offensive*

Through his marketing and communications policy the supplier's account manager tries to influence the customer's preferences. The buyer needs to be attentive to these matters and should continuously reflect whether the perceived differences in value of the product that is offered by the supplier outweighs his price variance and the risk of a larger dependency.

Demand side

In general three types of market structure on the demand side can be distinguished.

■ Pure competition. The description given above also applies here.

■ Oligopsony. This is the oligopoly situation in reverse: there are only a few buyers and a large number of suppliers. The (frequently large) buyers are aware of one another's behavior and in this way collectively occupy a position of power *vis-à-vis* the usually smaller suppliers. One example of this market structure is the automobile industry in its capacity of buyer of semi-manufactured products and components. Other examples are agricultural cooperatives or buying consortia which can be found in numerous branches. These organizations in fact coordinate the buying volumes of their members *vis-à-vis* usually much larger suppliers.

■ Monopsony. In this situation there is only one buyer of the product versus a large number of suppliers. In reality this is a very rare situation. Examples are the sugar industry, dairy industry, the railways (as buyer of locomotives and trains) and public utilities in some countries (gas, electricity, water supply).

The supply and demand situations described above can be placed in a matrix and the result is shown in Figure 4.4. Depending on the number of suppliers in the market and their positions relative to those of immediate competitors, the buyer's position can be dominant, equal or subordinate in comparison to the opposition. To assess one's position of power it is important to take into account one's position relative to the opposition. An airline company like SAS may be one of the few buyers of turbo-jet engines but, compared to a company the size of General Electric, SAS's negotiating position is minor. To take another example, DAF Trucks only has a minor power position compared to ZF, the largest German supplier of gearboxes. DAF Trucks orders add up to tens of millions of euros annually but, compared to Daimler-Chrysler, DAF Trucks is only a small player for ZF. One of the reasons to become part of Paccar in 1996 was to benefit from a leveraged negotiation position in its dealings with large, international suppliers.

When developing a purchasing policy, the purchasing manager should reflect on the following questions:

■ Which types of markets are we dealing with in relation to article X; how many (potential) suppliers are in the market, from whom we could, in principle, obtain this article?

■ What reactions will placing an order of volume Y and price Z with one supplier generate from the other suppliers?

■ What is the degree of differentiation for a particular product in the supplier market; which alternatives or substitutes are available?

■ What is our company's market share for product X in the supply market and who are our competitors with regard to this product? Who else is buying this product?

FIGURE 4.4 Typology of market structures.

Number of suppliers \ Number of buyers	One	Few	Many
One	Bilateral monopoly, 'captive market' (spare parts)	Limited supply-side monopoly (fuel pumps)	Supply-side monopoly (gas, water, electricity)
Few	Limited demand-side monopoly (telephone exchanges, trains	Bilateral oligopoly (chemical semi-manufacturers)	Supply-side oligopoly (copiers, computers)
Many	Demand-side monopoly (weapons systems, ammunition)	Demand-side oligopoly suppliers (components automobile industry)	Polypolistic competition (office supplies)

☐ = demand-side stronger than supply-side
☐ = Demand and supply more or less in balance
☐ = Supply-side stronger than demand-side

- What is likely to happen in the short and the long term with regard to the supply of product Q and what effect will the expected developments have on price setting and availability?

Knowledge of market structures is important to the buyer because these determine to a large extent the desired strategy on the one hand, and the negotiating strategies that will be used on the other. Chapter 8 discusses these strategic consequences in more detail.

PURCHASE OF GOODS

Raw materials and commodity exchanges

Raw materials are a substantial component of many companies' purchasing portfolios. In this context one can think of oil as the raw material for oil refineries and the chemical industry, vegetable oils and fats for the margarine industry and iron ore for the steel industry. These examples clearly show that a distinction can be made between natural raw materials (which include natural products such as cattle, corn, wheat, coffee, cocoa, sugar, cotton and soya), and minerals (for example coal, iron ore, copper and bauxite). The purchase of raw materials often involves large sums of money. In addition they partly determine the cost price of the finished product. For these reasons they will often be earmarked as strategic products.

The commodity exchange plays a significant role in the purchase of raw materials. The major commodity exchanges are in the United States, for example Comex in New York where precious metals are traded, and the Chicago Board of Trade where grain, rice and soya are traded. One major commodity exchange outside the United States is the London Metal Exchange (LME). This futures market deals primarily with non-precious metals such as copper, zinc, tin and aluminum.

The origins of these commodity exchanges are often historically determined. Past attempts to establish exchanges in Amsterdam, Paris, Singapore and Hong Kong were all in vain. The reasons why these efforts failed are to be found in the absence of one or several crucial conditions that must be fulfilled. The most important criteria for the effective functioning of a futures market are:

- A logical geographical location – this is important, bearing in mind the transportation of raw materials, coupled with a highly developed banking network, because it must be possible to conclude large numbers of financial transactions.

- Liquidity of the article – the raw material must be available in sufficient quantity, but also in manageable units. The manageability of crude oil has always presented a problem, because the quantities involved are usually too large to be able to achieve a standard quantity through the futures market. Furthermore, it must be possible to standardize the quality of the article.

- Liquidity of the market – there must be sufficient parties willing to participate in the futures market.

- Political stability – there must be a certain degree of political stability in the country where the exchange is established, because of the huge financial interests connected with the futures trade. For this reason a futures market in a politically unstable country is doomed to fail.

Futures trade is forward trade, which means that goods are purchased to be delivered at a future time, not with the intention to receive or deliver these goods at that agreed time, but to fulfill the contract by settling the price difference between the original and a new transaction. There is, therefore, no physical trading of goods on the futures market, but a trade in contracts concerning goods.

A futures market is used to hedge the price risk of a particular transaction (purchase or sale of a commodity), which will be concluded at some future date (for example a future receipt or delivery). Future trading is a complex, and for outsiders, not very accessible process.

Participants in a futures market always take 'an open position' which can be either long or short. A long position refers to the situation in which on balance a party buys more of the product or the futures (including stocks and options) than he has sold. The balance of purchases and sales is therefore positive. A short position is taken when there have been more sales than purchases so that the balance of purchases and sales is negative.

The futures market functions by means of the clearing house. This body guarantees the contracts and takes care of the financial settlement. Normally, trading is possible six to eight months ahead, based on delivery per calendar month, spread across the entire year, for example January–March–May–July–September–November, or any other combination of months. Each month, or rather, each position, has its own quotation, bid price, asking price, last traded price, daily high–low prices and closing value (see Table 4.1).

The quotations for all the major futures markets are published daily in the financial newspapers. Many trading houses and brokers have direct access to the rates by means of Reuters screens or the Internet, so they can monitor them by the minute.

Registration as a party is a precondition for buying or selling a standard quantity of the standard quality commodity/raw material in a previously determined month of delivery (delivery position) at any given moment during the opening hours of the market. After the month of delivery has been concluded, the participant should be back to a zero-position on that futures. He can achieve this by means of a counter transaction at a certain point in time: buying when he is short or selling if he is long. This is the principle of the futures market in a nutshell.

As a rule, four groups participate in the futures market: the producer, the trader, the buyer and the speculator. Each group has its own primary goals and so introduces a different element to the market process.

The producer will use the futures market to secure the yield of his crop. Farmers, for example, who have sold their grain crop to the cooperative for a fixed price in the spring, are confronted with the risk of a rise in prices. Had they waited until August, they might have negotiated a better price. This risk can be hedged by means of a forward transaction.

The trader is the main user of the futures market. He is both buyer and seller and is satisfied with small profits over large positions.

The main goal of the buyer is to limit the market or price risk. Breweries often purchase the barley harvest from the farmer when the seeds have only just been planted. This means that they run a price risk for several months, until the moment of delivery. By delivery time the prices can be substantially lower. The brewery can hedge this risk by means of a forward transaction.

The only goal of the speculator is profit. He operates on both sides of the market, buying and selling. Speculators provide the market with dynamics: the larger the number of speculators, the higher the liquidity of the market becomes.

How does a forward transaction work? Memo 4.1 shows an example of a hedge. To hedge means that price risks, which are related to a physical transaction, are covered by taking up a counter transaction on the futures market. The example indicates in what way buyer and seller can limit their risks of either a rise or a fall in prices.

Purchasing will make use of futures markets especially in the following situations:

- The raw material that is purchased is an essential constituent of the cost price of the finished product.

- It is almost impossible to pass on a price increase on the purchasing side to the sales price. If this is the case, using the futures market is to be recommended.

- The raw material which is used in the finished product cannot be substituted by other products (for example: natural rubber as a substitute for synthetics). If there are many possible substitutes it is less necessary to use a futures market. However, if one is dependent on one particular raw material, a futures market can be very useful.

TABLE 4.1 Examples of a futures quotation

Month	Last traded	Bid	Ask	Open	High	Low	Close
November	2350	2349	2352	2330	2360	2325	2345
January	2392	2385	2388	2361	2398	2358	2370
March	2428	2426	etc.				

Buying components

Components are parts which are to be built into the final product, to be sold by the manufacturer. They can be either standard or specific. Standard components are manufactured based on specifications provided by the supplier, e.g. tyres, light bulbs, fuses, small electric motors and condensers. Specific components are manufactured according to designs, specified by the buyer. Examples of specific components are forgings and castings, gears, gearboxes and axles.

Components are often purchased for serial production. This enables buyers to negotiate annual agreements with suppliers, or to negotiate even longer-term price and delivery agreements. This simplifies the administrative process significantly, because as the conditions have been agreed, orders can be placed directly at the supplier (through call-off orders or blanket orders).

Quality aspects play an extremely important role in buying components, for every defect in the production line can result in delays and production losses. Furthermore, the quality of the constituent parts determines the quality of the finished product.

It is for this reason that quality requires special attention in the purchase of components. In their pursuit of quality improvements, buyers increasingly take a preventive approach: before suppliers qualify for an order, they are first audited with regard to their prevailing quality system and production process (see also Chapter 11). A supplier is only included in the 'approved suppliers' file after it has been determined that he is capable of delivering a product of the required quality. The relationship with suppliers who repeatedly fail to meet the quality standards is terminated. After the evaluation there will be joint efforts to reach a quality agreement, which, among other things, establishes targets for quality improvement. If these targets are met, incoming inspection and quality inspection of the deliveries can be abolished, or the frequency of inspections can be lowered considerably.

MEMO 4.1 THE PURCHASE OF COFFEE

On 1 January a trader buys 50 tons of coffee from a producer at €1800 per ton. The consignment will be delivered on 1 April. The trader therefore runs the risk of a fall in prices from January through March. If the market falls to €1600 he would sustain a loss of €10 000. Therefore, the trader is 50 tons long. He can limit his price risk by entering into a forward transaction, doing this by taking a short position on the futures market for the same amount of money. In other words he can obtain 10 futures contracts of sale of 5 tons each on a three-month term; at that time the price of a three-month contract is €1800.

If by 1 April the market price for coffee has gone down from €1800 to €1600, he loses the €10 000; however, at that moment he sells his forward futures contract for 50 tons at €1800 while the current rate is €1600. In other words, he makes a profit of €10 000:

Effective purchase		Sale forward contract March	
50 tons at €1800	= €90 000	50 tons at €1800	= €90 000
Decreased market value:		Forward price:	
50 tons at €1600	= €80 000	50 tons at €1600	= €80 000
Market loss	€10 000	Profit futures market	€10 000

The balance of both transactions is zero. In this way the trader can limit his price risks by means of a forward transaction. Of course there are costs in connection with forward transactions, but compared to the total financial interest they are extremely low.

When a quality agreement has been entered into, it will be checked periodically as to whether all conditions are still being met. In case of doubt or in the case of proven quality problems, extra quality inspections will be carried out until the agreed quality level has been reached. Information on the quality behavior of suppliers is systematically recorded in a quality control system (part of the vendor rating-system). Based on this information action can be taken in the case of negative trends in the supplier's performance. Vendor rating can also be used to compare quality levels of suppliers. Chapter 15 will further address methods to assess suppliers.

Finally, the directive concerning liability for defective products is of importance. This directive has been established by the Council of the European Communities, to protect the consumer from damage which results from defective products. In addition this directive serves to harmonize the legislation regarding this subject between the various member states. When a purchased component is defective, both the supplier and the manufacturer of the finished product are liable for the entire damage. If one of the liable parties has compensated for the damage, then the aggrieved party cannot address the others.

Buying maintenance, repair and operating supplies

The buying of maintenance, repair and operating supplies has its own specific problems. The major purchasing-related characteristics of these goods are:

- Very extensive article assortment – in a medium-sized company an assortment containing 10 000 to 15 000 articles is no exception. This also results in an extensive supplier file. The turnover per article and per supplier is low.

- Varying degrees of specificity – some articles may be standard (such as office suppliers), other articles may be very supplier- or company-specific (for example spare parts for production or processing equipment).

- Many of these articles have a low, but irregular consumption rate – this implies that these articles usually have a very low inventory turnover rate.

- The user has substantial influence on the choice of the product.

In practice, MRO items take up 80 per cent of the product codes. At the same time they rarely make up more than 20 per cent of the purchasing turnover and, as a result of the characteristics mentioned earlier, quite often 80 per cent of the buyer's work concerns these articles.

Measures aimed at increasing purchasing efficiency should primarily focus on reducing the administrative work involved. Several measures may be used for this, including drastic reduction of product variety through standardization, outsourcing materials planning and purchasing to specialized distributors, electronic ordering and invoicing, working with electronic catalogs through e-commerce and Internet technology (see also Chapter 10). Arrangements with suppliers can be negotiated through so-called call-off agreements, which specify price, delivery terms and conditions and the contract period covered. Usually bonus arrangements are part of the contract specifying what bonus will be paid depending on the volume ordered by the company. Orders actually are placed by the users themselves, who refer to the overall contract terms that have been agreed. This frees the buyer from an important administrative workload.

A greater level of cooperation is afforded by the systems contract. A systems contract usually covers a plant or department's requirements for MRO supplies. It generally provides for the supplier to carry inventory and to make regular, timely deliveries. How to arrive at such a contract? Let's use office supplies as an example. First a particular product group or assortment (e.g. office supplies) is analysed. Based on a thorough inventory it is decided to reduce the product variety and standardize. This usually requires ample discussions between the users and the buyer involved, who for this reason work together by means of a buying committee. Also the number of suppliers is analysed. The idea is to bring the whole product group to only one specialized supplier, usually a distributor who will take stock and take care of all deliveries. Ordering routines are then established which, as a rule, mean that the internal users can order directly from the supplier (often through a detailed electronic product catalog), without intervention from the purchasing department. Also, a specific customer service level is agreed upon with the supplier, such as delivery of the assortment within three days at a 98 per cent delivery reliability, directly to the user. Finally, the supplier invoices the administration once a month and provides the manager of every department or the person responsible for the budget with an overview of the orders from that department on a monthly basis. It is clear that this solution prevents a lot of work and solves the so-called 'small-order problem' of many purchasing departments. Larger companies use this method for the purchase of office supplies, hand tools, electro-technical articles, fasteners and so forth. Although systems contracting seems to resemble other forms of contracts, it is characterized by the high degree of integration between the supplier and the customer organization. The recent upswing of e-commerce and the availability of Internet technology has improved the practical application of this type of thinking considerably. E-commerce provides not only electronic ordering right from the user's desk, but also electronic tracing and tracking of deliveries and, more importantly, electronic payment. One way of solving payment issues is to integrate the purchasing card within e-commerce.

In recent years corporate credit cards have widened in scope from travel and entertainment purposes to those of non-production buying, facilitating the incidental purchases that offices and plants make at the last moment. Such transactions are too small for national contracts, yet accounting for them costs a fortune in paperwork. Many companies in the US distribute the purchasing cards to foremen, clerks and secretaries. Companies can specify the use and billing so that they can be available, say, for only hardware items up to 500 dollars. The cards incorporate codes that set credit limits and restrict where they can be used and for what commodities (see Memo 4.2).

At the time of transaction the electronic checking process validates that the type of commodity is allowed, and the person buying is requesting a job code for the items being purchased. The credit card company pays the suppliers, eliminating thousands of purchase orders and cheques. At the end of the month the company receives one bill, hard copy and/or on tape, with all transactions sorted by purchaser, store, and/or job code. These systems greatly reduce cash use and provide cost control over the many small purchases often needed in the field or on the spot. Credit card companies generally provide quickly redigitized hard copies of any purchase slip for verification. In this way the purchasing card cuts processing costs to a minimum.

Buying investment goods

The process of purchasing investment goods takes place as described in Chapter 3. This section is therefore limited to a general outline. In general, the purchase of investment goods entails:

- the purchase of machinery, installations and services;
- monitoring the progress (expediting);
- ensuring the required quality and verifying that the requirements as specified in the order are met.

The purchase of investment goods usually takes place on a project basis, within an approved budget and established planning, in accordance with the agreed procedures. Often, a specific project team is installed. Such a team for larger investment projects is frequently composed of:

- A project leader, ultimately responsible for the optimal realization of the project in terms of technology, budget and planning.
- A project engineer, responsible for the coordination of the various technical disciplines.
- A planning engineer, responsible for setting up and maintaining up-to-date planning and documentation.
- A project administrator, responsible for budget management.
- A process engineer or environmental expert.

MEMO 4.2 GILLETTE AND THE PURCHASING CARD

Bob Edwards, manager corporate purchasing at The Gillette Company sees a bright future for the Purchasing Card. Purchasing in his view adds little or no value to the buying of non-production, maintenance, repair and operations (MRO) items. 'We just take a purchase requisition and convert it to a purchase order and pass it on to a supplier. We have become high-priced clerks'. The cost of processing an order is often more then the cost of goods/services Gillette is buying. 'My goal is to eliminate 50 to 80 per cent of non-value added work from the purchasing and accounts payable departments', says Edwards. 'First, I have to draw the people, i.e. requisitioners, in to using the Purchasing Card. I want a few restrictions at first on the card, i.e. dollar-limit per transaction, because otherwise they are not going to use it. I will let them buy almost anything that they have bought previously using a purchase requisition. I want them to get so used to using that Purchasing Card that they cannot live without it. Second, in a year's time I will do an analysis of what goods/services have been purchased, and from whom these were bought. After that analysis is done, purchasing will go out and negotiate national or international company-wide contracts and then restrict the use of the Purchasing Card only to those preferred suppliers under contract'.

Accounts payable will not pay an invoice without the issuing of a purchase order. Purchasing is not going to issue a purchase order, as long as they don't have a purchasing requisition, and if purchasing gets a purchasing requisition they will say: Hey, why a requisition? You have a Purchasing Card, buy it yourself! It's a closed loop. This eliminates the issuing of purchase orders, receiving reports, invoices and checks. Our credit card company pays the supplier within 72 hours and bills Gillette once a month for all transactions.

In the near future Gillette is going to set up electronic catalogs on their personal computers. When a requester wants, let's say, toothpicks, he or she types in 'toothpicks': the name of the supplier, contact person, telephone number and price will come up on their screen. The requester then calls the supplier and orders their toothpicks and gives them his Purchasing Card number. They buy it themselves. It doesn't come through purchasing anymore, it is automated. The purchase order processing costs can be reduced from approximately 125 dollars to less than 3 dollars per transaction. The credit card company has developed the software so they can send Gillette an electronic invoice once a month and Gillette can run it directly into their general ledger. Gillette pays this company once a month by doing electronic funds transfer. 'We have completely automated the process'.

Says Edwards: 'Now purchasing is going to add real value in the non-production (MRO) area, because we will have the time to negotiate better/more contracts, find better suppliers, and we have the leverage of the total dollars.'

Source: van Weele and Rozemeijer (1996), pp. 89–91

- Engineers as representatives of disciplines appropriate to the project, such as civil engineering, mechanical engineering, electrical equipment, instrumentation, accessories, pipeline systems and power supply.
- A project buyer, as representative of the purchasing department and responsible for all purchasing aspects, including order handling, inspection and quality inspection at the supplier's site, and monitoring progress/expediting.

The criteria used for selecting suppliers include:

- Production. What experience does the supplier or contractor have in projects like those in question?
- Organization. What is the state of the quality and experience of the staff that will be employed? To what extent is the supplier able to supply all required disciplines?
- Financial status. What about the supplier's financial reliability? What is the state of his liquidity and profitability? How pressing is his need for work?
- Design and manufacturing capacity. Which assembly instructions will the supplier use? How does he plan to monitor his costs? Does he have any experience with the materials that will be used?
- Quality assurance. What guarantees is the supplier willing to provide regarding design specification and technical specifications? What quality standards will he adhere to?
- Experience and references. What are the experiences of other client organizations with regard to the work done by the supplier? What references can the supplier provide?

After the supplier has been selected, a purchase contract will be drawn up, in which a large number of issues are set down. Quite frequently such an order consists of several hundreds of pages, including the project specifications. Many issues must be regulated, including:

- What is to be delivered, to be set down with extensive technical specifications.
- Where the goods are to be delivered or where the service is to be performed.
- The conditions under which the delivery is to be made; these concern price, delivery, payment and warranty.

Apart from these general issues there are several specific aspects involved in purchasing for investment projects, such as:

- Bank guarantees. Demanded of the supplier by the buyer to ensure that the supplier will fulfill the obligations which follow from the contract.
- Transfer of title. By means of which ownership of the material is transferred to the buyer when the supplier has received payment for these materials.
- Performance guarantees. In which the supplier guarantees that the performances specified in the order will be met in the circumstances described (frequently the supplier will have to demonstrate this in an acceptance test).

Buying services

Buying services takes place according to more or less the same principles as for the purchase of goods. Specific attention will also have to be given to matters such as the law concerning ultimate responsibility for the payment of taxes and social security, flexiwork, insurances, safety regulations, and ownership. Several types of services can be distinguished:

- services in the fields of architecture and civil engineering;
- services in the fields of machine construction, production equipment, transportation and generation of energy;
- services regarding electrical engineering, instrumentation, production automation, etc;
- facilities services regarding offices, laboratories, business computers and peripheral equipment, cafeterias, safety and health care;
- professional services such as IT-consulting, management consulting, legal, fiscal, accountancy.

A frequent question with regard to services is whether to 'do it yourself' or to buy these from suppliers. Buying of services may be necessary because of insufficient internal capacity to perform the work planned; this is called capacity buying. A lack of expertise to perform the planned work internally at an acceptable quality level or at a justified cost level gives rise to the need for specialist buying. Table 4.2 shows the advantages and disadvantages of subcontracting from suppliers.

In case of subcontracting the principal can choose between a fixed-price contract or a cost-reimbursable contract (see also Chapter 3). Popular methods for arriving at a fair selection of the best supplier are the open tender with pre-selection and the open tender without pre-selection. In the first case, the principal explicitly indicates which companies qualify for the activities and only invited companies can submit proposals. With an open tender, every supplier can submit a proposal, because the principal makes no pre-selection.

One feature that regularly leads to misunderstandings in this type of contracting is the surplus work – the unforeseen activities for which often no price has been agreed. This work is frequently an unwelcome surprise for the buyer.

When work is contracted out, the principal must take into account that the laws have been tightened up. Important regulations in some European countries are those related to payment of social securities and taxes in the case of subcontracting. Put simply, these are arrangements applied by national government to prevent 'moonlighting' and illegal recruitment or contracting practices. The essence of these regulations is that the principal is liable for payment of social insurance premiums and taxes. This does not only apply to the activities executed by the contractor – the principal is also responsible for payment of

TABLE 4.2 Advantages and disadvantages of contracting out

Advantages	Disadvantages
Investments can be focused on core activities	Increased dependency on suppliers
Optimal use of knowledge, equipment and experience of third parties	Constant monitoring of costs related to contracting out is necessary
Flexibility is increased; fluctuations in workload can be absorbed more easily	Risk of communication and organizational problems during transfer of activities to third parties
Contracting out leads to a more simple primary process in the organization	Risk of information 'leaks' (confidential information)
Input of an independent vision prevents organizational shortsightedness	Risk of social and legal problems in case of execution of activities by third parties
Part of the company risk is transferred to third parties	

the premiums and taxes of the subcontractors that are engaged by the contractor! In some European countries this law may apply to all sectors.

Other laws that require attention in the context of buying services are laws related to flexitime, foreign labor, health, safety and the environment, general labor conditions, collective labor agreements which may be present within a specific sector, income and company tax and social insurances.

SUMMARY

To be able to purchase effectively, the buyer must have a sound knowledge of the supply-markets in which he operates and of the products he buys. Supply market structures determine the buyer's tactics – his attitude towards a monopolist will differ greatly from the attitude he adopts when dealing with an oligopoly situation. When deciding on his tactics the buyer will take into account the demand side and the supply side of a specific market. A sound analysis of the buyers' power position requires understanding of the behavior of both buyers and suppliers.

This chapter has described the purchasing process related to raw materials, components, MRO items, investment goods and services. The descriptions show that the buying of each of these goods requires its own knowledge and experience - there is a world of difference between buying raw materials, hedging price risks by means of futures contracts, and buying for investment projects. In the purchase of services, it was seen that in addition to the specialist aspects, legal requirements play an important role. Due to some EC directives, legislation in this area is subject to change and it is essential for the buyer to keep informed of changes which are going on.

ASSIGNMENTS

4.1 This chapter has discussed four different supply side market structures. Explain how price elasticity would relate to each of them. What market structure would have the largest price elasticity and why?

4.2 As business to business markets have become more concentrated, this has led to less competition. As a buyer you are preparing your negotiations with a major, large supplier who has a strong market position and who is, in your opinion, charging you outrageous prices for his products. How would you prepare for this in order to get the best out of the dealings with this supplier?

4.3 Your company, a firm with 150 people employed at one location, is considering replacing its five small and medium volume copiers, producing about 300 000 copies a year. Traditionally, the management would consider buying the equipment and hence paying later for the accessories, paper and services. However, they have asked you to come up with a proposal. The objective is to arrive at a sourcing solution enabling the company to go for the lowest total cost of ownership (TCO). What would your sourcing proposal look like? What cost aspects would you need to cover in your proposal and how would you select the best possible supplier for this job?

4.4 In the purchase of MRO goods there is the small-order problem: the smallest part of the turnover is made up by a very large amount of low-consumption articles which are bought from a large number of suppliers. Name some examples of MRO articles and their major buying characteristics. What measures ▶

would you as purchasing manager take to make the purchase and/or ordering of these articles as effective and efficient as possible?

4.5 One of the unsolved problems in many companies is who should be responsible for the purchase of services. Indicate who in your opinion should take care of the purchase of the following services. Describe how you see the involvement of the purchasing department for each situation:

(a) buying consulting expertise

(b) hiring temporary labor

(c) buying advertising and PR material

(d) buying technical design expertise

(e) buying automation services.

After studying this chapter you should understand the following:

- The major tasks and responsibilities of purchasing.
- The basic principles on which purchasing policy can be based.
- The major policy areas in purchasing.
- How purchasing may develop over time as a business function.

CASE STUDY   PURCHASING'S NEW MUSCLE

'The role of purchasing has changed dramatically in the last 25 years. Back in the early days, requisitions were sent "down" to the purchasing department – it seemed that purchasing always was in the basement. People did not know to whom they were sending their requisitions; they certainly never spoke to anyone down there. They simply sent down a piece of paper that said "Buy five of these".

'In the 1970s and 1980s, companies like AT&T downsized and reengineered to stay competitive, but they ignored the importance of their purchases. In most companies, purchases consume 40 to 60 per cent of total revenue. Fortunately, the last few years have witnessed a revolution that *Fortune Magazine* referred to as "purchasing's new muscle".

'I would have preferred a different title for a couple of reasons. First, we at AT&T call it "procurement" rather than purchasing because our process goes far beyond what is traditionally known as purchasing. Second, I do not like refer-

ring to this new influence as "muscle" because it implies the use of force. Rather than raw power, purchasing's new status is based upon respect for what it can contribute to the business. Clearly, businesses are waking up to the real value of purchasing. In other words, purchasing has finally risen from the basement.

'Nothing is more important than purchasing but few executives understand the size of the opportunity. For example, one result of our restructuring will be the formation of a systems and technology company. This $20 billion business will spend $10 billion, half of its total revenue, on outside suppliers. If there is anything in that business that is more important than purchasing, it is a well kept secret.'

Source: Interview with William B. Marx jr, executive vice president Multimedia Group Products, AT&T, as quoted from 'Purchasing's New Muscle', in *Strategic Purchasing: Sourcing for the Bottom Line*, The Conference Board, 1996, pp. 9–10.

INTRODUCTION

There are major differences between organizations in the area of purchasing and supply management. Observations from business practice have shown that tasks, responsibilities and the degree of authority, assigned to the purchasing departments, differ. These differences can be traced to differences in the purchasing portfolio, the characteristics of supplier markets, the production technology and organizational structures. However, differences also stem from the way in which purchasing actually is being managed.

The objective of this chapter is to systematically answer the question as to how an organization's purchasing policy can be structured, building on the concepts presented in Chapter 1.

Tasks and responsibilities assigned to the purchasing department vary widely among companies. In one organization the purchasing department may simply represent an ordering agency, whose main activity is processing purchasing orders, whereas in another organization purchasing is considered a strategic activity which is integrated into all major business processes. This chapter describes the major tasks and responsibilities of purchasing and supply management, the basic principles on which purchasing and supply strategies can be based and the elements of the purchasing management process. Moreover, the way in which purchasing and supply management may develop as a business discipline over time is discussed.

PRIMARY TASKS AND RESPONSIBILITIES

Based on the framework of concepts developed earlier, the following responsibilities are considered to be core to the purchasing function in any organization:

- Contribution to the continuity of the company's primary activities (see also Chapter 1). The materials and services which are to be purchased must become available in line with the requirements of purchasing's internal customers. Purchasing's primary task is, therefore, that of securing supply from reliable suppliers at consistent quality at reasonable (total) cost. Effective and efficient supply is mandatory. If this task is not executed effectively the buyer, or the purchasing department, will lose credibility. The internal customers, such as engineering, manufacturing and technical services, will then bypass the purchasing department and start doing purchasing on their own. Effective purchasing therefore requires an explicit supply orientation.

- Control and reduction of all purchasing-related costs. Having secured supply, purchasing needs to make sure that goods and services are supplied at the lowest total cost of ownership. Total cost of ownership consists of two major elements: direct materials cost and all (indirect) costs related to the handling of these materials (costs related to incoming inspection, materials handling, inventory, administration, and scrap, etc.) Of course, a major task is to make sure that materials and services are bought at fair and competitive prices from the best suppliers that can be found.

    However, buyers should also attempt to reduce or prevent indirect costs. They can do so by reducing the 'buffers' or 'waste' that may be built into the materials process or supply chain (e.g. safety stocks, incoming inspection, quality inspection, field expediting, etc.).

    In view of the fact that on average 60 per cent of the production value of industrial companies consists of purchased products, it is obvious that purchasing's contribution on this aspect is a major one.[1]

---

1 See also Chapter 1 on purchasing's impact on the company's return on net assets (DuPont analysis).

- Reduction of the company's risk exposure in relation to its supply markets. If possible, the company should avoid becoming too dependent on just a few suppliers, both in terms of supply and technology. 'Captive' sales situations must be prevented or reduced and it is important to have access to reliable suppliers because high quality and punctual delivery are often more important than price. In order to minimize its technological and supply risks in the long term, the company's management preferably should aim to spread its purchasing requirements among different suppliers.

- Contribution to product and process innovation. Suppliers are often a source of new products and production technologies. In many industries technological developments take place at such a rate that even large enterprises, such as General Motors and IBM, are unable to generate all the investments needed to keep up with technology development in every area. In some cases this leads to partnerships with suppliers in the research and development field. The Smart Car, which was developed by Daimler-Chrysler in cooperation with Swatch company, is one example; another is the development of high precision wafersteppers (for the manufacture of microchips) by ASM Lithography in The Netherlands with Carl Zeiss, manufacturer of high-tech lenses, from Germany.

The company's image is partly determined by what it communicates to its customer markets and the financial community. It is certainly also influenced by what it communicates to its suppliers. A fair and open attitude towards suppliers can help the company position itself as an attractive business partner. Buyers must make sure that the company actually meets its contractual obligations towards suppliers. It is therefore important that purchasing works according to a minimum set of purchasing procedures which describe how orders are placed, who is authorized to make purchasing decisions and how to structure the purchasing process (see Chapter 3). The ways of working should be described preferably in purchasing procedures, which are simple to use and easy to communicate. Examples of such procedures are the simple rule that no invoice will be paid to suppliers unless it can be matched by a purchase order. Or, another example: that all purchases beyond a certain amount of money (for instance, €5000) need to be covered by at least three quotations from suppliers. Of increasing importance are some clear rules of conduct on how to deal with supplier relationships, on what is allowed when accepting gifts and other fringe benefits from suppliers. As cooperation with suppliers becomes more intensive the need for this kind of formal arrangement grows.[2] The importance of a clear and professional communication on the company's purchasing policies is increasingly being recognized by mainly larger companies (see Memo 5.1). Most of them have developed brochures to explain their policies both internally and externally.

Having described the most important tasks and responsibilities of purchasing, the following observations are worth mentioning.

- Acceptance of these ideas implies that in order to be successful, an explicit (internal) customer orientation is adopted. Buyers need to support the business the company is in.

MEMO 5.1 'SELLING' THE PURCHASING POLICY

Many large companies now have sometimes very attractively designed brochures which explain their purchasing policy. By means of these brochures both internal staff and suppliers are informed of the methods used by the company's purchasing department, the way in which it is organized and also of the division of the different commodities among the buyers.

---

2 See also Chapter 16 on 'rules of conduct' and 'purchasing ethics'.

Buyers should therefore spend a substantial part of their time in contact with internal users, such as production, product development and engineering. Bureaucracy ('this order must be placed according to our purchasing procedures') and too strong an emphasis on price aspects ('let's see what discount we can get!'), which many buyers are accused of in practice, are incompatible with a true customer orientation. Experience shows that internal users will only consider costs when they are convinced the buyer will ensure timely delivery and/or availability at the quality they want. Those aspects should be of primary concern to them (see Memo 5.2).

- The various purchasing tasks cannot necessarily be applied collectively, and in certain situations they can even be contradictory. Single sourcing is often based on the objective of reducing materials costs – by placing all purchasing requirements with one supplier it is often possible to negotiate substantially better conditions. However, this policy certainly has its price in that it will lead to increased supply risk and/or dependency on one supplier. Balancing the pros and cons of this particular problem exceeds the authority of a buyer. This is one reason why strategic supplier decisions need to be made by top management.

- The idea that buyers can indeed make significant contributions to product and process innovation, implies high demands on buyers' technical competences and personal qualities. Cooperation between engineering or research and development on the one hand, and the purchasing department on the other hand, can often not be realized in practice. Engineers and developers don't believe that buyers can make a significant contribution to their work because buyers often lack the required technical background and have insufficient affinity with product development and design and engineering problems. In those cases the purchasing department's professional staff should be upgraded to bring it in line with the level of professionalism which is present in the surrounding business areas.

POLICY PRINCIPLES

In this section the major principles on which purchasing policies are grounded are described. Preferably purchasing policies should be based on a sound business orientation, reflect a cross-functional approach and be directed at improving the company's bottom line.

Business orientation

Developing a purchasing and supply strategy requires a thorough understanding of the company's overall business policy. What end-user markets is the company targeting and

---

MEMO 5.2   VALUE VERSUS PRICE

It is unwise to pay too much, as it is unwise to pay too little. When you pay too much, you lose a little money, that's all. When you pay too little, you sometimes lose everything, because the thing you bought was incapable of doing the thing you bought it to do.

The common law of business balance prohibits paying a little and getting a lot. If you deal with the lowest bidder, it's well to add something for the risk you run. And if you do that, you will have enough to pay for something better.

Source: anonymous

what are the major developments going on in those markets? What competition is the company suffering from and what leeway does the company have in setting its own pricing policies? To what extent can materials price increases be passed on to the final customer or is this impossible? What changes are happening in the company's product, production and information technologies? What investments will be made by the company in terms of new products and technology and what products will be taken out of the market for the years to come? Understanding these kinds of questions is important since it will determine how purchasing and supply strategies will need to support the company in meeting its goals and objectives.

Integrated, cross-functional approach

Purchasing decisions cannot be made in isolation, and should not be aimed at optimization of purchasing performance only. Purchasing decisions should be made taking into account the effects of these decisions on the other primary activities (such as production planning, materials management and transportation). Therefore, purchasing decisions need to be based on balancing total cost of ownership. When buying for instance a new packaging line, it is important to consider not only the initial investment, but also the costs which will be incurred in the future for buying accessories, spare parts and services. Moreover, unplanned downtime needs to be guaranteed by the supplier to be kept to a minimum during the packaging lines' technical and economic lifespan. The selling of equipment by a supplier is one thing: servicing that same equipment satisfactorily over a large number of years by that same supplier is often something different. This example illustrates the complexity of this type of purchases and the different kinds of decisions that need to be made. Careful decision making in those circumstances, therefore, requires a cross-functional and team-based approach among all the business disciplines affected by it. Purchasing and supply strategies can only be developed effectively in close cooperation with all disciplines and top managers involved. The purchasing and supply manager will lead the developing of such views and visions.

Bottom-line orientation

The author does not share the view that purchasing should only operate as a service function which works on behalf of and complies with its customers' requirements without asking too many questions. Rather, purchasing should provide a healthy commercial opposition *vis-à-vis* its internal customers. Through their activities buyers should make the company more cost aware. They should consistently look for improving the price/value ratio of the goods and services bought by the company. To accomplish this, purchasing should be able to suggest alternatives to existing product designs, materials or components to be used, and alternative suppliers. Experience with companies in which purchasing is recognized as a bottom-line-driven activity shows that this function contributes to a permanent reduction of the cost price of the end product, whilst stimulating innovation from suppliers at the same time.

PURCHASING MANAGEMENT PROCESS

It has been argued that purchasing policies and strategies should be based on the company's overall (financial) objectives and product/market strategies. A company that operates in a highly competitive end-user market (e.g. the automotive industry), will beyond doubt have a strong focus on cost reduction and innovation. Hence, its purchasing and supply strategies should reflect those aspects and the purchasing activities will be directed through detailed materials budgets and well-prepared cost reduction projects. Constantly looking for new and more competitive sources of supply on an international basis (global sourcing) will be part of these projects. As an example, Volkswagen AG, since 1993 has pursued an aggressive sourcing strategy for its components. Having sourced traditionally from German suppliers, its flamboyant purchasing director Ignacio Lopez changed its sourcing strategy into one based upon global sourcing. Volkswagen's international purchasing offices nowadays invite quotations from suppliers worldwide, which are compared by an executive board which convenes weekly at Wolfsburg. As a result Volkswagen reported significant materials cost savings. Important savings (up to 20 per cent of initial materials costs) were reported during 1994–95; after these years however, severe delivery and quality problems occurred: most suppliers were not capable (or willing) to keep up with Volkswagen's growing materials volumes. Hence, this led to many disruptions in production.

A high-tech company operating in a niche market where it sells unique products, however, will have other concerns in the area of purchasing and supply strategy. Early supplier involvement, securing proprietary knowledge, reducing development lead time and development cost, will be of prime interest to the technical management. Apart from that the purchasing and supply function needs to secure flawless delivery of components and materials required. Innovation and supply come first; next, price and cost aspects are considered. Philips Medical Systems, manufacturer of advanced medical equipment, may serve as an example here. This company has gone to great lengths to involve purchasing and suppliers at an early stage of development. Suppliers are primarily selected on their technological capabilities and invited to take an active role during the development stage. After development, suppliers are requested to submit quotations which, in most cases, are very competitive due to the fact that the suppliers have gone through their learning curve earlier than their competitors. ASM-Lithography, a manufacturer of high-tech wafer-steppers in The Netherlands, is also practising this approach in its purchasing policies.

In order to describe the elements of the purchasing management process, much can be learned from the literature available on marketing management (e.g. Kotler, 1997). There are some striking similarities between marketing and purchasing:

- the primary focus of both company activities is on the exchange of values between two or more parties, resulting in the sell–buy transaction;
- both activities are externally oriented, i.e. aimed at outside parties;
- neither activity can be done adequately without sound knowledge of markets, competition, prices, technology and products;
- as a result of the amounts of money involved, both activities have great impact on the company's bottom line;

Analogous to marketing management, the following successive elements are identified in managing purchasing and supply:

- purchasing and supply (market) research
- determining purchasing and supply objectives
- determining strategy
- action planning
- implementation
- control and evaluation.

The purchasing management process is schematically illustrated in Figure 5.1. Each of these elements is discussed briefly now.

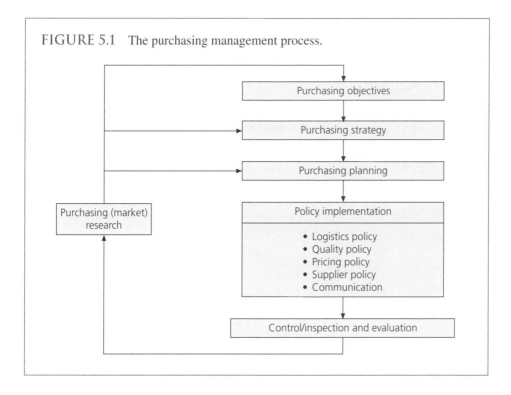

FIGURE 5.1   The purchasing management process.

Purchasing and supply (market) research

Purchasing and supply (market) research refers to the systematic study of all relevant factors which may affect supply and demand of goods and services, for the purpose of securing the company's current and future requirements.

Purchasing (market) research is used first of all to support purchasing policies and decision making; it must generate data and alternatives on which the buyer and/or management can base better purchasing decisions. Purchasing research can have both an external and an internal focus. Examples of the former are supplier studies, supply market studies and materials cost and price analyses. Examples of the latter are analysis of the company's purchasing portfolio and analysis of the costs that may be related to holding inventory and the quality costs of incoming materials.

A detailed description of the role and significance of purchasing market research is included in Chapter 6.

Purchasing and supply objectives, strategy and planning

Based upon the company's overall objectives, purchasing objectives will relate to cost-reduction, reduction of the supplier base, improving product quality, lead time reduction and so on. Through these objectives the company directs, manages and controls its purchasing activities and relationships with suppliers. In line with these purchasing and supply objectives purchasing management can focus on different areas for action (see Figure 5.2).

Important decisions need to be made in terms of supplier strategies. How many suppliers are needed per product category? For what product categories are we going to reduce or increase the number of suppliers? Are we going to pursue a relationship based upon partnership or one based upon competitive bidding? For what products do we need to source globally and for what products do we need to find local suppliers? These and other aspects are covered in the commodity sourcing strategy document.

Implementation of purchasing policy

Important areas to consider when implementing purchasing and supply policy are supply, product and supplier quality, materials costs and prices, supplier policy and communication policy (see Table 5.1).

■ Supply. Supply is aimed at the optimization of both the ordering process and the incoming materials flow. Purchasing order processing entails handling of purchasing requisitions, order processing and expediting, and development of efficient, computer-supported order routines with regard to the order-to-pay cycle. Materials and supply

---

FIGURE 5.2   Examples of areas for action in purchasing.

Sourcing policy – determining dependency on suppliers and designing plans to reduce this dependency.

Direct versus indirect buying – determining the (possible) cost benefits of buying from importers and distributors, or buying directly from the manufacturer.

Make-or-buy analysis – analysis of savings opportunities by eliminating particular production activities and buying the required products from third parties; buy-or-lease may be considered as an alternative.

Integration between purchasing and other functional areas – plans aimed at removing interface problems between purchasing and materials management, purchasing and engineering, and between purchasing and financial administration or treasury.

Setting up a purchasing information and control system – analysis of purchasing's information needs and design of an automation plan; possibilities of linking this system with existing information systems in other functional areas.

Centralized or decentralized purchasing – balancing cost benefits and strategic considerations related to a centralized or decentralized organization of purchasing.

Standardization – determining possibilities to achieve standardization in order to reduce product and supplier variety; balancing savings and risks.

TABLE 5.1 Aspects of purchasing policy

Tools	Aspects
Supply policy	Purchasing order processing
	Materials and supply planning
Product and supplier quality policy	Early involvement in development
	Improving suppliers' quality performance
Materials cost policy	Control of materials costs and prices
	Reduction of materials costs and prices
Supplier policy	Sourcing policy
	Improvement of supplier performance
Communication policy	Internal contacts
	External contacts

planning relates to issuing materials delivery schedules to suppliers, reducing supplier lead times, troubleshooting in case of delivery problems, reducing (pipeline) inventories, and monitoring supplier delivery performance.

- Product and supplier quality. Central to this aspect are the materials specifications. Two important subjects of concern here are purchasing's early involvement in design and product development and improving product and supplier quality performance. Activities which may contribute to both areas are:

  - standardization of materials – by striving for simplification or standardization of product specifications, the buyer may reduce product variety resulting in both cost reduction and a lesser supplier dependence at the same time;

  - a purchasing policy focused on the life cycle of the end products – there is not much point in investigating material quality improvements used in products which will be eliminated shortly;

  - specific quality improvements – negotiating targets on improving reject rates, reducing incoming inspection, and negotiating quality agreements;

  - agreeing on and gradually extending permanent warranty conditions that are to be provided by the supplier;

  - initiating special programs in the field of value analysis to simplify product design and/or reduce product costs.

- Materials cost policy. The objective of materials cost policy is twofold: first, to obtain control of materials cost and prices in such a way that suppliers are unable to pass on unjustified price increases to the company. Second, to systematically reduce the supplier's materials cost through joint, well-prepared action plans. In order to be successful on both aspects a thorough knowledge of the supplier's pricing policies and cost structure is required. In this context, understanding and knowledge of market structures and of the susceptibility of the price paid to market and cost factors is necessary. It should be decided for what products to build detailed cost-models, for what products to monitor underlying cost factors, and for what products to develop detailed materials budget estimates.

- Supplier policy. The supplier policy is focused on the systematic management of the company's supplier base. First, decisions need to be made for what commodities to pursue a multiple sourcing strategy or to go for single sourcing or a partnership relationship. Suppliers who actually perform best should be rewarded with more business in the future. Targets and possible projects for future cooperation should be determined carefully. Relationships with suppliers who consistently fail to meet the company's expectations should be terminated. However, such decisions need to be made based on detailed data on how the supplier performed in the past and be implemented carefully.

- Communication policy. The company's purchasing policies need to be communicated both internally and to suppliers. Increasingly, companies use their Intranet for the former. At this time many companies employ their own purchasing website (see Memo 5.3) in order to communicate their future materials requirements and ways of working to their suppliers. The next step is that preferred suppliers have access to the customer's Intranet through which internal users can order directly from them using their electronic catalogs. The facilities to communicate both internally and externally for buyers have considerably improved over the past years. Most companies at this time are only beginning to discover the vast opportunities in purchasing and supply that the new electronic media offer.

- Control/inspection and evaluation. Purchasing management must see that both results and activities that have been planned are realized within the available financial resources. To this end the actual performance, obtained through purchasing activities, must be periodically checked against the purchasing plans. In most cases reports are required about the savings and costs reductions realized through (cross-functional) purchasing activities. Furthermore, the performance of suppliers should be checked periodically through vendor performance reports. These subjects need to be reported to management through a consistent procedure so that management is able to assess overall purchasing performance.

As Figure 5.1 shows, the purchasing management process in fact is a closed loop. If one of the elements gets insufficient attention, the effect will be that activities get out of control. When objectives and concrete targets are absent, this will lead to a situation in which purchasing activities will lack clear guidance. When objectives and targets have not been translated into detailed action plans, this will lead to a lack of understanding of who is responsible for doing what. The absence of a management reporting structure often is a prime reason why managers do not understand what purchasing has contributed to the company's bottom line. In many companies, elements of this purchasing management process are ill-structured. This is one of the reasons why purchasing in those companies has little professionalism. Most problems related to purchasing and supply management, therefore, are problems of management rather than being related to the purchasing area itself.

MEMO 5.3   REVERSE MARKETING AT SONY

The Internet site of Sony (see Figure 5.3) provides an interesting example of how large manufacturers communicate with their suppliers nowadays. New suppliers are explicitly invited to study Sony's purchasing policy, structure and pre-qualification procedure. In fact, Sony uses the Internet as a marketing instrument to inform suppliers about their current procurement vision and strategy. Through this website future 'partners' (as Sony like to refer to suppliers who are capable of meeting all Sony requirements) can subscribe and inform themselves about what it takes to become a prospective Sony supplier.

Other progressive manufacturers also have a purchasing website on the Internet. Usually the following information is communicated to their supplier communities:

- description of company policy, strategy and structure
- vision on procurement and supplier relationships
- what it takes to qualify as a prospective supplier
- structure of the procurement organization
- list of persons that may be contacted
- invitation to submit quotations for certain products or services
- description of the supplier quality assurance program
- general procurement conditions and compliance to laws and regulations
- recent press information that may be relevant for suppliers.

Contrary to some years ago, most parts of these sites are now confidential and only open to suppliers who are part of the company's established supplier community. Many sites now provide facilities for buyers to closely monitor the incoming materials flows from suppliers.

FIGURE 5.3 Sony procurement window.

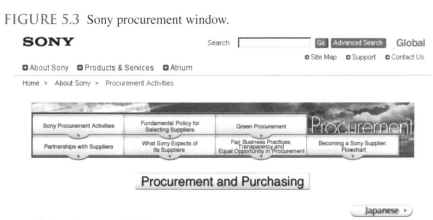

Procurement and Purchasing

Japanese ›

▶ Sony Procurement Activities

Sony's procurement activities are based on two main principles.

One is meeting the expectations of Sony customers worldwide. Customers expect Sony products and services to offer a high level of value. They also expect Sony to be a good corporate citizen through its operations. Sony's procurement activities are no exception in meeting these expectations.

The other is relationships with suppliers. Sony procures parts and materials for its products from numerous suppliers worldwide. Sony's worldwide procurement activities require smooth relationships with suppliers based on mutual trust and cooperation. Sony therefore places importance on creating such relationships with suppliers.

Sony believes that both Sony and its suppliers need to be good partners: in order to provide highly appealing products that satisfy customers, and to be good corporate citizens through such activities as green procurement.

Partnerships with Supplier ›

⊕ About this Site   ⊕ Terms of Use
⊕ Change Text Size

Copyright 2004 Sony Corporation

HOW PURCHASING AND SUPPLY MANAGEMENT DEVELOPS OVER TIME

Purchasing structures in large companies nowadays are very different from those structures in place during the 1970s or 1980s, and they will, beyond doubt, be different in the future. Two decades ago concepts like purchasing portfolio management, total cost of ownership, supplier-partnerships, early supplier involvement and cross-functional buying teams were not known. Since then many new strategic and organizational concepts in the field of purchasing and supply chain management have been developed. The professional development of the purchasing function in organizations can be analyzed from different angles and/or aspects. Over the past years many authors have suggested conceptual models on this subject.[3] Most authors assume a stage-wise or step-wise development of purchasing and supply management within organizations with the following characteristics:

- Integrated final stage. Most authors assume the existence of a final stage of excellence towards which all improvement efforts should be directed. Almost all models show a final phase where purchasing is integrated in the major lines of business. At this stage line management is actively involved in purchasing strategies and tactics. Also at this stage it is assumed that purchasing processes are organized around multi-disciplinary, team-based structures.

- Purchasing's organizational status. Most models point out that purchasing initially reports rather low in the organizational hierarchy. Next there may be some degree of centralization, which in a business unit structure will turn to some form of co-ordinated purchasing (where responsibility for purchasing policy resides within the individual business units).

- Supplier management. The development of supplier management is another similarity in the different development models. In the first stage, supplier management seems to be reactive ('opportunity driven'). In the next phase, it becomes more proactive ('supplier performance improvement'), and in the last phase it becomes relationship management ('partnership').

- Supplier relationships. Most authors assume that, as purchasing moves through the different stages of development, relationships with suppliers will change. The process starts with a purchasing department handling many suppliers at 'arms length'. In the next stage, purchasing has reduced its number of suppliers considerably so that closer relationships with a smaller number of (preferred) suppliers are able to develop.

Major drivers, which influence how purchasing and supply management will develop over time, are considered to be:

- Business context. It is generally assumed that the more competitive the business context, and the more mature the technology in the industry in which the company is operating, the higher the pressure on purchasing to contribute to the bottom line will be.

- Company strategy. The more explicit the company is about the goals and objectives it wants to realize and the more formalized the planning process, the larger the chance that purchasing issues are integrated into the overall company strategy.

- Systems development. Modern information and communication technologies are considered to be important enablers for the implementation of modern purchasing and supply management concepts.

---

3 See van Weele *et al.* 1998 for an overview.

- Top management commitment. This relates to the degree to which top management shows active interest in, and is actively involved with, purchasing strategy and supply issues.
- Functional leadership. This relates to the personality of the purchasing manager, his management style and prominence.

The approach that has been described by Keough (1993) is one of the most interesting ones. It is very detailed; it identifies five stages of development and assumes a direct causal relationship between the industry a company is in and the stage of development in purchasing. For the remainder of this chapter this model is taken as the point of departure. The author has tried, however, to integrate and combine some valuable insights from other contributors in order to arrive at an integrated purchasing developmental model.

Based upon these general parameters the following six-stage purchasing developmental model has been identified (see Figure 5.4).

Stage 1 'Transaction orientation; serve the factory'

In this first stage the primary task of purchasing is to find appropriate suppliers and ensure that the plant does not run out of raw materials and supplied components. There is no explicit purchasing strategy in place. Formulation of purchasing goals is very rudimentary and intuitive. The main contribution of the purchasing function is considered to be securing the availability of the right materials and goods for the company's primary purpose. The organizational structure can be characterized by a decentralized sub-department at plant level, mostly under the responsibility of a production or logistics manager. The purchasing function is strongly orientated on operational and administrative activities. Non-production buying is predominantly done by users themselves, and is considered by purchasing as of secondary importance. There is very little knowledge of what is exactly the total purchasing spend of the company. The culture is 'reactive'. Management is based on complaints. No complaints means purchasing does a good job. The information systems, if in place already, are developed by purchasing and very much administratively oriented. The purchasing staff consists usually of operational and administrative buyers, strongly task oriented, and with little education for the job.

Stage 2 'Commercial orientation; lowest unit price'

At this stage a pro-active type of purchasing manager is recruited who can negotiate credibly with suppliers for lower prices. Striving for the lowest unit cost requires some independence from functions like product development, engineering and manufacturing. As a result purchasing, while reporting to a senior executive, has more autonomy at lower organizational levels. Purchasing strategy at this stage is characterized by a sharp focus on low prices. The purchasing function has its own department at plant level, reporting directly to the plant manager, who is interested in the savings purchasing adds to the bottom line. At this stage the purchasing function more and more becomes a specialist function. Specialist buyers are organized around different product groups. Buyers are concentrating on negotiating and contracting 'good deals'. The culture is that of playing hard negotiations with many suppliers. Management monitors on low prices and savings. Performance measurement is focused primarily on price (-variance) and delivery performance of the suppliers. Cost savings are used as a prime performance indicator for assessing purchasing's overall effectiveness. Purchasing staff consists of operational and initial buyers with 'hands on' experience. Important skills are negotiating skills and the ability to make price comparisons.

Stage 3 'Co-ordinated purchasing'

Led by a strong central purchasing department to implement uniform buying policies and systems, the emphasis here lies on cross unit coordination and compliance with nationally negotiated contracts. This stage may lead to purchasing bureaucracy and lack of responsiveness from the decentralized business units. At this stage for the first time there is some kind of strategy formulation, aimed at capturing the benefits from internal coordination and synergy. Apart from price and costs, the purchasing function is seen as having an important influence on the quality level of purchased products. The importance of the non-production buying becomes recognized by purchasing. Slowly the purchasing function is getting some attention from top management. However, the rest of the organization is still not convinced of the value adding potential of the purchasing function.

FIGURE 5.4   Towards a coherent purchasing and supply development model.

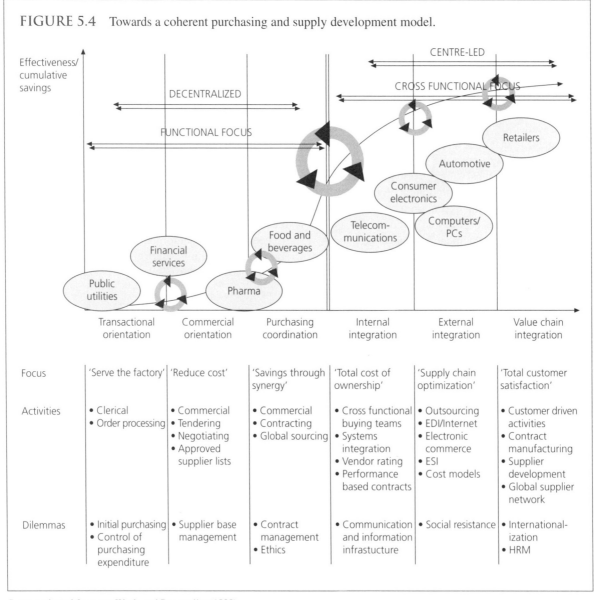

	Transactional orientation	Commercial orientation	Purchasing coordination	Internal integration	External integration	Value chain integration
Focus	'Serve the factory'	'Reduce cost'	'Savings through synergy'	'Total cost of ownership'	'Supply chain optimization'	'Total customer satisfaction'
Activities	• Clerical • Order processing	• Commercial • Tendering • Negotiating • Approved supplier lists	• Commercial • Contracting • Global sourcing	• Cross functional buying teams • Systems integration • Vendor rating • Performance based contracts	• Outsourcing • EDI/Internet • Electronic commerce • ESI • Cost models	• Customer driven activities • Contract manufacturing • Supplier development • Global supplier network
Dilemmas	• Initial purchasing • Control of purchasing expenditure	• Supplier base management	• Contract management • Ethics	• Communication and information infrastructure	• Social resistance	• Internationalization • HRM

Source: adapted from van Weele and Rozemeijer (1998)

Supplier management is a central issue at this stage and is characterized by looking for synergy by bundling purchasing power of the different divisions and adoption of differentiated supplier strategy based upon portfolio-analysis techniques. The organizational structure of the purchasing function is a centralized purchasing department on divisional level. Formalization of the purchasing process and procedures is at full speed. The purchasing organization is still strongly product oriented. The culture is characterized by a great amount of attention for communication and the intention to cooperate more internally between business units. Computerized information systems are in place now, but still not linked to each other. The stand-alone databases are linked over the divisions, but not yet fully integrated. Purchasing staff have a specific purchasing background and training and there are a large number of different purchasing jobs in place. Training is aimed at analytical skills, total quality management and communication skills.

Stage 4 'Internal integration: cross-functional purchasing'

At this stage the emphasis is on cross-functional problem-solving with the objective of reducing total systems cost and not just the unit cost of purchased components. These cross-functional efforts often include key suppliers as joint problem solvers and a move from confrontational to partnership sourcing. Until this stage the purchasing function was very much functionally oriented, and trying to organize the company around the purchasing function. At this stage purchasing is becoming more process-oriented, trying to organize the purchasing function around the internal customers. In this stage there is serious attention for non-production purchasing. The strategic importance of the purchasing function comes to full recognition, and purchasing is involved in strategic issues like core/non-core questions and make-or-buy decisions. The structure is 'centre-led'; operational buying disappears in the line, i.e. is integrated with materials planning and/or scheduling or line planning. The culture is characterized by team-based management, often by means of cross-functional teams. Improvement actions are aimed at integrating the purchasing processes over the different divisions. In this stage the focus is still internal, however, process oriented. Information systems are integrated with that of other departments/functions and divisions, but not yet with those of the most important suppliers. Purchasing performance measurement is done in the form of internal customer satisfaction surveys and benchmarking. People involved in the purchasing process have a broad business perspective and a high educational level. Skills looked for at this stage are strong team-building abilities, strong communication skills.

Stage 5 'External integration; supply-chain management'

This stage is characterized by an outspoken outsourcing strategy combined with extra attention to cooperation with supply partners on product development and preproduction planning. The purchasing function concentrates on the effects the supply chain has on the resources of the company. Non-production buying is fully supported and/or executed by the purchasing function. Users order themselves against corporate contracts through advanced, web-enabled catalog systems to which some major suppliers have been hooked up. This is especially true for the non-production area. Purchasing works hard to make things simple for their internal customers, by using systems contracting, purchasing cards, electronic business and catalogs and/or EDI. Supplier management becomes supply chain management at this stage. Companies invest heavily to involve supply partners in different business processes, instead of just buying goods and services from them as efficiently and effectively as possible. Responsibility for initial purchasing resides with cross-functional teams (inter-divisional and inter-organizational) and is no longer executed by a separate department. There are residential engineering teams, and improvement teams with members from different disciplines, divisions and organizations (suppliers). Integration with other disciplines, divisions and especially suppliers is at full speed, to enable integrated supply chain management. The management style is results driven, though supportive and coaching at the same time. The culture is characterized by participation and consensus style decision making. Important skills are knowledge of total-cost-of-ownership principles, strategic supply chain management, and general managerial and leadership abilities. Information systems are not only integrated internally, but also with those of the partner suppliers.

Stage 6 'Value chain orientation'

The 'purchasing' strategy in this stage will be based on the recognition that most important for success is delivering value to the end customer. To satisfy the needs in end-customer markets, subcontractors seek support from their suppliers. Suppliers are consistently challenged to support their customer's product/market strategies and to actively participate in product development. The goal is to design the most efficient and effective value chain possible to serve the end-customer. Purchasing strategy is evaporated in the total business strategy. The orientation is both stream upwards as well as downwards. In fact the traditional marketing and purchasing functions are integrated, and have become 'virtual' in the company. The functioning is based on a shared vision carried by all organizational members. The culture is entrepreneurial. Information systems are integrated as much as possible.

Although this model may seem rather straightforward, some critical remarks must be directed towards it. First, the model has never been tested by thorough academic research. It is important to question and test the validity and reliability of this model. Is the process of development in purchasing a rational process, as the model suggests, or rather an irrational one? Does purchasing development really take place as a process of continuous change or is it in reality characterized more by step-changes and discontinuity? What change strategies underlie purchasing development processes in organizations? Do all organizations follow the stages identified or can some stages be skipped? To what extent are purchasing managers the most decisive actors in the process of purchasing development? Or are they rather receptive in general and are the real change agents coming from other disciplines? More research is warranted in order to use this model as a term of reference for guiding purchasing and supply's organizational and professional development.

SUMMARY

In summary the argument is that most companies have a large potential for improvement in the area of purchasing management. A systematic approach of the purchasing policy can help make this potential visible and accessible.

The tasks, responsibilities and authority of the purchasing function must be established first: securing supply of required materials and services at consistent quality from reliable suppliers is the prime task and responsibility for purchasing. However, activities should not be exclusively limited to this. Purchasing and supply management has more to do. Purchasing and supply management should also strive to continuously improve the price/value ratio in the relationship with suppliers. Materials price control and cost reduction are therefore important policy areas. At the same time the risk exposure, in terms of the company's dependence on suppliers, should be minimized. Furthermore, the buyer should be alert to technological innovations that take place in his supplier markets, which may be beneficial to the company.

Professional purchasing requires effective communication both internally and externally. Purchasing procedures and policies should be approved by top management and communicated to the internal users. Simple brochures and leaflets, which explain how purchasing prefers to work with suppliers and what may be expected in terms of professional support, may be helpful. The new electronic media also provide new and vast opportunities in this respect.

Managing purchasing implies that all elements of the purchasing management process are defined. Purchasing objectives need to be derived from the overall company policy and should support this. They need to be translated into detailed sourcing strategies and action plans, indicating what performance will be targeted for in terms of cost reduction, quality improvement, improving supply performance and internal efficiency. Finally, purchasing management should provide periodical, detailed management reporting.

Putting these elements of the purchasing management process in place takes time, however. This explains why differences exist in purchasing operations between companies, even if they operate in the same type of industry. The purchasing development model, which has been presented in this chapter, provides a picture of the stages companies may go through when they want to develop purchasing professionalism. However, this model should be used carefully, for all stages may not be relevant for all types of commodities, companies and industries, as some authors may want us to believe.

ASSIGNMENTS

5.1   In this chapter four major tasks and responsibilities have been described which can be attributed to purchasing and supply management. What are these? It has been argued that these four tasks and responsibilities should not necessarily be in line with each other. Provide at least four situations where two or more of these tasks and responsibilities may be conflicting. How would you solve these conflicts?

5.2   Why would communications both internally and to suppliers be so important for effective purchasing? Who would you see as the most important 'competitor' of a buyer? How would you prevent 'back-door selling' from a supplier's representative?

5.3   A reporting structure has been presented as an essential part of the purchasing management process. If you were a purchasing manager, what would you report to your superiors on a monthly basis? Would you report the same thing to your production and logistics manager? Discuss!

5.4   This chapter discussed a six stage purchasing development. It suggests that as purchasing as a discipline in companies moves from one stage to another, purchasing managers need to prepare for resistance from the organization. What kind of problems and/or resistance may purchasing managers expect when companies move from stage 1 to stage 2, from stage 2 to stage 3 and so on?

▶

5.5 Management has requested you to develop a cost-down program for your organization related to non-production buying. What would such a cost-down program look like? What structure would you give to it? How would you execute it? Describe and present.

CASE STUDY   SUPPLY MARKET RESEARCH THROUGH THE INTERNET

Using the Internet to locate and evaluate suppliers just got easier. Finding a supplier and determining its adequacy, often two separate endeavors, can now be combined into one 'net-based chore'. Renowned business information company Dun & Bradstreet has teamed with SupplyBase, a San Francisco-based web-directory firm, to offer online supplier directories that include detailed information on supplier performance and manufacturing capacity.

According to *Purchasing*'s recent Internet-usage survey … researching potential suppliers is the number-one reason buyers log on to the Internet. Chris Golec, vice president of marketing at Supply Base, noticed a similar trend. 'Manufacturers were looking for reliable third-party information to differentiate suppliers based on performance, risk, and other business factors,' says Golec.

Dave Otterness, director of supplier management for Flextronics International, an electronics contract manufacturer, has used the D&B/Supply Base directories. 'It is difficult to determine if a supplier's information is accurately portrayed on the Internet, or if the company has sufficient expertise to handle high-volume projects,' says Otterness. 'Integrating D&B's supplier-evaluation tools with SupplyBase's industry-capability information will reduce business risk and increase sourcing productivity.'

Finding and assessing a supplier on one of these sites is quite a seamless process. For example, a buyer in search of recycled plastic materials might have an experience like this: from a list of five supplier categories, the buyer chooses 'materials', and then from a menu of more specific industries, 'recycled plastics'. The buyer can choose to narrow the search by geography and the next screen contains relevant suppliers. By clicking on one of the suppliers, the buyer comes to a profile page containing a brief company profile, product showcase, RFQ option, and contact information. Included prominently on this page is the supplier's standard

D&B D-U-N-S number, hyperlinked to D&B's information store on that company.

According to Chris Golec, once the buyer has identified a prospective supplier, detailed D&B reports, including the supplier evaluation report (SER) and the supplier performance review (SPR), are available for purchase. The SER measures the financial stability of a supplier and quantifies the risk of doing business with them. The SPR determines how well a supplier performs in key areas, such as quality, tech support, and delivery, relative to the industry average.

Source: Vigoros (1998)

INTRODUCTION

O ver the past years the Internet has become available to buyers as a professional tool for investigating supplier markets. A wide variety of supplier databases is available nowadays, providing links between supplier directories and providers of financial and supply market information. Through this and the rapidly improving search facilities business-to-business markets have become much more transparent. The Internet even provides consumers and professional buyers with new tools which facilitate tendering, ordering, shipment and payment. Through these new tools the productivity of many purchasing departments has increased, whilst at the same time the quality of purchasing decision making has improved.

This chapter covers the subject of purchasing and supply market research. A major objective of purchasing market research is to ascertain sound decision making. Just as for other types of research, purchasing market research has to identify and analyse the risks related to important purchasing decisions. Purchasing market research will not reduce the risks related to decision making. However, it makes these risks more visible and transparent.

Some authors make a distinction between purchasing research and purchasing market research. Purchasing research, then, refers to subjects concerning the internal organization (such as research on the composition of the purchase assortment, its pricing, research on the buyers' workload, the internal efficiency).[1] Purchasing market research refers to the external suppliers' market. It contains analyses of macro-economic developments in supplier countries, analyses of supply and demand of important raw materials, and assessments of the financial strengths and weaknesses of the individual supplier organization. In this chapter the focus will be on purchasing market research only; it will show what areas and aspects to consider. Also some research techniques that can be used will be discussed. At this point we will present the possibilities, opportunities and risks related to using the Internet for this purpose. Finally the subject of how to organize for purchasing market research will be discussed.

WHY PURCHASE MARKET RESEARCH?

The need for systematic purchasing market research has been increasing in recent years. Many large companies, like IBM, Honda of America, Lucent Technologies and Philips Electronics have introduced corporate commodity teams which are responsible for the worldwide sourcing of strategic parts and materials. Relentlessly, these teams look for the best-in-class suppliers for their materials and service needs. Originally supported by

---

1 A better term to indicate this activity is 'purchasing control'.

specialized staff departments, the corporate commodity buyers increasingly commit to conduct purchasing market research themselves. The Internet increasingly provides better and more up-to-date information on supply markets in a faster and more convenient way. What factors have led to a greater need for active supply market research? The major ones are:

- Continuing technological developments. As was seen earlier, every company, whether industrial or trade, has to concentrate on product innovation and quality improvement in order to stay competitive. When investing in new technologies the question arises: should we develop new technologies ourselves or should we buy them? Strained financial resources often lead managers to the latter option. The make-or-buy decision demands a lot of research, as does the final supplier selection decision once the decision has been made to buy. Buyers have to refresh their knowledge constantly about new technological developments which are going on in their supply markets, through product and supplier research.

- Supply market dynamics. International supply markets are constantly on the move – export facilities can suddenly be limited because of changes in political arrangements between countries, suppliers can disappear as a result of bankruptcy, suppliers may be acquired by a competitor with several consequences for the price level and continuity of supply. Demand side changes may similarly occur – demand for a product can increase enormously (for example demand for Pentium microprocessors in the mid-1990s) resulting in a scarcity situation. Buyers, then, have to anticipate likely changes in a product's demand and supply situation and thus develop a better understanding of the price dynamics of their commodities.

- Changes in Western society. The relatively high wages level in Western Europe has led to changes in the suppliers' market. An example is the change in textile supply for most European retailers, who shifted from local to European suppliers and who now have shifted their primary supply base to the Far East due to much lower wages. The same trend can be recognized for many industrial products (varying from television glass to car tires). For many products, industrial production has shifted from Western countries to the Far East (especially to China) or the developing countries, and this development will probably continue.

- Monetary developments. The ever-increasing volatility of some major currencies poses new problems for buyers who operate internationally. High inflation in some countries, large governmental budget deficits, rapidly changing currency exchange rates may all require immediate action from buyers in terms of a reallocation of their materials requirements.

These are some of the factors which underline the importance of systematic purchasing market research.

PURCHASING MARKET RESEARCH: DEFINITION

Purchasing market research can be defined as the systematic gathering, classification and analysis of data considering all relevant factors that influence the procurement of goods and services for the purpose of meeting present and future company requirements in such a way that they contribute to an optimal return.

Some aspects of this definition warrant further explanation:

- Purchasing market research can relate to research which is conducted at regular intervals, such as monitoring market prices of strategic commodities. However, it may also be conducted on a project-basis. Examples of this type of research are: developing a detailed cost model for a strategic commodity; auditing suppliers; or conducting a specific country study against the background of global sourcing initiatives.

■ Purchasing market research can be qualitative or quantitative in character. Qualitative research is research based on gathering views or opinions on trends and developments going on in a specific industrial sector. Usually this type of research is based upon interviews with industry experts. Quantitative research is based on numerical data possibly derived from general statistics and other public sources. For example: what is the market share of a specific supplier? How do supply and demand develop over time? How can supply and demand patterns be clarified by other macro-economic indicators? Other examples are cost-breakdown analyses which explain whether the price charged by a given supplier is fair or not. Most supply market research covers both aspects. Supplier benchmark studies are examples of both quantitative and qualitative research.

■ Purchasing market research can focus on short-term as well as long-term issues. Concentration tendencies and materials shortages, which are to be expected, in certain industries may require that the company covers its materials needs for a longer period and may foster long-term relationships with suppliers. Short-term supply market analysis may be required when a major supplier is unexpectedly suffering from production problems or goes bankrupt.

As demonstrated in Chapter 5, purchasing market research is an essential element of the purchasing management process. Its major benefit is that the data gathered through it may serve as a thorough and objective basis for key purchasing decisions.

HOW TO STRUCTURE PURCHASING MARKET RESEARCH

Figure 6.1 shows the most important steps to be made when conducting purchasing market research. These are in more detail:

1 Determine objectives. What exactly is the problem to be solved? What information is desired? How accurate does the information have to be? These questions are not a problem if the research is carried out by the buyer himself. If, however, the research is delegated to others a good briefing is of great importance, in order to generate useful information from it. Are we talking about a global market review or is an extensive analysis of the suppliers' financial and market positions required? When does the answer have to be available? These aspects should be covered in a concise briefing.

2 Cost-benefit analysis. What will be the costs of the research? How many man-hours are required for the research? Will the value of the obtained information outweigh the expense?

3 Feasibility study. What information is already available within the company? What information is available from publications and statistics? There may be more information readily available than originally expected. A good (computer-based) documentation service can be invaluable. On many issues international electronic databases exist (see Memo 6.1) – and specialized agencies may conduct market and product studies at limited costs. If a public database cannot be found directly, it is worthwhile asking for such a survey at university libraries or economic information services. The next research step should only be taken once it is confirmed that the required information is unavailable in the form of publications or statistics.

4 Design of a research plan. Specific action is sometimes needed to obtain information, as for example, in the case of auditing a specific supplier. Another example is an investigation to analyse possibilities for a 'catalog buying' contract - a situation in which the buyer looks for opportunities to transfer a coherent assortment of products (e.g. fasteners, computer supplies) from many suppliers to only one supplier. In addition to desk research, interviews with buyers and suppliers will be required, followed by field research. It is important to prepare well for such research through a detailed project plan.

5 Execution of research activities. In the execution stage it is important to follow the project plan prepared earlier. Decision making is often dependent on a certain amount of information being available. Excuses for delays in research activity cannot be accepted – potential problems should have been anticipated while designing the time plan and estimating the workload.

6 Preparing research report and evaluation. When the research is finished a report has to be prepared – this has to contain the assignment, as well as the obtained results. Did the buyer get an answer to his questions? Is the report drawn up in a comprehensive manner? What assumptions underlie the obtained results? These are issues that require

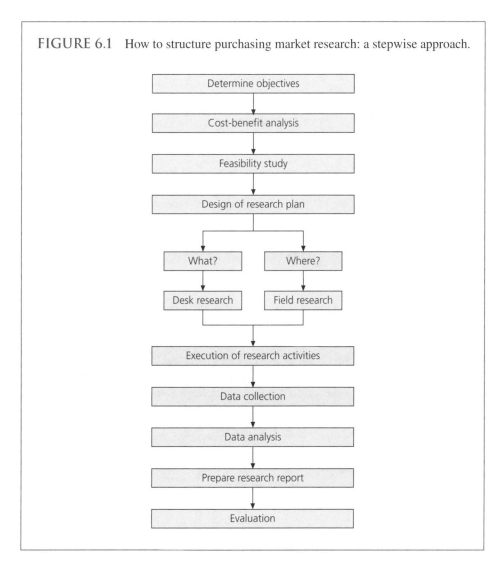

FIGURE 6.1   How to structure purchasing market research: a stepwise approach.

MEMO 6.1   ELECTRONIC SOURCES OF SUPPLY MARKET INFORMATION

There are about 1000 e-marketplaces for businesses in the world today, but only a handful have the participation of the world's biggest companies and handle large trading volumes. Some of the most important e-marketplaces are listed per industry here.

Automotive

Covisint (www.covisint.com)
Established in February 2000, Covisint provides a platform for original equipment manufacturers (OEMS) and automotive suppliers to trade with some of the world's major automotive companies.

SupplyOn (www.supply.com)
Established in mid 2000 by leading companies within the automotive supply industry (e.g. Bosch, Continental, INA and ZF along with SAP as a technology partner). At the end of 2001, Siemens VDO also joined the company

Aviation

Aeroxchange (www.aeroxchange.com)
Founded on 1 October 2000 by 13 airlines. 19 additional airlines have since joined the founding group. Among the founding airlines are Air Canada, Air New Zealand, Cathay Pacific, FedEx, KLM, Lufthansa, SAS and Singapore Airlines. The e-marketplace is focused on streamlining the buying and selling process of products such as airframes, avionics, engine components, maintenance services as well as airline specific goods and services.

B2B-Aero.com (www.b2b-aero.com)
Founded in February 2000 the e-marketplace's mission is to connect airlines, OEMs and aviation repair facilities to streamline the overhaul and repair business using the Internet.

Exostar (www.exostar.com)
Founded by Bae Systems, Boeing, Lockheed Martin Group, Raytheon Co. and RollsRoyce. The e-marketplace is an electronic business service provider built for the aerospace and defence industry.

Building and construction

BravoBuild (www.bravobuild.it)
Founded in July 2000 by Italcementi Group, one of the most important cement producers and distributor in Italy.

Edilportale (www.edilportale.it)
Online from March 2001, Edilportale was founded by Italian private investors and venture capitalists. The e-marketplace offers a good industry directory and it is rich in news, industry laws and events.

Citadon (www.citadon.com)
Although not strictly an e-marketplace, Citadon provides a web-based software application for project collaboration, document access, sharing and business process automation for the global engineering and construction industry. Its members are some of the world's major engineer, procure, and construct (EPC) companies including Alcoa, Bechtel Corp., Fluor Daniel, Marriott, Halliburton, GE Power Systems and Kvaerner Oilfield Products.

Chemicals

Elemica (www.elemica.com)
Founded in August 2000 by 22 of the world's biggest chemical companies including: BASF, Bayer, BP, Dow, DuPont, Mitsubishi Chemical Corporation, Mitsui Chemicals, Rhodia, Rohm and Haas, Shell Chemicals, Sumitomo Chemical and Royal Vopak.

ChemConnect (www.chemconnect.com)

Founded in 1995, ChemConnect is a global trading hub for chemical products such as: petrochemicals, industrial chemicals, plastics and polymers, pharmaceutical inputs, fine and speciality chemicals, industrial gases and agrochemicals.

Energy and fuels

Eutilia (www.eutilia.com)

Eutilia is a European e-marketplace for the sale and purchase of electricity and related equipment. Eutilia was set up in March 2001 by 11 of Europe's leading utility companies including Electrabel, Electricité de France, Endesa, National Grid Company, RWE, Vattenfall and Nuon.

Trade-Ranger (www.traderanger.com)

Founded in 2000 by a number of major multinationals in the energy and petrochemical industries, Trade-Ranger's shareholders include ConocoPhillips, The Dow Chemical Company, ENI, Equilon Enterprises, Mitsubishi Corporation, Motiva Enterprises, Repsol YPF, Royal Dutch/Shell, Statoil, Total, Unocal, Occidental Petroleum and BP.

Food and beverages

Transora (www.transora.com)

Transora's investors include more than 50 of the world's largest consumer packaged goods manufacturers including PepsiCo, Coca-Cola, Mars, Kellogg's, Danone, Procter & Gamble, Unilever NV, Quaker Oats and Heineken. Operating in seven languages Transora has interoperability projects underway with CPGmarket and GlobalNetXchange (GNX).

CPmarket.com (www.cpgmarket.com)

Founded by Nestlé, Danone, Henkel and SAPmarkets in March 2000. Investors in the e-marketplace are leading players of the consumer packaged goods industry in Europe, both manufacturers and suppliers. Significant manufacturers using the e-marketplace include The Coca-Cola Company, L'Oreal and Pernod Ricard.

Healthcare and pharmaceuticals

Global Healthcare Exchange (www.ghx.com)

GHX was founded in March 2000 for hospitals, manufacturers and wholesalers. Products traded include medical and healthcare equipment, products and services and pharmaceuticals. Members include Siemens, 3M Medical, Arrow International, Bayer Diagnostics, Boston Scientific Corp. and GE Medical Systems.

Retail and consumer goods

Globalnetxchange (www.gnx.com)

Founded in March 2000 and operating in six languages (including Chinese and Japanese), GlobalNetXchange (GNX) facilitates the trade of all types of products and services for the retail sector ranging from perishable foods to clothing. Members include Carrefour SA, Coles Myer Ltd., Karstadt Quelle AG, The Kroger Co., METRO AG, Pinault-Printemps-Redoute SA, Sainsbury's plc, Sears, Roebuck and Co. and Federated Department Stores

WorldWideRetailExchange (www.wwre.com)

WWRE was founded in March 2000 for retailers and suppliers in the food, general merchandise, textile/home, and drugstore sectors. Members include Edeka, Tengelmann Group, Rewe, K Mart, Target, Marks & Spencer, Tesco, Seibu Dept Stores, Jusco, Woolworths and others.

Transportation and logistics

Transcore (www.transcore.com)

TransCore's freight exchange, powered by DAT Services, is an e-marketplace for the matching of freight shippers with carriers. With installations in 37 countries and 1800 employees Transcore handles over

▶

2.5 million transactions monthly. The e-marketplace is based in Beaverton, USA and was established in 2000.

In the case of purchasing market research it is common to differentiate between desk research and field research. Desk research is the gathering, analysis and interpretation of data that serve the research assignment, but which have already been gathered by others. In purchasing, this type of research is used the most. Large companies in most cases have a special documentation service that continuously gathers general and market-specific technical information. Much of this information is published and made available to buyers nowadays through a special purchasing intranet (see Memo 6.2).

Source: this list was taken from e-Market Services, December 2003. At the time of publishing the e-marketplaces which are mentioned here may have undergone significant change.

MEMO 6.2   PURCHASING INTRANET DAF TRUCKS

DAF Trucks, the leading truck manufacturer located in The Netherlands, was acquired in 1996 by Paccar, a leading manufacturer in the US. Important brands of Paccar are Peterbilt and Kenworth. One of the reasons for Paccar to acquire DAF Trucks was to realize a strong foothold in the European truck market. Another reason was to create significant global leverage in purchasing and supply. Today buyers at DAF Trucks work with an advanced purchasing information system, which supports them in their strategic and operational activities (see Figure 6.2).

FIGURE 6.2 Excerpt from DAF Trucks purchasing information system.

Source: DAF Trucks Purchasing Department (2003). Reprinted with permission.

attention in the report; finally, what is the opinion of the research after it has been carried out? Have the method and the result been satisfactory? These questions have to be considered to prevent mistakes being repeated in the future.

A differentiation can be made between:

- The different applications that buyers can use for their tactical activities. Here you will find vendor rating information, corporate purchasing information (standard presentations and contract templates), travel information, access to DAF Trucks' Supplier Net.

- Contact list and contact information for all DAF Trucks and Paccar commodity managers enabling them to communicate quickly and efficiently worldwide.

- Purchasing toolkit including templates for developing commodity plans and conducting supply market surveys, supplier risk assessment tools, a labor costs calculator, a fixed costs calculator (see below).

- Detailed order information related to OEM orders, rerouted orders, parts, non product related purchases.

- Detailed supplier data related to supplier performance, financial data with regard to suppliers and general supplier information.

- Supplier database providing all kinds of information with regard to DAF Trucks' suppliers.

Notable are the labor costs calculator and the fixed costs calculator. The first allows the buyer to quickly calculate the extra cost that is incurred when he changes from a local supplier to a foreign supplier. The calculator compensates for higher transportation cost, pipeline inventory, risk of late delivery etc. The fixed cost calculator allows the buyer to calculate the effect, based upon the percentage of fixed cost in the cost price of a specific part, of a higher order volume. When the buyer is going to order a higher volume this tool calculates the net effect on the supplier's salesprice. Purchasing and supply market research are prime tasks for the buyers and commodity managers of DAF Trucks. Among other things they keep a sharp eye on the supply chain structure and developments of DAF's main competitors.

Field research is the gathering, analysis and interpretation of information that cannot be obtained by means of desk research. It tries to track down new information; visits to industrial exhibitions and suppliers are examples of field research methods.

Not every research project will follow the phases described above exactly. The available time usually places restrictions on research design and each project will require its own approach so that a standard method is hard to provide.

SUBJECTS OF PURCHASING MARKET RESEARCH

It will be clear by now that purchasing (market) research covers a wide variety of subjects. In general three main areas of investigation can be identified:

- Materials, goods and services. This kind of research aims at realizing savings or at reducing purchasing-related costs. It can also attempt to reduce the risks incurred by the firm with regard to supply by searching for alternative supply sources.

- Suppliers. Supplier-related research is concerned with the relationship with a supplier. Questions to be addressed here include, for example, 'Will the supplier continue to be able to satisfy both future technical requirements and our requirements concerning reliable and flexible supply?'

- Systems and procedures. A good purchasing information system is of great importance to all buyers and efforts should be directed constantly at improving the supply of information. Information and communications technology offers great possibilities for this, but it has to be guided on the basis of buyers' needs. In connection with this, purchasing research can also focus on simplification of administrative procedures in the relationship between buyers and suppliers.

Another distinction is the one between macro-, meso- and microeconomic research (see Figure 6.3).

- Macroeconomic research. This refers to the general economic environment and focuses on factors that can influence the future balance between supply and demand. Examples of these factors are developments in unemployment in a country, labor costs, inflation, consumer price index, order position.

- Mesoeconomic research. This focuses on specific sectors of industry and at this level a lot of information is often available at central statistical offices and industrial agencies, established in many countries. They have specific information on profitability of the sector, technological developments, labor cost, indirect cost, capacity utilization, order position, energy consumption etc.

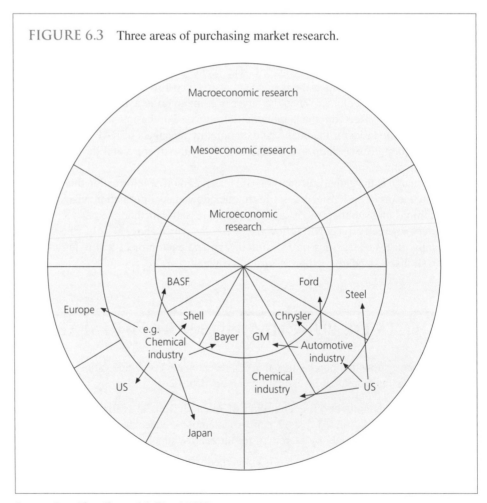

FIGURE 6.3   Three areas of purchasing market research.

Source: adapted from Faes and de Weerd (1983)

TABLE 6.1 Main parameters to be addressed in purchasing market research

Level	Parameter
Macroeconomic	Business cycle and economic growth
	Development of industrial production
	Average utilization rate in industry
	Price development (e.g. currencies, inflation)
	Interest rate
	Development of wages
	Productivity development
	Political climate
Mesoeconomic	Supply-and-demand analysis
	Utilization rate
	Order situation and sales
	Inventories
	Market structure
Microeconomic	Financial situation
	Organizational structure
	Quality of delivered goods
	Delivery performance
	Delivery lead time
	General conditions
	Service quality
	Ownership and shares
	Cost–price structure
	Price level

Source: adapted from Van Eck and De Weerd (1981)

- Microeconomic research. This focuses on assessing strengths and weaknesses of individual suppliers and products. Examples are financial audits of suppliers, quality audits as part of a supplier certification program, supplier cost analyses, etc. The objective here is to get a thorough understanding of the supplier's specific capabilities and its long-term market position.

Table 6.1 shows typical subject areas for each of the three categories of purchasing market research.

PURCHASING MARKET RESEARCH AND INFORMATION TECHNOLOGY

At the beginning of this chapter it was illustrated how Internet technology may be used to conduct purchasing market research. Currently, companies are discovering the many ways in which this new technology may support their purchasing operations and strategies. The following examples further illustrate this point:

- Company's like Saint Gobain, the French conglomerate, which is active in a wide range of products ranging from glass manufacturing to insulation and construction materials, have installed a worldwide purchasing Intranet enabling exchange of product, supplier and contract information among all sites and operating companies. Investment: less than $35 000 for software (licences) and three months' preparation. Other manufacturing companies, ranging from automotive and computer industry to the beverage and food industry, have built similar systems based on Lotus Notes or Microsoft Outlook software.

- Data-suppliers like Yellow Pages, ABC, Kompass and Wer Liefert Was have now available through their websites vast supplier bases covering supplier addresses in all major EC-countries enabling buyers to conduct market surveys in a very short time. For commodities, long lists of potential suppliers may be developed in just a few minutes. Supplier information (with regard to product assortment, references, financial stability) may be asked for through extensive database searches and directly through e-mail from the supplier. Requests for quotations may be submitted through simple, computer-supported ordering systems or directly through e-mailing the supplier concerned.

- Some companies use their purchasing website to attract new suppliers for certain commodities. Suppliers are requested to react for components which are short of supply or for which new suppliers are wanted. Suppliers may act through filling in the SQA-questionnaire and sending it through e-mail directly to the purchasing department of the prospective customer. In this way the Internet is actively being used for 'reversed marketing'.

- Companies like FedEx, DHL Worldwide Express and UPS provide linkages through the Internet which enable companies to keep track of their deliveries. Some of these sites enable cost breakdowns per port of destination enabling buyers to find their most competitive source of supply for shipment and transportation.

- Although electronic payment is still troublesome and far from safe, developments are moving fast in this area. In the consumer goods business some companies have posted impressive turnover figures and financial results (such as CD Direct, Amazon and DELL). Although legally not yet approved in all countries in Europe, it is expected that electronic commerce and payment will grow rapidly in the years to come.

Other examples can be added to this list. Memo 6.3 summarizes how the Internet may be used in the purchasing area nowadays. It will be clear from this list already that the electronification of purchasing is developing very fast. New IT-supported tools will become available for the coming years, and not only for buyers. The same tools will also be available to all other disciplines in the company (who in general are computerwise and much better equipped than their counterparts in the purchasing organization), which will call for a sometimes drastic review and reorientation of the traditional role of the purchasing function in companies.

ORGANIZING FOR PURCHASING MARKET RESEARCH

Every purchasing department possesses a large amount of purchasing market knowledge and information. The issue for managers is how to make this knowledge and experience available to other departments in an efficient way. In principle, there are three possible methods of establishing purchasing market research in a company.

- Create a separate staff department. One possibility is to locate all purchasing market research activities in a separate staff department or section. The big advantage is that purchasing market research can then be assigned to specialists, who have knowledge of specific research techniques. If this option is chosen, good communication between researchers and buyers must be ensured to prevent the research from becoming too detailed and/or theoretical.

- Market research conducted by the buyer. The advantage of this arrangement is that research will only be done on issues which buyers consider relevant; this also enlarges their involvement in the activity. However, a major drawback is the buyers' lack of time to do the research systematically because they are constantly forced to spend their time on pressing issues. Other disadvantages are the lack of knowledge that most buyers have of market research techniques and potential sources of information, and the lack of a central collection point for all the gathered knowledge.

- Work with research teams. A compromise solution is that of forming *ad hoc* research teams, consisting of both buyers and researchers; after the assignment is finished the team is broken up. The advantage of this method is the involvement of the team in the

MEMO 6.3   INTERNET AND INTRANET APPLICATIONS IN PURCHASING SUPPLY MARKET RESEARCH

The Internet may provide buyers with different kinds of information related to each step of the purchasing process:

- Purchasing market research and supplier selection. Examples are Wer Liefert Was, Yellow Pages, Industrynet, all of which may be used to find new suppliers.

- Getting the right product specifications. Product descriptions may be derived from Purchasing Extranet.

- Checking supplier references. Supplier financial and performance references may be checked from Dun & Bradstreet.

- Sending requests for proposal. This may be done through e-mail directly to the supplier or through the websites of supplier data-providers.

- Bid information is exposed through specialized intermediaries such as BidCast or Tender Daily.

- Virtual auctions. Free Markets Online, Ariba, Procuri provide software and services to organize auctions among suppliers for individual buyers. Some large retailers (such as Wehkamp in The Netherlands) have daily auctions for merchandise on sale.

- Reversed marketing. Some large subcontractors and manufacturers (such as NASA and Sony) have a special purchasing website on which they expose products for which they seek new suppliers. Initial screening is done through filling out a detailed questionnaire.

- Commodity buying. Some major commodities can now be traced online through the Internet, allowing buyers to manage their commodity buyers from hour to hour and enabling them to buy at the right moment.

- Shipment tracking. FedEx, DHL Worldwide Express and UPS have extensive websites where tariffs may be requested for express freight and shipments and deliveries may be tracked and traced.

- Electronic payment. Payment may be tied to credit cards or special Purchasing Cards, enabling paperless invoice handling.

- Education and training. Some universities and professional organizations have websites which present training and educational programs and virtual programs in purchasing and supply management.

research and, when required, other specialists can be invited to contribute, depending on the progress made. Another advantage is the task orientation of such teams, provided that a clear working plan has been prepared. Although this approach is preferable from a costs point of view, there are some objections. In practice, it is difficult to work on a research project in combination with day-to-day activities because the latter receive priority, thus affecting the market research. It is for this reason that good project planning is essential. Experience shows that a small, specialist staff department is to be recommended for large companies; for smaller companies the team approach is best. When left to the buyer, market and supplier research will only be carried out during the buyer's spare time. Not surprisingly, the experience is that companies with dedicated researchers carry out more market research and this undoubtedly has consequences for the knowledge of the supply markets in these companies.

SUMMARY

The ever-increasing turbulence in global supply markets makes purchasing market research a crucial activity. Purchasing market research is required in order to keep informed about changes going on in technology, supplier markets, competition and supplier organizations. It is also necessary to assess the competitiveness of the current supply base and to keep track of changes in currency rates, to name just a few. These subjects can be investigated by using different techniques. A distinction has been made between qualitative and quantitative research. Purchasing market research can be aimed at providing data on short-term and long-term policy issues.

In setting up research a stepwise approach is recommended. First, the objectives of the research should be clearly formulated. What questions should be answered by this activity? Will the value of the information to be gathered probably outweigh the costs? What information is already known about the subject? In most cases desk research will be sufficient. In some specific cases field research and surveys may be necessary, although these will add to the costs of the activity and its lead time. Finally, the results should be presented in a concise report.

As discussed, the Internet provides ample opportunities for buyers to conduct purchasing market surveys. For some commodities and services, information may be found covering all aspects of the purchasing process, just by using Internet technology. And these opportunities and facilities expand every day! Therefore it is very important for buyers to keep informed about this medium, since it will make supply markets more transparent than ever before. This is not only true for macro-economic research, but also for sector studies and individual supplier research.

Most research will probably be done by the buyers themselves. For specific subjects support staff will be convenient. In specific cases, purchasing market research may be done by a specialized outside market research agency. A specialized purchasing staff is usually only found in large, multinational companies.

ASSIGNMENTS

6.1 Your purchasing manager has requested you as a buyer to develop a commodity strategy for the product group that you are responsible for (stamped, steel components). In your commodity plan you should come up with a future sourcing plan. What information would you need in developing a sourcing plan for your commodity group?

6.2 Investigate the websites of some large data suppliers such as Wer Liefert Was, Yellow Pages, Kompass etc. What kinds of functionality do these data suppliers provide to the buyer today? How do these suppliers support the purchasing process model that was described in Chapter 2?

6.3 A distinction is made between macro-, meso- and microeconomic research. Name some sources of information to be consulted in each of these types of purchasing market research.

6.4 You are working for a large supplier in the automotive industry. Your purchasing manager has requested you to investigate whether it is worthwhile to participate as a member in Covisint. What kinds of solutions does Covisint offer to the medium-sized automotive supplier today? Would you recommend your purchasing manager to take part in this important electronic, automotive marketplace?

6.5 Internet technology is open to everyone. Not only to buyers, but also to users and budget holders within organizations. Today, every employee is able to buy from the Internet without interference of a buyer. What would you consider to be the most important threats and opportunities from buying through the Internet? What recommendations would you make to companies in order to benefit from modern web-enabled buying opportunities?

STRATEGY AND PLANNING

After studying this chapter you should understand the following:

- Why companies outsource part of their business processes.
- How to structure the process of outsourcing.
- The most important risks and pitfalls related to outsourcing.
- How to deal with the most important downside risks related to outsourcing.

CASE STUDY   OUTSOURCING OF IT

The telecom market in many European countries has been the playing field of fierce competition over the past decade. Traditional, state-owned telecom companies have been privatized and new players have entered the field. The period of un-precedented growth for mobile phones in many European markets has come to an end. As new tech-nologies and applications have become more mature, value propositions have standardized among the different providers, enabling consumers and businesses to shop around for the most attrac-tive prices and rates. Facilitated by the Internet, consumers have better access to benchmark infor-mation, enabling them to go for the best rates and deals. This has put significant pressure on the fat margins of the providers, who as a result are desperately seeking for opportunities to slash cost. Moreover, most of them are seeking opportunities to improve their cash position due to their ill-considered decisions in the recent past to win gov-ernment initiated tenders to obtain new technology licences (such as UMTS and GPRS). The participa-tion in these tenders, requiring billions of euros, has consumed most of these players' cash.

Against this background a major telecom player in Europe looked for drastic measures to both re-duce its operational cost dramatically and improve its cash position. After a careful selection of projects it was decided to outsource all of its IT activities and call-centres to outside parties. The outsourcing deal for IT, which was closed in 2000 (just before the economic recession) with one of the large IT providers, encompassed the sale and lease back of all hardware, peripherals and other IT infrastruc-ture, and all software. The IT provider, selected after a competitive tender, also had to take over most of the company's IT staff. The future relation-ship was based upon a thorough long term, service level agreement, which consisted of a detailed description of the activities to be performed by the IT provider, and the costs and rates that could be incurred. Of course the agreement described the impressive sum of money to be paid to the telecom company. It was agreed that rates and fees would be paid to the IT provider based upon a limited number of critical key performance indicators (KPIs), which would be monitored and discussed on a monthly basis between the parties involved. For this an impressive communication structure was built up at both organisations, involving several working groups, technical committees and steering platforms.

▶

After two years it became clear to the telecom account team that things had not worked out as intended. First of all the IT provider was dissatisfied about the sums that were paid; in hindsight, since prices of hardware and software had gone down significantly, the IT provider thought it had paid far too much when buying the hard- and software. In order to secure its margin and recoup part of the investment it started to cut costs in its services to the telecom company: by putting inexperienced, lower-paid staff on crucial service functions (such as helpdesks) the service level to the telecom's internal staff declined to a surprisingly low level, leading to all kinds of disruptions in simple, but crucial operational processes. Next, although the contract stipulated the use of leading-edge technology and although investment schedules were agreed upon, the IT provider postponed investments in new solutions. Furthermore, there was a constant debate about extra allowances, rates and fees to be incurred by the IT provider. They warned that if bills were not paid by the telecom provider in time, this would lead to disruptions or even a temporary stop of services. All this led to a situation where internal staff constantly started to challenge the outsourcing decision that had been made. Most of the staff felt that the IT provider was not up to its tasks and wanted to insource most of the IT activities again.

INTRODUCTION

This Case Study explains what can happen to firms that act too fast in the area of outsourcing. Identifying and deciding between core and non-core activities within a firm is one thing; bringing this concept into practice is another matter. Companies must realize that when complex activities such as IT are outsourced to an outside specialist based upon a single source agreement, the risk profile of the company will change dramatically. It appears, then, that decision making exclusively based upon economical and financial considerations may have dramatic consequences. Later, at the stage of implementation, the perceived and expected savings and economies are frequently more than outweighed by the price the company has to pay for its total dependence on the selected partner. In such a situation things cannot be made better in a short period of time.

The objective of this chapter is threefold: (1) to determine whether and under what circumstances outsourcing is a successful business strategy, (2) to determine what the critical success factors of outsourcing then are on strategic, tactical and operational level; and (3) to identify the most important risks related to outsourcing decisions and how these can be managed. In this chapter, first the concept of outsourcing will be introduced by presenting the factors behind the growth of outsourcing as a strategy and the different activities that can be outsourced. Next the different definitions and concepts of outsourcing are presented, followed by the rationales for outsourcing. Finally, the risks related to outsourcing are discussed.

OUTSOURCING AS A BUSINESS CONCEPT

In an attempt to enhance their competitiveness, organizations are increasingly turning to outsourcing. Not only are changes in the business environment drivers behind the rise of outsourcing as a business strategy, also new management concepts such as business process re-engineering, organizational restructuring, benchmarking, alliance management and lean management have stimulated the trend towards outsourcing.

The Outsourcing Institute (2000) reports that outsourcing in the United States has become a standard business practice across small and large companies in about every industry. From 1996 onwards, outsourcing has grown at a tremendous rate. Outsourcing expenditures in 2000 in the US were around $340 billion and were expected to grow at a rate of 15 per cent annually.

This trend is not only visible in the US but in Europe and Asia as well, where the market for outsourcing is expected to grow into double digits (Corbett, 2002). The reason for this growth is that companies view outsourcing as a way to achieve strategic goals, reduce costs, improve customer satisfaction and provide other efficiency and effectiveness improvements. This makes outsourcing a mandatory business strategy for companies to compete in today's competitive market environment. In general, outsourcing is viewed as one of many approaches to maintain or develop competitive advantage (Quinn and Hilmer, 1994; Bailey et.al., 2002; Gilley and Rasheed, 2000).

The types of activities that are outsourced have evolved over time. Starting with *activities* more and more entire business *functions* are being outsourced. The type of activities and functions that are outsourced by companies in the US are depicted in Figure 7.1.

As outsourcing for many firms is not just a trend but more and more a viable business strategy, the questions on how to successfully engage in outsourcing and how to stay successful in an outsourcing relation are very important. These are addressed in the next section.

DEFINITIONS

Definitions on outsourcing are abundant. In general, outsourcing can be described as the transfer of activities, that were previously conducted in-house, to a third party. Ellram and

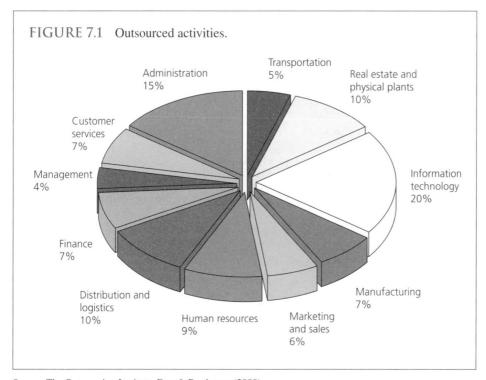

FIGURE 7.1   Outsourced activities.

Source: The Outsourcing Institute, Dun & Bradstreet (2000)

Billington (2001) see outsourcing primarily as 'the transfer of the production of goods or services that had been performed internally to an external party.' A wider definition is reported by NEVI (2000):

> *Outsourcing means that the company divests itself of the resources to fulfill a particular activity to another company to focus more effectively on its own competence. The difference with subcontracting is the divestment of assets, infrastructure, people and competencies.*

We favor the definition as provided by Axelsson and Wynstra (2002), who define outsourcing as: 'The decision and subsequent transfer process by which activities that constitute a function, that earlier have been carried out within the company, are instead purchased from an external supplier'. Major characteristics of outsourcing are: (1) activities that initially were performed in-house are transferred to an external party; (2) assets and, in some cases, people go over to that external party; (3) there will be an extended relationship between the parties involved over a longer period of time; (4) in transferring the activity to the external party the buyer is exposed to both a cost- and risk profile, both of which are new to the companies involved.

Now that the definition of outsourcing has been discussed two different types of outsourcing can be presented. In line with Chapter 3 we differentiate here between turnkey (integral) and partial outsourcing. Turnkey outsourcing applies when the responsibility for the execution of the entire function (or activities) lies with the external supplier. This includes not only the execution of the activities, but also the coordination of these activities. Partial outsourcing refers to the case in which only a part of an integrated function is outsourced. The coordination of the function and activities still lies with the outsourcer (the buyer). Here a major problem is of course how to demarcate the responsibility for the final performance of the outsourced activity between the parties involved.

TABLE 7.1 Forms of outsourcing services

	Labor outsourcing	*Mixed outsourcing*	*Complete outsourcing*
Contractor provides	Some employees	Some or all of the following: Employees Materials Process and systems Technology and equipment Facilities Management/supervision	Employees Materials Process and systems Technology and equipment Facilities Management/supervision
Host firm provides	Some employees Materials Process and systems Technology and equipment Management/supervision	Some or all of the following: Employees Materials Process and systems Technology and equipment Facilities Management/supervision	Program management

Source: Allen and Chandrashekar (2000), p. 26.

Allen and Chandrashekar (2000) provide an interesting typology for outsourcing (see Table 7.1).

This categorization is essentially the same as the two types that we identified, because 'labor outsourcing' essentially can be considered as a specific form of partial outsourcing.

Table 7.2 gives an overview of the advantages and disadvantages of the two concepts of outsourcing.

Two important dimensions of outsourcing are the decision to outsource and the transfer of the function being outsourced. Both usually are highly complex processes in organizations. A company that opts for outsourcing can decide whether it prefers partial or turnkey outsourcing, based on the advantages and disadvantages each type has.

RATIONALES FOR OUTSOURCING

Research shows that there are different reasons for firms to engage in outsourcing. Due to the development of outsourcing as a business strategy, these reasons may range from merely tactical to more strategic (Figure 7.2).

TABLE 7.2 Partial versus turnkey outsourcing

	Advantages	Disadvantages
Turnkey outsourcing	Buyer has minimal responsibility for outsourced processes	The buyer has limited influence on the determination of the price and little insight into cost structure of provider
	Buyer doesn't need to have experience with similar projects	The buyer has limited influence on the staff, technology and materials used and their quality
	The project generally goes smoothly for the buyer	Large dependence of buyer on provider resulting in high commercial, technical and performance risks
Partial outsourcing	The buyer has more influence on prices, rates and costs	The buyer is required to have knowledge of the separate parts of the outsourced functions/ activities
	The buyer has more influence on the staff, technology and materials used and their quality	The buyer is required to have the organizational capacities to coordinate and integrate the outsourced functions/activities
	Specific advantages can result in cost reductions	Communication and coordination problems between parties involved can be a cause of delay and disappointment

Tactical reasons are: to reduce control costs and operating costs, to free up internal resources, to receive an important cash infusion, to improve performance and to be able to manage functions that are out of control. Strategic reasons may be: to improve company focus, to gain access to world-class capabilities, to gain access to resources that are not available internally, to accelerate reengineering benefits, improve customer satisfaction, increase flexibility and share risks.

All these reasons underlie one overall objective: to improve the overall performance of the outsourcing firm, or from another perspective, to enhance the value of an organization's offerings to its customers.

The considerations underlying outsourcing may be either capacity orientated or expertise orientated. When the company has not enough capacity to perform the requested service it can opt for outsourcing. This type of outsourcing is defined as 'capacity outsourcing'. When the expertise to perform the activity at the required quality level, or for an acceptable cost level, is not present any more the company can also opt for outsourcing. This type of outsourcing is referred to as 'specialistic outsourcing'.

As the Case Study at the beginning of this chapter illustrates, there are risks and disadvantages associated with outsourcing. These may relate to loss of control, loss of critical skills, loss of intellectual property, loss of security, service quality drops, increase in cost and loss of innovative power.

Table 7.3 provides a general picture of the advantages and disadvantages of outsourcing.

The next section deals with the outsourcing process. The rationales of outsourcing are important in the decision-making stage of the process. Essential in this part of the outsourcing process is to assess both the advantages of outsourcing, and the risks, disadvantages and costs that will be related to this decision.

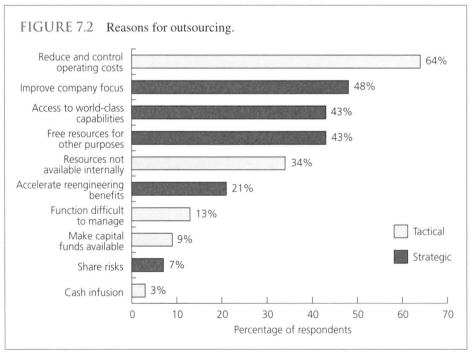

FIGURE 7.2   Reasons for outsourcing.

Source: The Outsourcing Institute (2000)

SUCCESS OF OUTSOURCING AS A BUSINESS STRATEGY

It is difficult to determine the success of outsourcing as a business strategy, because the external factors in the before and after situation may have significantly changed. Determining the success of outsourcing in terms of cost savings is not an easy task, because often it is almost impossible to determine the costs of the function/activity before it was outsourced due to all kinds of hidden costs that are involved. When outsourcing has been selected as a favorable business strategy due to different reasons other than obtaining cost savings, it is even more difficult to assess the success of outsourcing in an objective manner. This is probably one of the reasons for the fact that in the literature not much evidence can be found on the success or failure rate of outsourcing as a business strategy. Another reason might be the fact that outsourcing is often poorly evaluated so that data is just not available. Since academic research is scarce on the actual results of outsourcing decision making, we need to turn to the research that has been conducted by some international research agencies. Tarlo Lyons (2001) reports that:

Seventy-six per cent of the outsourcers rate their outsourcing as either good or extremely good value for money. The rest thinks that the value is average. Nobody considers it to be poor. The IT sector is least likely to rate their outsourcing as good value.[1]

Gartner (2003) reported that:

Satisfaction with the business benefits from outsourcing contracts fell from 86 per cent in 2001 to 50 per cent in 2002 among board-level executives in Western Europe

TABLE 7.3 Advantages and disadvantages of outsourcing

Advantages	Disadvantages
Freeing up of cash: investments can be concentrated on core activities	Increased dependence on suppliers
Optimal usage of knowledge, equipment and experience of third party	Continuous follow-up and monitoring of the supplier relationship is necessary
Increased flexibility: fluctuations in the workload can more easily be absorbed	Risks of communication and organizational problems during the transfer of activities to a third party
Outsourcing leads to easier and more focused primary processes in the organization	Risk of leakage of confidential information
Input through an independent party's point of view which reduces the risks of introvert short-sightedness in the organization	Depending on balance of power between parties: inability to execute contractual performance incentives and penalties
	Risk of losing essential strategic knowledge

---

1 As reported from a survey among 71 financial directors in the FTSE 1000 in the IT, finance, engineering, logistics/distribution and business consultancies.

. . . European companies wasted 6 billion euros due to poor deal structures and poorly managed relationships with IT outsourcing companies in 2002 . . .[2]

And finally, Corbett (2002) reports that:

The use of outsourcing is growing stronger . . . Satisfaction with service providers is strong but there are some concerns. Only 60 per cent of executives are satisfied with their outsourcing initiatives and only 11 per cent of the executives are very satisfied . . .[3]

Obviously, the success of outsourcing as reported by the various consultants varies enormously. However, most reports conclude that in more that half of the cases outsourcing projects does not seem to produce the results that were expected from them.

Based upon the foregoing, we may conclude that both in the US and in Europe outsourcing as a business strategy and therefore as a market is growing at a fast rate. It appears that a large variety of functions and activities are being outsourced. Based upon the rationale behind outsourcing, we have identified different types of outsourcing, each having its advantages and disadvantages. There are a number of reasons why companies choose to outsource activities, 'reducing costs' being the number one reason. Although these factors have been discussed in detail by many authors, it is striking that little empirical evidence can be found on the success of outsourcing. The sources that have been found, however, report mixed results of outsourcing.

Now, let's have a closer look at the process that will determine the success of outsourcing as a business strategy.

THE OUTSOURCING PROCESS

This section presents critical success factors of outsourcing through an analysis of the outsourcing process. First, the outsourcing process and its importance is introduced. Then the three different phases of the outsourcing process will be discussed and the factors that contribute to their success. In the next section the critical success factors derived from the discussion on the outsourcing process and other literature will be presented.

The outsourcing process can be structured around different elements. Most authors would agree that essentially three distinct phases can be identified: a strategic phase (why, what, who?), a transition phase (how?) and an operation phase (how to manage?). Based upon these phases, Momme and Hvolby (2002) present a framework that identifies six generic steps of outsourcing that provide guidance to the outsourcing process (Figure 7.3).

Strategic phase

During the strategic phase three essential questions have to be answered. The first question relates to the objective of the firm with regard to its intent to outsource a certain activity. The next question that has to be answered is what activities are considered for outsourcing. Finally, the question of what qualifications a supplier should be able to meet, in order to qualify as a potential future partner for providing the activity concerned, must be answered.

---

2 Press release from Gartner Inc, a research and advisory firm on its annual outsourcing and IT services summit in London.

3 Data from the 1999 Outsourcing Trends Study. The data from this study reflects the opinions of a variety of private and public sector executives, industry experts, and a small number of non-US managers.

Companies may have, as we have seen earlier, many motives for outsourcing. Whatever reason will be given, the decision to outsource should support and enable the company's overall strategy. The motives that are cited most are: (1) focus on core competence, (2) focus on cost efficiency/effectiveness and (3) focus on service (Brandes *et al.*, 1997). This implies that the strategy of the outsourcing company should be aligned with these three motives and that the outsourced activities should contribute to this strategy.

The second question relates to *what* should be outsourced. In other words: which activities or functions are candidates for outsourcing? In the literature two important approaches are used to answer this question; the transaction cost approach and the core-competence approach.

The transaction cost approach is based on the idea of finding a governance structure aimed at arriving at the lowest cost possible for each transaction that is made (Arnold, 2000) and comparing whether to perform an activity internally or outsource the activity in the market. Williamson (1983, 1985) is one of the founders of the transaction costs theory. He defines transaction costs as the costs that are associated with an exchange between two parties. The assumption of the transaction costs approach is that an exchange with an external party is based upon a contract. The (potential) costs associated with establishing, monitoring and enforcing the contract, as well as the costs associated with managing the relationship with the external party, are all considered to be part of the transaction costs as well as the costs associated with the transaction itself. Therefore, all of these costs should be taken into account when deciding between make or buy options.

The level of the transaction costs depends upon three important factors (Ellram and Billington, 2001). These factors are the frequency of the transaction, the level of the transaction specific investments and the external and internal uncertainty. The frequency of the transaction is an important factor because the more frequently exchanges occur between partners, the higher the total costs that are involved. The level of the transaction-specific investments also determine the level of transaction costs, because transaction-specific investments are investments that are more or less unique to a specific buyer–supplier relationship. Examples are investments in specific supplier tooling (such as molds and dies) by a large automotive manufacturer and the change costs involved when choosing a new accountant (internal staff need to get accustomed to the new accountant, the new accountant needs to be thoroughly briefed to get acquainted with the company etc.). These examples show that investments are made in assets as well as in human capital. Obviously the higher these investments are, the higher the transaction costs will be. The last factor that determines the transaction costs is the external and internal uncertainty. Uncertainty is a normal parameter in the decision-making process. It can be defined as the inability to predict contingencies that may occur (Williamson, 1983). The higher these uncertainties, the more slack a supplier wants to have in presenting his proposal and rates, and the more difficult it will be to make a fixed price or lump sum contract that deals with all

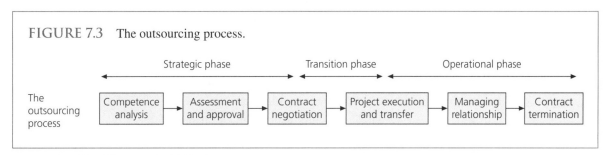

FIGURE 7.3   The outsourcing process.

Source: adapted from Momme *et al.* (2002) p. 71

uncertainties beforehand. Therefore, the higher the level of uncertainty, the higher the transaction costs will be.

As said before, the transaction cost approach assumes that costs for each transaction are incurred depending on the three factors mentioned above. When there are high overall transaction costs the most favorable governance structure to be recommended is vertical integration; when these costs are low, outsourcing is considered to be the most favorable structure.

The other approach on which an outsourcing decision can be based is the core competence approach. This theory is based, among others, on the work of Quinn and Hilmer (1994). The core competence approach is based on the assumption that, in order to create a sustainable competitive advantage, a company should 'concentrate its resources on a set of core competencies where it can achieve definable pre-eminence and provide a unique value for customers ... (hence, it should) strategically outsource all other activities' (Quinn and Hilmer, 1994, p. 43). The important question to be answered here is: What are the firm's core competencies? Quinn and Hilmer (1994) suggest that characteristics of core competencies are:

- skills or knowledge sets, not products or functions
- flexible, long term platforms that are capable of adaptation or evolution
- limited in number: generally two or three
- unique sources of leverage in the value chain
- areas where the company can dominate
- elements important to the customer in the long run
- embedded in the organization's systems.

The competencies that satisfy these requirements are the core competencies and provide the firm with its long-term competitive advantage. These competencies must be closely protected and are not to be outsourced. All other activities should be procured from the markets if these markets are totally reliable and efficient.

Long and Vickers-Koch (1992) distinguish five categories of a firm's activities, instead of two categories, core or non-core, (Quinn and Hilmer 1994). These five categories are:

- 'Cutting edge' activities. The activities that determine the competitiveness of the organization from a long-term perspective.
- Core activities. The activities that create the foundation and main processes for the organization and its possible competitive advantages.
- Support activities. Those activities that are directly connected to the core competences.
- Separable activities. The activities that are part of the main processes, but easily separated from that process and not related to the core competences.
- Peripheral activities. The activities that do not concern the main process.

Arnold (2000) also makes a further distinction in a firm's activities. He distinguishes between:

- Company core activities. Activities that are necessarily connected with a company's existence.
- Close-core activities. The activities that are directly related to the core activities.
- Core distinct activities. The supporting activities.
- Disposable activities. Activities with general availability.

Both studies imply that the outsourcing decision framework based upon the work of Quinn and Hilmer (1994) needs adjustment. Arnold (2000) has developed a general model for outsourcing decisions. He combines the transaction cost approach and the core competence approach into one framework, Figure 7.4. This model provides a good guidance for the answer to the *what* question. The functions or activities that are candidates for outsourcing are those that can be found in the right part of the model, i.e. the functions or activities that have low transaction costs and that are non-core for the existence of the firm.

The first two of the three questions have been discussed. Now the last question will be discussed: to whom the function should be outsourced. After the decision to outsource has been made, it is essential that the right supplier is chosen. A supplier has to be selected who has the necessary technical and managerial capabilities to deliver the expected and required level of performance. Also the supplier should be able to understand and be committed to these requirements.

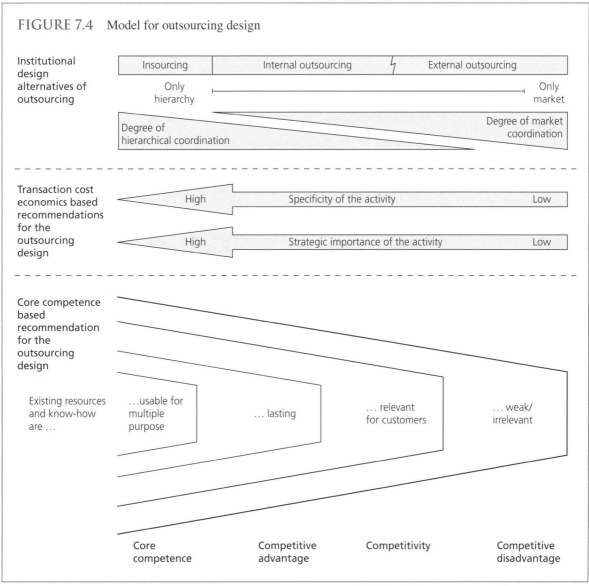

FIGURE 7.4 Model for outsourcing design

Source: Arnold, 2000, p. 26

The supplier selection process is key to the success of the buyer–supplier relationship. Companies that make extensive use of supplier selection and monitoring practices in supplier partnerships seem to be more successful than the companies that do not (Ittner *et al.*, 1999). An adequate supplier selection model is crucial for the success of the outsourcing decision.

Momme and Hvolby (2002) present a four-phase model (Figure 7.5). This model gives guidance on how to identify, evaluate and select outsourcing candidates and therefore is an appropriate tool to use in the strategic phase (see Figure 3.2, phases 1 and 2). It also gives a brief guidance for the transition (phases 2 and 3) and the operational phase (phase 4), but needs to be elaborated for that purpose.

Wynstra (2002) also emphasizes the importance of the supplier selection process and provides some important aspects to consider, such as supplier market structure, supplier capabilities, supplier improvement capacity, strategic fit, conditions for collaboration and others.

This discussion of the strategic phase of the outsourcing process can be concluded with the observation that successful outsourcing depends on (1) having the right strategic reason to outsource, (2) selecting the right functions or activities to be outsourced and (3) selecting the right supplier to outsource to. The next section will discuss the transition phase.

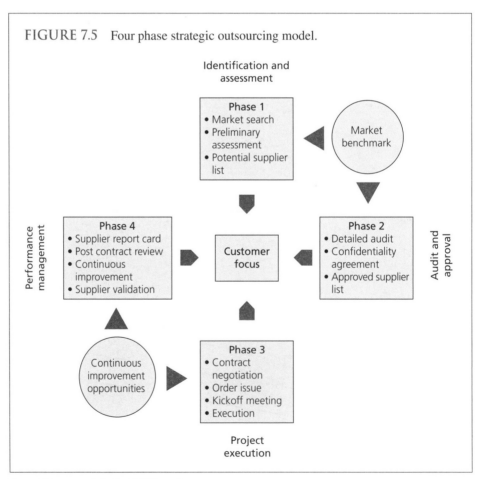

FIGURE 7.5   Four phase strategic outsourcing model.

Source: Momme and Hvolby (2002) p. 191

The transition phase

After the strategic phase in which the outsourced activities and supplier have been identified, the transition phase starts. The transition phase consists of the contract negotiation and the project execution and transfer (see Figure 3.1). The most important issue in the contract negotiation is the contract itself. Also it is important to keep in mind that the contract negotiation in an outsourcing agreement is often the start of a long-term relationship, so not only the contractual issues should be dealt with but the people issues and the importance of a sound and cooperative relationship should be covered as well.

The contract is the legal basis for the relationship and is therefore the key document in the outsourcing process. It allows both organizations to maximize the rewards of the relationship, while minimizing the risk. This makes the outsourcing contract a key success factor for the establishment of a strategic outsourcing relationship (Deckelman, 1998). The contract and the type of contract should reflect the business plan (the goal of the co-operation) the two parties have and should be reasonable for both parties.

There are different types of contracts. The type chosen depends on the characteristics and the scope of the contract and the functions or activities that are outsourced. NEVI (2000) suggests eight types of contracts (Table 7.4).

As said before, the contract has a great impact on the success of the joint operations. One of the key issues in the contract phase is whether to use incentives and/or penalties (a negative incentive) or not. The idea of using incentives and penalties in a contract is generally supported and seen as a critical success factor for the output of an outsourcing agreement. Incentives help the provider to work as a partner and enable the partners to work together towards joint goals, so that both parties can profit from successful achievement of the goals. Incentives motivate the outsourcing provider to perform beyond targets. The use of incentives however is only possible when both parties agree on the goals of the contract, the level of service that has to be provided and the performance measurement system.

The type of contract and the use of incentives are just two of the many issues to be discussed in the contract negotiations. There are many other 'ingredients' in an outsourcing agreement. We mention here the following:

- Scope of services. The description of the services that will be provided.

- Term of the agreement. The duration of the contract, this depends on the objective of the outsourcer. Usually, short-term contracts are favored.

- Service level agreement (SLA). (Performance measurement). This is one of the key documents in the outsourcing agreement. It defines the required (minimum) service that the supplier has to provide. The SLA should have the following requirements: (1) reflect the overall business goals, (2) objective, (3) measurable, and (4) comparable against pre-established criteria. The SLA should be a living document and be able to change when business conditions or client requirements change. Also the contract should specify the required actions if the service level is not achieved.

- Rates, fees, incentives. The pricing and fee structure should be clear to both parties.

- Termination plan. When the relationship is terminated, it should be executed in a fair and equitable manner, without resulting in disruption of service. Also items such as ownership of data, intellectual property and so on should be agreed upon beforehand.

- Conflict resolution. It is very important to manage the relationship in such a way that conflicts are resolved in a cooperative manner, in the contract an informal conflict resolution method can be arranged. But the formal dispute resolution method should also be arranged.

- Communication. A communication plan is a key document of the contract. It should contain guidelines on reporting, staff communication etc.

- Management and control. The parties should develop procedures for managing and performing the services. This part of the contract can contain many different subjects, such as a manual for day-to-day operations, guidelines for subcontractors, the supplier's obligation to work with customer's standards etc. This document should also contain a section on how changes in the contract should be handled. The mandate, the degree to which the supplier is empowered of the supplier, should be defined.

- Other. A contract can contain many more items than discussed above. These include warranty, confidentiality, audit rights, transfer of assets, escape clause, etc.

After the contract is signed and all the issues in the preceding phases have been dealt with, the outsourced function has to be transferred to the supplier. The key activities in this phase are establishing the basis for supplier integration, defining the workflow interfaces and adapting the organization as a result of the transfer of activities to the supplier.

TABLE 7.4 Types of contract

Lumpsum turnkey	Contract is based upon a fixed price (per period) for executing the project or a certain activity.
Reimbursable turnkey*	In this situation the provider is compensated for all costs that he incurs for executing the project or a certain activity.
Semi lumpsum turnkey	Part of the work is compensated for on a fixed price basis; the other part is compensated on a reimbursable basis.
Lumpsum fixed price	The supplier agrees to complete the work against a fixed price based upon a predefined, detailed scope of work. Everything that is not included in the scope of work is settled between parties on an *ad-hoc* basis.
Cost reimbursable	The supplier agrees to complete the work on open book, open cost basis based upon a general scope of work. There is no sharing of savings.
Guaranteed maximum contract	The same as a cost reimbursable contract, only the outsourcer pays to a certain agreed maximum. The extra costs are for the supplier.
Share the savings/loss (target price contract)	The services are paid for on a reimbursable basis. When the contract costs are higher or lower than the original budget (target price), the difference is shared between parties on a pre-agreed basis.
Unit rate	Rates are agreed for regular, routine activities, the size of which cannot be anticipated. Rates are defined per m^2 of paint, meter of cable to be installed etc. Payments are made based upon the actual number of units consumed during the completion of the wor*k*.

* Note: in some cases also referred to as 'time and materials contract'.
Source: adapted from Jurg (1997).

The outsourcing transition can be a very complex event. The transfer should be conducted using project management principles. This approach includes the assignment of a dedicated project manager by the provider. The project transition manager should in fact manage all phases of the implementation and thus act as the central point of contact. Furthermore he will see to the preparation of a sound transition plan. This plan is a document that identifies the steps that must be taken to accomplish a successful transition. A project timeline also needs to be set up, with designated milestones that need to be formally signed off. The last phase before going live is a test phase in which the supplier's organization is tested against the contract requirements. Obviously an important task for the outsourcing company is to provide training and support for the supplier's staff if necessary.

The operational phase

After the transition phase has successfully ended, the operational phase of the outsourcing process starts. This operational phase consists of two processes: (1) managing the relationship and (2) contract termination.

Managing the buyer–supplier relationship management is one of the, if not *the*, critical stage in the outsourcing relationship. Achieving the goal of the outsourcing relationship is impossible without close cooperation. When the relationship is not properly managed the conditions for close cooperation will not be present and the outcome of the outsourcing relationship will be far from optimal. In an article from Greco, a director of strategic resources of a large brewery is quoted:

> *the true value of outsourcing comes after the relationship has had time to develop and additional synergies have emerged. Creating a sustaining, long relationship with a supplier is exciting; it's where the win–win is really beginning to show.*
>
> *(Greco 1997, p. 54)*

Many researchers have written on the characteristics of a successful buyer–supplier relationship. The top five include the factors trust, flexibility, team approach, shared objectives and open communication. In a study in a sales environment between manufacturers' and their principles, McQuiston (2001) identifies a conceptual model for building and maintaining the relationship between these two parties. It identifies six core values as being critical to the success of these relationships. These six core values are strengthened by four supporting factors. The parameters in this conceptual model seem to be consistent with other outsourcing literature. The factors found by McQuiston to be core to a successful outsourcing relationship are presented in Table 7.5.

TABLE 7.5 Core values and supporting values of an outsourcing relationship

Core values	Supporting factors
Shared goals and objectives	Developing a personal relationship
Mutual dependence	Having professional respect
Open lines for communication	Investment of effort by top
Concern for the other's profitability	management
Mutual commitment to customer	Commitment to continuous
satisfaction	improvement
Trust	

Successful outsourcing relationships focus on results. The performance of the services provided should be measured against the agreed service level on a regular basis and be benchmarked against the performance of other providers in the same business or competitors when possible. Both the buyer and the supplier are responsible for this process. But in an outsourcing relationship it has to be clear which party is responsible for what. A common mistake made by a buyer is not only to feel and act responsible for the measurement process, but also feel and act responsible for the execution of the contract. Successful outsourcing requires a shift in mindset for the buying organization. The contract manager, the person responsible for the relationship, should manage paper rather than people. However, he should be careful not to be too detailed in specifying what is needed to the supplier. Quinn (1999) gives the following opinion: 'A primary reason for outsourcing is to leverage the supplier's greater skills, knowledge bases, investments and processes. If the buyer specifies the job in detail, it will kill innovation and vitiate the real advantage.' So the buyer must explain what is wanted, in terms of services and results but leave it to the supplier to determine how these results are achieved.

The contract review process should be a recurring process in which the outsourcing organization assesses the alternatives to prolonging the relationship with the outsourcing provider. These alternatives are either to replace the current supplier with a new supplier, obviously based on proper research, or sourcing the activity or function in-house again. This is only a viable option when the knowledge and capacity in the organization has not disappeared and when the business environment has changed so much that the decision to outsource this function apparently has to be reviewed.

RISK ASSESSMENT

Based upon the foregoing it will be clear that managing outsourcing relationships goes far beyond dealing with traditional buyer–seller relationships. Due to the fact that both parties engage in a long-term relationship many aspects need to be taken into consideration. This is particularly true for those outsourcing relationships where the parties involved have no history or have not built up experience (see also Chapter 2 on organizational buying behavior). In those cases companies will try to cover for all kinds of risks and uncertainties that they perceive to be associated with their future relationship. In such cases, where trust and interpersonal relationships are not present, parties try to arrange for dealing with these risks and uncertainties by detailed contracts. It is unnecessary to state that the discussions and dealings of these contracts (and the many contract clauses involved) will require a lot of stamina and energy from the executives that are involved. When legal specialists (lawyers) enter the scene too early, it appears that negotiations and discussions get lost due to the fact that the letter of the text of the contract becomes more important than the intention with which it was initiated.

Based upon our experience, we feel that outsourcing contracts are associated with the following kinds of risks:

■ Technical risks. These risks are related to the extent to which the provider is able to provide the desired functionality and performance. The degree of risk is related to whether the actual performance to be delivered by the provider can be stated in objective terms. Outsourcing contracts should be preferably performance-based contracts rather than contracts where the activities to be conducted by the provider are specified. Technical risk is related to the question of how to maintain crucial knowledge in the company over the time needed to manage the outsourced activity effectively; how to ensure that the supplier will apply leading-edge technology and solutions; and how to make sure that supplier staff are capable and remain capable of doing their job.

- Commercial risks. Commercial risks are related to the uncertainty, with regard to the price we will pay and the costs that we will incur, when having outsourced our activities to the supplier. Covering this type of risk requires an in-depth knowledge of the cost structure of the activities that are conducted by the supplier, the key cost drivers and the underlying cost parameters. Commercial risk also relates to the extra cost and allowances we have to pay when the supplier needs to deviate from the agreed scope of work (allowance for extra work or paying less for less work). Commercial risks can be reduced by using incentives and penalties for above average or below average performance. A final aspect relates to Intellectual Property (IP): how to prevent sensitive information leaving the company uncontrolled or, even worse, becoming known to our most important competitors

- Contractual risks. Does the contract describe in sufficient detail the performance that is expected from the supplier? Do the performance indicators that have been defined sufficiently cover what needs to be accomplished by the supplier? Have sufficient arrangements been made in cases that: (1) the scope of work or (2) the resources that have been agreed upon to be used by the supplier, have changed? Are there sufficient possibilities, when things may turn out wrong, that the penalties actually can be enforced in the relationship with the supplier, without destroying the relationship or without putting the service delivery by the supplier in immediate jeopardy? Did we make sufficient arrangements for dealing with subcontracting issues? These are aspects that need to be considered when assessing the contractual risks.

- Performance risks. These risks relate to the chance that the supplier is not capable of doing the job he was hired for. Does the supplier have sufficient capacity and flexibility to meet our fluctuating requirements? Do we have sufficient capacity and information to trace and track the supplier's operational processes? What if the supplier is not able to meet the agreed targets on service levels, quality and cost?

The risks that are described here are related to the change in the balance of power between the contractor and the provider. As a result of outsourcing, the contractor becomes much more dependent, and usually for a long period of time, on the provider, who after the initial period (when people, assets and knowledge have been passed over to him) may find himself in a more powerful position. In deciding about outsourcing, therefore, this dependency and associated risks need to be carefully balanced against the anticipated cost savings.

Many authors over time have pointed out, that in dealing with these risks, detailed contracts will not solve the problem. The importance of trust and partnership in the relationship must be stressed. Developing trust and an atmosphere of partnership, however, is easier said than done. It is our observation that the level of trust seems to be conversely related to the size and complexity of the contract: the more suspicious parties are, the higher the need for an all encompassing, legal contract. The more mature the relationship between the parties, the lesser the need to put everything in writing. Therefore, we feel (in line with Chapter 2) that chances for successful outsourcing relationships are predominantly present between parties that have been dealing with each other already for a long time in other business areas or activities. The less familiar buyer and seller are, the more they should refrain from complex outsourcing deals. In the next chapter we will see that having historical bonds and a good personal relationship are necessary, but not sufficient conditions, for making partnership in general and outsourcing in particular a success. Rather, a careful strategic positioning and a sound balance of power between the parties seem to be just as important.

CRITICAL SUCCESS FACTORS OF OUTSOURCING

At the end of this chapter we provide an overview of the most important critical success factors that should be considered prior to engaging in an outsourcing relationship with an external provider. Here, we take the ideas that were originally suggested by the Outsourcing Institute (1998) as a point of departure for our discussion. This Institute considers the following factors as critical for success in outsourcing:

- Understanding company goals and objectives. The motive for starting an outsourcing process has to be in line with the overall business strategy. When a company has decided to outsource part of its manufacturing, since it considers this activity as non-core to its business, it should not reconsider this decision when going through an economic recession.

- A strategic vision and plan. Outsourcing should not be conducted to solve just an operational problem e.g. solving people and capacity problems related to IT. The activity or function that is a candidate for outsourcing should be assessed thoroughly and the potential benefits, risks and resistance to be met from the internal organization should be analyzed beforehand..

- Selecting the right vendor. An exhaustive supplier selection process is recommended. The future provider should be selected on the basis of a cohesive and consistent set of criteria related to the supplier's technical and managerial capabilities, as well as the extent to which future visions and strategies and culture aspects at different levels of the organization are shared.

- A properly structured contract. The contract that is negotiated should be fair for both parties, the basis of it being a SLA that reflects the overall goals of the relationship. Preferably the performance to be delivered by the provider need to be translated into a limited set of objective, measurable performance indicators that are comparable over time. The contract should support the idea of going for a long-term relationship. The goal of the contract therefore should not be a win–loose, but a win–win situation. In the contract all the aspects of the relationship such as procedures, communication, termination etc. should be arranged.

- Open communication with the individual groups involved. A communication structure requires frequent interaction at regular intervals among different levels of the organizations involved. Also reporting schedules need to be agreed upon from both sides. Both parties could agree on joint training programs in order to make everyone aware of the new environment and new ways of running the processes involved.

- Ongoing management of the relationship. Performance incentives should be considered in order to motivate the supplier to meet and exceed expectations. Contract management is vital to the success of the outsourcing agreement. A contract manager has to learn not to manage the people, but to manage the contract. Management and people issues are to be left to the project managers. The procurement department should be sufficiently equipped to deal with the outsourcing environment.

- Senior executive support and involvement. Since outsourcing usually relates to complex decision making, large sums of money and a long-term commitment from the company, together with top management support, is crucial for making it happen.

- Careful attention to personnel issues. Outsourcing will affect the ways of working and routines of all people involved. Jobs will change or even disappear. New tasks will emerge. It is therefore important that staff are informed and well prepared on what management expects from them. Management of people issues therefore is crucial.

Here, we would like to add that one of the most important factors for successful outsourcing is the way the company is strategically positioned *vis-à-vis* its future provider. It is our view that the company strategically should be in a position where it can exert some control over its provider. When the company becomes totally dependent on the provider, in a situation where the provider is not very dependent on its customer, the outsourcing relationship may backfire. It may show that when people, assets and knowledge have been transferred to the provider, the provider will after some time engage in discussions on raising prices and rates (often with a fair percentage!). The provider may actually slow down its services in order to enforce concessions from its customer. Therefore the essence of making sound outsourcing decisions lies in a careful analysis of the expected cost economies and operational benefits against the change in risk profile and supply market dependencies. In the next chapter we will introduce a portfolio method which can be used to assess these risks and dependencies.

SUMMARY

This chapter has shown that the market for outsourcing is growing at an enormous rate, not only in the United States but also in Europe and Asia. From the type of activities that are outsourced it can be derived that the confidence in outsourcing as a business strategy is growing, because more and more entire business functions are being outsourced. Based upon its popularity, it might be concluded that outsourcing is a successful business strategy. However, as we have seen in this chapter, it is difficult to determine the actual success of outsourcing. There are many reasons for a company to choose to outsource certain activities and business functions and an evaluation of the success of outsourcing should depend on a review of the outsourcer's expectations/reasons against the actual outcome of the outsourcing project. Based upon studies by consultants in this field, outsourcing leads to mixed results which is why we feel it should be approached with great caution and care.

   Although it is difficult to measure the success of outsourcing, it is still possible to determine the factors that can influence the success of outsourcing. A comprehensive outsourcing process determines the success of an outsourcing relation. This process consists, as we have seen, of three important phases, i.e. the strategic, transition and operational phase. In the strategic phase the outsourcing decision and supplier selection process are a central point of attention. In the transition phase deciding on the proper contract form and the actual contract negotiation should receive the most attention and in the operational phase managing the relationship is the central issue. From these three phases the most important overall success factors have been identified. It is important to align the outsourcing strategy with overall corporate strategy. At this stage expectation and objectives to be met by the outsourcing project need to be defined in detail. First, the issue of what activities should be considered core to the company needs to be addressed. Next, potential cost savings through outsourcing non-core activities or business functions should be validated using a transaction cost analysis approach. Then, a project proposal can be prepared outlining what activities should be outsourced and what performance should be expected from an external provider. Based upon this information the supply market should be thoroughly analyzed in order to be able to find the partner that meets all qualifications. Apart from technical competences, the vision and strategy, management style, and organizational culture should fit with those of the outsourced company. Since trust is an important element, providers with whom the company already has a relationship should be favored. The basis of the future relationship consists of a detailed service level agreement in which the most important key performance indicators are defined, which are used to validate and monitor actual supplier performance. Penalties and incentives may be part of this contract to stimulate the supplier to exceed expectations. It is the role of the contract manager to monitor progress based upon this contract and to regularly review whether actual performance levels are being met by the supplier. In this way he/she should support the project manager, who primarily deals with operational and people issues.

As a result of outsourcing, the traditional balance of power between the outsourcing company and its provider changes dramatically. It will become much more dependent on this provider, which is why a careful risk assessment should be part of the preparation. Here, we have differentiated between technical risk, commercial risk, contract risk and performance risks which are all affected when entering into a complex outsourcing relationship. These analyses should result in a picture of how dependent and vulnerable the company will be *vis-à-vis* its future partner. In all cases the company should avoid a too large dependency and vulnerability, which is why outsourcing should be avoided in some cases.

ASSIGNMENTS

7.1 In business many terms are used to describe purchasing and contracting activities. What would you consider to be the most important differences between purchasing, subcontracting and outsourcing? Discuss.

7.2 Looking at the Case Study at the beginning of this chapter what went wrong at the telecom company? What would the telecom company need to do in order to get more control over its provider?

7.3 What would you consider to be the most important elements of an outsourcing contract? Provide at least 15 subjects that you would need to arrange for apart from the usual contract terms and conditions (such as price, delivery, quality).

7.4 When outsourcing an activity that was conducted in-house to another firm what kinds of resistance would you be likely to meet? What would be the consequences of organizing for this kind of event? What would you consider to be the role of the buyer, i.e. contract manager?

7.5 As a result of outsourcing the outsourcing company may become more dependent on the supplier. What could a company do in order not to become too dependent on a specific supplier? What would you recommend to the outsourcing company to enable them to exert some degree of control over their supplier?

After studying this chapter you should understand the following:

- The changing international business context and how companies strategically respond.
- The increasing strategic role of the purchasing function.
- How purchasing can support the company's overall competitive strategy.
- How to develop a differentiated purchasing and supplier strategy

CASE STUDY   CESSNA SOARS . . .

Integrated supply chain management has become a way of life at Cessna Aircraft Co., Wichita, Kansas, USA.

As recently as 1997, the aircraft manufacturer had little strategic supply chain process. Relationships with suppliers were adversarial (except in engines and avionics) and it showed. Contract prices rose 3 per cent per year, incoming quality was running at 50 000 parts per million (ppm) and on-time delivery was 65 per cent. Buyers spent their time placing purchase orders and expediting orders.

While Cessna was successful at producing and marketing business jets (it had 50 per cent of the market), shareholder and customer expectations were rising. Management realized that if it wanted to maintain the company's leadership position, Cessna would have to shift gears. Charles B. Johnson, president and chief operating officer, recalls, 'As our supply chain processes house the majority of our cost, it was necessary to create a more strategically aligned supply chain that yielded the most competitive quality, delivery, flexibility and value.' His strategy: transform a tactical materials department into an enterprise-wide supply chain process.

The man for the job was Michael R. Katzorke, senior vice-president, supply chain management, a seasoned purchasing veteran who had worked for such companies as AlliedSignal and Honeywell. Under his leadership, the supply chain management organization at Cessna has created a long range strategic plan and cross functional commodity teams that have worked to rationalize the company's supplier base; developed a tool called Maturity Path Development that aligns supplier strategy with that of Cessna; revamped the company's sales, inventory and operations plan (SIOP) improving performance to customer expectations and reducing inventory turns; implemented use of Malcolm Baldrige National Quality award criteria and Six Sigma quality tools to drive improvement in supplier performance; and introduced a value analysis/value engineering process that encourages supplier involvement in removing cost from the supply chain.

Katzorke and the supply chain management team have involved the company and its suppliers in supporting Cessna's corporate 'High Five' objectives of total customer satisfaction, world quality standard for aviation, breakthrough operating performance, top 10 company to work for and superior financial results.

In the past five years, these activities have yielded such outstanding improved business results as:

- 86 per cent improvement in supply chain quality.
- 28 per cent improvement in material availability.
- 113 per cent improvement in production inventory turns.
- Significant cost take-out in the supply chain through a strategic supply chain management process integrated into Cessna's overall business plan.
- 62 per cent reduction in production suppliers from the transition of phase-out to growth suppliers.

'These achievements have translated directly into improved customer satisfaction and improved financial results for the shareholder,' says Johnson. Aircraft quality is significantly improved. Defects resulting from supplier quality issues are down, reducing the number of production test reflights. Parts availability – which five years ago was about 65 per cent to schedule – is consistently at 99 per cent, while inventory turns continue to improve.

Cessna concluded 2002 with the highest revenues ($3.2 billion) in its 75-year history. While the aircraft manufacturer experienced some challenges related to the economy in 2003, it still introduced two new aircraft (Citation Mustang and Citation CJ3) late last year to ensure future growth.

'Perhaps the biggest achievement of Katzorke and his team,' says Johnson, 'has been the engagement of the organization in the Cessna supply chain transformation process from a transactional purchasing organization to an integrated full supply chain process.'

For these reasons Cessna Aircraft Co. was the 2003 recipient of *Purchasing* magazine's Medal of Professional Excellence.

Source: Susan Avery, *Purchasing*, 4 September, 2003, pp. 25–35.

INTRODUCTION

Increasingly, suppliers are being acknowledged as important sources for competitive advantage. This chapter discusses the strategic role that purchasing and supply management may represent to manufacturing companies and how to develop differentiated supplier strategies to support the company's overall product/market and business strategies.

PURCHASING AND COMPETITIVE STRATEGY

Over the past decades the competitive situation of West European industry has changed dramatically. First, European manufacturers experience far more competition from countries that were not considered as major producers until recently (e.g. Korea, Hong Kong, Singapore, Thailand, Taiwan and China). Second, industry in Western Europe seems to be under-represented in the areas of new technologies and emerging new industries (e.g. the computer industry, telecommunications, microchips). Looking at most industrial sectors in Europe it seems that many industries are at the stage of market saturation or decline (see Memo 8.1).

As a result of this situation, the long-term strategy of many companies nowadays focuses on 'selective growth', i.e. a combination of enhancing the core activity and starting up new, promising activities. One consequence of this strategy is that companies sell off those activities that are not considered to belong to their 'core business'.

In general, the following reasons may underlie this trend.

- Increased subcontracting, as a result of make-or-buy studies. Based on internal and external cost price studies, carried out in the context of a so-called 'competitive bench-marking program', a manufacturer of office equipment discovered that particular manufacturing activities could not be carried out competitively any longer. The internal manufacturing costs appeared to be much higher than the costs of external suppliers. This prompted the manufacturer to start a 'make-or-buy' program. As a result the company decided to focus its manufacturing on a higher level of assembly. At present, modular components are being sourced from a limited number of preferred suppliers. The company focuses on design, assembly, marketing and sales, and most component manufacturing has ceased. The same trend is observed in other companies. For example, a manufacturer of domestic appliances expects he will be making more use of flexible, universal production equipment in the near future and so specialized activities such as stamping, lathe work and plastic moulding will be contracted out.

- Buying of finished products instead of components. Due to the high labor costs level in some European countries, it is hard for some enterprises to compete. For example, Western Europe is expensive for the clothing industry to operate in. This industry is experiencing heavy competition from 'low-wage countries' and in recent years there has been a shift of production capacity to developing countries. Large retailers buy the

MEMO 8.1   HOW INDUSTRY LIFECYCLES AFFECT THE ROLE OF PURCHASING AND SUPPLY MANAGEMENT

The competitive situation of West European industry has changed dramatically over the past two decades. As a result of improved transportation, the rapid progress in information technology and the increased *globalization* of markets, competition (from the Far East in particular) has increased. This competition is manifest in both conventional and new products, and their associated technologies.

Looking at the industrial structure of most European countries, a relatively large number of industries are in the phase of saturation or decline. There are relatively few European companies with a strong position in new, emerging industries, i.e. industries that are in the introduction or growth phase (see Figure 8.1). Most industrial activity (and employment opportunities!) in Europe seem to be situated in the latter two stages of the industry lifecycle.

There are apparent differences in competitive strategy depending on the stage in the industry lifecycle. In the stages of introduction and growth, companies obtain a market position through research and development, product development, the introduction of new models and varieties and improvement of existing products. Research and development and, of course, marketing, aimed at tailoring products and services to the requirements of specific market segments and target groups, are key success variables here. In the stages of saturation and decline, however, the company can only maintain or reinforce its market position if it is able to sell end products (of basically the same quality and service level) at very competitive prices. Technology in these stages is mature and not subject to significant changes. In other words, during these stages of the industry lifecycle measures aimed at cost reduction, quality improvement and lead time reduction play a major role in maintaining or reinforcing the market position. Contracting out non-core activities to specialized suppliers can serve all these objectives. This explains the rising purchasing-to-sales ratio of many industrial enterprises, including Xerox, Electrolux, Philips Electronics, DAF Trucks, Alcatel, Volvo, over the past few years. This in turn results in an increased awareness among top-management of the strategic value of the purchasing function. This Memo also demonstrates the lasting nature of this interest, since no major changes in favor of European companies are expected in the international competitive situation over the next few years.

raw materials, which are then sent together with the design to low-wage countries, where the end products are made.

- Turnkey delivery. Manufacturers of specialized optical instruments often have to supply their products including sophisticated measuring devices. As a rule these costly devices need to be purchased by the manufacturers from specialized suppliers. To cite another example: manufacturers of industrial fences need to deliver their products turnkey (at the buyer's request), which means that they have to take care of all installations including safety and surveillance equipment (cameras, keyless entry systems). These relatively expensive products also need to be obtained from specialist suppliers. As a result the purchasing share for these manufacturing companies in the project cost is gradually increasing.

- Technological development. In some industries the technology develops at such a pace that even large manufacturers cannot afford the investments needed to keep up. Take for example the computer manufacturers who obtain their microprocessors from specialized suppliers, or the manufacturer of compressors who has to rely on specialized foundries to be able to benefit from new developments in casting technology.

In summary, the changed competitive situation in many West European industries requires management of many manufacturers to focus on their core activities. Specialist activities outside the scope of these core activities are increasingly farmed out. As a consequence, purchasing's share in the cost price of many end products will rise. Hence, purchasing decisions will have an even greater influence on the company's financial result. That is why management has become increasingly aware of the purchasing function. The consequences of these developments for integrating purchasing in the company policy will now be discussed.

FIGURE 8.1 The industry life cycle.

Introduction	Growth	Saturation	Decline
		Chemicals	Textiles
		Food products	Clothing
		Rubber, plastics	Leatherware/shoes
		Automobile industry	Steel
		Machine construction	Shipbuilding
		Computers	
		Telecommunications	
	Pharmaceuticals		
	Medical equipment		
Optical industry			
Biochemistry			

COST LEADERSHIP AND DIFFERENTIATION: CONSEQUENCES FOR MANUFACTURING AND PURCHASING STRATEGY

Every company's goal is to develop a distinctive, sustainable competitive advantage. Only then will the company be able to guarantee its long-term survival. In recent years the question of how to obtain such a position has received a lot of attention in the literature. One of the most interesting books on this subject still is the classic written by Porter (1980). According to this author, there are three basic strategies that can lead to a distinguishing market position:

- Cost leadership. The main focus of this strategy is to continually work at reducing the cost price of the end product. If a company succeeds in marketing products at a lower cost price than its competitors, it will achieve a satisfactory return. Companies that employ this strategy usually have a strong financial-economic orientation, expressed in meticulous budgeting and reporting procedures and strict control of overheads. This type of strategy is usually only successful if a large market share can be obtained. This makes it possible to manufacture in large volumes, on streamlined production lines, with specialized production equipment.

  This strategy must also pay attention to aspects such as quality and service, but costs come first. Its application is illustrated by some automobile manufacturers (General Motors, Daimler-Chrysler, Ford), a few computer manufacturers (manufacturers of PC-clones) and some manufacturers of domestic appliances.

- Differentiation. This strategy aims at marketing products which are perceived by the customer as being unique. Product individuality can be in the design (Swatch watches), the logo (Lacoste), the technology (Apple), service (American Express) and many other dimensions. Combinations are also possible; in addition to a high quality technical product, most truck manufacturers have an after-sales service organization that can supply parts within 24 hours all across Europe. In this way these manufacturers anticipate and respond to the problem of downtime which is experienced by every hauler: every hour the truck does not run costs a lot of money! A differentiation strategy aims at creating customer loyalty and brand preferences, thereby reducing the importance of price. If the size of the target group that responds to the unique advantage of the product is limited, the company may have to settle for a smaller market share.

- Focus strategy. This strategy aims to serve a particular, clearly defined group of customers in an optimal way. Examples are to be found primarily in the industrial sector (relatively small paper finishing companies that concentrate on finishing the products supplied by printers), or in transportation (some haulers are equipped specifically for the transportation of clothing, furniture or computers). A focus strategy means that the company studies the activities of the customer group, becomes familiar with the main problems, and provides specific solutions.

The importance of Porter's (1980) division is that the company will have to make a clear choice between these strategic alternatives. The consequence of not making a choice is that the company will be unable to build up a sustainable competitive advantage in the end-user markets. This will probably result in a mediocre return accompanied by a small market share.

This reasoning seems simple, but applying it in practice is something else again. Many entrepreneurs have a hard time in making a choice. They frequently want everything at the same time – very high quality and high customer service at the lowest price!

Limiting ourselves to the first two strategies, in Porter's view a company cannot realize both simultaneously because the necessary support in terms of organization and company culture is different for each of the strategies.

A company that strives for cost leadership will emphasize cost reduction. Since stocks raise costs, they are kept as low as possible; investments in automation are analysed with regard to their efficiency; strict budget systems and budget reports prevent cost overruns. The production tasks are prepared in detail and, to run as efficiently as possible, breakdowns must be prevented. Because everything has been prepared so thoroughly and high-quality technical production equipment is used, there is no reliance on improvization or human creativity. Production managers are judged on the capacity utilization of their machines and changes in production planning are not really acceptable, because they would result in production loss and therefore increased costs. Production companies that aspire to cost leadership are usually large, integrated companies that take advantage of effects of scale through vertical integration (textile industry, food products industry).

The company that applies a differentiation strategy operates in a completely different way and there is far less attention to costs although they are not ignored. A company that wants to respond flexibly to customer requirements is constantly searching for opportunities to reduce internal lead times.

Production utilization may vary over time, which means that personnel must be able to perform different tasks. Flexibility, a high level of education, and a strong identification with the company are important here. Budgeting can be less detailed since it is known that capacity planning is never fully realized.

A company that wants to differentiate in the area of technology must invest continuously in its people and machines. A well-equipped development and design function guarantees a steady stream of up-to-date products and the quality of the end product.

In practice, elements of both cost leadership and differentiation will often be found. However, the descriptions demonstrate that the choice between them has far-reaching consequences for the design of the production strategy and structure. It goes without saying that the consequences for the production organization will have to be translated in terms of purchasing policy. Cost leadership and differentiation require different types of purchasing strategies.

In the case of cost leadership, price and costs are central in the negotiations with the supplier. An important criterion for supplier selection is not so much delivery time, but delivery reliability. Regular failure by the supplier to comply with delivery requirements results in production failures, which in turn means high costs. Rejection of incoming materials should be prevented for the same reason.

In the case of differentiation the emphasis is on close cooperation with the supplier. This cooperation can be in the area of process and product improvement, quality control, lead time reduction and exchange of information. It is important that there is a direct relation between the supplier and the user, which is why a central purchasing department can have a disruptive effect in this type of company. The buyer is more or less the intermediary between production and the supplier market.

In the cost leadership situation, communication with the supplier takes place via a formal, administrative route. Much time is invested in optimizing or developing the ordering routines.

LEAN MANUFACTURING

Porter's ideas on competitive strategy have influenced management thinking for a long time. Over the last few years these basic beliefs about competitive strategy have been put to the test by some major Japanese and US manufacturers, who seem to have been able to combine the elements of a low-cost strategy with the advantages of a differentiation strategy. The core concept through which they are able to do this seems to lie in what has been designated as lean management. This concept originated first in an extensive study on the automotive industry, conducted by the Massachusetts Institute of Technology (MIT) during the 1990s. Lean management is a philosophy concerning how to run a manufacturing organization, which entails all aspects of the business system in general, and design, manufacturing and supply management in particular. The practices applied in these areas differ significantly from those applied in mass production by most American and European manufacturers. Significant changes in management style are also implied. Fundamental to lean management (Womack *et al.*, 1990, p. 99) is that:

> *it transfers the maximum number of tasks and responsibilities to those workers actually adding value to the car on the line, and it has in place a system for detecting defects that quickly traces every problem, once discovered, to its ultimate cause.*

Important features of lean management are:

- Teamwork among line workers, who are trained in a variety of skills to conduct different jobs within their working group. These not only relate to manufacturing tasks; workers are also trained to do simple machine repairs, quality checks, housekeeping and materials ordering.

- Simple, but comprehensive information display systems that make it possible for everyone in the plant to respond quickly to problems and understand the plant's overall situation.

- Total commitment to quality improvement on the shop floor. Workers are encouraged to think and act positively on how to improve the effectiveness of their work, whereas their supervisors need to provide active support to bring these ideas to fruition.

Japanese manufacturers devote considerable time and effort to the design of new products. First, the manager in charge of new product development has far greater authority to make decisions than his Western counterpart. Second, product and process engineering are integrated responsibility areas. Third, the engineering manager decides on who he wants to involve in his engineering team and for what period. These are significant differences compared with how engineering projects are organized in Western manufacturing companies.

The most important differences are apparent, however, in the way that Japanese manufacturers manage their supply chain (see also Lamming, 1993).

- The average supply base is much smaller than for Western manufacturers. Most Japanese manufacturers are dependent for a large part of their business on their suppliers and the power balance is definitely to the former's advantage. As a result OEMs have organized their suppliers into regional supplier associations which meet several times per year in order to learn about the future product/market plans of their customers.

- Most Japanese OEMs have a 'layered' supplier structure, which is often three or more tiers deep (see also Chapter 12 for more background information on this subject). Assemblies and subassemblies (such as seats, engines and gearboxes) are assigned to first-tier suppliers ('main suppliers'), who in turn rely on a team of second-tier suppliers for specialist components, and so forth.

- Suppliers are usually involved in new product development at a very early stage. It is not uncommon for Japanese OEMs to delegate half of the engineering hours to their first-tier suppliers. Engineers from the manufacturer and the supplier may work full time at each other's premises when solving technical problems and/or working out improvements.

- Suppliers are confronted with well-defined targets in terms of quality improvement, lead time reduction and cost reduction and are, by means of a simple though effective grading and performance measurement system, fully informed as to whether they meet their contractual obligations.

Since the principles of lean management extend to marketing, design, manufacturing and supply management, Japanese manufacturing companies have been able to obtain impressive results, which has put them at a safe distance from their foreign competitors. In the context of this book it is important to acknowledge that supply and supplier management is definitely considered to be the cornerstone of their competitive strategies! Most impressions on lean management are related to the Japanese automotive industry and we have to be careful about generalizing. However, for this type of manufacturing environment, the ideas of Porter clearly need to be refined.

In previous sections the influence of the corporate strategy on the purchasing policy has been discussed. It has become clear that the contents of the purchasing strategy depend on whether the company in question pursues a cost leadership strategy, a differentiation strategy or lean management. The next section shows how to obtain a view of a company's strategic vulnerability in relation to its purchasing markets.

INTEGRATING PURCHASING INTO COMPANY POLICY

In designing their overall business strategy, top management will have to make explicit decisions about the company's positioning *vis-à-vis* its three major stakeholders. Some authors have added a fourth group of stakeholders, namely 'employees' or 'unions'. As more and more companies see knowledge and human capital as key success factors for their organization, the 'strategic triangle' may develop into a 'strategic quadrant' in the future. The following stakeholders constitute what we would call the 'strategic triangle'.

1 Primary customer groups or target groups. This touches upon the issue of market positioning and segmentation. Products and services will have to be tailored increasingly to the needs of more differentiated customer target groups, which requires specific product/market strategies. This subject is not elaborated here but can be studied in the specialized marketing literature, for example Kotler (1997).

2 Major competitors. Companies must not only be able to respond to customer needs; they also need to respond in such a way that they achieve a so-called 'distinctive, sustainable competitive advantage'. This may explain why customers are turning to the company, instead of its competitors. As we have argued earlier, a competitive advantage may be derived from a superior cost position (South-east Asian car manufacturers), a superior brand image (many top consumer brands), superior product quality (RollsRoyce), superior logistics performance and customer service (DHL, UPS, Federal Express). To guarantee that customers will turn to the company, they must be able to clearly differentiate the company's products and services from the offerings of their direct competitors. In order to be able to do so continuous benchmarking of the company's overall performance is required against that of direct competitors and those companies who are considered to be best-in-class in a specific activity.

3 Major suppliers. Developments within the supplier markets necessitate continuous review of the company's core activities. Management will have to ask itself continually to what extext core and non-core activities (both production activities and support services) are carried out competitively. If the conclusion is that current (production)

activities cannot be carried out competitively in the long run, it will be necessary to investigate subcontracting options and/or possible partnerships with suppliers in the shape of so-called 'focused sources'. As a result supply chain strategies and specific supplier strategies need to be developed.

One example is a European automobile manufacturer who transfers the design and production of compressor valves for the automatic gearboxes of a new generation of cars to a specialized supplier. With financial support from the subcontractor, this supplier has built a factory to enable just-in-time deliveries based on call-off orders. Both parties are completely dependent on each other for the supply of this type of components; the relationship has developed from an adversarial, arm's length relationship into a long-term partnership relationship.

The conclusion from the foregoing is that the ultimate competitive position of a company is thus a result of (a) the company's positioning relative to its major customers; (b) its sustainable, distinctive advantage compared with direct and indirect competitors; and (c) its positioning versus its major suppliers and its supply chain strategies.

This is expressed in Figure 8.2. Although many companies have an explicit customer orientation and competitive strategy has become a major theme, there are only very few companies that systematically benchmark the performance of their key processes against those of specialist suppliers. This may explain the growing interest currently seen for supply chain management and supplier strategy.

In shaping the relationship with suppliers two elements play a major role. The first is 'costs'. Large companies are looking increasingly for suppliers who can produce at minimum total cost of ownership. In trying to find the most competitive sources of supply most manufacturers have adopted a global sourcing approach at the expense of their

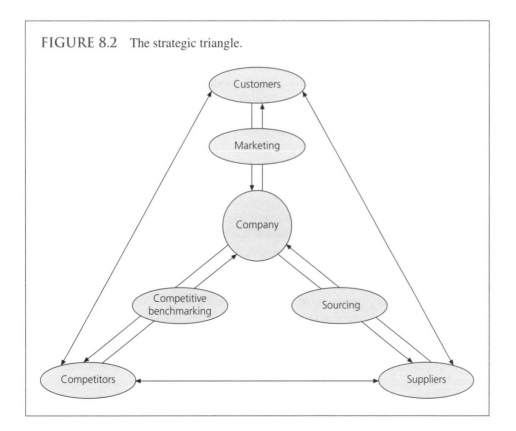

FIGURE 8.2   The strategic triangle.

traditionally 'nationally' oriented sourcing strategies. The second element is superior customer service. At the same time manufacturers are looking for suppliers who can support their logistics and just-in-time programs. Some authors, for example Fisher (1997), have demonstrated that in structuring their supply chain and supplier strategies, manufacturers need to differentiate between basic products and customized products. Basic products have a rather predictable demand and have a rather long lifecyle, whereas demand for customized products barely can be predicted due to their short lifecycle. Managing supply chains for the latter requires a responsive supply chain and a highly structured, local supplier network. Due to the fact that customer demand can be predicted much better for basic products, supply chains need to be less responsive. Hence, global sourcing for this type of product is an option. For this type of product an efficient chain would be preferred.

In many cases manufacturers develop and sell a mix of both functional and innovative products. Therefore, they need to manage different supply chains at the same time. This obviously explains why most companies have adopted both a local and a global approach in their dealings and relationships with suppliers.

TOWARDS LEVERAGED PURCHASING STRATEGIES

In the previous paragraphs the relationship between business strategy and purchasing and supply management has been described. As companies pursue different types of business strategies, the role of purchasing will be different. It has been argued that purchasing strategies definitely need to be linked to overall business strategies. The following paragraphs describe how purchasing and supply strategies can be designed and what steps can be helpful in formulating them.

In doing so the author is following the ideas of Monczka and Trent (1991, 1992), who have published extensively on this subject. Based at Michigan State University, Monczka launched a Global Procurement and Supply Chain Benchmarking Initiative in the early nineties. The idea behind this initiative was that companies participating in it would be able to compare their purchasing and supply processes, to exchange experiences and to learn from 'best-practices'. A number of large manufacturing companies, such as Shell, Philips, Motorola and Coca-Cola, subscribed to this initiative and worked with the researchers from Michigan State University to leverage their purchasing and supply strategies. In doing so they went through several stages or cycles of the program (see Figure 8.3).

- Insourcing/outsourcing. During the first step companies need to decide what activities to handle inside or outside the company. The decisive criterion is the question of whether the activity concerned contributes to achieving a competitive advantage. If this is not the case the company should decide to bring that specific activity outside the company. The reverse, however, may also be true. Insourcing means that the company may decide to take over strategic activities that previously were performed by suppliers.

- Develop commodity strategies. At this stage the company needs to develop a clear and detailed picture of its purchasing spend. On what commodities do we spend the most money? And on what suppliers? How many suppliers do we have per commodity and are we happy about the outcome of this analysis? Commodity is used here in its broadest sense since it may relate to raw materials, technical and high-tech components and standard, off the shelf products. A commodity strategy should then be developed. Such a strategy provides guidelines on whether or not to pursue product standardization and reduce the product variety, whether or not to reduce the number of suppliers, what type of relationship should be developed, etc. Of course the strategy for each commodity should be in line with and support the company's overall business strategy. It should be absolutely clear what benefits can be expected when the commodity strategy is implemented. Therefore a commodity plan maps out who will be responsible for each activity, a detailed timeframe and how progress will be monitored.

- Establish and leverage world class supply base management. Supply base management is part of every commodity strategy. Supply base management covers how many suppliers will be dealt with for a certain commodity, what conditions and qualifications the best-in-class suppliers should meet and how the best suppliers will be selected. At this stage suppliers are investigated and benchmarked and, often, submitted to a detailed audit.

- Develop and manage supplier relationships. In order to do so suppliers need to be grouped into distinctive categories. Philips Electronics may serve as an example here, as a company which differentiates between:

  - commercial suppliers: these suppliers just need to deliver the goods and services according to the agreed terms;

  - preferred suppliers: mutual objectives and improvement programs are developed and agreed by both parties. The preferred status is reciprocal;

  - supplier partners: these suppliers work intensely with Philips to develop new technologies, products and business opportunities. Usually, it concerns a limited number of suppliers, who are considered to be crucial in supporting Philips' overall business strategies and core-technologies.

As will be seen later, developing partnerships is a very difficult issue and takes a long time to develop between parties. In general a major step forward is reached when suppliers no longer suspect that their customer is simply trying to find out and cut back their profit margins.

FIGURE 8.3   Leveraging purchasing and supply management.

Source: adapted from Monczka (1999)

- Integration of suppliers in product development. Having carefully selected the best-in-class suppliers, companies next should focus their efforts on building constructive relationships with suppliers in the area of new product development. This implies that technical experts from the suppliers will become part of the research and development teams and other project teams and vice versa. Often both parties are confronted with difficulties in collaborating effectively together, which relate to differences in working methods, management style and culture. This subject will be discussed in more depth in Chapter 11.

- Supplier integration into the order fulfillment process. Motorola is one of the few companies which integrates suppliers into their customer focus teams. The idea behind this is that manufacturer and supplier in the end have one mutual objective which is to satisfy the final consumer as best they can. Joint teams work on issues like how to increase responsiveness and customer service, how to improve asset utilization, how to reduce pipeline inventories in the supply chain and how to improve communications and transaction flexibility by applying modern information and communication technology (ICT).

- Supplier development and quality management. At this stage suppliers are challenged actively to provide new ideas for improvement. These ideas may relate to product design, manufacturing technology and other business processes. Ideas and suggestions from suppliers are carefully considered and action is taken to implement them. Suggestions from suppliers are no longer considered as criticism but as sources for innovation and improvement. Motorola refers to this process as the 'Open Kimono' approach. This is the reason why it often asks its suppliers to value Motorola as a customer to work for. As experience has shown, adopting such a practice is not without risk. If suppliers feel that ideas are not taken seriously or good ideas simply are not being implemented, they will no longer support this type of program (see van Weele and Rozemeijer, 1998).

- Strategic cost management. This concept includes the identification of all costs, cost drivers and strategies aimed at reducing or eliminating costs throughout the supply chain (see Chapter 15 for more details on these subjects). Developing cost models and value stream mapping are important concepts and vehicles at this stage. The idea behind this is that both parties (or clusters of suppliers) work jointly with their customer to realize cost savings. Obviously, this will only work when each party may share some benefits of this exercise. Otherwise, this will lead to a clear lack of motivation for such initiatives in the future.

Through this eight-step process some leading-edge manufacturers have actually been able to integrate suppliers into their business processes. Based upon experience the author, in general, agrees with the approach as suggested by Monczka. However, in most cases it is felt that supplier development and quality management need to have a higher priority in the procedure. Preferably, it should be placed after the third part of the suggested program.

PURCHASING PORTFOLIO ANALYSIS

When designing commodity strategies, the portfolio approach originally suggested by Kraljic (1983) in his classic article, is recommended. Fundamental to his approach is the idea that, since suppliers represent a different interest to the company, purchasing managers need to develop differentiated strategies towards their supply markets.

Key in developing purchasing and supply strategies is the issue of influencing the balance of power between the company and its key suppliers. In the author's view the balance of power should preferably be in favor of the subcontractor. If the situation is the reverse, the subcontractor may suffer from an overdependence on a specific supplier, who may be able to pass his requirements and conditions onto his customers. Obviously, when a company is too dependent on a supplier, something should be done to change this situation. In developing effective supplier strategies, the following questions may be helpful:

- Does the present purchasing strategy support our business strategy and does it meet our long-term requirements? Are opportunities for benefiting from synergies between divisions/business units fully exploited, for example by joint contracting for common materials requirements?

- What is the balance of power between our company and our major suppliers? For which products/materials does the company have a dominant position on the supply market and for which products/materials is the company dependent on one single supplier?

- Are the strategic products and services sourced from the best-in-class suppliers? To what extent have the purchasing requirements and volumes been evenly spread over several suppliers and geographic regions?

- What percentage of our purchasing requirements is covered by long-term contracts? What percentage is covered by spotmarket transactions or short-term contracts?

- To what extent are internal operations benchmarked against those of specialist suppliers?

- What difficulties or interruptions in supply can be expected in the near future and how can these problems influence the profit and growth objectives of our company?

- What opportunities exist for collaboration with suppliers with regard to product development, quality improvement, lead time reduction and cost reduction? Are these opportunities sufficiently being used?

An analysis of the company's purchasing spend per category, and its supplier base in general, will show that the 20–80 rule applies: 20 per cent of the products and suppliers will represent about 80 per cent of purchasing turnover. This analysis is a first step in identifying the company's strategic commodities and suppliers. It also reveals the often huge number of small expense items and small suppliers, who in general are responsible for 80 per cent of the company's internal handling costs. After this step the analysis can be refined using Kraljic's (1983) purchasing product portfolio approach. In this approach the purchasing turnover and the supplier base are analysed based on two variables:

- Purchasing's impact on the bottom line to the company. The profit impact of a given supply item measured against criteria such as cost of materials, total costs, volume purchased, percentage of total purchase cost, or impact on product quality or business growth. The higher the volume or amount of money involved the higher the financial impact of purchasing on the bottom line.

- The supply risk. This is measured against criteria such as short-term and long-term availability, number of potential suppliers, cost of changing a supplier, competitive structure in supply markets, make-or-buy opportunities, storage risks and substitution possibilities. Sourcing a product from just one supplier without an alternative source of supply represents a high supply risk. Supply risk is low when a (standard) product can be sourced from many suppliers, whilst so-called switching costs are low.

Combination of these variables yields a two-dimensional matrix with four quadrants; these represent the product groups or suppliers, each offering different interests to the company (see Figure 8.4).

- Strategic products. These are high-tech, high-volume products, which are often supplied to customer specification. Only one source of supply is available, which cannot be changed in the short term without incurring considerable costs. Usually this type of product represents a high share in the cost price of the end product. Examples are engines and gearboxes for automobile manufacturers, turbines for the chemical industry and bottling equipment for breweries. Communication and interaction between subcontractor and supplier are usually intensive, and, as they relate to different aspects of the relationship, complex. Looking at the balance of power between the parties involved one can differentiate between three different sub-segments:

– Buyer-dominated segment. Here requirements are in fact imposed on the supplier by the subcontractor/manufacturer. Although some of these manufacturers have developed partnership programs for their suppliers, suppliers will experience the relationship as rather one-sided. This situation is common in the automotive industry. The

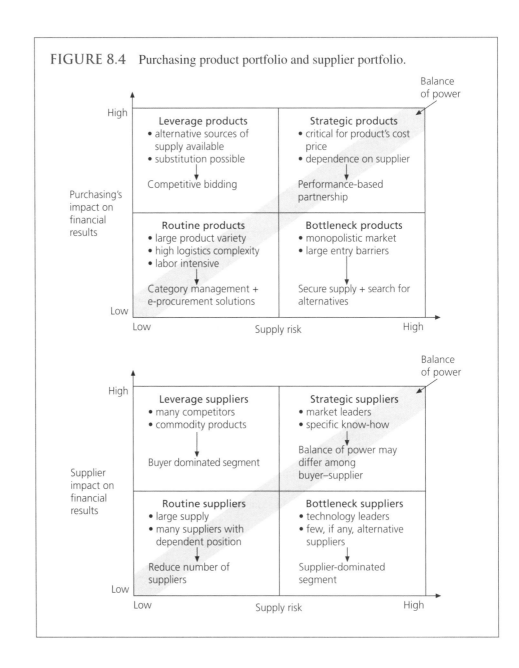

FIGURE 8.4   Purchasing product portfolio and supplier portfolio.

relationship between supplier and contractor is not a balanced one. The manufacturers dictate their demands to the suppliers, who just have to meet their requirements.

- Supplier-dominated segment. Here the situation is different. Through its technology and carefully designed marketing strategies the supplier actually has the customer 'locked in' a relationship. This is often the case in the business information technology industry, where IT providers have made their customers totally dependent on them in terms of supply of hardware, software and services (SAP, Oracle, Microsoft). Customers buy their hardware and software at one single supplier, only to find that the same supplier charges enormously for these. Usually the performance guarantee is only valid if products and services are bought from that same supplier. The customer has little leeway in general; he/she only can accept the conditions the supplier imposes on him.

- Balanced relationship. In this situation neither of the two parties dominates the other. They have a mutual interest in keeping the relationship stable. In this situation a 'partnership relationship' may develop over time.

■ Leverage products. In general these are the products that can be obtained from various suppliers at standard quality grades. They represent a relatively large share of the end product's cost price. A small change in price has a relatively strong effect on the cost price of the end product. This is the reason why the buyer exerts aggressive sourcing and tendering among a small sample of prequalified suppliers. Using e-auctions may be useful here to arrive at competitive prices in an efficient way. Examples are bulk chemicals, steel and aluminum profiles, packaging, steel plate, raw materials and standard semi-manufactured commodities.

Characteristic for this situation is that the contractor has freedom of choice regarding his selection of suppliers. There are various suppliers and the 'switching costs' are low. Abuse of this power, however, can lead to cooperation among the suppliers. Cartels and price agreements, though forbidden under EC-law, may develop in these situations, shifting the commodity to the right side of the matrix.

■ Bottleneck products. These items represent a relatively limited value in terms of money but they are vulnerable in regard to their supply. They can only be obtained from one supplier. Examples are catalytic products for the chemical industry, pigments for the paint industry and natural flavorings and vitamins for the food industry. Spare parts for equipment also fall into this category. In general the supplier is dominant in the relationship with the contractor, which may result in high prices, long delivery time and bad service.

■ Routine products. These products produce few technical or commercial problems from a purchasing point of view. They usually have a small value per item and there are many alternative suppliers. In practice most items fall into this category; examples are cleaning materials, office supplies, maintenance supplies, fasteners, etc.

The problem with this group of products is that the handling often takes more money than the value of the products itself. Usually, 80 per cent of the time and energy of purchasing is used for these products: a reason why purchasing is often seen as an administrative job. The purchasing of these normal products should be organized efficiently, in order to spare time for the other, more interesting products.

Depending on the product segment of the portfolio, the supply strategy will differ. The emphasis should lie with the strategic and leverage products. Work related to normal products has to be limited as much as possible.

The purchasing product portfolio provides an opportunity to identify and analyse the risks of the company in its purchasing markets. This is illustrated below.

Four basic supplier strategies

For every segment of the portfolio a different strategy is possible. The strategies are:

- Performance-based partnership. Strategic products together with the leverage products make up 80 per cent of total turnover. Minor changes in price levels will have an immediate impact on the end product's costs, so price and cost changes, as well as developments in the supplier market, must be monitored closely. At the same time, the supply risks are high. These arguments justify a central or coordinated purchasing approach. Depending on the relative power position of the different parties involved, the purchasing policy for strategic products will be aimed at partnership or collaboration. The goal is to create mutual participation based on preplanned and mutually agreed cost and operational improvement targets. A relationship based on 'open costing' is preferred. With the suppliers, efficiency programs are developed to achieve cost reduction, quality improvement, process improvement, and improved product development. Such co-operation can in the end lead to the fading of borders between the different companies.

  An essential aspect of this partnership strategy is the thorough selection of the supplier. Early in the development, the market is scanned for the 'best-in-class' suppliers. These suppliers are screened on their references, financial stability, the present research and development potential, production capacities, the quality of their logistics and their quality systems, and of course their research and development and engineering capabilities.

- Competitive bidding. For leverage products a purchasing policy based on the principle of competitive bidding or tendering will be pursued. Since the suppliers and products are basically interchangeable, there will be, as a rule, no long-term supply contracts. Long-term contracts and annual agreements will be combined with 'spot' purchasing. In most cases buyers will adopt a multiple sourcing strategy. Buying at a minimum price while maintaining the required quality level and continuity of supply will take priority here. Small savings (small in terms of percentages) represent a large sum of money. This justifies an active market scanning through continuous market and supply research. Regularly, outsiders will be introduced so as to avoid price arrangements between the present suppliers.

  Buying of leverage products justifies a corporate or coordinated approach where corporate agreements with so-called preferred suppliers are negotiated which can be used by decentralized units. Price changes caused by, for example demand and supply changes, are monitored closely in order to estimate the effect on the cost price.

- Securing continuity of supply. The purchasing policy concerning bottleneck products has focused on securing continuity of supply, if necessary at additional cost. At the same time activities are conducted aimed at reducing the dependence on these suppliers. This is done by developing alternative products and suppliers. However, the costs involved in these actions (for example, tests in laboratories) often exceed the cost savings obtained, which is why management often has difficulty in approving this type of action.

  A risk analysis to determine the most important bottleneck items in the short-, middle- and long-term supply is necessary. Based on this analysis contingency plans are made. With contingency planning, measures are prepared in case one of the established risks actually occurs. Examples of measures are consigned stock agreements aimed at keeping stock of the materials concerned at the supplier's, or the company's own premises, preparing alternative modes of transportation and actively investigating product alternatives.

- Category management and e-procurement solutions. For reasons mentioned earlier, routine, MRO-products require a purchasing strategy which is aimed at reducing administrative and logistic complexity. Buyers will have to work out simple but efficient ordering and administrative routines with the suppliers, in the form of electronic catalogs, through which employees can order directly from the pre-selected supplier. A few aspects relevant to the policy for these products are: standardizing the product assortment (article catalog), reducing the number of suppliers, pursuing systems contracts for categories of MRO items (office supplies, technical maintenance products, cleaning products, catering, etc.), working with electronic catalogs, ordering through Internet-technology, electronic payment or using the Purchasing Card. A final example is to contract out the purchasing of these articles to specialized purchasing offices and/or trading houses.

The use of the purchasing portfolio leads to a differentiated purchasing strategy. It points out that suppliers represent a different interest for a company. The different supplier strategies that have been discussed are summarized in Figure 8.5.

In Chapter 9 we see how the relationship with suppliers can be structured and developed. An illustration of how the purchasing portfolio can be applied is given in Memo 8.2. Figure 8.6 provides an illustration from Siemens.

FIGURE 8.5   Basic characteristics of the four supplier strategies.

Strategies / Characteristics	Partnership	Competitive bidding	Secure supply	Category management and e-procurement solutions
• Objective	• Create mutual commitment in long-term relationship	• Obtain 'best deal' for short term	• Secure short- and long-term supply • Reduce supply risk	• Reduce logistic complexity • Improve operational efficiency • Reduce number of suppliers
• Suitable for	• Strategic products (gearboxes, axles, optics, engines)	• Leverage products (commodities, steelplate, wire)	• Bottleneck products (natural flavors, vitamins, pigments)	• Routine products (consumables, supplies)
• Activities	• Accurate forecast of future requirements • Supply-risk analysis • Careful supplier selection • 'Should cost' analysis • Rolling materials schedules • Effective change-order procedure • Vendor rating	• Improve product/market knowledge • Search for alternative products/suppliers • Reallocate purchasing volumes over suppliers • Optimize order quantities • 'Target-pricing'	• Accurate forecast of future requirements • Supply-risk analysis • Determine ranking in supplier's client list • Develop preventative measures (buffer stock, consigned stock, transportation) • Search for alternative products/suppliers	• Subcontract per product group/product family • Standardize product assortment • Design effective internal order delivery and invoicing procedures • Delegate order handling to internal user
• Decision level	• Board level • Cross-functional approach	• Board level • Purchasing	• Purchasing • Cross-functional approach	• Purchasing • Cross-functional approach

MEMO 8.2   OUTSOURCING PISTONS AT CUMMINS

The decision to outsource a strategic component is one of the most wrenching for any company. However, it is precisely this willingness to lose a battle in order to win the war that separates industry leaders from the followers. Managers at Cummins were faced with just such a choice in the mid-1980s. Confronted with a need to develop much more advanced piston designs to meet emissions legislation, they discovered the need to make enormous investments in order to upgrade capabilities. The financial payback appeared dubious since Cummins could buy pistons from several suppliers. On the other hand, pistons were the very 'guts' of an engine, and there was an understandable reluctance to relinquish control of this component to a supplier.

An emotional debate raged for over three years. Should Cummins strive to rebuild its piston capability or turn to the best worldwide sources for piston technology? To quell the debate, senior management commissioned a team with representatives from engineering, manufacturing and purchasing to develop and implement an appropriate piston strategy. Engineers first identified the key technologies and capabilities that would be required to specify, design and manufacture pistons. The team visited the four leading piston suppliers and benchmarked internal capabilities relative to these suppliers.

The team discovered that Cummins's internal design and manufacturing capabilities lagged behind those of two suppliers who were world-class technologists. Moreover, these two companies were aggressive innovators. Their scale allowed them to invest more than 20 times as much as Cummins did in product and process research and development. In fact, both suppliers had their own machine-tool divisions and foundries and developed highly specialized machines and metallurgical processes. Cumulative volumes that were many times larger than Cummins's allowed them to ride down the experience curve much faster.

Thus not only was Cummins's piston design and manufacturing capability low in relation to the suppliers; but so also was its relative rate of learning. In light of this disparity, it was unlikely that Cummins had any chance of matching the capabilities of these suppliers without substantial investments that were difficult to justify. This objective fact-finding mission confirmed that the right decision was for Cummins to outsource pistons.

Source: Venkatesan (1992).

FIGURE 8.6   Siemens purchasing portfolio.

SUMMARY

One of the reasons why purchasing management is being assigned a more prominent position in corporate policy is closely connected with the strategic reorientation that many companies are involved in. After the diversification strategy of the 1970s, today's motto seems to be 'concentrate on your core business'. The advantages are self-evident: many activities can be carried out at lower cost by specialized suppliers, the company gains flexibility, and management's attention can focus on the 'core business'. These considerations are the reason why purchasing activity is receiving more attention from top management circles now than it did a few years ago. As companies have sourced out more of their activities, they have become more dependent on the competitiveness of their supply base. Purchasing's strategic role therefore is to develop a worldwide competitive supply base and to integrate these suppliers effectively into the company's business processes.

The purchasing strategy that is to be developed cannot be separated from the corporate policy nor from competitive strategy. As we have seen the extremes of the strategic continuum are cost leadership and differentiation. These strategies cannot be pursued simultaneously, as their organizational requirements are completely different.

Whatever business strategy is developed, they need to position the company against its three major groups of stakeholders, i.e. its customers, competitors and suppliers. Over the past decade there has been great interest from managers and academics for marketing management and competitive strategy. The interest for purchasing and supply (chain) management as a prime concern for top management is fairly recent. However, it is growing fast.

In the discussion on how to develop leverage in purchasing and supply management, the author has followed the ideas as developed by Monczka. A program where companies would preferably go through eight different steps is suggested. Key to these ideas is that purchasing and supply management is recognized as a major area of business and is managed that way. Elements of this approach are to develop corporate commodity strategies and article group strategies, to develop a supplier base which is 'world class' and to actively manage this supplier base. Supplier integration in new product development processes and the operational processes of the company are part of this activity.

When developing supplier strategies Kraljic's purchasing product portfolio may be very helpful. It recognizes that different products require different supplier strategies. It starts with a thorough analysis of both product groups and supplier base based on two criteria: (1) purchasing's impact on company profitability and (2) the degree of supply risk associated with the purchase of a specific item. An analysis of these aspects provides the first clue for the purchasing strategy which has to be developed. The second step is to further analyse the four product categories: (1) strategic products, (2) leverage products, (3) bottleneck products, and (4) normal products. For each of these products different supplier strategies can be developed. The value of this approach is that it explains that partnership and competitive bidding should be seen as complementary strategies rather than mutually exclusive. It also shows that the four basic supplier strategies serve different objectives.

ASSIGNMENTS

8.1 At the beginning of this chapter the industry lifecycle was introduced. Explain the characteristics of the purchasing strategy that would be most appropriate for each of the four stages that have been identified. What focus would each purchasing strategy have in each stage?

8.2   Consider a manufacturer of food products (macaroni and spaghetti products, dry soups and sauces). Analyse the purchasing portfolio based on Kraljic's portfolio analysis. Indicate which products can be characterized as strategic products, leverage products, bottleneck products, and normal products.

8.3   Global sourcing has become more popular among manufacturing companies. For what segments of the purchasing portfolio would you recommend a global sourcing strategy? Discuss the advantages and disadvantages of global sourcing.

8.4   Many large manufacturers have tried to develop partnership relationships with their key vendors. How would you define a partnership relationship? Do you think a true partnership approach is feasible in manufacturing industry? What conditions would buyers and sellers need to meet in order to be able to develop effective partnership relationships?

8.5   Some time ago the microprocessor market was characterized by considerable scarcity. The demand for products was enormous, and the supply was limited. Those manufacturers who were able to secure supply of essential parts could increase their production volume. As a result, these manufacturers realized a larger market share than their immediate competitors. Describe the optimal purchasing strategy in this situation. In answering this question, use the purchasing portfolio approach.

LEARNING OBJECTIVES

After reading this chapter you should understand the following:

- The reasons why suppliers do not always think and act in the interest of their customers.
- Sourcing-strategy and contract-strategy as basic elements of supply management.
- Measures that have to be taken in order improve the performance of suppliers.
- How to develop partnership relations with suppliers.

CASE STUDY   OCÉ PURCHASING STRATEGY

Océ and its suppliers are entering a period in which we will work together in new ways. In this brochure we document the key elements of Océ's new purchasing vision.

Océ enables people to share information by offering products and services for the reproduction, presentation, distribution and management of information.

Because of the changing environment we are changing the scope and focus of purchasing activities. There will be a greater focus on the overall quality of our suppliers in terms of engineering capacity, the core competences of the suppliers, their role and attitude in the value chain and their capacity to support Océ in its future developments.

The impact of this changed orientation is that suppliers will be involved in new ways. Key words will be long-term relationships, systems buying, simultaneous engineering and continuous improvement.

The main issues of our purchasing strategy are:

- We prefer to leave design and part of the industrialization to suppliers who can design to functional requirements.
- We are going to increase the strength of our supply base, raise supplier networks and find more world class suppliers.
- We are going to work more closely together with selected world class suppliers and we are going to establish more long-term relationships.
- We will be very selective in choosing suppliers and will do more business with less suppliers.
- The purchasing department will focus on value sourcing and strategic management of quality and logistics issues, will increase the access to know-how and technology from main suppliers, will analyze suppliers from a competitiveness point of view and will focus on overall cost.

We will continuously be looking for the best suppliers in the world and want them to perform better. We will constantly benchmark our suppliers' performances. We will set challenging targets on cost, quality, logistics and functionality. We have to reduce our total value chain related costs by double digit percentages. In doing so we will create a world class supply base from which we all will benefit.

Source: Océ Purchasing Strategy, 1998.

INTRODUCTION

This Case Study shows how Océ, a leading manufacturer of copying and design equipment, intends to integrate suppliers into its business strategy. Other large European manufacturers have also discovered the strategic importance of an effective purchasing and supplier strategy. In the early 1990s, Ignacio Lopez, the flamboyant purchasing director of successively General Motors and Volkswagen, stirred up the European supplier industry. As a result of his unorthodox and aggressive purchasing approach, he realized 'double-digit' savings on the materials costs of the companies he worked for. Lopez's methods have not been undisputed, but they show that a well-prepared purchasing strategy can reap significant benefits.

This chapter discusses the management of supplier relationships and will build on the purchasing portfolio technique which has been described in the previous chapter. Active and professional management of supplier relationships is an important topic now that many companies have contracted out the greater part of their activities. The basic assumption is that when manufacturers are not capable of managing their supplier relationships, they without doubt will be managed by them! The author's experience with suppliers in many companies has shown that suppliers often do not think and act in the interest of their client. This chapter shows what the underlying reasons are and what companies can do about it. Therefore, the cornerstones of effective supply management will be described. In doing so we will also describe what companies can do to foster collaboration with their suppliers and how they may develop partnership relationships.

WHY SUPPLIERS DO NOT ALWAYS THINK IN THE INTEREST OF THEIR CUSTOMERS

The cost down programs that have been set up over the past few years by an increasing number of companies have resulted, almost without exception, in large purchasing cost savings. Impressive savings have not only been reported in the area of production-buying, but most certainly also in the area of non-production buying. This, notwithstanding the often long-established and often highly-valued relationships between the parties involved! How were these cost savings realized? What activities have generated these? What reasons may explain the slack that apparently exists in the prices paid for the purchased materials and services? In general most manufacturers and suppliers are reluctant to share this type of information with the outside world. Based on experience the following reasons why slack in materials costs and prices may exist are mentioned:

- Price increases automatically passed on to the next in line. This phenomenon is referred to as the 'french fries principle' (see Memo 9.1). According to this principle suppliers will pass on cost increases to their clients, who in turn pass these increases in costs on to their final consumers. This happens not only with materials cost increases: increases in wages, social insurance and other labor costs ultimately will also be passed on to the customer next in line. As recent examples in the automotive and consumer electronics industry have shown, this practice cannot go on for ever. In some cases this practice has led to customer prices that simply were no longer accepted by consumers, resulting in lost sales and significant financial losses.

Some visionary purchasing and supply directors have emphasized that manufacturers and suppliers in fact share a common goal: serving the final consumer in the best way possible. The more products are sold by the manufacturer, the more business will be generated from suppliers. This premise underlies the total customer satisfaction program of Motorola (manufacturer of microchips and telecom equipment), where suppliers are working in integrated customer teams to improve customer satisfaction.

- Overspecification. As opposed to Japanese and some American companies, concepts such as 'concurrent engineering' and 'early supplier involvement' are hardly developed in Europe. This is a consequence of the highly functional structure of European companies. As a result, technical specifications for purchased products are being defined by research and development departments only, without any input from purchasing specialists or suppliers. In most cases this leads to 'overspecification'. In this situation technical requirements are imposed on suppliers, which are not necessary for the functioning of the product. An example is the boxes for food products, as used by a large food manufacturer, with full six-color print, which only serve for transportation to the retailer's distribution centre. In general, the more specific the requirements for a given product, the fewer suppliers can be found for delivery. In some cases it may even lead to monopolistic supply situations (i.e. single sources), where manufacturers are very dependent on one specific supplier. The disadvantages of overspecification are obvious:

  - products become unnecessarily expensive;
  - supplier knowledge for improving or simplifying product design is not used;
  - it limits opportunities for competitive bidding amongst suppliers.

These disadvantages illustrate the need to work with cross-functional teams. However, this often requires a drastic change in the company's organizational culture.

MEMO 9.1   THE 'FRENCH FRIES PRINCIPLE' IN PURCHASING

The passing on of cost increases can best be described by the price developments of potatoes. A bad potato harvest has direct consequences for the price of a bag of chips. A good harvest has hardly any consequences. If the harvest of potatoes in a given year is bad, supply will decrease. However, demand usually stays the same. As a result of the stable demand and shortages of supply, the price per kilo will increase. The prices per portion of french fries at the cafeteria will also increase.

What happens in the case of an abundant harvest of potatoes the next year? Then supply of course will increase, whilst demand remains the same. As a result the price for potatoes per kilo will decrease. One would expect that this in turn will result in a price reduction for a portion of french fries. However, in real life this is rarely the case! The idea of this principle is that cost increases, which have been incurred by suppliers, immediately are passed on to the customer. However, materials prices reductions and productivity gains are to be kept from the customer in order to improve supplier profitability. In most European economies this phenomenon is very visible as can be seen from the tariffs charged for gas, oil and energy, or for paper and corrugated board, petrol and gasoline, etc.

- Mechanistic competitive bidding amongst a fixed group of suppliers. This means that purchasers regularly sound out competition amongst their well known suppliers by playing them off against each other. The procedure here is that out of five bids, you take the lowest one, just to start a negotiation to reduce the price even more. Then, the buyer will go with the lower price to the next supplier and also negotiate with him, and so on. When applied regularly, it is clear that suppliers will anticipate this opportunistic buyer behavior. First, they probably will refuse to offer their lowest possible price in their quotations, since they will keep some leeway in the 'game' of give and take, which will follow. These ritual dances between purchaser and supplier usually deliver limited results. Moreover, this process often consumes valuable time. Second, when applied among a small group of suppliers, it promotes silent agreements between them and cartels may be formed. This type of purchasing behavior is widespread in the construction industry in some European countries. It explains why relationships in this industry usually are at 'arms' length' and why collaboration between construction firms and their suppliers is often ill-developed.

- Supplier cartels in (international) supply markets. In spite of the agreements made at EC level and the EC laws concerning competition, cartels are very common in most European economies. In many industries, such as the paper industry, packaging industry, some construction materials (concrete, bricks), pharmaceutical industry and some food ingredients (e.g. sugar and some fragrances), concentration is very high. There are only a very limited number of players around, which makes it easier to make some silent agreements on pricing behavior and division of markets. Usually, such a situation results in product prices which are not in any way related to the underlying cost structure of the manufacturers.

- Traditional purchasing. In many companies purchasing is managed in a traditional way. This means that buyers are involved late, if at all, in the purchasing decision-making process, and the company actually deals with a fixed group of familiar suppliers. Specific policies on purchasing or on how to deal with suppliers are hardly developed. If available, purchasing plans usually are not very ambitious. It might be that products are purchased for years without any knowledge of the underlying cost structure of the suppliers involved. Supplier representatives have free access to the company. In such a situation much benefit can be gained from adopting a more businesslike way of working with suppliers.

- Suppliers' customer relationship programs. Many suppliers avoid discussion on how to improve their performance for their clients. Rather, they spend time and money on 'customer management programs' trying to influence the preferences of decision makers in their favor. The activities related to such programs are abundant! Tactics vary from invitations for in-company seminars (banks) and product presentations (car manufacturers) and personal gifts and presents, to straightforward bribes. All these activities aim to influence the personal preferences of decision makers on 'soft' aspects and to avoid an objective client testing the products and services. Given the often aggressive and personalized marketing and sales policies of many suppliers, most companies would benefit from a company-wide policy on business ethics.

These points explain why in most cases suppliers have considerable slack in their price setting. Some of these points are related to the manufacturer, other points relate to characteristics of the supply market and the sales and marketing activities as applied by suppliers. The next section deals with the issue of how to identify slack in supplier prices and how to capture this cost reduction potential.

MAIN ELEMENTS OF SUPPLIER MANAGEMENT

In order to be effective a supplier strategy should be able to answer the following questions:

- For which commodities should the number of suppliers be reduced?
- For which commodities should the current number of suppliers be maintained?
- For which commodities should the number of suppliers be increased?

In answering these questions, conducting the purchasing portfolio analysis (see Chapter 8) can be a first step. Over the past few years many companies have focused their sourcing strategy on reducing the number of suppliers. However, obviously this cannot go on for ever. Reducing the number of suppliers should never be considered as a goal in itself. Rather, it should be seen as a vehicle to reduce costs and/or complexity.

Next, the supplier strategy should describe per commodity what type of relationship with the supplier needs to be pursued. Here, a distinction can be made between the sourcing strategy and the contract strategy that preferably needs to be followed. Considerations concerning the sourcing strategy are:

- Global versus local sourcing. Is an international, global supplier orientation required for this product or can a local, national orientation suffice? The answer depends on the type of product. Factors in favor of local sourcing are when it concerns a high-tech product for which the product specification often changes, when a high flexibility and precision is required in terms of delivery, and when intensive personal communication is required in the relationship. Factors in favor of global sourcing are when it concerns bulk products or standardized products, when large price differences among suppliers exist for the same commodities, when products can be bought in large quantities in order to benefit from transport economies, etc. These examples show that decisions on global versus local sourcing should always be based on considering the total cost of ownership.

- Single vs multiple sourcing (see Memo 9.2). Does the company wish to purchase the product from one supplier or are several suppliers for that same product necessary? If the company purchases the product from one supplier, the company becomes dependent on that supplier. Supply risk is usually less when the same product is or can be sourced from more than one supplier.

- Partnership or competitive bidding? Does the company wish to buy the product from a supplier with whom a partnership relation is preferred, or is the supplier to be kept at a distance and focused by regularly sounding out competition? Entering a partnership relationship has far-reaching consequences for the ways of working of the companies involved, the openness and willingness to share sensitive information and the contractual arrangements. These aspects will be discussed later in this chapter. Competitive bidding means putting out a 'tender' amongst a limited number of previously approved suppliers. Depending on the propositions, the total volume is spread over the most attractive suppliers. For the individual supplier the allocated volume may differ from year to year. This tactic is mostly used when commodities are purchased or when the products are purchased in large volumes.

A second aspect of supplier strategy is deciding on contract strategy. Developing a contract strategy requires a decision on the following aspects:

- Buying on contract or buying on spot basis. Is the total volume of purchased products to be covered by a contract or is part of the volume to be bought on a spot basis (at the current market prices)? The advantage of buying under contract is that the volume is bought at a previously agreed price. The buyer is also certain of delivery. The disadvantage of covering the total volume under a contract is that the company loses its contact with the market. The suppliers who dropped out are aware that the company has secured the delivery of the products and therefore they will not continue to inform the company about the latest developments on the market. In case of expected price increases, a contract covering the greater part of the total purchasing volume is preferred. In case of expected price decreases, the opposite applies. As a rule, most companies choose a combination of both contract and spot buying.

- Price agreement versus performance agreement. What kind of contract is preferred? How detailed should it be? Should it be confined to a price agreement only? This may be sufficient when buying fabrics with certain standard qualities. Or is a detailed service level agreement (SLA) with specific arrangements on time of delivery, tests, maintenance, guarantees, etc. to be preferred? This is appropriate when contracting for specific process equipment or other investment goods. When buying services, service level agreements have increasingly become popular. Another development can be found in the automotive industry. Most automotive companies, as an example, use a 'life of type' contract for their suppliers of components which states that the prices have to decline a certain percentage every year and that the supplier should be able to deliver the specific component during the total economic life span of the car.

These issues have to be well considered before searching the international supply market.

GETTING BETTER RESULTS FROM SUPPLIERS

How to secure superior service from suppliers? How to develop a relationship with a supplier? How to enter into a partnership relationship with a supplier? These questions are addressed in this section.

MEMO 9.2   SINGLE SOURCING

Single sourcing is the deliberate choice of one supplier. *Sole sourcing* refers to the situation in which the company could not make a free choice of any supplier because it concerns a monopolist. Generally, a company will prefer single sourcing when it concerns: (1) the production of a small series of complex components with high tooling costs, (2) contracting out small volumes of client specific products which are produced under licence or with specific know-how, (3) products that need to be delivered with very short lead times, (4) when the technological knowledge is simply not available within their own organization.

One advantage of single sourcing is the involvement of the supplier, which makes it easier for the supplier to open up to the customer since there is no fear of competition. Being dependent on the supplier, the contractor is often willing to involve the supplier more and more in his new product development process. However, this can result in losing contact with the supply market and a greater dependence.

For these reasons most large companies prefer a sourcing strategy based on multiple sourcing in order to have several alternative suppliers at their disposal for a certain product group. However, it is possible that within the product group, one specific supplier is responsible for one particular item. For example: Toyota has several suppliers for their automobile seats; however, the seat for the Toyota Carina is delivered by one supplier, while the one for the Yaris is delivered by another.

Single sourcing does not automatically lead to a partnership relationship. This depends on the relative power between supplier and contractor. The concepts 'single sourcing' and 'partnership' therefore are by no means synonymous.

Usually, the following step-wise approach will provide a useful vehicle:

- Contract review. This step concerns a thorough analysis of current contract arrangements with existing suppliers. Often, this results in some search activities, since it appears that contracts are difficult to find and have not been accurately documented. This is particularly true for contracts which are made without the involvement of the purchasing department. Often the supplier has to be contacted to provide a copy of the contract. The contract documents are analyzed at this stage and checked for completeness and functionality. The main objective is to determine which price agreements have been made, whether the actual performance and satisfaction with the supplier have been documented and to assess the risks and responsibilities involved. Usually, such an analysis leads to a new, up-to-date and complete contract outlining the product and service performance required from the supplier. The objective of this step is to conclude a performance-based contract. Experiences have shown that this activity alone can lead to substantial savings (5–10 per cent). An example is a food company where such analysis revealed a maintenance contract which was still being paid for while the machines had been sold and scrapped years ago!

- Competitive bidding amongst current and new suppliers. This step focuses on analysing the international supply market and sounding out competition. The objective here is to get a competitive bid from a large number of new suppliers. An important element is that the number of possible suppliers is not limited to well-known companies. Before the market research, the company must decide which requirements the suppliers have to meet (supplier profile). Then a shortlist is made of all the suppliers who conform to this profile. Based upon a detailed request for quotation the prequalified suppliers (8–15) are asked to present their proposals; a few international suppliers are deliberately included. Formal tendering procedures such as e-auctions may be used here to organize and speed up the process (see Chapter 10).

  Some companies do not use a tender or an e-auction and nevertheless are able to arrive at very competitive prices in their dealings with suppliers. After suppliers have been preselected, they are in a first round invited to come up with their proposals. Next, the three most promising suppliers are invited for a number of creative sessions together with the specialists from the customer. During these sessions the participants are challenged to come up with creative ideas for cost reduction, improvement of the product design and quality improvement. At a later stage, the customer team will visit the supplier in order to determine possible means of improving the product process, using a detailed company audit. The ideas that grow out of this workshop are presented to the management of the supplier at the end of the workshop. Honda of America developed a 'best practice program' for this purpose (see Memo 9.3). After these ideas have been processed in a final purchasing order specification, the suppliers are invited during a second round to present their final quotations. The final choice for a supplier is based on these quotations. The objective of this step is to identify the 'best-in-class supplier' for the required product or service, on a performance-based contract. Given the effort that this approach requires, it is only applied when buying key commodities and major investment goods.

- Optimizing the supplier relationship and value chain mapping. As a result of the previous steps the company now has a performance-based contract with the 'best-in-class supplier'. From now on, the focus is on continuous improvement within the supplier relationship. The premise here is that in the balance of power there is a relationship, or that the balance of power is at the advantage of the contractor. At this stage concrete objectives and targets on price and cost reduction, quality improvement, lead time reduction and improvement of customer service are settled. These objectives and targets are often prepared by supplier improvement teams or supplier alignment teams, consisting of specialists from several disciplines from both parties. A major objective is to exchange ideas for improvement activities on both sides. Both parties exchange sensitive technical information and cost information. Often, contractors find out that the greater part of the homework has to be done on their side! Working this way leads to a situation where the supplier becomes gradually integrated in the customer's business processes. This is the reason why Daimler-Chrysler uses the term 'extended enterprise program' (Dyer, 1996). They see their suppliers as an extension of their own company that need to be equally, or even better managed, than their internal operations. This approach can result in the early involvement of suppliers in the development of new products. During that period of time, specialists of the supplier are actually working within the organization of the contractor (residential engineering). *Vice versa*, engineers of the contractor can be present in the organization of the supplier when the first trial production runs take place, supporting them in solving start-up problems. This subject will be further discussed in Chapter 11. At this stage, some advanced contractors will analyze the entire supply chain with help from their suppliers. The instrument used is value chain mapping: per component, the source of origin of every part is determined. Then, per sub-component, the purchasing contracts are analyzed and possible simplifications for purchasing or logistics are identified. In many cases, this results in the contractor helping the supplier with improving his contracts with the next tier of suppliers. This approach is used by Japanese and some American manufacturers. In Europe this approach is still in its infancy. Characteristic for this stage is that the improvement activities are initiated and managed by the contractor and followed through progress meetings. Detailed vendor rating schedules showing the achievements of suppliers are discussed in these meetings.

The major objective underlying this way of working is to develop and optimize the operational relationship with the best-in-class supplier and to integrate him in the new product development processes and projects. In this way suppliers are systematically challenged

MEMO 9.3   WORKING ON SUPPLIER QUALITY AT HONDA OF AMERICA

Honda of America deals with suppliers. The cooperation with suppliers is characterized by simplicity. Dave Nelson, vice-president purchasing says:

When we receive a promising quotation from a new, unfamiliar supplier, we invite him to come and explain his proposal. At this meeting, a team of Honda specialists is present. If this meeting passes satisfactorily, one of Honda's younger engineers will visit the supplier's factory. The task of this engineer is to organize the working space of the supplier. He will start cleaning the machines and the tooling warehouse. Molds and dies are inspected, cleaned and categorized so people will not have to search for them anymore. Then the factory is whitewashed to make it spotless. At first the engineer works alone, but after a while a few employees of the supplier cannot bear to see him working alone and will give him a hand. And that is precisely the intended plan. Eventually, we want to create a situation in which the supplier incorporates our management philosophy, which is based on respect for the individual and the full utilization of the creativity of employees. If that is accomplished, we are both working with common views, and barriers between the supplier and us automatically fade away.

Honda of America work with their 'best practice program', which stands for 'best practice', 'best price' and 'best process'. The purpose of this program is to show suppliers how to eliminate the seven wastes in their production organization: standstill of machinery, moving materials, defects and failures, production disturbance, over-production, lead time and stocks.

and mobilized to support the company's overall business strategies and to secure business success.

THE MYTH OF PARTNERSHIP

This chapter would be incomplete without a discussion of the issue of 'supplier partnership'. In recent years, large international manufacturers have spent a lot of time and money in the development of supplier-partnership programs. One of the first companies in Europe to focus on partnership was Philips, which introduced the term 'co-makership', i.e. 'the building of long-term relationships with a limited number of suppliers based on mutual trust'.

A major objective underlying this type of cooperation is to achieve significant improvements in:

- Logistics. By giving the suppliers insight into the supply needs and materials schedules for the coming months, they can anticipate much better the future requirements, which will lead to a higher level of service and lower logistics costs for both parties.

- Quality. Early mutual agreement on quality requirements enables zero defects deliveries, which in turn result in a reduction of quality costs for the contractor.

- Product development. By introducing product and process engineering knowledge and experience of the supplier early into the development process, the time-to-market and start-up costs may be reduced.

The subject of partnership has been widely covered by academic research. In recent years, many concepts have been developed. Interesting views come from the research done by Ellram and Hendrick (1993). In their investigations these authors used the following definition of partnership:

> A 'partner' is defined as a firm with whom your company has an ongoing
> buyer–seller relationship, involving a commitment over an extended time-period, a
> mutual sharing of information and a sharing of risks and rewards resulting from the
> relationship.

Based on this definition, the researchers concluded that, within the examined companies, less than 1 per cent of the total of supplier relations could be defined as partnership relationships. These suppliers, however, were responsible for as much as 12 per cent of the total purchasing volume of the examined companies.

Another interesting study on partnership was conducted into the British automobile industry (DTI, 1994). This study shows that the mutual trust between supplier and contractor is still out of reach. This research reports that 'many years of broken promises, abuse of trust, and conflicts', made close collaboration in general and partnership between (car) manufacturers and their suppliers impossible. The researchers concluded: 'In developing new working agreements with their suppliers most vehicle manufacturers still appear to deal more in rhetoric than reality' (p. 5).

Reviewing the current practice of purchasing, these results do not come as a surprise. Cooperation with suppliers requires internal teamwork between all the disciplines. The functional structure in many companies interferes with an effective internal cooperation and as a consequence interferes with a close and effective cooperation with suppliers. Of course, there are some examples of successful partnership relationships. However, it must be acknowledged that these were the result of many years of muddling through, disappointments and perseverance. Developing partnership relationships with suppliers takes

FIGURE 9.1 How producer–supplier relationships may develop over time.

Aspects	Supplier	Preferred supplier	Supply partner	Design partner
Relationship characteristics	• Operational	• Operational	• Tactical	• Strategic
Time-horizon	• From order to order	• 1 Year	• 1–3 Years	• 1–5 Years
Quality	• As requested by producer • Qualitity control by producer	• As requested by producer • Quality control by producer and supplier	• 'Sign-off' by supplier • Quality assessment by supplier (process quality)	• 'Sign-off' by supplier • Early supplier involvement in design • Quality assessment by supplier (design quality)
Logistics	• Orders	• Annual agreements + call-off orders	• Periodical scheduling of materials requirement by producer	• Electronic document interchange
Contract	• From order to order	• Annual agreement (1 year)	• Annual agreement (>1 year) • Quality agreement	• Design contract • Life of type responsibility (product liability supply)
Price/cost	• Price	• Price + rebate	• Price + cost-reduction targets	• Price based on open calculation • Continuous improvement (design, quality, cycle time)

time as illustrated in Figure 9.1 which shows the large differences in the relationships with a supplier and design-partner.

The author considers partnership to be the result of the contractors' continuous effort to improve results in the relationship with suppliers, rather than a technique which can be adapted and applied in a short time. This probably explains the small number of really successful partnership relationships in practice.

SUMMARY

Effective supplier management is another cornerstone for a successful business strategy. The way this policy is executed in organizations increasingly determines its shareholder value. Companies like AT&T, Ford, General Motors, Motorola and Volkswagen use purchasing and supply strategies as an integrated part of their company policy. They are proof of the huge savings and significant improvements in operational processes that can be made through dedicated, effective supplier management.

The international competitive arena forces manufacturers to look continuously for ways to improve their customer value. Product costs need to be maintained at a competitive level. At the same time, they have to work continuously on product and process innovation. Suppliers are able to, and should, contribute to both objectives. The author's view is that this cannot be done automatically. This chapter has explained why most suppliers do not automatically think in their clients' interest for reasons that are due to both the contractors' organization and the suppliers' marketing and sales policies. It is fair to say that if contractors are not able to manage their suppliers, the suppliers without doubt will manage their customers. Successful companies tie their purchasing and supplier strategies to their overall business strategies. Suppliers should support their customers' business strategies in the best way possible. If the manufacturers do well in terms of growth and volume, so will the suppliers. Successful contractors will try to overcome conflicting interests in the relationship with their suppliers which may have developed over the years. This is done by developing carefully designed sourcing programs which focus on where to go for single sourcing, global sourcing and/or partnership. These sourcing programs always result in detailed action programs which will highlight contract review, competitive bidding and cooperation with suppliers at the same time.

The road to partnership is long and difficult. There are no easy ways or short cuts to success. Supplier strategies should be supported by the top management. Activities are to take place in cross-functional teams from both sides. This often requires a complete change of view on traditional purchasing practices. Purchasing needs to become more and more integrated into line management and the major business processes. The buyer, then, becomes just one of the team's players. Firm rules on ethics and on how to deal with suppliers are needed in order to limit the effects of their often aggressive marketing and sales programs.

ASSIGNMENTS

9.1 In the Case Study described at the beginning of Chapter 5, AT&T (a company with a purchasing share of 55 per cent) states: 'Purchasing is by far the biggest activity at AT&T. Nothing else is more important.' How do you feel about this statement? Do you agree with AT&T?

9.2 This chapter focuses on the necessity of cross-functional teamwork during the stage of product development. What do you think are the benefits of such cooperation? Why does cross-functional teamwork often require a complete cultural change?

9.3 This chapter states that the reduction of the number of suppliers should not be a goal in itself: it should be seen as a means for other goals. Which objectives are served with the reduction of the number of suppliers? Why does the reduction of the number of suppliers mostly result in cost reductions?

9.4 What is the difference between single and sole sourcing and partnership? Give examples. Discuss how these terms interrelate.

9.5 What benefits and risks would you see to be related to the use of e-auctions? Answer this question from the perspective of both the buyer and the supplier.

After reading this chapter you will be able to:

- Explain the differences between e-procurement as defined in its broadest sense and its narrowest sense.

- Cite possible electronic solutions that are open to purchasing and supply managers and categorize them.

- Identify the different kinds of electronic marketplaces that are relevant for purchasing and supply managers.

- Outline how electronic marketplaces and e-procurement may support purchasing and supply strategies and what savings can be generated from these.

- Assess the value of electronic auctions for purchasing.

- Delineate the risks associated with implementing electronic procurement solutions and the conditions that should be met within organizations in order to do so effectively.

CASE STUDY   SUN SHINES BY COMBINING TWO SUPPLIER STRATEGIES

Sun Microsystems, like a lot of high-tech companies, spent much of the mid-1990s outsourcing its manufacturing operations to electronics manufacturing services providers in the US and abroad. The strategy was aimed at reducing costs but also increased the complexity of Sun's supply chain and made it more difficult to communicate supply and demand issues to suppliers throughout the tiers.

'As we outsourced more and more of our manufacturing, we found the ability to communicate with our supply chain partners became more important,' says Kurt Doelling, vice-president of supplier management and worldwide operations strategy. 'We had gone from building 100 per cent of our systems internally to building about 10 per cent of our systems internally in a span of three years. That drove the need to communicate better with our supply chain partners. When we built everything internally and a plan changed, we could put the changes through our material requirements planning (MRP) system and the next day all the component suppliers would know about the plan changes. But now (after outsourcing most of our manufacturing) when we run changes in MRP, we send the plan changes to contract manufacturers building systems for us. Then they have to send the plan changes to their suppliers who may be building boards, and the board makers send the changes to the component suppliers. What used to be a one-step process suddenly has several steps or tiers in it and if you aren't really careful, these changes can take three or four weeks to get down the line.'

In an effort to minimize the negative impacts of the more complicated supply chain, Sun established its e-operations initiative with two primary goals. First, increase the effectiveness of supplier communication in the more complex, multi-tiered supply chains. Second, develop stronger partnerships with Sun's existing supply chain partners while making them more competitive for contracts.

The first thing Sun needed was an infrastructure to foster communication directly with its diverse supply base. Some suppliers were EDI-proficient and moving on to XML while others were not so advanced and needed a tool that worked only with a browser. To address these various levels of e-enablement, Sun created a portal framework that made it very easy for all suppliers and buyers to access the tools and information they needed. Information available on the portal is classified into several categories. There is public information targeted at companies that might want to be Sun suppliers. There is also information for existing Sun suppliers such as terms and conditions for doing business with Sun and specific contacts. And there is supplier-specific information, e.g. purchase orders and forecasts.

The entire portal framework was completed in about 18 months. Today, 40 suppliers use 18 different applications available through the portal, from demand planning to supplier performance to logistics tools.

Source: *Purchasing*, 6 May, 2004.

INTRODUCTION

Modern information technology is the great enabler behind the plans to set up electronic market exchanges. By using Internet technology, large manufacturing companies can communicate and trade both with their customers and suppliers faster, more efficiently, and on a larger scale.

After the initial euphoria at the start of the new millennium, we have witnessed a turnaround. It seems that investors are becoming increasingly realistic in their appraisals for their portfolios, with a sharper eye for what is and is not possible with regard to e-business applications.

Within the various Internet applications, those in the field of purchasing are especially important. There is a rapidly growing interest both on the part of purchasing and supply managers and top managers. Is all this attention justified? Which electronic applications are we talking about exactly? Are they of equal use to all businesses? What electronic purchasing solutions should enterprises invest in and how sustainable will these investments be? What are the risks and what kinds of losses can be expected? This chapter reviews the most important insights into the field of purchasing management, supplier relations and the Internet.

INVESTING IN E-PROCUREMENT SOLUTIONS

A large, international company was approached some time ago by an international consultant who planned to work together with similar companies to set up a joint electronic marketplace for purchasing. The idea was that their joint forces would lead to considerably lower purchasing prices. In addition, transaction costs would be lowered by forcing suppliers to use the standardized protocols of the electronic marketplace for their transaction processing. As a result, transaction processes would be faster and would suffer from fewer problems. The initiative was not only to the advantage of the manufacturers involved; suppliers could also profit from the arrangement. It was to be a win–win situation. It seemed a plan that was too good to be true. Each participant had to be prepared to invest a couple of million euros. In fact, setting up the marketplace required an investment of about 100 million euros in total.

If you were a purchasing manager, what would your decision be? Would you ignore the proposal and run the risk of missing an important development and the accompanying purchasing advantages? Or would you invest and run the risk that this sketchy initiative would turn into hot air and only produce a fraction of the savings it proposed to do?

In this chapter, we first indicate how enterprises in such situations could respond. Top executives and purchasing managers, as we see it, would need to take several aspects into account. In our opinion the initiative must first support the procurement strategy of the enterprise, and the procurement processes and accompanying information systems will have to be brought up to date. This finding is quite significant. It is assumed that enterprises do indeed hold a strategic view concerning the field of purchasing. If such a view, however, does not exist, investments in an electronic marketplace may become isolated without being adequately embedded in the purchasing processes of the enterprise. Hence, a basic question is: to what extent will participation in such an electronic marketplace differentiate the corporation from its competitors? If the competition gains more from such a project, is it wise to participate?[1]

Next, it is necessary to consider what investment one is prepared to make, what yields are set off against this investment, and within what period one expects to see profit being realized. This aspect focuses on the cost-benefit ratio of the initiative. In practice this proves to be an extraordinarily difficult exercise, which makes it all the more important to use a scenario analysis for it (best case–worst case scenario). One of the difficulties is that supplier relationships are much harder to change than generally assumed. Another issue is that, when reducing transaction costs, it will appear that most of these costs are fixed, since they relate to labor and investments in information systems which are, again, difficult to influence.

In addition, one needs to know what type of technology platform is chosen for implementing an electronic marketplace. More important than the technology platform is the question of what purchasing functionality is sought. Are solutions sought in the field of global sourcing, auctioning and tendering, or are solutions needed that simplify the transaction flows between the enterprise and its suppliers? Combinations are possible too, of course. Does the proposed initiative sufficiently deal with the needs and issues of the enterprise?

Once these questions have been answered, the purchasing manager is left with the question of how to take the first step. How can you get the ball rolling? Memo 10.1 summarizes the most important initial questions.

In this chapter we will refer to e-procurement solutions in two notions. We will differentiate between e-procurement in the narrow and the broad sense. In the broad sense it is a collection of web technology-based purchasing solutions aimed at simplifying commercial transactions within and between organizations. In a narrow sense it entails information technology solutions for ordering, logistics, and handling systems, as well as payment systems. Examples include electronic ordering systems and catalog systems. E-procurement solutions come in three different ways, i.e. electronic marketplaces, electronic catalog

---

1 This finding was reason enough for General Electric to go its own way regarding electronic marketplaces. *Purchasing*, 15 June, 2000, p. 14.

MEMO 10.1 INITIAL QUESTIONS RELATED TO INVESTING IN AN ELECTRONIC MARKETPLACE

- To what extent does electronic purchasing support current purchasing and supplier strategies?
- To what extent will electronic purchasing contribute to the realization of a sustainable competitive advantage?
- What are the technological implications of the initiative for the enterprise and how dependent will the company become on its IT provider?
- Which investments are necessary, how long will it take to earn them back and what are the chances of success?
- Which electronic solutions can be imagined in the field of purchasing and which are the most suitable for the enterprise?
- How can one obtain a view on these questions and what is the first step one needs to take?

solutions and e-auctions. We will discuss each of these topics in the remainder of this chapter. We will also shed some light on the implications of these new tools for IT-strategies and structures in purchasing.

ELECTRONIC MARKETPLACES AND ELECTRONIC PROCUREMENT

There are various types of marketplaces that can be found on the Internet. Here, an electronic marketplace is defined as a place on the Internet where actual transactions can take place between buyers and sellers. A visitor to such a marketplace may find one of the following variants (see Figure 10.1):

- Website. A place where a buyer finds a single seller or *vice versa* (1–1). A website is characterized by a one-to-one relationship between the buyer and seller.
- Buyer-centric portal. A marketplace set up by several sellers with the objective of offering the potential buyer an integrated product line (n–1). The buyer is not aware of the

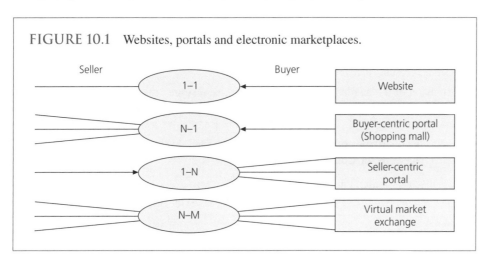

FIGURE 10.1 Websites, portals and electronic marketplaces.

presence of the other buyers (n–1). Shopping malls and market plazas are examples of this kind of portal.

■ Seller-centric portal. A place where a seller finds several buyers at the same time (1–n). The buyers are aware of the presence of other buyers. Examples here are auctioning sites run by large department stores where individual consumers can bid. Other examples are the auctions run for companies by independent providers such as FreeMarketsOnline and e-Breviate.

■ Electronic market exchange. A marketplace where several sellers and buyers are present at the same time (n–m).[2] These may be organized per type of industry (ChemConnect. com, Covisint.com) or per type of commodity (MRO.com, AtYourOffice.com).

A distinction can be made between vertical and horizontal marketplaces (also referred to as e-hubs by some authors). *Vertical marketplaces* aim to encourage, facilitate, and realize transactions between parties that belong to the same value chain. For example, take www.Transora.com, which was set up by food manufacturers to facilitate the communication with their suppliers. Other examples are Covisint.com, e-Steel.com, ChemConnect.com, and PlasticsNet.com. *Horizontal marketplaces* focus on facilitating relations between parties which operate in different value chains. Examples here are MRO.com and Atyouroffice.com, which both aim to facilitate transactions between sellers and buyers in the field of office articles. Horizontal marketplaces basically are an electronic version of the *buying consortia* that arose in the United States in the late 1990s, in which various large companies worked together to close joint contracts for a particular purchasing product category. These consortia can be found in the field of energy and in healthcare, where a number of hospitals combined their forces in the area of purchasing.[3] The *buying community* is a less strict variant of a consortium, in which a number of buyers join forces only temporarily to purchase certain products. Examples of buying communities can be found in business-to-consumer relationships. Early attempts were www.letsbuyit. com and priceline.com. However, these initiatives have not been very successful in most cases. An interesting classification of electronic marketplaces has been presented by Kaplan and Sawnhey (2000). Memo 10.2 gives more details about this interesting scheme.

To conclude this section Memo 10.3 provides a description of some frequently used terms.

POSSIBLE IT STRATEGIES FOR PURCHASING

Companies may follow different strategies to implement information technology for e-procurement. Here are some examples:

■ Purchase of a separate front office application that is integrated into the back office systems present (e.g. PurchasingNet).

■ Extension of the available back office enterprise resource planning (ERP) system with an e-procurement function, which stops integration from being an issue. Known ERP suppliers such as SAP, Oracle, Peoplesoft and Baan have developed this functionality.

■ Make use of a front office application that is available within the marketplace (e.g. Ariba, Netscape, or CommerceOne).

Essentially, e-procurement systems must enable their users to specify their purchasing requirements, to conduct purchasing market research, to pre-qualify suppliers, and if poss-

---

2 In the following we will use the terms 'portal' and 'electronic marketplace' interchangeably.
3 See also Corsten and Zagler (2000) for a detailed discussion of this subject.

ible allow for the running of tenders. Besides remarkable differences in the functionality offered by the various applications which currently are available, the efforts necessary for integration differ greatly. To realize the savings claimed by the providers of these applications, a high degree of integration is required between the front office and back office[4] on the one hand, and between the back office and the supplier's systems on the other.

MEMO 10.2 CLASSIFICATION OF ELECTRONIC MARKETPLACES

Kaplan and Sawhney differentiate between *manufacturing inputs* and *operating inputs* on the one hand and how the products are purchased on the other. Here they make a distinction between *systematic sourcing* and *spot buying*. Systematic sourcing involves negotiated contracts with qualified suppliers. Because the contract tends to be long-term, the buyers and sellers often develop close relationships. In spot sourcing the buyer's goal is to fulfill an immediate need at the lowest possible cost. Commodity trading for products such as oil, steel and energy exemplifies this approach.

Based upon these two criteria a matrix is presented in which the following electronic marketplaces can be identified (see Figure 10.2):

- *MRO-hubs*. Horizontal marketplaces which enable systematic sourcing for indirect, non-production-related goods and services.

- *Yield managers*. Horizontal marketplaces which enable spot buying for indirect goods and services.

- *Exchanges*. Vertical marketplaces allowing spot-buying for direct, product-related goods and services.

- *Catalog hubs*. These marketplaces allow systematic sourcing for direct, product-related goods and services.

FIGURE 10.2 Business to business matrix.

Source: adapted from Kaplan and Sawhney (2000), p. 98–99

---

4 Front office relates to the actual ordering cycle between the requisitioner and the buyer. Back office relates to all transaction processing activities between buyer and supplier.

The applications discussed here can be acquired by the user in various ways:

- Purchase and implementation of e-procurement software. Take for example, Philips, where in 1999 the decision was made to base the e-procurement solution on Ariba. Philips actually decided to buy the software from Ariba and installed it on their own servers and systems. Their biggest hurdle in this case was the implementation, integration, maintenance and management of the application in compliance with their different ERP systems. After several attempts to solve this issue they abandoned the initiative.

- Hosting of the e-procurement application by the ASP on behalf of the user. In this situation, the user puts his product catalogs on the ASP system, which takes care of the technical management. Content management and development are in the hands of the

---

MEMO 10.3 THE JARGON WITHIN E-PROCUREMENT

- *Application Service Provider (ASP)*. A firm which operates a technology platform and allows users to use it against a pre-arranged license fee and/or an allowance per transaction. Examples in the purchasing area are: Ariba, CommerceOne, Netscape. Companies may place their own product catalogs on these platforms or use the ones provided by the ASP.

- *E-commerce*. The whole of business actions carried out electronically to improve the efficiency and effectiveness of market and business processes. In practice, however, e-commerce is usually understood to be 'Marketing, sales, and purchasing of products and services via the Internet and/or other open electronic information networks'. The term e-business is used for the collection of activities aimed at the improvement of business performance through the application of electronic solutions in and between value chains.

- *E-procurement*. There is a distinction between e-procurement in the narrow and the broad sense. In the broad sense it is a collection of web technology-based purchasing solutions aimed at simplifying commercial transactions within and between organizations. In a narrow sense it entails information technology solutions for ordering, logistics, and handling systems, as well as payment systems. Examples include electronic ordering systems and catalog systems.

- *Electronic Data Interchange (EDI)*. This is related to the exchange of information between the information systems of trade partners by means of standardized communication protocols and data entities.

- *Intranet*. This term relates to an internal computer network within a given organization, which is only accessible to employees of that organization, and is primarily intended for internal communication and message exchange. An intranet is often connected to the Internet via a so-called gateway.

- *Extranet*. This is an extension to the intranet that allows external parties (customers, suppliers, dealers, etc.) to make use of the same facilities as internal employees of the organization. Thus, electronic message exchange is possible between parties using communication standards set by the organization in question.

- *Maverick buying*. This term refers to a phenomenon which can be observed in many large organizations where centrally negotiated contracts are only used by the operating units to a small extent. A variety of reasons may be the cause of this (lack of knowledge, no realtime contract library available, resistance to corporate initiatives, etc.). Enforcing contract compliance by systems discipline may result in siginificant savings.

- *Open Buying on the Internet (OBI)*. A communication standard that was developed upon the initiative of a number of large American purchasing organizations together with their suppliers. It is especially focused on facilitating electronic transactions of indirect or non-production related goods.

user. One example is WorldWideMarketExchange, in which Ahold participates. Supplier and product databases and files, as well as transactions Ahold carries out with suppliers, are only visible to Ahold and not to its competitors.

■ Make use of an application including content. A third option is for the user to not only make use of the technological platform of the ASP but also the product and supplier catalogs that are in its care. Naturally, a company's own catalogs can be integrated into those of the ASP and be tailored where necessary.

These examples make it clear that, when choosing a specific electronic platform, a company may become very dependent on the ASP. Purchasing managers, therefore, need to verify at a very early stage the technological stability and the financial strengths of their future partner. We shall return to this point later in this chapter.

DIFFERENT PURCHASING SOLUTIONS FOR DIFFERENT PURCHASING OBJECTIVES

Our description makes it clear that a great diversity of electronic tools are already available in the field of purchasing. These tools can be used for different purposes. Electronic marketplaces facilitate the searching of and actual tendering among suitable suppliers. One important advantage is that supplier markets, as a result, become more transparent. Another is that large firms can move away from traditional supplier relationships and find new suppliers. The present broadening of their supplier markets has major consequences for the balance of power and pricing mechanisms in the B2B markets.[5] Modern information technology makes new types of purchasing possible as well. Consider electronic auctions for example (in the shape of upward or downward auctions[6]), computer-supported tendering, and best bid analysis. ERP systems and catalog systems may offer efficient solutions in the field of more efficient order control, goods logistics, and payment systems. The present information technology already makes in possible to deal with transaction flows between organizations without human intervention. Cisco claims that 55 per cent of its customer orders (stemming from more than 34 000 customers for a sum of about 4 billion dollars) are handled without intervention from Cisco employees. As well as considerable savings this also results in a major reduction in order throughput time (from six to eight weeks down to one to three weeks).[7] Examples like Cisco, however, are rare. For most enterprises this picture may remain a utopia.

Which solutions are available for which type of product or supplier? Using the purchasing portfolio, we have attempted to provide a systematic view on this topic (see Figure 10.3).

The purchasing portfolio shows that different solutions can be imagined for the various purchasing segments. For more commodity-oriented products, which can be specified easily and are bought against standard qualities, such as the well-known MRO articles,[8] we would suggest catalog systems and electronic payments solutions (i.e. Purchasing Card). This segment particularly focuses on the lowering of transaction costs. For strategic products and services, which are often tailored to customer needs, EDI is often favored as a solution, due to the frequent transactions and interactions, and the fact that automatic

---

5 B2B markets = business-to-business markets.

6 The latter are also referred to as reverse auctions.

7 Elisabeth Fee, Supply Chain Management at Cisco, e-Motion Conference, Eindhoven, October, 2000.

8 MRO stands for maintenance, repair and operating supplies. See also Croom (2000) on how Internet technology could support MRO-buying.

materials requirements planning systems trigger purchasing orders. The yield from electronic auctions is largest for so-called leverage products, which does not lessen the fact that these can be equally applied to the segment of routine articles. However, we expect that catalog systems and e-procurement solutions will mostly be used for the latter segment (see also Memo 10.4). For the bottleneck segment, usually, there is little to choose from the side of the buyer. Given the dominant position of the supplier *vis-à-vis* the buyer, the supplier in most cases will impose his ordering systems on the buyer.

On the basis of Figure 10.3, we believe that most companies in the area of purchasing need to apply a variety of electronic solutions. In other words, we do not place great stock on an all-encompassing information system that supposedly offers every possible type of functionality in the field of purchasing. The reason is that because of the position of suppliers in the portfolio it is highly unlikely that they all will be willing to cooperate in integration. Powerful suppliers with strong positions will force their systems upon their customers. Customers in those cases will unfortunately have to adapt to their suppliers rather than the other way around. Obviously, the story is completely different for purchasing segments where the customer holds a dominant position with respect to the supplier.

Consultants and suppliers of these solutions have great expectations of the possible profits resulting from these solutions. The following is claimed:

- Important advantages can be gained from electronic sourcing through electronic marketplaces. Increased market transparency and the accompanying improved options in the field of competition can lead to considerably lower purchasing prices. The advantage for direct and indirect goods differs. For direct goods the percentages are between 1 and 5 per cent; for indirect goods potential savings are estimated at between as much as 15 to 30 per cent.

- By using electronic catalog systems, more purchasing transactions can be contracted so that the percentage of maverick buying[9] can be drastically reduced. This again would lead to considerable savings.

FIGURE 10.3   Different electronic solutions for different purchasing purposes.

---

9 This refers to the share of the purchasing volume that is bought without a contract (often a considerable share of the total purchasing expenditure).

- The transaction costs can be reduced (from a hundred to just tens of euros per transaction) by using integrated ordering and goods handling systems. Here we see the third source of potential savings in purchasing.

These estimations sketch a picture that has to catch the eye of any reasonable manager. However, perhaps some warnings should be given too. With regard to the first issue, it is true that a broader market orientation and greater competition can be expected to lead to lower prices.[10] However, this only applies to enterprises that have had a poor and unprofessional purchasing policy in the recent past. In our opinion this is the reason why a number of enterprises with very professional purchasing policies have been rather reluctant to participate in electronic marketplaces. In addition, we believe that advantages gained in this way will be of a temporary nature: after an initial period all participants will level out to the same price level regarding their purchasing. Based on this argument we do not believe marketplaces exclusively aimed at pricing will survive for very long. But there is more. Recent surveys[11] show that top managers generally are more positive about the options offered by electronic procurement and electronic marketplaces than their purchasing managers. The latter continue to refer to the importance of good suppliers, who score well on the basis of a good business relationship founded on total cost of ownership. The purchasing managers resist the opportunistic attitude and short-term advantage that can be achieved.

MEMO 10.4   WHAT PROBLEMS ARE SOLVED BY E-PROCUREMENT SYSTEMS?

E-procurement systems[12] enable users within organizations to order directly from an electronic catalog without interference from a purchasing department. Orders are acknowledged automatically by the supplier. The user can verify the order status online, when desired (When will the order be delivered? What terms and conditions apply?). There is no need to contact the purchasing department with these kind of questions. Many suppliers nowadays offer detailed tracking and tracing facilities which enable their customers to monitor order follow up and delivery real-time. Besides this, e-procurement systems enable electronic invoicing, invoice matching and payment. As a result the traditional purchasing cycle is reduced and simplified considerably (see Figure 10.4).

Implementing e-procurement systems allows companies to reap significant benefits in terms of both lower materials prices and lower organizational costs. E-procurement systems represent an important productivity tool for both purchasing managers and departments, since these will lead to a significant reduction of administrative workload. At the same time customer service levels will improve since internal customers now will have responsibility and authority for ordering the materials they need through pre-arranged and efficient order routines. Finally, savings may result from the fact that common material requirements are grouped in homogeneous product families, which are ordered from electronic catalogs from far fewer suppliers. Concentration of a larger volume among fewer suppliers, again may lead to better prices. However, implementation of e-procurement systems is a far from simple matter. It requires a high level of purchasing professionalism, clearly spelled out purchasing procedures and a seamless integration with the general ledger system and other systems within the company. Next, these systems need to match with the administrative systems of suppliers, which in many cases is a big problem!

▶

---

10 See also Chapter 10.

11 See also the special issue of *Purchasing*, 15 June, 2000, which is exclusively dedicated to procurement (pp. 6–13).

12 Here the term is used in the narrow sense. See also Kalakota (2001), Chapter 10, for a detailed discussion.

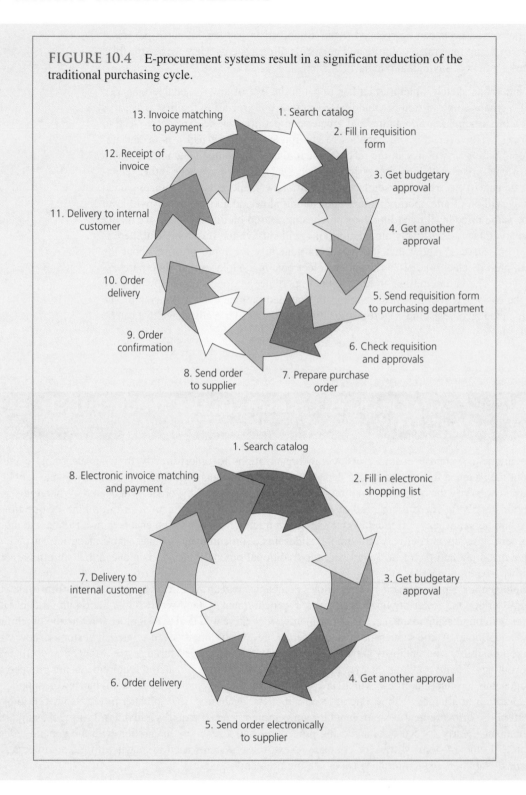

FIGURE 10.4 E-procurement systems result in a significant reduction of the traditional purchasing cycle.

Reducing maverick buying is a good resolution and nearly always pays off. However, it is hard to realize due to all sorts of political considerations and sensitivities in the field of purchasing within enterprises. The introduction of electronic ordering and catalog systems requires a properly defined purchasing structure, which is still lacking in many companies.

With regard to the potential savings that can be obtained in transaction processing, we would like to point out here that the costs related to this mainly consist of personnel and system costs, which are very inflexible in most European countries. Cost advantages in either field can only be realized slowly within the European social structure and legislation. This means the advantages listed are only realized after a far longer period than that sketched by most consultants.

Reverse auctions

Electronic auctions have developed today into the most popular e-procurement solutions. They are, however, not without criticism. Auctions are not new to the business community. Most of us are familiar with antique auctions, organized by reputable companies such as Christies or Sotheby's. Most agricultural products, e.g. corn and wheat, are sold on large, international commodity exchanges where buyers and sellers trade large volumes. Other examples are flowers and vegetables that are in most cases sold daily through auctions. The Internet today allows buyers and purchasing managers to benefit from online auctions. These may come in different forms. Here we differentiate between:

- Open request for information (RFI). In this case potential suppliers are requested to qualify before the actual auction. The buyer wants to validate whether suppliers are actually capable of meeting his requirements beforehand. Apart from that he may need some background information, such as financial status and performance, references, expertise. Or, prior to the actual auction, he may want some initial offer from the supplier in order to test his competitiveness, request for quotation (RFQ).

- Reverse auction. In this type of auction the buyer sets an initial price which suppliers need to meet. Also visible is a target price which the buyer wants to arrive at. If this price level is not reached the contract will not be awarded. During the auction suppliers may be able to follow the actual bids made (see Figure 10.5 for an example). However, the buyer may decide to reveal the actual prices that are provided by the supplier; in these cases the supplier may only see his ranking on the screen.

- Forward auction. Here the seller sets the price. Several buyers need to provide bids to the auctioneer. Also in this case a target sales price may have been indicated. The seller may decide on the same parameters as in the case of a reverse auction.

Needless to say, the reverse auction is most popular among buyers. However, in some cases they may decide to use a forward auction. This type of auction is appropriate when selling salvage or old equipment and inventory.

Auctions may not always be useful. Products and markets should meet certain criteria. Auctions may be used for high volume, standard products that can be supplied by many suppliers. The supply market should be characterized by free competition. The buyer should not show a specific preference for one supplier. The market should be preferably characterized as a buyer's market: there should be sufficient capacity. Finally, the buyer should be sufficiently interesting to a supplier to compensate for the effort needed to engage in a reverse auction.

Benefits for the buyer are numerous. First and foremost the auction generates competition among suppliers that previously may have not been in competition with each other. New suppliers, provided that they qualify, can easily be involved in the auction process. Depending on the work that is needed for preparing the auction, considerable savings both in terms of money and throughput time are possible. Savings have been reported by companies as a result of auctions ranging from 5 per cent to 40 per cent. Another advantage is that since all communication is done electronically the process is well documented which allows for easy tracking and tracing afterwards.

Obviously, there are also some drawbacks which explain why electronic auctions have not expanded as rapidly as many consultants believed at the beginning. All parties involved need to be carefully briefed beforehand; in most cases buyers and suppliers need to be trained in order to get acquainted with the auction software. Next, the buyer should prepare all documentation (including a detailed purchase order specification) and communicate this well in advance. As experience has shown, last-minute changes in specifications and requirements may considerably reduce the willingness of suppliers to participate in the auction. For this reason some people believe that there is nothing new to auctions. Most savings will come, they say, from the preparation that is needed, rather than from the auction itself!

Both the supplier and buyer community seem rather reluctant to adopt this new purchasing technology. Buyers, since they feel that changing from one supplier to another may lead to higher costs and risks than their managers are aware of. Suppliers, since they do not appreciate markets will become more transparent and also because they criticize the lack of ethical behavior from their clients. Examples are known where the buyer still favored his current supplier, notwithstanding the fact that he was not the lowest bidder.

We feel that reverse auctions are going to belong to the standard tool-kit of the future buyer. This tool, however, will need to be used selectively based upon the considerations that have been stated in this section. Buyers should see to it that auctions are executed with the highest of professional standards, based upon fair play. If not, auctions will most certainly damage the relationships buyers have with their suppliers.

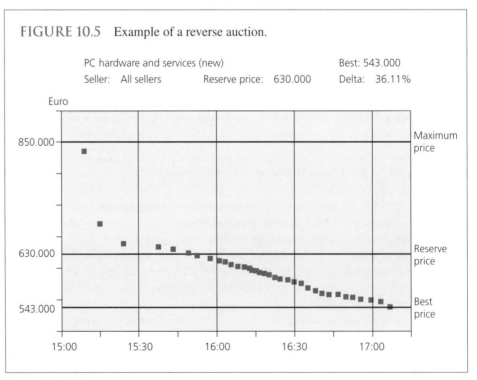

FIGURE 10.5   Example of a reverse auction.

Source: Ariba (2003).

AGENT TECHNOLOGY AND THE INTERNET

So-called software agents are expected to play an important role within e-procurement in the near future. A software agent is a piece of software that can operate more or less independently, is capable of learning (intelligent agents), and in some cases can move across the Internet (mobile agents). These agents are presently used to locate web sites that offer the best price for a given product. They are also used in auctions, where the agents independently participate in the bidding process within the boundary conditions as specified by a given buyer and/or seller. A well-known example is a Spanish academic experiment with an electronic fish market, where homemade agents can participate in the bidding process (http://www.iiia.csic.es/Projects/fishmarket). Agents reduce the workload for users, who would otherwise have to spend considerable time carrying out Internet searches, or standing by to participate in the bidding processes. Some infamous viruses are perhaps the most known example of software agents. Their effects may be very negative, but they are an illustration of the new opportunities which are constantly arising on the worldwide web.

SUMMARY

Independent of whether the various phenomena in the field of e-procurement[13] will prove successful, it is obvious that the traditional B2B landscape is going through fundamental changes. Anticipating and using these means is far from easy and requires a carefully designed corporate strategy, which should give priority to how to arrive at an integrated supply chain. In this chapter we have demonstrated that neither entrepreneurs, nor purchasing managers should rush into things. Rather, they should make a thorough study of what electronic solutions have to offer to realize and support their overall business objectives. Here a distinction can be made between electronic marketplaces and e-procurement systems. Electronic marketplaces can have different forms: we have identified buyer-centric portals, seller-centric portals and electronic marketplaces on the one hand and horizontal and vertical marketplaces on the other. As we have seen, electronic market-

MEMO 10.5   ARE YOU READY FOR E-PROCUREMENT?

- Does the organization have a fully understood purchasing and supply strategy that matches and supports the business strategy of the corporation?
- Is article or commodity management adequately structured through cross-functional buying teams?
- Is an objective procedure available for the selection of suppliers?
- To what extent are operational purchasing/order systems compatible with the electronic solutions that are considered? Is seamless integration possible with current general ledger systems?
- Are structured and documented purchasing procedures in place and adhered to?
- Is purchasing authorization organized?
- Are there clear ordering and handling procedures available supported by work flow document control?
- Are supplier and purchasing contracts regularly revised?

---

13 Here the term is used in the broad sense.

places may support buying consortia and buying communities. E-procurement systems may be based upon different technical solutions. Companies may choose to purchase and implement specific e-procurement software, hosting an e-procurement application at a ASP or using the software, including product catalogs and supplier databases, from the ASP for a license fee.

Much attention should be paid to the question of to what degree the introduction of the solutions mentioned will contribute to the realization of a sustainable and defendable competitive advantage. Based upon the purchasing portfolio, different electronic solutions are available for different portfolio segments. In dealing with routine products e-procurement catalog systems may be most promising. For leverage products reverse auctions have made inroads into the international buying community.

As we see it, the Internet is not a miracle cure for poorly working purchasing organizations. Before large-scale investments are made into e-procurement solutions and electronic markets, it is necessary to check whether the conditions for their successful application within the organizations are present. Using the points listed in Memo 10.5 may be useful. Even if the conditions for a successful introduction are present, the introduction of e-procurement will nevertheless be a tough process. In general it will take much time and effort to ensure the compatibility of the systems involved and, hence, generate the savings that can accrue from them.

Very few enterprises will have the luxury of putting their house in order to make effective use of e-procurement. However, in our opinion there is little choice. Purchasing and supply managers will be forced to invest and to gain experience with the new electronic tools in the field of purchasing. We advise managers to keep their investments low and to control them.

ASSIGNMENTS

10.1 This chapter describes how electronic marketplaces develop within different types of industries. Electronic marketplaces can be initiated by different parties: sellers, buyers and/or intermediary organizations. What factors explain the success of electronic marketplaces? Which of the three marketplaces, mentioned here (initiated by sellers, buyers, intermediaries) will be the most successful in your opinion? Discuss!

10.2 A large manufacturer of handtooling equipment is considering implementing an e-procurement system in one of its manufacturing locations. Describe what it will take to be able to do so effectively. What role would the purchasing department have in such a process?

10.3 Find European examples for each of the types of electronic marketplaces that have been identified by Kaplan and Sawhney.

10.4 Implementing electronic solutions in purchasing should, according to some leading consultants, lead to impressive savings. What sources do these savings come from? Mention at least three possibilities. How easily can these savings be realized?

10.5 Why do companies report such high savings from the application of e-auctions? Mention at least five reasons for these. Discuss why both suppliers and buyers may be reluctant to apply e-auctions.

After studying this chapter you should understand the following:

- The possibilities and impossibilities of integrating the purchasing function into technical design and new product development processes.
- The most important concepts concerning purchasing and quality control.
- Purchasing's role in and contribution to quality management.
- The elements necessary for an approach aimed at improving supplier quality.
- The consequences of the implementation of total quality management for the purchasing organization.

CASE STUDY   SUPPLIERS AS A SOURCE OF INNOVATION: PSA'S PLURIEL PROJECT

PSA started the development of the Citroen C3 Pluriel at the beginning of 1999. The Pluriel was positioned as a fun car for youngsters, offering a stylish design based upon the C3. The Pluriel would feature a flexible roof system: drivers could instantaneously transform the car from a small sedan with an open roof, into a coupe or even into a cabriolet. When the concept was shown at the IAA 1999 auto fair in Frankfurt, the reactions were overwhelming. Shortly after that PSA decided to bring the car out in the market. Given the positive reaction already received, a fast track development project was required and it was decided to start production mid-2002. An incredible time to market! As the basic design of the C3 body was available, the design and construction of the roof system posed the most challenge. PSA knew that for its development they had to rely on one of the larger roof systems manufacturers. At first they con-

sidered the two market leaders, Meritor and Webasto. Given the Pluriel's unique features, Webasto had the impression that they were the only feasible supplier for this one-off roof system. The price proposal they made was identified by PSA purchasing specialists as not realistic. In the meantime, Inalfa, a Dutch specialist supplier of roof systems, with manufacturing facilities in many countries through its newly established office in Paris, had heard about the Citroen C3 Pluriel and was desperate to make an offer to PSA for this unique project. Inalfa's management team decided to bring in a highly challenging business case and competitive pricing. PSA's engineering team was impressed by Inalfa's thorough preparation; after a careful review of Inalfa's technical capabilities it was decided to award the order to them.

In the project, different stakeholders were involved. In order to work out the design, Italdesign was selected by PSA as lead designer and engineer. Italdesign is an Italian company that designs and builds prototypes and niche-models for large car manufacturers.

At their Milan headquarters, Italdesign set up a concurrent, highly international, engineering team, consisting of about 60 engineers from different organizations (25 from PSA, 25 from Italdesign, and 10 from various suppliers). PSA staff from Spain were involved since the new car was to be produced in the Spanish assembly plant. From the outset it was intended that the Citroen C3 and the special C3 Pluriel would be produced on the same production line. Inalfa was one of the suppliers that was represented in the project team. Other suppliers were Wagon for the arches, Hutchinson for the seals and Gestamp for stamped parts.

The Pluriel project was a far more complex undertaking than the projects Inalfa had previously carried out. Several functionalities, like the folding roof, the electrical release, the full-size rear window, and the back door had to be integrated. Tight time schedules challenged Inalfa in finding new ways of working. Intensive collaboration with several development partners was necessary. Furthermore, extensive theoretical validation and computer simulations, with the emphasis on kinematics and strength, preceded practical verification. In this way, Inalfa was able to solve important engineering challenges and time constraints at an early phase of the project. Through endurance and functional tests the folding roof system was further verified and improved. Early supplier involvement was considered a necessity for several suppliers, especially for the sealing system that would be used. For this system, Inalfa involved a German supplier Saargummi. For the other parts four or five main suppliers were selected. In a later phase the concept turned out to be more complex than anticipated, which forced Inalfa to initiate a collaboration with yet another supplier for the rotation frame.

A major challenge in the project has been managing the efforts of all parties involved. In particular, communication became a major issue with so many nationalities involved. Communication took place in five languages: Dutch, French, German, English, and Italian. Differences in working styles between the companies involved posed another challenge. Italdesign has a more practical approach, in contrast to the much more theoretical approach of PSA, leaving Inalfa inbetween on many occasions. In addition, PSA used some unique design methodologies, like FMEA analysis, that had to be used in the integrated development process. Eventually, Inalfa hired some French expertise in this field to master the technique.

Finally, at the beginning of 2003, the manufacturing start-up took place from 30 to 350 units per day. In May 2003 the Citroen Pluriel was produced at full capacity.

The price for the roof system was initially based upon 220 parts. Eventually, the design turned out to consist of 480 parts, of which 80 per cent were new to Inalfa. Notwithstanding the increased complexity of the product, the price per unit remained close to the initial offer. Due to this innovation PSA has entered a new niche market. The Pluriel has been received very well by the market and contributes to PSA's reputation for building cars of extraordinary designs.

Source: Author interviews

INTRODUCTION

The Pluriel Case Study reflects several issues. First of all it shows that to be able to remain in a competitive position, PSA must pay considerable attention to reducing the 'time-to-market' of new car models. This is the period between the time the development of a product is started and the time it is introduced to the market. Japanese companies need considerably less time for this than European companies. And this situation, unfortunately, is not limited to the automotive industry! Second, this Case illustrates the importance of suppliers' contributions in the early development of new products. Suppliers are a major source of ideas at this stage: working together instead of working at arm's length not only leads to a considerable result in terms of engineering lead-time reduction, but also to important cost benefits. If suppliers are involved in the product design at an early stage, they can provide their suggestions about simplification of the design and substitution of materials with components that are easier to process, etc.

This chapter addresses the role and significance of new product development in companies. The role assigned to purchasing in this context will be described and the contribution that purchasing can and/or should make to the company's quality policy will be discussed extensively. It will become clear that the implementation of total quality control generally has far-reaching consequences for the purchasing organization.

PURCHASING AND NEW PRODUCT DEVELOPMENT

Many companies attempt to track down new technologies and products through systematic market research. The results of this research are usually translated by the marketing department into several new product ideas which are then discussed with research and development, and the engineering department. These discussions are often the starting point for projects aimed at improving current products or the development of new ones.

Depending on the nature of the product and the type of company, the development process, starting with conceptualization and ending with introduction to the market, will pass through several stages.

- Product development. In this phase the ideas supplied by the marketing department are translated into a few concrete, but still relatively abstract, functional designs. Such designs describe the functions that the product to be developed will have to fulfill for the user. From these functional designs, the most promising design is selected to be elaborated further.

- Product design. In this phase the functional design is worked out in detail – proposals are made about the materials to be used, the physical properties that the product must satisfy, etc. Often, several product designs are produced which meet the functional design and these can be presented to potential clients at an early stage, in order to get their first reactions and impressions (concept testing). This information enables the engineers to focus on the most promising design. Subsequently, the product design is elaborated in the form of a prototype or mock-up. If necessary this prototype can also be presented to potential buyers and users.

- Preproduction planning. The manufacturability of the product has already been considered during the product design stage. At this stage the production requirements are taken into account. After the prototype has been approved, preparation for production can be started. If it concerns a technically complex product, this phase may take a lot of time and it may be necessary to purchase new production equipment. The capacity requirements of this new equipment will have to be determined based on, among other things, market exploration and sales forecasts. Preproduction planning frequently ends with a number of preproduction series.

- Start of the production. Products from the preproduction series are subjected to thorough examination; based on the results of this examination the product design or the settings of the machines might be adapted so as to limit future production and quality problems to a minimum. One of the problems that might occur in this phase is changing the specifications. Every change is documented in a change-order sent by the engineering department to the purchasing department in order to discuss this with the supplier. This phase means a lot of work for the purchaser involved in the project.

Every change in the specification has to be approved by the supplier, the consequences for the total costs have to be analyzed, the changed product needs to be tested again, etc. This is one of the reasons why it takes so long for a new product to become available for customers. Only when the problems have been taken care of, can actual production commence.

It goes without saying that it is possible to refine this sequence of steps, depending on the nature of the product and the type of company. As the product development process advances, the specifications become more rigid and it becomes more difficult to introduce changes. The consequence for purchasing is that its latitude decreases and the costs of technical changes introduced at a later stage in the process become higher (see Figure 11.1).

Many engineers and developers usually play it safe: their primary interest is in materials and components that solve the technical problem they are faced with. Once a suitable material or construction has been found, tested and approved, the willingness to consider any alternatives (in the form of a different material, component or a substitute product from another supplier) will be limited at a later stage. Any alternatives will have to be tested and approved again, which implies not only a lot of work, but also risks. This desire to to reduce technical risk may result in specific components being channeled in the direction of one particular supplier because of positive experiences with this supplier in the past (see Memo 11.1). The buyer is put in a difficult situation since it is very awkward to negotiate with such a supplier, if one can speak of negotiating at all. Based on his job perception, a buyer will always attempt to have more than one supplier to fall back on. For the buyer to be able to go out into the market, the product preferably must be described in terms of functional specifications (rather than in terms of supplier or brand specifications). There exists, therefore, a kind of natural conflict in the way designers and buyers operate (Figure 11.2) which can only be solved by means of cross-functional development teams.

How do large manufacturers communicate with their first-tier suppliers in product development projects? Some possibilities are:

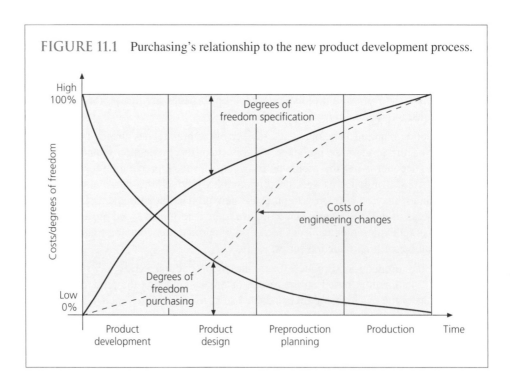

FIGURE 11.1   Purchasing's relationship to the new product development process.

- Purchasing engineering. This is a specialist function to provide the liaison between the engineering department and the purchasing department. Purchasing engineers are members of the design teams, where they will evaluate designs against purchasing-specific criteria. It is their task to bring in specific supply market knowledge and new suppliers at an early stage of design.

- Early supplier involvement (ESI). Suppliers who have proved in the past to be 'best-in-class', are invited to participate in the company's development projects at an early stage. In this way they are able to criticize future designs, suggest alternative materials, come up with ideas for more efficient manufacturing, etc. at a stage where engineering changes can be made without severe cost consequences.

- Residential engineering. A next step is to co-locate engineers from the supplier on a more or less permanent basis within the organization, in order to work on design or

MEMO 11.1 THE VALUE OF SUPPLIER CATALOGS

Some suppliers cleverly take advantage of the uncertainty that engineers experience in their design activities. They make it easy for them by providing a catalog with all the information about the product assortment they carry. Examples are European distributors of technical components who provide electronic catalogs to their clients which list all their products. These concern small articles, such as switches, condensers, resistors, fasteners, etc. The most important technical data are presented for all these articles, together with the article number which can be used to order them.

To specify the technical description of these articles is, of course, a very labor intensive task and, for the sake of convenience, many designers just list the article number from the catalog on their design. The result is that the articles, described in that way, can only be ordered from that specific distributor.

Through this practice some distributors have been able to build captive customer relationships against handsome margins. Electronic catalogs prove to be very successful. They often go with handy terminals, from which orders for materials can be placed directly at the distributor. Obviously, this type of relationship and ordering procedure is facilitated by Internet technology.

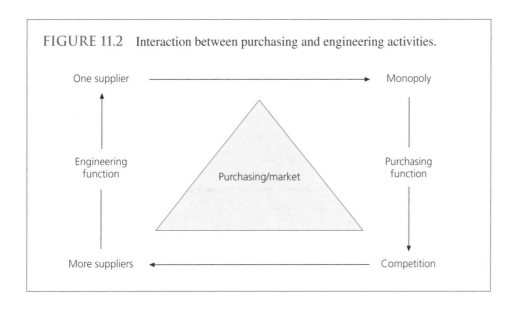

FIGURE 11.2 Interaction between purchasing and engineering activities.

TABLE 11.1 Involving the supplier early in new product development can result in considerable saving

Stage of product design	Degree of design complexity or product uniqueness (%)		
	Low	Average	High
Initial design	2–5	10–25	30–50
Changing existing design	1–3	3–15	15–25
Redesigning to improve quality	10	15–30	40–60

Note: The figures indicate the percentage of savings on the cost price. See Wijnstra (1998) for more research on this subject.

manufacturing problems which appear during the successive stages of development. Residential engineering also relates to a situation where a large original equipment manufacturer has placed engineering specialists at the supplier's premises in order to resolve a variety of technical problems (sometimes referred to as supplier support teams). This is quite common at some large car manufacturers like Honda and Daimler-Chrysler.

Buyers are important scouts for any organization when it comes to spotting new technical developments; in their professional capacity they come into contact with suppliers, products and technologies much more frequently than engineers and developers. Buyers are generalists, while engineers are specialists. Involving buyers in development processes at an early stage can result in the contribution of new knowledge and a better understanding of construction, suitable materials, suppliers, and also the early introduction of supplier knowledge. Practice has shown that early supplier involvement can result in considerable cost reductions and product improvements (see Table 11.1) This is the reason why, for example, Philips Electronics speaks of co-design in addition to co-makership.

Development projects require careful project management. Targets on design-to-cost and time-to-market need to be carefully translated in detailed action plans and cost-budgets. Ideally, the project planning for a new product development project will identify at what stage suppliers will be involved. Memo 11.2 shows how Océ has solved this problem: the company differentiates between four possible relationships with their supplier during the design and development process. A distinction is made between co-design (where a supplier engages in developing specifications), co-development (joint development of a prototype that meets the specifications) and co-making (manufacturing the product according to specifications and production schedule). In this case the term early supplier involvement relates only to the first two situations.

BENEFITS AND RISKS RELATED TO EARLY SUPPLIER INVOLVEMENT

Although early supplier involvement has important benefits for companies, it appears that in practice it is difficult to apply and implement. In some cases companies have found that involving suppliers early in new product design actually has increased development cost

MEMO 11.2   EARLY SUPPLIER INVOLVEMENT AT OCÉ

Océ's range of products contains copying, printing, plotter and document handling systems. Océ develops and produces the main part of these products by itself (see also Case Study at beginning of Chapter 9). The company is heavily research-oriented: annually about 7 per cent of the turnover is invested in research and development. For its new line of copiers Océ has started a technological cooperation with KMWE Precisie Eindhoven and Nedal Aluminum in order to develop a new photocarrier cylinder. This part is one of the high-tech, key components of any copier.

Nedal Aluminum is the supplier of the basic aluminum and KMWE shapes this into the cylinder with high precision. KMWE has been a supplier for Océ for many years, but this new product has many new and much higher technical requirements. For this reason KMWE was selected after a thorough and careful selection process.

For the supplier selection Océ has developed a special questionnaire: the Questionnaire for Preventive Supplier Evaluation. Through this the engineering capacity and capabilities of potential suppliers are assessed and documented. The questionnaire covers the following subjects:

- *Identification details*: relates to subjects like ownership and shareholders of the company, organizational structure, major clients, breakdown of turnover, investments made recently and major suppliers.
- *Technical competence*: relates to the production process, type of machinery and equipment available, transportation equipment and type of manufacturing systems in place, type of materials requirements planning systems used.
- *Financial situation*: here Océ want the supplier to provide detailed financial figures and records.
- *Quality control*: questions here relate to the quality control systems in place, quality certificates, organization of quality function, manuals which are available, method of evaluating suppliers.
- *Price information*: here questions are asked on method of cost price calculation, allocation of overhead costs, and the willingness to cooperate based on open calculations.

Océ has a very clear strategy on product development and the involvement of suppliers in the new product development process. Prior to actually developing a new product, all parts, key components and subassemblies are plotted down into a matrix (see Figure 11.3). The technical aspects and costs of every part are analyzed. Furthermore the supply risk and the availability of each specific component is assessed. Based on this analysis, four quadrants usually apply:

- *Strategic products*. In this quadrant Océ pursues a relationship with prospective suppliers based upon co-development. The example of the photocarrier cylinder fits into this category. Suppliers for this type of components are selected at a very early stage in order to be able to let them participate in the development teams as early as possible. Part of the development and design work is done by the suppliers.
- *Leverage products*. Here Océ pursues a relationship with the supplier based upon early supplier involvement. Actual development of the component is done by Océ itself. The suppliers involved are contacted in the engineering phase, before starting pre-production. At this stage suppliers bring in their ideas on how to manufacture the parts involved in the most efficient way. This may lead to some minor technical changes in the original design of the parts. Next, suppliers will provide prototypes which will be tested by Research and Development.
- *Routine products*. Suppliers of routine products are involved when all design and development work and engineering activities have been finished. In fact they need to submit their proposals based on detailed designs and specifications, as provided to them by Océ. Relationships with suppliers here can be characterized as jobbers or routine suppliers.
- *Bottleneck products*. This type of component normally causes a lot of trouble given the large dependence on the supplier. When identified early during the design and development process it is assured that sufficient alternatives are considered.

▶

Through this Development portfolio (see also Wijnstra and Ten Pierick, 1999) the joint purchasing and R&D teams are able to decide which supplier to involve for what component at what time. Experiences are that only a very limited number of suppliers are invited to participate in the new product development process at a very early stage. However, their activities may easily cover 80% of the targeted cost price of the new product!

whilst time to market targets were not realized. It is therefore clear that companies need to think about the conditions that should be in place in order to develop effective collaborative relationships with suppliers.

In assessing the benefits of early supplier involvement, companies need to differentiate between short-term and long-term benefits (Van Echtelt, 2004).[1] Short-term benefits may result from improved product quality, reduction of product cost, reduction of development time and reduction of development costs. These benefits result from the suppliers' in-depth knowledge of components and technologies, which enables them to match component designs better with their manufacturing capabilities. Long-term benefits may consist of more efficient and effective collaboration in future new product development projects, the alignment of future technology strategies, a better access to the technology resources of the supplier and the contribution of suppliers to product differentiation. The Senseo coffee machine that resulted from a joint development between Sara Lee DE and Philips may serve as an illustration here. Since in most European countries the market for coffee is saturated, Sara Lee DE was looking for a new coffee concept. In particular, they were looking for a concept that was more upmarket to satisfy the increasing needs of Dutch consumers for quality coffee. Italian espresso machines were meeting these needs but they

FIGURE 11.3   Development portfolio as used by Océ.

---

1 Van Echtelt (2004), 'New product development: shifting suppliers into gear', PhD thesis, Eindhoven University of Technology, Eindhoven.

were laborious, expensive and troublesome to operate. The new concept would need to be efficient, affordable and easy to operate. Since, Sara Lee DE did not have any experience with designing and manufacturing coffee machines, they turned to Philips to find out their willingness to participate in this challenging project. Based upon the initial idea, Philips set out to develop a new coffee machine enabling Sara Lee DE to present an innovative, new coffee concept based upon so called 'coffee pads' that could be easily exchanged and would come in different tastes. The product was introduced to the market and immediately became a tremendous success. After a careful market introduction, the concept has now been rolled out to other European countries. Introduction to the US market was considered from the start. The Senseo project is a nice example of a profound product innovation that would not have been feasible without the active participation from the outset of an large, experienced and knowledgeable supplier. Needless to say, the relationship between Sara Lee DE and Philips extends far beyond the traditional buyer–seller relationship. Both companies benefit from the value that the concept has created for them.

However, collaborating with suppliers in new product development is not without risks. In most cases companies are afraid of losing crucial product or process knowledge and skills. Moreover, they fear becoming locked into a specific supplier's technology which may make them totally dependent on him in the future. Some large companies expect that early supplier involvement will lead to higher relationship costs, since they need to meet and discuss with the supplier intensively. Therefore they are afraid that involving suppliers early will actually slow down the development process. Finally, risks are perceived to result from diverging objectives and levels of commitment to the outcome of the project. In general, companies establish inter-organizational relationships when they think these are beneficial to them. The presence of mutual interest is an important incentive to remain committed to the inter-organizational relationship. However, the expectations of the customer and the supplier about the way the collaboration takes place, and its outcome, may change over time and they may even may end up in conflict with each other. Regular review meetings between supplier and buyer are therefore necessary to make sure that perceptions and expectations between the parties involved are still in tune.

As research has shown companies that want to involve suppliers in new product development need to develop a long-term view on their make or buy policies, supplier selection and other strategic supply processes. Moreover, they should be experienced in applying modern project management techniques. Finally, they should be able to develop partnership relationships with suppliers that go far beyond the traditional buyer–seller relationship.[2]

PURCHASING AND QUALITY CONTROL

Definition of terms: quality and quality assurance

After the product specifications have been released the purchasing department must ensure that they will be met by the supplier. The products that are to be manufactured must remain within these specifications. In addition, the purchasing department has to ensure that the suppliers will honor their agreements on other points, such as delivery time, delivery quantity and price. In this way buyers need to reflect total quality management approaches in their ways of working.

What exactly is quality? The literature on the subject contains almost as many definitions as there are authors who have written about it. A distinction is made between con-

---

2 See for more on this topic Wijnstra (1998) and Van Echtelt (2004).

cepts such as 'functional quality', 'physical quality', 'fitness-for-use', etc. One common definition of quality is: 'The total of features and characteristics of a product or service that bear on its ability to satisfy a given need' (American National Standards Institute). Without wanting to do any injustice to this definition, we favor IBM's simple definition of quality:

> *Quality is the degree in which customer requirements are met. We speak of a quality product or quality service when both supplier and customer agree on requirements and these requirements are met'*

The requirements mentioned in this definition can relate to the technical properties of a product. However, they can also relate to user-friendliness, ease of maintenance, delivery agreements and packaging instructions. Here, we propose to take a broad view in that the quality concept is related to more than just the physical properties of the product.

Most large companies initiate quality programs for the purpose of effecting a change in attitude towards quality. These programs also address the issue of quality control. Quality control is defined as: 'Making sure that the requirements are met' and being able to demonstrate this objectively. This implies that for every transaction between customer and supplier, they need to agree on:

- the basic requirements of the transaction;
- the way in which the requirements are to be realized;
- how to check that the requirements are (being) fulfilled;
- the measures to be taken when the requirements/expectations are not met.

These steps form the four basic elements of the requirements-verification cycle, which is shown in Figure 11.4.

In summary, quality control entails all activities and decisions aimed at taking the organization's products and services to the desired quality level and to maintaining that level. Quality control therefore requires intensive consultation and sound tuning between the various departments in the organization and with outside suppliers and customers. After the desired quality level has been established, the complete production process must be organized in such a way that this level of quality is reached and maintained in a con-

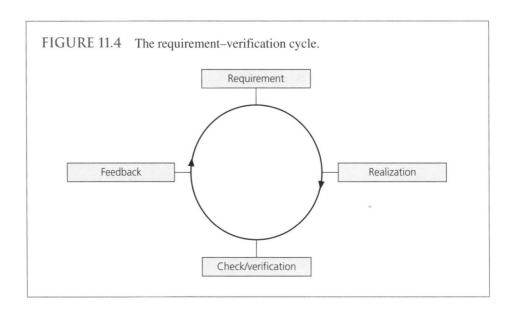

FIGURE 11.4   The requirement–verification cycle.

trollable manner. To accomplish this, quality management has at its disposal four inter-related functions: setting standards, assessment, control, and assurance. This last function will now be addressed in more detail.

Quality assurance is an important criterion for supplier selection. What guarantees can the supplier give with regard to design and technical specifications? According to what quality standards is it proposed to operate?

Quality assurance concerns keeping up the methods and procedures of quality control, i.e. systematically checking that they are efficient, that they lead to the desired objective, and that they are applied correctly. Internal company assessment of these issues is often called auditing; external assessment is referred to as verification. An external assessment establishes the degree to which the methods and procedures used satisfy the conditions which have been recorded in national and international standards. The best known are the ISO-9000 standards, which are accepted in many European countries. These will be discussed later.

The collection of methods and procedures used for quality control is called the quality system, which is usually recorded in a quality handbook. This handbook should be the formal reflection of the way in which quality control, including quality assurance, actually functions in practice.

THE COSTS OF QUALITY

Crosby (1984) pointed out that it is not so much quality, as the lack of it, that costs money. The concept of quality costs can be used to initiate quality improvement initiatives. In many companies a considerable number of man hours are spent on the inspection of incoming goods and on solving acute quality problems (troubleshooting). The costs involved are often invisible and many companies have absolutely no idea what the lack of quality is costing them. Making these costs transparent starts with classifying them. In practice three types of quality costs are distinguished:

- prevention costs – the costs of preventing errors;
- assessment costs – the costs related to the timely recognition of errors;
- correction costs – the costs that result from rectifying mistakes.

Prevention costs are all costs that are related to actions in the context of preventing quality errors. Prevention costs therefore include the expenses related to the development, implementation and control of the system of total quality control. This concerns matters such as:

- conducting systematic product inspections;
- executing process controls;
- ensuring that product inspections and process control (auditing) are conducted systematically and periodically;
- investigations to uncover the causes of errors and mistakes;
- establishing the internal organization of quality control;
- drawing up specifications, procedures, instructions and regulations for the total quality control system;
- the development of special testing and measuring equipment and other tools in support of quality assessment;
- education, training and motivation of personnel on quality management.

Assessment costs are incurred to minimize the consequences of errors. Examples are:

- incoming or acceptance inspection of purchased goods;
- inspection of intermediate and semi-manufactured products;
- sorting the production (100 per cent inspection) to track down faulty products and to separate them from good products;
- final inspection of products and quality assessment of finished products;
- registration and processing of and reporting on the measuring data.

Quality can be present in various degrees. This must be taken into account during the inspection procedure of a product series. Some of the rejected items may be made suitable for the client's production process by minimal treatment. However, these corrections come with a price-tag. The so-called error costs are usually divided into internal and external categories. Internal error costs (including wastes and losses) emerge as a result of mistakes which are noticed in time, i.e. before the product is delivered to the customer. These include:

- the costs of corrective measures;
- losses due to product downgrading;
- losses due to a reduced speed or even standstill of production, to the extent that they are caused by quality deviations in materials or components.

External error costs are a result of flaws identified by the customer. This group includes:

- the costs of processing complaints;
- costs made for settling customer claims and disputes;
- costs of processing return shipments from customers;
- loss of 'goodwill'.

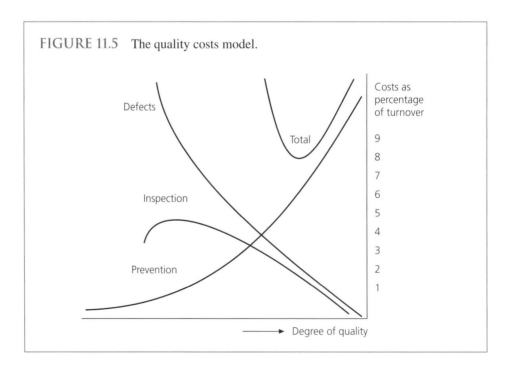

FIGURE 11.5   The quality costs model.

Over many years the emphasis has shifted from correction to prevention. In an attempt to reduce the total quality costs, preventive quality control has been enhanced. This is illustrated by Figure 11.5 which shows the quality costs model.

SUPPLIER QUALITY ASSURANCE

An important role in the implementation of total quality management is reserved for the purchasing department. This is because the quality of the finished product is determined to a large extent by the quality of the raw materials and components. Working on improving the quality offered by the suppliers is therefore a main task for buyers. For this reason many large manufacturers in Europe have established supplier quality assurance (SQA) programs (see Memo 11.3).

To improve the quality of their products, many companies opt for an approach based on prevention. Cooperation is required from every department in the company, and this also applies to the purchasing department. With regard to purchasing, the objective of prevention is to maintain and/or improve the quality of goods and services to be purchased. This is based on selecting the supplier who can guarantee a sufficient level of quality. It is important that the supplier can also guarantee this quality level for the future. The preventive approach is expressed by the following measures.

- Preparing the purchase order specification. A sound preparation is half the battle. Many problems can be prevented if there is an up-to-date, complete purchase order specification and it goes without saying that this specification contains a technical

MEMO 11.3 SUPPLIER QUALITY ASSURANCE AT IBM

Large companies devote a lot of attention to improving cooperation across business functions. In this context IBM started developing a program to achieve 'zero defects' in cooperation with Philip Crosby. Top managers in all IBM branches took quality courses. These managers developed zero-defects programs in every production plant. The first initiatives were aimed at shifting attention from the detection and correction of errors to the prevention of errors.

The suppliers were invited to participate in the seminars, for the purpose of acquainting them with IBM's objective of zero defects, and to convince them of the importance of this objective. The role of the suppliers in all this was strongly emphasized. The supplier's employees were the next link that had to be made aware of the quality message.

Potential suppliers were selected on the basis of a checklist. The total quality performances of the supplier were considered: conformance, quality of production, the supplier's attitude towards quality and response to quality problems, facilities and personnel.

The quality performance (in a broad sense) of existing suppliers is evaluated continuously. One important parameter is the so-called quality-conformance of the supplier. Conformance in percentages is the ratio of the number of accepted deliveries divided by the total number of deliveries in one month. A delivery is accepted when inspected samples meet the standards. The suppliers are audited periodically. In addition, delivery reliability is measured and assessed, as are the price and cost behavior and the administrative accuracy of the supplier!

Most production plants inform their suppliers about their performance on the subjects mentioned on a monthly basis. Every year the best supplier receives an award (the IBM Supplier Award). All of these measures are aimed at one objective: motivating suppliers towards continuous product and process improvements.

description, supplemented with designs. It will also contain an estimate of the materials requirements for the short and middle term, and additional logistic requirements such as packaging and transportation needs. At this stage clear sign-off procedures are important. The release of designs to suppliers cannot take place without the purchasing department's approval. This procedure also encompasses (future) engineering changes.

- Preliminary qualification of (potential) suppliers. Here the distinction between potential and existing suppliers must be made. Potential suppliers are sent a questionnaire before they can qualify for an order. The purpose of this questionnaire is to gain insight into the delivery possibilities of these suppliers. After a positive evaluation of the responses, a second round takes place. A team consisting of a buyer, a quality expert and a production manager visits the supplier and subjects the quality system in particular to an investigation (quality audit). A statement is then made about a possible order. As a rule, manufacturers document the results of their investigation and report on these to the supplier's management. Weaknesses found in the supplier's quality organization and process are discussed. Corrective measures are suggested and agreed upon. These are to be written down by the supplier in a quality improvement program. The activities recorded in this program are checked in periodical progress meetings. Based on the observed progress it is determined whether a supplier qualifies for orders related to new (development) projects or if he can only supply for existing projects. Of course there is a third possibility: that the relationship will eventually be terminated.

- Sample inspection procedure. The next step on the road to acceptance of a new supplier is the sample inspection procedure. The supplier is requested to manufacture a sample product in cooperation with the design department. This product will then be assessed on its conformance with the requirements as agreed beforehand. Suggestions to achieve improvement of the product can be elaborated by the supplier as well as by the development team. This type of cooperation results in a certain degree of co-design. A number of large manufacturers use the number of times that the sample has to be offered for final approval (the initial sampling reject rate) as a measure for the supplier's design quality. The most important objective at this stage is to establish the degree to which the tools (molds, templates) that will be used to produce the products, will meet the requirements.

- Delivery of first and subsequent preproduction series. The next step is to have the prospective supplier manufacture a preproduction series. Specialists from the customer company will be present during production to audit the process. Attention is paid specifically to the degree of process control and the functioning of the quality control organization. Afterwards both strong and weak points of the process are analyzed and agreements are made about adjusting the process. In the end this cooperation can result in a partnership agreement.

- Manufacture of the first production series. This is the moment of truth. Has the supplier lived up to his agreements? Is he capable of really meeting the zero-defects requirement? The customer checks the process completely: all products are inspected for quality (100 per cent inspection). If everything is satisfactory, then the level of inspection is reduced. The ultimate goal is to reach a situation of direct acceptance of delivered products, i.e. without prior inspection. In this way the customer avoids the incoming inspection, which is a major source of costs.

- Quality agreement and certification. As a rule, a quality agreement is closed when the objective of zero-defects has been reached. This agreement determines that the supplier will manufacture the products involved in the way agreed upon with the manufacturer. It also describes the change procedures, which are so very important: i.e. in what way should the manufacturer and the supplier act if it is necessary to change the design and/or specifications. The quality agreement usually involves one product (article code). The supplier who proves able to supply, without any defects or mistakes, all deliveries of all products which are purchased from him is awarded a certificate by the manufacturer. The certified supplier is placed on the final list of preferred suppliers which means he is also eligible for new, future projects. If there are no problems, these suppliers' deliveries are subjected to inspection only a few times each year.

■ Periodic verification. The extent to which the tasks which have been agreed upon with the supplier in the context of product and/or process improvement are being realized, must be checked periodically. Should it turn out that the tasks were set too high, adjustments can be made. If the tasks are fulfilled, then this results in new tasks being formulated. In this way the concept of continuous quality improvement (or *kaizen*) in the relationship with the supplier is given substance. At this stage many large manufacturers work with computer-supported supplier rating systems, which are used to record and report on the suppliers' performances on several points (see Memo 11.4).

A few closing remarks in conclusion of this section now follow.

■ Supplier selection. Selection of new suppliers is a cross-functional issue. Ideally, the following functions should be involved: purchasing, design, quality, production, production planning. Considering Ford, for example, the cross-functional product

---

MEMO 11.4   SUPPLIER RATING AT ALCATEL BELL ANTWERP

'Alcatel Bell only buys from sources which have been selected on the basis of their ability to meet requirements' (ISO 9001, par. 4.6.2.). These sources are registered in the Procurement Management Systems Database as 'approved', 'potential', or 'discontinued'. Any buyer can purchase from the approved sources. Purchase from suppliers with the status of 'potential' or 'discontinued' are subjected to the approval of senior buyers.

The quantity and identity of purchased goods is always verified at the receiving gate. Whether or not additional incoming inspection is performed depends on the nature of the purchased materials and the confidence Bell Alcatel has in the supplier; this confidence is indicated by the Incoming Inspection Category (IIC) which once again features in the Procurement Management System Database.

The IIC ranges from 0 to 9. The IIC provides us with a steering mechanism enabling us to optimize the incoming inspection resources. We judge quality performance of a supplier by comparison with others who supply similar components. This comparison is based on two indices:

1 The IIC, which is a measure of the amount of incoming inspection we still have to perform and which consists of an average of the evaluated IICs.

2 The Quality Index (QI) based on the quality of actual deliveries. This QI takes into account the percentage of deliveries with a problem and the percentage of delivered products with a problem.

For each percentage point, 5 points are deducted from a level arbitrarily set at 1000. Based on this score suppliers are at present considered to be:

very good   QI > 990
good   990 > QI > 950
poor   950 > QI > 900
bad   QI < 900

Source: Bell Alcatel, *Quality On Time Magazine*, 1st Quarter, 1991 development teams request two or three qualified suppliers to make a proposal for the design of new components. Following analysis, the buyer negotiates with the supplier. If this negotiation leads to acceptance of the proposal, the supplier usually remains solely responsible for the delivery during the lifecycle of the product ('life-of-type responsibility').

■ Functional design. Industrial customers must enable their suppliers to study the design of the complete subassembly beforehand. This is in line with the growing trend of drawing up only functional specifications. Based on these specifications, the supplier can submit a design proposal. The customer's designers should concentrate on the design of essential parts and not on designing, for instance, valves and switches.

■ Feedback and recognition. Feedback and recognition are prerequisites to motivate suppliers towards a better performance. Looking at a company such as Hewlett-Packard, it is seen that they assess their suppliers every 3 months, every 6 months and every 12 months, depending on the nature of the delivered components. In the assessment they judge technology, quality, response time, reliability and costs. In addition there are consultations between members of the Hewlett-Packard purchasing teams and the major suppliers, in which the results and possibilities for improvement are discussed in detail. Just as for IBM (see Memo 11.3) and other large manufacturers, Hewlett-Packard provides an annual award to the best-performing supplier.

■ Dependency. Raising quality requirements leads to a reduction of the number of suppliers. For many buyers, this development has resulted in the fear that suppliers might be gaining a more powerful position *vis-a-vis* the buyers. This fear is not completely justified because, as a result of the new cooperative relationships, many suppliers are also becoming more dependent on large manufacturers. Companies that start to function as 'single source' suppliers get involved in a product policy they have no control over, and as such they have no guarantees that the lifecycle of the product is long enough for them to recover the investments they make. Large manufacturers must not lose sight of the fact that it is of vital importance to the suppliers that they keep making profits. Both parties would suffer if the supplier's financial means were insufficient to invest in R&D, process innovation, training, etc.

■ Testing relationships. To uncover the suppliers' needs, Ford Supplier Relations conducts a confidential survey annually. Several suppliers are asked to describe in detail how they experience their cooperation with Ford. The information gathered in this way is passed on to all management levels of the departments of quality control, design, production control and purchasing. To motivate suppliers towards just-in-time deliveries, Ford also organizes regular seminars in areas such as statistical process control and total quality management.

ASSESSING SUPPLIER QUALITY: DIAGNOSTIC METHODS

Several methods are available for the evaluation or assessment of suppliers' quality policies. Earlier, a distinction was made between internal and external assessment. As a rule, the following methods for assessing a supplier's resources are at the buyer's disposal:

■ product audit

■ process audit

■ systems audit.

The product audit provides an image of the degree to which a company succeeds in making everything run perfectly, i.e. according to the standards and demands established by the company itself. The product is judged and every flaw is registered, the cause located and removed. Frequently, the observed deviations are awarded defect points in terms of reject rates. The total score provides, to some extent, an image of the quality level of the entire production process.

The process audit is a systematic investigation of the extent to which the (technical) processes are capable of meeting the established standards in a predictable way. It is also checked whether the raw materials, semi-manufactured materials, etc. are satisfactory, and whether the job instructions and process instructions are complete and clear. In short, the process audit investigates whether the process operators have at their disposal all the facilities (including expertise) required to ensure sound and controlled production. This is also sometimes called a 4M audit (man, materials, machines, methods).

The systems audit compares the quality system to external standards. A standard, or norm, is used which is a generally accepted guideline. Standards can be either general standards or company-specific standards. Examples of general standards are the Allied Quality Assurance Publications (AQAP), originating from the military, and the European NEN-ISO standards. The latter are presented in Table 11.2.

One major company-specific system standard that is used for auditing suppliers is the Ford Q101 procedure. The supplier is required to answer questions related to some 20 subjects. Questions are answered by means of awarding a score between 0 and 10. The total score gives an indication of the quality of the production process. Volvo employs a systems audit which is based on the Ford Q101 system. Table 11.3 shows the subjects that are addressed in such an audit.

External verification contributes to the assurance of the quality system or, as the case may be, to keeping up the quality system, and it also demonstrates that the system meets the required standards.

Many suppliers strive to live up to the standards, especially the NEN-ISO standards. A supplier who meets these standards becomes eligible for certification. Whether or not the candidate-supplier possesses one or more certificates plays a major role in purchasing's decision to use this particular supplier.

Many companies have their organization assessed by an independent organization in the context of a quality certifying program. In most European countries Certification Councils have been founded during the last 10 years. These councils are the central (national) institutions that confer competence on certifying organizations to give out NEN-ISO 9001, 9002 or 9003 certificates to organizations that meet the relevant standards. Such

TABLE 11.2 The ISO 9000 series of quality assurance standards

Standard	Title
ISO 9000	Guidelines for selection and application of ISO 9000 through 9004
ISO 9001	Requirements concerning quality control in purchasing, development, production and sales (equivalent to AQAP 1)
ISO 9002	Requirements concerning quality control in purchasing, production and sales (equivalent to AQAP 4)
ISO 9003	Requirements concerning quality control of final inspection and testing (equivalent to AQAP 9)
ISO 9004	Guidelines for the organization of a quality system
ISO 8402	Terminology and definitions

a certificate is evidence of the company's capability with regard to the quality of the system, at least for the period of its validity.

Not all manufacturers attach the same value to these general standards and accompanying certificates. Some continue to use their own company-specific standards, which suppliers must meet to qualify for cooperation. Examples are the military AQAP standards and the Ford Q101 standards mentioned earlier. Even during a long-term agreement between supplier and manufacturer, periodical checking (especially of the system, the process and the product) against the standards, is necessary. Based on the results of the audits, the decision is made to either continue the agreement or to start looking for an alternative supplier.

TABLE 11.3 Structure of systems audit automobile manufacturers

		Action plan						
No.	Subject	Jan	Feb Mar	Apr May	Jun July	Aug Sept	Oct Nov	Dec
1.	Organization							
2.	Planning							
3.	Documentation and management of technical changes							
4.	Manufacturing equipment control							
5.	Production – procedures – instructions							
6.	Inspection – procedures – instructions							
7.	Standards							
8.	Means of inspection							
9.	Quality assurance purchased components							
10.	Process parameters							
11.	In-process inspection							
12.	Final inspection							
13.	Sampling instructions							
14.	Nonconformance							
15.	Quality and inspection status							
16.	Materials handling							
17.	Training personnel							
18.	Documentation and registration							
19.	Corrective measures							
20.	Volvo inspections at suppliers							

Classification		Required points
A1	Qualified	825–855
A2	Qualified, with comments	755–820
B1	Acceptable	645–750
B2	Acceptable, with reservation	535–640
C	Not acceptable	

IMPLEMENTING SUPPLIER QUALITY ASSURANCE: CONSEQUENCES FOR PURCHASING

As a rule, the implementation of total quality management requires considerable adjustments in terms of structure, systems and patterns of communication. The same applies to the purchasing department that wants to pursue a specific policy with regard to supplier quality assurance. Some of the most important changes that will have to be prepared for are:

- Clear task descriptions. There is not much point in formulating a general policy without formulating clear and unambiguous tasks. For that reason it must be very clear what supplier quality assurance is expected to yield in terms of, for example:
  - maximum rejection percentages per article code or per supplier;
  - the average term in which rejection reports must be dealt with (per buyer);
  - number of quality agreements closed with suppliers;
  - number of certified suppliers, etc.

- Clarity concerning supplier selection. As the demands made on suppliers increase, there are also higher demands on the manufacturer's entire organization, and on the purchasing department in particular. It must be clear who within the company is competent to enter into relationships with suppliers. In particular it must be clear who is responsible for the ultimate selection of suppliers. Requirements must be communicated to the suppliers from one central point so as to prevent misunderstandings.

- Quality first. Taking responsibility for quality also means being accountable and being judged on it. If the ultimate selection of suppliers is made by the purchasing department, then it must also be possible to call this department to account on the quality these suppliers deliver. This means that rejection percentages, the number of quality agreements, etc. are becoming part of the buyer's annual assessment.

- To measure is to know. It is essential that suppliers receive feedback on their performance. This is done in the form of a report on the findings of the audit which has been carried out, but is also needed in the form of a supplier rating score on subjects such as rejection, too late or too early deliveries, administrative errors, etc. This requires the appropriate administrative procedures, which should be computerized where necessary. Producing such data is not necessarily a simple matter, because the basic information is often stored in different systems and in various locations within the company.

The implementation of quality control in organizations is frequently a process of trial and error, with many ups and downs. The same goes for introducing a supplier policy based on quality principles. The extent to which problems occur regarding these aspects provides an indication of the extent to which suppliers are really seen, or experienced, as an essential link in the business chain.

SUMMARY

In this chapter the interfaces between purchasing, new product development and quality assurance have been shown. As the competitive environments of organizations become more turbulent, issues such as time-to-market, flexibility and product and service quality become more important. In these circumstances it is crucial to do things right the first time, because every error leads to time loss and extra costs.

It has been shown that cooperation between engineering, purchasing and suppliers offers considerable opportunities. As the product development process advances, the product specifications become more and more fixed, and it therefore becomes more difficult to introduce changes. Furthermore, changes made at a later stage will make the costs rise exponentially. Buyers are important scouts when it comes to spotting new technological developments that occur in the supplier market. Buyers are generalists, while designers and engineers are predominantly specialists. To them, the technical solution is often more important than supply. To prevent technical problems in the future, designers will tend to operate as specifically as possible and to record their designs in detail. This may go against the buyer's interests: he would like to see the product design drawn up in functional terms, so he can use different sources of supply in the future.

Suppliers increasingly are considered as a major source of new product innovation. As competition becomes more intensive, companies need to constantly improve and innovate their existing product offerings. Given the stringent targets on development cost and time-to-market, suppliers are more and more involved in the new product development processes of their customers. This, however, poses higher demands on the purchasing function in that suppliers need to be selected and screened thoroughly in terms of their technical capabilities. Next, they need to be integrated in the new product development process effectively. Here, companies may differentiate between co-development, early supplier involvement and a situation in which the supplier just has to meet the customer's specifications. Timing when to involve a specific supplier in the new product development process therefore is crucial. In doing so buyers need to balance the benefits of introducing a supplier early in the new product development process against the risks associated with this activity.

The product design is the basis for product quality. The term 'quality' has been taken in a broad sense, i.e. as 'the degree in which the requirements are met'. It has been seen that this concept entails more than just the technical properties. Quality control contains all activities and decisions whose purpose is to bring the organization's product to the desired quality level and to keep it there. These terms are central in the discussion of supplier quality assurance. The purpose of supplier quality assurance is improvement of supplier quality in the broadest sense. Some elements involved in a quality approach towards suppliers are:

- preparation of the purchase order specification;
- preliminary qualification of (potential) suppliers;
- sample inspection procedure;
- inspection of first and following preproduction series;
- inspection of first and following production series;
- quality agreement and certification;
- periodic verification.

Several methods used by manufacturers to assess the qualities of their suppliers were considered and the distinction between the product audit, the process audit and the system audit was explored. With regard to the latter it is general practice to follow the ISO standards. The most widely known and followed systems audit developed by manufacturers is Ford's Q101.

ASSIGNMENTS

11.1 What kinds of risks are related to involving suppliers early in new product development projects? Answer this question from the perspective of (a) the buyer and (b) the new product development engineer.

11.2 What kinds of benefits would you as a manager of a company require in order to make up for the risks that were mentioned when answering the previous question?

11.3 In order to establish an effective collaboration with suppliers in a new product development project, who would you engage from your firm and the suppliers involved? What would you need to arrange for previously, before kicking off the project, in order to prevent misunderstandings and problems?

11.4 What activities would be needed in order to arrive at a situation in which a supplier is able to deliver zero defects?

11.5 Which types of quality costs can be distinguished? Provide at least two examples of every type. To what extent can the purchasing department contribute to a reduction of the quality costs?

After studying this chapter you should understand the following:

- The definition of supply chain management and the basic supply chain concepts.
- The most important steps in the materials planning cycle.
- How supply chain activities can be structured within organizations.
- Characteristics of just-in-time scheduling and purchasing.
- The most important elements of a purchasing information system.

CASE STUDY   SUPPLY CHAIN MANAGEMENT HONG KONG STYLE

The impact and significance of an integrated approach towards purchasing and supply chain management can be illustrated by means of the development of Li&Fung from Hong Kong. As a result of a drastic reorientation in recent years, this trade company has expanded enormously.

Li&Fung started in 1906 as a traditional purchasing agent. Simple household and consumer goods were purchased at a provision rate for customers in the US and Europe. Production orders were allocated by Li&Fung among suppliers from the Chinese mainland on the basis of competitive tenders.

Today, the company has 62 purchasing offices in over 35 countries, most of which are situated in South-east Asia. Based upon the specifications of the western customer (predominantly American and European department stores) Li&Fung designers may develop a range of products under the customer's private label. After approval of the design by the customer, the best manufacturer for the production order is selected within the network of manufacturers in South-east Asia. Given their

volume, Li & Fung works with a large number of carefully selected manufacturers. The company always makes sure it has about 50 per cent of the turnover of a specific supplier in order to make sure that it is always treated by its suppliers as a preferred customer. A dedicated quality inspector will be on site to supervise the production order and to ensure that the products meet the agreed specifications and to monitor social and environmental conditions. The purchasing offices of Li&Fung supply all necessary raw and other materials (textiles, yarn, buttons, zips, packaging) to the manufacturer. Because of its scale, Li&Fung can stipulate far better conditions and qualities for their raw materials and components than the individual manufacturers can. After production, Li&Fung takes care of the shipment and transportation. The advantage lies in the consolidation of deliveries: different shipments for different customers may be consolidated into one container so that transport costs for the customer are as low as possible. Here, too, the company profits from its expertise and scale. Li&Fung make no secret of their network. If required, the customer can visit the production facilities. Li&Fung's integrated way of working allows them to work at 40 per cent lower costs, compared to when departments stores would take care of their business themselves. Li&Fung's success is reflected in their financial figures: over the past decade the company produced double digit growth figures annually.

Li&Fung is an example of a new generation of logistics business integrators, such as we expect to see many more of in the coming years. These business integrators will turn the traditional supply chains upside down. Companies will arise that own nothing and nevertheless control everything. They will not be very capital intensive and have few assets. They will, however, have superior logistics and financial information systems, and will work with a great deal of discipline. They will have broad supplier networks at their disposal with which they

maintain long-lasting relations that they continue to develop. What is essential to their business model is to create the position of chain director – a position that has to be carefully developed and strengthened.

This example also demonstrates the key factors to success for effective and successful supply chain management: a strong position in the customer-supplier network, supported by advanced information technology and creative entrepreneurship. The key element is not the price that Li&Fung offers its customers, but rather the integrated value proposition for the design, purchasing, and logistics for a complete production line. It is an example of an enterprise that is capable of successfully linking customer networks directly to its supplier networks.[1]

Source: Margretta, J. (1998), 'Fast, global and entrepreneurial: supply chain management Hong Kong style', *Harvard Business Review*, September-October, 103–114.

INTRODUCTION

This chapter addresses the relationship between purchasing and supply chain management. In this context the focus is on several important concepts and developments in the field of logistics management. The materials planning cycle is described, which will make clear how materials planning processes affect the purchasing order cycle and the incoming materials flow. In discussing this subject the chapter will differentiate between different supply structures that can be encountered in industry. Hence the distinction will be made between order-based materials processes and forecast-based materials processes. Given its importance there will be ample discussion of the subject of just-in-time manufacturing (JIT), lean supply and the impact of these concepts on purchasing and supplier relationships. Finally, this chapter discusses the major elements and principles in designing effective purchasing information systems.

PURCHASING AND SUPPLY CHAIN MANAGEMENT: DEFINITIONS

Today companies use the term supply chain management to denote the way in which supply processes are managed and structured. Supply chain management relates to the way in which materials processes are managed within the company. However, the term relates also to the way in which the external materials processes are managed. Here, we can differentiate between the outgoing materials flow and the incoming materials flow. The former relates to the way in which finished products are distributed by the company to its

1 van Weele (2003).

customers. This activity is commonly denoted as physical distribution. The incoming materials flow, obviously, covers all activities needed to optimize the goods flows up from suppliers to the point of consumption within the company itself. This activity used to be referred to as materials management. In many cases, the scope of supply chain management goes one step further in that it also relates to optimizing the materials flows from the supplier's suppliers to the company. As we will see later, supply chain management has matured due to the fact that advanced information systems have become available, which are able to trace and track complex materials flows in a great detail.

Supply chain thinking started several decades ago with logistics management. The term 'logistics' originally stems from the military organization and was already in use in the days of Louis XIV of France. Even then it was clear that the effectiveness of any military organization or operation did not depend solely on the weapons, the power and the fighting spirit of the soldiers. It was also affected by the possibilities of transportation and the efficient supply of ammunition and food. The rationalized consideration of the transportation and supply of materials, food and ammunition was called logistics. The French military successes of that time were mainly due to the importance that was given to logistics.

Logistics and flexibility go hand in hand. Flexibility receives a lot of attention in many companies today where functional thinking still dominates. In a functional organization individual departments such as sales, production, product development administration, purchasing and personnel, essentially are managed as separate entities. In most cases the managers responsible for each of these business areas report directly to the board. Each department has very specific tasks which are established in annual departmental budgets. Realization of these budgetary targets is an important factor in the assessment of managers and they therefore often strive to realize their own budget targets, even at the expense of other departments.

This practice can easily lead to departments operating fairly autonomously so that coordination of the whole is left to the interplay of forces between the departments themselves.

Logistics and supply chain management aim to counterbalance the shortcomings of functional thinking, by focusing on those processes through which customers can be better served. Logistics and supply chain management favor a process approach rather than a functional approach. All processes are focused on providing maximum customer satisfaction. Superior customer service, efficient customer complaint handling, customer driven product development and innovation are important cornerstones of logistics and supply chain management.

Logistics management is related to all materials flows, from the flows of purchased materials into a facility, through the manufacturing process, and out to the customer. The starting point for any logistics process is the short-term sales plan and the related product plan. The total logistics function therefore includes short-term materials planning, the supply of raw materials and other purchased goods, internal transportation, storage and physical distribution.

Speed and flexibility demand very close cooperation between these materials-related functions. Logistics management therefore applies to a very broad area of activities and is sometimes also referred to as materials management and/or integrated business logistics. Figure 12.1 illustrates the relationship between these and other materials concepts.

The following features are relevant to an understanding of the importance of a holistic view of the company's materials processes:

■ Design, engineering and development activities can strongly affect logistics processes, for these activities determine the structure of the (future) manufactured products. The tolerances and specifications of products and the components they are made of, can be defined in such detail that they can only be obtained from a few suppliers. One question in the context of the design activities, is to what extent one strives for standardization of components. If new components are specified for each new end product being developed, then this irrevocably leads to a very extensive article assortment. This will have considerable consequences for logistics complexity and therefore the degree of sophistication of the materials planning and control systems.

- The production department also determines the effectiveness and efficiency of the logistics function to a large extent. The production department will usually aim for a high-capacity utilization of its assets. Disruptions of the production process as a result of rejection and shortages of materials are undesirable. A production manager will take certain measures to prevent such disruptions, for example by building up buffer stock. Although these measures may reduce the threat of production stops, the cause of the problem remains. In other words, these 'solutions' (which used to be applied in many companies) are an example of sub-optimization – although the measure is a solution for one department, it is not for the entire organization.

- Logistics management starts with the customer. If the sales organization, for the sake of landing an order, promises a delivery time within the internal production lead times, materials problems are likely to occur! This frequently results in 'rush work' in production planning, production, and purchasing. It leads to a situation in which purchasing must exert considerable pressure on suppliers to get the required materials earlier – and often at considerable extra costs!

Some authors describe logistics management as the management (i.e. the planning, execution and control) of all factors that affect the materials flow, the financial flows related to it and the related information flows, seen from the perspective of customer requirements, in such a way that the highest delivery reliability, the best order fulfillment and the shortest delivery time are realized. Based upon this description we can differentiate between logistics management and supply chain management. This latter term is interesting, because the relationship between the supplier and the customer is also included in this concept. It has become clear that suppliers can make important contributions to the improvement of logistics management. This was illustrated when a manufacturer of cleaning materials and detergents decided to analyze its low customer service levels. The supply organization repeatedly was not able to meet promised delivery dates in their relationship with some major customers. The analysis revealed that 75 per cent of the reasons were related to the bad delivery of their suppliers! The analysis came to the appalling conclusion

FIGURE 12.1   The business chain and some related items.

that, where the company had to meet stringent delivery schedules as imposed by its customers, and evaluated on its customer service levels, the suppliers to the manufacturing organization were not monitored and evaluated at all on this key performance indicator. Based upon this finding the company started to put the same performance measures in place as those that were used by their customers. This immediately led to an improvement of the suppliers' delivery performance.

Apart from suppliers, customers also may have considerable influence on the effectiveness of a company's supply chain. If customers are willing to give up or adjust certain requirements (for instance with regard to packaging and minimum delivery quantities) considerable savings in, or simplification of, supply processes can be the result. When customers are willing to share important planning information with their suppliers, this will enable them to anticipate much more effectively on future customer orders. Since both customers and suppliers can exert considerable influence on supply processes, we favor an expanded view on business logistics. Therefore, we will use the term supply chain management throughout this book.

Over the past decade more and more attention has been given to the concept of supply chain management (SCM). Stevens (1989) looks at the supply chain as the connected series of activities which is concerned with planning, coordinating and controlling materials, parts and finished goods from suppliers up to the customer. This author extends the concept of business logistics to other tiers in the supply chain. This is also recognized by Cooper and Ellram (1993) who present supply chain management as an integrative philosophy to manage the total flow of a distribution channel from suppliers to the ultimate user. Like vertical marketing systems SCM represents a systems approach to viewing the channel as a whole rather than as a set of fragmented parts. SCM differs from traditional approaches on inventory control and focuses on the management of inventory control through the entire supply chain. Successful SCM relies on forming strategic partnerships with trading partners along the supply chain, with one partner playing a key role in coordinating and overseeing the whole supply chain . . . (*ibid.*, p. 3).

This last description proves that supply chain management should be considered as a logical extension of earlier logistics concepts. It says that in order to be able to manage cost throughout the supply chain, effective and cooperative supplier relationships are required. Hence, purchasing and supply management (including supplier management) can be seen as an integrated part of supply chain management. In fact, the latter concept encompasses both the logistics and the purchasing and supply function. Now that we have provided some definitions, let's have a closer look at how materials processes in organizations can be structured and managed.

MATERIALS REQUIREMENTS PLANNING

Materials requirements planning (MRP) starts in the sales department with drawing up a sales plan. This plan provides an estimate of the volume that management thinks can be sold in the following months or the year to come. Data are presented both at product-group level and at the product/article level. Comparison of the sales plan with the available finished product stock yields the volumes to be produced. This information is the input for the manufacturing planning and control system (see Figure 12.2) in which the following elements can be distinguished.

- Master planning. In the master plan the manufacturing plans at the level of the product families (product groups) are established in consultation with the departments of sales, product development, manufacturing, finance and administration and logistics. In the master plan the customer orders, the sales plan, the planned stocks of finished products and the production and purchasing plans are linked together.

- Manufacturing resources planning (MRP-II). The resources needed to realize the master plan are recorded in the manufacturing resources plan, from which the required composition of manufacturing resources is derived. In the process it may become clear that particular production series are not feasible because production capacity is insufficient. This necessitates adjustment of the master planning and/or adjustment of the manufacturing capacity. In the latter case an investment plan needs to be prepared for adding additional production capacity.

- Master production scheduling (MPS). The master production schedule translates the master plan into specific materials requirements. The MPS is also the basis for computing the quantities of materials, semi-manufactured products and components which

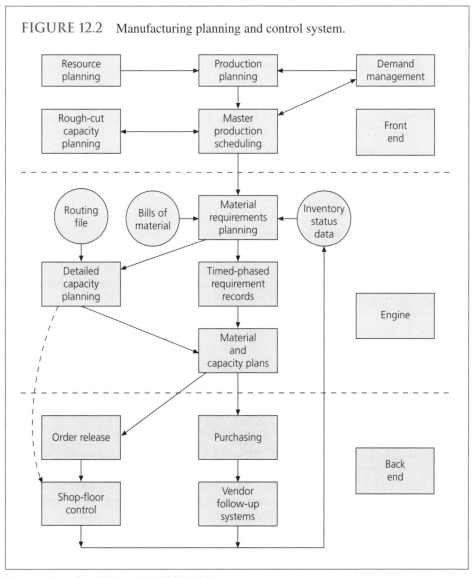

FIGURE 12.2 Manufacturing planning and control system.

Source: redrawn from Vollman *et al.* (1984) p. 25

must be manufactured. In this way the MPS provides the input for calculating the net materials requirements

■ General capacity testing. The MPS must also be tested for capacity limitations. This should be done for all potential bottleneck capacities. Such a check may reveal that the internal capacity is insufficient to produce certain components. If that is the case, the possibilities of contracting out the production of these components, or buying them, must be investigated.

■ Materials requirements planning (MRP-I). The materials requirements planning 'explodes' the requirements of the MPS level, step-by-step, in accordance with the bill of materials. It determines the materials requirements at the different levels of product structure and, finally, at the materials (item) level. If, at some level, identical requirements emerge from different MPS items, then these are grouped and added up per period. These needs are called the gross requirements and are converted into net requirements per period. This is accomplished by deducting the stock in hand from the gross requirements and subsequently deducting the manufacturing orders and purchasing order volumes that have already been placed. The net requirements are then plotted, taking into account the ordering procedures that have been developed. In this way the materials requisitions are built up. These requisitions must be available in time, to be ordered from the supplier, or to be manufactured by the company's own manufacturing departments.

■ Capacity requirements planning. Capacity requirements planning is conceptually comparable with materials requirement planning. The current and planned manufacturing orders from the materials requirements planning provide the input for the detailed production line planning. The required capacity is compared with the available capacity per production line (machine). The capacity requirements planning spots, at an early stage, where and when utilization problems will occur, so that preventive/alternative measures may be taken. If it is impossible to solve these problems, then the MPS must be adjusted.

■ Order release. Order releases change the status of the manufacturing orders and purchase orders from 'planned' to 'released'. The decision to release is based on the availability of the required materials and capacity. If a manufacturing order is released by a planner, the information system automatically allocates the required materials to this order, which prevents these materials being allocated to another process or manufacturing order. The system generates documentation for issuing the materials and components required to feed the manufacturing orders; in case stock is insufficient it generates materials requisitions for purchasing (i.e. purchasing requisitions).

■ Priority management. The priorities are derived directly from the master production schedule. Each unit receives a priority sheet which lists all manufacturing orders for that production line or machine centre. Orders with the highest priority should be given preference; regular 'overdue' reports indicate which manufacturing orders and purchasing requisitions will not be executed on time.

■ Capacity management. The issue of managing lead times, work-in-progress (WIP) and capacity is a complex one. To prevent under-utilization, manufacturing always tends to take on more work. However, when the expected workload (the input) exceeds the available capacity, long waiting periods ensue. The various manufacturing orders will be waiting longer, the lead times increase, the amounts of work in progress grow and delivery reliability decreases. This is why it is of the utmost importance that the waiting times per processing group are controlled. Input/output reports have an important function here: to compare the realized output for a production unit against its planned output.

The literature makes a distinction between MRP-I and MRP-II. MRP-I stands for materials requirement planning; this type of management system aims at releasing manufacturing orders and purchasing requisitions and at managing them. MRP-II stands for manufacturing resources planning and entails more than MRP-I. It is an integral system that controls relevant materials flows and production capacity, while also taking into account the relationship between these materials flows and the required capacity.

BASIC LOGISTICS STRUCTURES

The systems described above are characterized by the fact that they are forecast-based. The more accurate the sales forecasts, the more accurately production planning and materials requirements can be determined. It will be clear that in practice the unpredictability of sales orders is the stumbling block in the application of these systems. Furthermore, industrial manufacturing and logistics practice often shows much more variation than we have outlined here. Many companies have order-based production (as in the shipbuilding industry) instead of a forecast-based production (as is the practice in the petrochemical and processing industry). In customer-order-controlled manufacturing companies, production and materials planning are derived directly from the customer order. Every order is customer specific and therefore requires individual handling. Each sales order in fact represents a unique project. The customer's requirements tend to become known only at the last moment, which results in high time pressure. In such a situation the project approach to production is much more effective than an approach based on the MRP method. In other words, the application of MRP systems is limited to (small and large) series and process production.

In practice there are numerous hybrids between those production companies managed solely on the basis of customer orders and those based on forecast alone. Most manufacturing companies, unfortunately, have to deal with both types of manufacturing and goods flows. The order decoupling point (or order penetration point) concept is of major importance when organizing for efficient manufacturing and logistics. The order decoupling point indicates how deeply the customer order penetrates the firm's materials flow.[2] It defines from what moment on a production order becomes customer specific. The order decoupling point separates the activities based on order information from the forecast-based activities. This is important because these two types of activity require totally different planning techniques. In general, the following situations can be distinguished:

- Making and sending to stock (MSS). Products are manufactured and distributed to various distribution points which are dispersed and located close to the customer. Manufacturing is based upon forecasts and on the expected stock turnover at the points of distribution. Examples are the manufacture of sweets, foods, beverages.

- Making to stock (central stock) (MTS). Finished products are kept in stock at the end of the production process and from there are shipped directly to many geographically dispersed customers, as in the manufacture of dairy products.

- Assembly to order (ATO). Only systems elements or subassemblies are in stock at the manufacturing centre and final assembly takes place based on a specific customer order. In other words, manufacture of components takes place based on forecasts, and final assembly takes place based on customer orders. Examples are the manufacture of cars, computers, materials handling equipment.

---

2 This discussion was originally based upon Hoekstra and Romme (1985), who carried out pioneering research into supply chains and customer order decoupling points.

- Making to order (MTO). Only raw materials and components are kept in stock. Every customer order is a specific project. Examples are the manufacture of beer and lemonade cans, basic construction materials.

- Engineering and making to order (ETO). In this situation there is no stock at all. The purchase and order of materials takes place on the basis of the specific customer order and the entire project is carried out for this one specific client. Examples are construction companies and shipyards.

Figure 12.3 presents these situations in diagrammatic form.

The question of where the order decoupling point should be located in the company's primary processes is a major issue when designing the manufacturing and logistics organization. The answer to this question also determines where in the process inventories should be located and in what quantities. The role and position of the purchasing function will differ in each of the situations described above. In the first situation the planning of the quantities to be purchased per period is fairly predictable. Based on expected volumes, annual (bulk) agreements can be negotiated with suppliers, or price agreements with a long

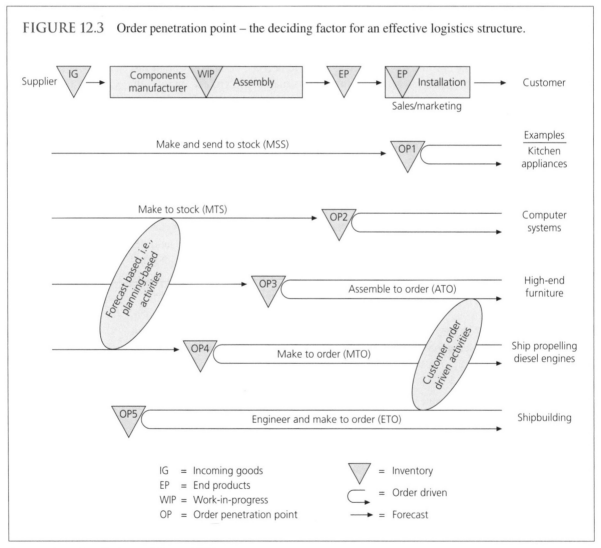

FIGURE 12.3   Order penetration point – the deciding factor for an effective logistics structure.

IG   = Incoming goods
EP   = End products
WIP = Work-in-progress
OP   = Order penetration point

▽ = Inventory
     = Order driven
⟶ = Forecast

Source: redrawn from Hoekstra and Romme (1985)

period of operation can be made. Based on the production planning, delivery schedules can be drawn up and made known to the supplier.

In the last situation purchasing strongly resembles project purchasing. Every project is new – new suppliers have to be found for every production order, the products that are to be manufactured must be discussed in detail with suppliers, and intensive consultation between the design and engineering department is necessary. On-time delivery and quality are more important than price! Purchasing must be able to respond to changes in design and project planning quickly.

JUST-IN-TIME MANAGEMENT

Characteristics of just-in-time management

The principle of just-in-time management (JIT) means that all materials and products become available at the very moment when they are needed in the production process, not sooner and not later, but exactly on time and in exactly the right quantity. The major objective underlying this approach is to continuously tackle and solve manufacturing bottlenecks within, and interface problems between, consecutive steps in the manufacturing processes. Incoming inspection, buffer stock and extensive quality control procedures on incoming materials are primarily considered as 'waste'. The basic idea is to strive continuously to reduce these often 'hidden' costs in the factory.

Just-in-time management implies that nothing is produced if there is no demand. The production process is 'pulled' by customer orders. The 'customer' is in fact the organizational entity which is 'next-in-line'. This concept, therefore, may relate to other departments within the company itself. However, it may also relate to external customers, outside the organization. When no customer orders have been received, manufacturing activities will come to an end and the spare time is used to do minor repairs/maintenance, housekeeping and/or prepare for materials planning. The spare time may also be used to discuss how to improve on the work currently being conducted within the organizational entity ('small group activities'). No production, therefore, does not imply that the time is used unproductively.

Because they contract out a considerable amount of work, many large Japanese producers work closely with a limited number of suppliers, who are sometimes organized in supplier networks or supplier associations. The bulk of the materials requirements are sourced from these suppliers. It is not uncommon that one manufacturer is responsible for more than 50 per cent of a supplier's turnover. At the same time this same supplier may deliver 80 per cent of the manufacturer's specific materials requirements. This leads, contrary to many European manufacturers, to a large interdependence between manufacturers and suppliers. As a result Japanese manufacturers are able to benefit much more from the supplier's expertise and capabilities. Another aspect is that Japanese manufacturers in general focus on assembly only. All component manufacturing is outsourced to specialized suppliers. Since the producer frequently represents a large share of the supplier's turnover, a maximum effort by the supplier is ensured. Obviously, there is some risk involved for suppliers when engaging in this type of relationship: if there is no market demand for the customer's product, there will be less work for the supplier. In this way part of the business's economic risk is transferred to the suppliers. However, if the producer can guarantee a certain production volume for a number of years, it becomes appealing for the supplier to invest in new technology. Japanese supplier relations are characterized by their long-term orientation (three to five-year contracts).

Order quantities and batch sizes

Continuity in production demands a constant availability of the required materials. Manufacturing managers continuously need to decide when and how much should be ordered from their suppliers. There are several models that can be used for optimizing the incoming materials flow. One very well-known model is Camp's formula. The variables used in this inventory model are:

S	fixed usage per period
t	delivery period
Q	order quantity
C_0	costs per order
C_i	inventory carrying costs for one unit during one time unit.

The economic order quantity is where the sum of inventory costs and ordering costs per unit is lowest. Ordering large quantities from suppliers has the advantage that the ordering costs (fixed costs) can be spread out over a larger number of products. Hence, large order quantities will lead to a lower order cost per unit. The disadvantage of ordering large quantities, however, is that larger quantities of the product must be kept in stock for a longer period of time, which naturally implies higher inventory carrying costs per product.

Starting with the order quantity Q and a usage rate per period S means that in a given period S/Q orders are required. The order costs for that specific period therefore will amount to $S/Q \times C_0$.

The average inventory level, measured over one period, is $1/2\ Q$ and the total inventory costs for the considered period are $1/2\ Q \times C_i$.

The total ordering and inventory costs will be:

$$\frac{S}{Q} \times C_0 + \frac{1}{2}\ Q \times C_i$$

The economic order quantity can now be calculated (Camp's formula) as:

$$Q_0 = \sqrt{\frac{2S \times C_0}{C_i}}$$

Although this formula has received significant interest from practitioners, it is only of significance under the following conditions:

- the consumption of the component at hand is fairly stable;
- the consumption of the component is evenly spread over the course of time;
- the delivery time of the product is fixed and not due to fluctuation;
- the ordering costs per order are fixed;

the inventory carrying costs do not depend on the ordered quantity, etc.

The just-in-time approach basically challenges each of these assumptions. For example, order-related costs are analyzed in terms of costs related to:

- negotiations with the supplier;
- administrative processing;
- follow-up and expediting of orders;
- incoming and quality inspections.

Suppliers are now classified in categories, depending on the degree to which they represent work for the buyer. Suppliers who comply with the stringent JIT conditions require no more investigation. This saves costs on the four items mentioned above. By systematically considering how savings can be accomplished for each separate cost item, the buyer succeeds in reducing the optimal order quantity. A graphic representation is provided in Figure 12.4.

The reasoning used for determining the economic order quantity can also be applied to determining the (optimal) batch size in production. This issue arises when one production line is used to produce different products or product varieties. Changing production from one product to another means that the production line needs to be reset, a process which usually costs time and money. In general, four steps in the process of setting up a production line may be identified.

- Preparation. This includes gathering tools, molds, spare parts, work instructions, etc. and transporting them to the machine or production line concerned.
- Conversion. This is the dismantling and rebuilding of the machine or production line, mounting the appropriate tools and molds, and, if necessary, cleaning.
- Setting up. This refers to setting the machine in such a way that the desired quality and speed is achieved; a trial run may be necessary.
- Finishing. Finishing may consist of removing, cleaning and storing the used tools and spares, and removing the finished product.

While the machines are being reset nothing is produced. Many companies therefore regard setting-up production lines as a necessary evil. In practice the easy solution is frequently chosen: the production line is used to make the same product for a longer period of time, so that less frequent resetting is required. In other words, the batch size is enlarged to benefit from economies of scale achieved as the result of a lower set-up cost per unit produced.

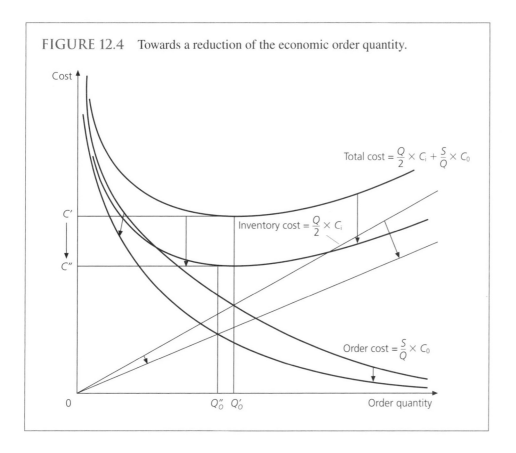

FIGURE 12.4   Towards a reduction of the economic order quantity.

Moreover, this practice leads to a much better capacity utilization in production (yield). Clearly, one disadvantage of this way of working is that the size of the stocks related to semi-manufactured products and finished products and the associated inventory carrying costs increase. The decision about the optimization of batch sizes must therefore be based on balancing set-up costs against inventory costs. The optimal batch size is achieved when the sum of the inventory costs of work in process and set-up costs per unit produced is lowest.

Thinking based upon economies-of-scale and production yields, which still can be observed in many manufacturing organizations, limits production flexibility and fast response to customer requirements. This poses a problem for manufacturers when customers demand short lead times, which happens in many markets today.

By systematically striving for reductions in set-up times, the optimal batch size can be reduced considerably. Often, when calculating the optimal batch size, the set-up costs of the production machinery, among other things, are considered fixed. These costs can be very high. Japanese production thinking has continuously focused on the question of whether these fixed costs can be made variable. Japanese producers have constantly looked for ways to minimize their set-up costs and times. Much has been achieved by means of organizational measures, and new machines have been designed that are easier to handle and set up. As a result, optimal batch sizes have been reduced considerably, enabling Japanese producers to benefit from low costs per unit together with a high product mix flexibility in their production.

Quality and zero defects

Another characteristic of the just-in-time principle is related to quality awareness. Smaller batch sizes make it necessary to detect quality defects at an early stage. In most Japanese companies every employee is responsible for the quality of his/her work. If a production employee notices that a particular part does not meet the specifications, he/she immediately notifies his/her colleague in the previous link of the production process. It may be that the conveyor belt has to be stopped. The advantage of this procedure is the fast response time – corrective action is taken immediately following a complaint. This situation is in sharp contrast with the practice of some European companies, where defective material is first put aside, then handed over to the quality department, which in turn contacts the production department in question in order to solve the problem.

It is clear that the JIT approach must be supported by all functions within the company. Top management should actively support foremen and shop floor workers in providing the resources necessary to improve manufacturing operations. Adopting a JIT approach will take considerable time; it took Toyota 15 years to implement its famous *kanban* philosophy. Considerable attention is paid to quality in Japan because there is almost no slack in the production process. This means that a defective product may threaten the continuity of the whole production process.

Traditional quality control procedures were often based on inspection after a set number of parts had been manufactured. The rejected parts were dismantled and, when appropriate, repaired. Just-in-time management requires that everything goes right the first time. In Chapter 11 this principle has been referred to as the 'zero defects' principle. It will be clear that just-in-time production and scheduling cannot be successfully implemented without a 'zero defects' philosophy.

Having discussed the major characteristics of just-in-time management, the question of what its introduction means for the purchasing department and for the performance of suppliers is now addressed.

JIT and the purchasing function

The JIT concept cannot be limited to production only. It must be supported and implemented in every functional area in the organization. Applied to purchasing, JIT is a philosophy that aims to make exactly the required materials and products available at exactly the time they are needed, so that value is added only to the product which is to be manufactured, and indirect costs are avoided.

What does the introduction of JIT mean for the purchasing function? JIT has a major impact on both the quality and the quantity of the materials to be purchased. Table 12.1 lists the main differences between the traditional purchasing approach and the JIT approach.

The JIT approach is characterized by regular but flexible supply. Ordered materials are delivered frequently (sometimes, in an assembly environment, several times a day) in different quantities. To facilitate this, the supplier is informed of the production planning and the related purchasing requirements on a daily, weekly and monthly basis through delivery schedules which are available online. In this way he is able to anticipate his customer's future requirements. Hence, he will be able to plan his production and materials requirements more effectively. Apart from this, there are some other definite advantages of working with suppliers in this way. The producer uses in general long-term contracts, against which periodic call-off orders are placed. Once a year (or more often) the conditions are renegotiated with the supplier. Targets for productivity improvement and cost reduction, as required by the producer, are also part of these negotiations. Agreements on these issues are documented and communicated to the supplier. In essence, they are the standards against which the future performance of the supplier is going to be monitored and measured.

TABLE 12.1 Differences between the traditional approach and the JIT approach in purchasing

Purchasing activity	Traditional approach	JIT approach
Supplier selection	Minimum of two suppliers; price is central	Often one local supplier; frequent deliveries
Placing the order	Order specifies delivery time and quality	Annual order; deliveries called off as needed
Change of orders	Delivery time and quality often changed at the last moment	Delivery time and quality fixed, quantities are adjusted within predetermined margins if necessary
Follow-up of orders	Many phone calls to solve delivery problems	Few delivery problems thanks to sound agreements; quality and delivery problems are not tolerated
Incoming inspection	Inspection of quality and quantities of nearly every delivered order	Initial sample inspections; later, no inspections necessary
Supplier assessment	Qualitative assessment; delivery deviations of sometimes up to 10 per cent are tolerated	Deviations are not accepted; price is fixed based on open calculation
Invoicing	Payment per order	Invoices are collected and settled on a monthly basis

As far as quality is concerned, the guiding principle is zero defects. Imposing quality targets upon suppliers may represent large savings to the producer, both in terms of a reduction of the number of incoming quality inspections and a reduction of buffer stock. In this way the supplier is educated towards a better quality performance.

The practices described above are still different from the traditional purchasing practices of most European companies. Traditionally these are aimed at creating optimal competition between suppliers. Relations with suppliers are, in this approach, mostly focused on the short term; dependency on a single supplier is considered to be fundamentally wrong. Traditional purchasing theory prescribes multi-sourcing, i.e. obtaining materials from various suppliers. The underlying idea is that a company must not become too dependent on one single supplier. Therefore, many manufacturers prefer multiple sourcing in their supplier relationships. Where possible, single sourcing (see also Chapter 10 on this subject) should be prevented.

Looking at the characteristics of JIT it is clear that traditional buyers must radically alter their views and policies on two important aspects, in order to adopt this approach:

- willingness to consider single sourcing as an appropriate strategy;
- willingness to arrange longer term contracts instead of 'one-shot' deals.

The criteria used to select and assess suppliers must also be adjusted. The demands made on suppliers are different and generally considerably higher. These refer to both product and process quality (zero defects) and delivery reliability (just-in-time). The purchase price, traditionally a prime issue in the negotiations, usually will get a lower ranking within the selection criteria used.

The JIT approach was initially introduced to the USA and Europe by subsidiaries of Japanese companies. Nowadays, many European companies are attempting to follow their example. Philips Electronics and Alcatel Bell were among the first companies to introduce the just-in-time approach in their European plants in relationships with their suppliers (see Memo 12.1).

CONSEQUENCES FOR SUPPLIERS

Advantages and disadvantages for the supplier

The JIT concept has some specific advantages and disadvantages for the supplier. This section will start with the advantages.

With the JIT approach the supplier is regularly informed about the quantities to be delivered. The supplier is able to plan his future production volume more accurately because of this information. The same holds for the planning of materials. As a result the pipeline inventory may be reduced. This advantage will be even larger when the supplier succeeds in implementing JIT principles in the relationship with his own suppliers.

JIT can, besides better planning, lead to administrative savings for the supplier. All handling of transaction documents is done through electronic information systems. Suppliers are able to connect their production and materials planning systems with those of their customers. This requires, of course, some sophistication of the computer systems which are available on both sides – this is why some large manufacturers shun those suppliers from their business, who do not have sufficient EDI capabilities. When the supplier is notified in case of quality defects, he immediately should take corrective action. Claims and bills will be avoided.

The constant communication between supplier and manufacturer on quality and cost improvements can lead to product and process innovations. These innovations can be very profitable for the supplier in other markets.

A last advantage for the supplier is his investment policy. JIT contracts are signed for a long period of time. A certain volume and turnover are guaranteed. This makes it easier to decide whether and when to invest in new production technology and equipment.

However, engaging in JIT relationships with a manufacturer obviously also has some disadvantages for the supplier. In Japan these types of relationships have affected not only supplier relationships, but also the industrial structure of the nation. In many industrial sectors a strong hierarchy can be observed in the different links of supply chains. In general the large manufacturers, at the top of the supplier pyramid (see Figure 12.5), have imposed their demands and requirements rather ruthlessly on the often much smaller suppliers. Given the large dependence on these large manufacturers, suppliers have had to comply with these demands, at the risk of losing their entire business.

In general, it may take some time for a supplier to deliver at zero defects, or to achieve zero defects. In the beginning the supplier has to conduct many quality checks and many products fail the test. To deliver just-in-time with zero defects takes great effort and therefore initially requires high costs. These investments are not being paid for by the large manufacturers; they come at the expense of the supplier.

MEMO 12.1   SUPPLIER RELATIONSHIPS AT PHILIPS ELECTRONICS

The relationship with suppliers is a central issue in the purchasing policies of many companies. Philips introduced the term co-makership.

The Philips companies in Belgium and The Netherlands operate in an international and dynamic market. A characteristic of this market is the demand for a variety of products which are subject to rapid technological change. In addition, demands for short delivery lead times and a high customer service are greater than ever. Only an organization which can respond quickly to this fast-evolving and changing market – in which there is intense competition – will be able to maintain its position. For this reason the Philips organization has decided to introduce an integrated manufacturing resources planning (MRP) concept. This management system produces quick feedback from the market to product development, manufacture and logistics planning, thereby ensuring a flexible supply capability to Philips' customers.

The purchasing organization should contribute to the achievement of the required results by means of more intensive cooperation with its internal and external suppliers. Philips refers to this approach to suppliers as 'co-makership'. This co-makership relationship must produce the following results:

- improved product quality
- increased flexibility of response to market demand
- shorter delivery lead times
- quicker implementation of product changes
- increased reliability of orders and deliveries
- reduced stock levels
- lower integral cost prices.

We have found similar programs that focus on the ideas described in other companies, such as IBM's 'First Time Right' program, Xerox's 'Leadership through Quality' program and Alcatel-Bell's 'Quality on Time' program.

Source: Philips Electronics (1989), Co-makership (internal brochure).

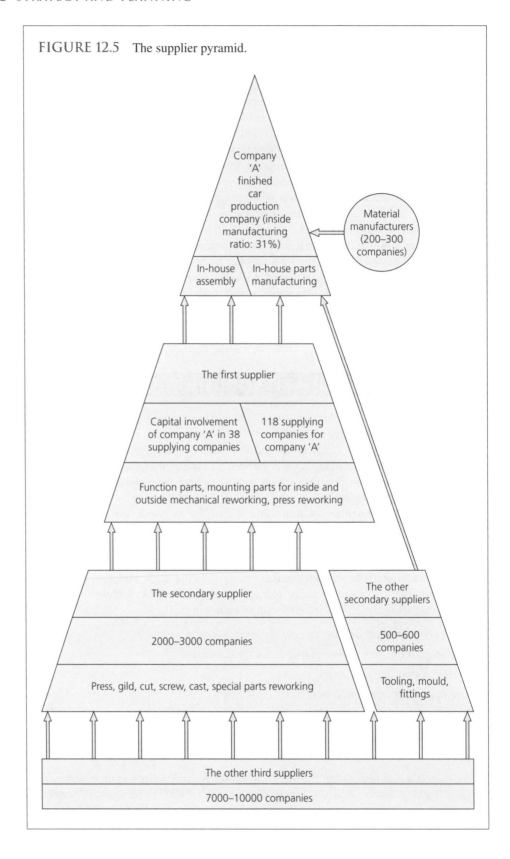

FIGURE 12.5   The supplier pyramid.

Another disadvantage is that the supplier can become very dependent on only one manufacturer. If the supplier focuses too much on the business of one or two manufacturers, this can become a threat to its continuity. After a long-term contract has ended, circumstances may have changed which can result in the end of the relationship. Given its large dependence on that one manufacturer the supplier will go to great lengths in order to get a new contract. Obviously, when a supplier is not able to keep up with competition and has missed the contract, it will not be easy to regain the lost territory.

JIT principles in supplier relationships may affect the industrial structure of a nation. In Japan it has resulted in a pyramid shaped supply. In this structure original equipment manufacturers (OEMs) work closely together with main suppliers responsible for the development and delivery of complete subcomponents (dashboard units, transmission systems). These system suppliers buy their own materials from a second tier of suppliers. These suppliers, in their turn, do business with smaller suppliers who work on components. At the bottom of the pyramid are the often large and powerful suppliers of basic, raw materials.

This structure is criticized by both Japan and Europe. OEMs often make extreme demands on the system suppliers who shift these demands to their own suppliers and so on. In the end the smaller companies have to work very hard to be able to survive, therefore the smaller suppliers at the bottom of the pyramid are often referred to as 'sweatshops'.

The system suppliers are in many cases strong specialized and international companies who work closely with their customers. In some cases this cooperation means not only delivering systems or components, but also assembling these into the end product. The system supplier is made responsible for the planning of delivery and the logistics involved. This principle is also referred to as JIT II (see Memo 12.2). Another principle which is applied in dealings with these systems supplies, is 'pay for production'. The equivalent of this principle is 'pay for consumption'. The manufacturer only pays the supplier for the components which actually have been consumed during the production of a given day or batch. At Whirlpool and Xerox, suppliers of key-components and packaging are no longer paid for the products they deliver, but for the products that actually have been consumed in a day at a certain production line. Through EDI a supplier can monitor every day which components have been consumed at the production lines of the manufacturer. At the end of the day the balance is made and the amount due paid electronically. Pay for production is closely related to JIT.

Manufacturing organizations in Europe do not wish to follow the example of Japanese industry. The main objection to the Japanese situation is the dependence on too few

MEMO 12.2 JIT II

JIT II is a concept pioneered by the Bose Corporation. In sales, purchasing and material planning applications, the customer planner, buyer and supplier salesman are replaced by an 'in-plant' supplier employee who is empowered to place customer purchase orders with his company. Supplier access and linkage to customer computers is also utilized. The in-plant supplier also performs concurrent engineering with customer engineering departments from within the customer company. 'Vendor managed inventory' and 'automatic material replenishment' are features of JIT II.

JIT II has been featured in front page articles in the US and European *Wall Street Journal* and other worldwide business periodicals. US corporations such as IBM, Intel, AT&T, Honeywell and many other major corporations have implemented JIT II nationally in scores of supplier relationships. *Business Week* named Bose one of the 'world class champs' in supplier management. Many corporations have adopted JIT II nowadays as a sales and customer support program.

suppliers. In Japan, exclusiveness is demanded from suppliers: a supplier may deliver a product only to one company. Most organizations in Europe do not encourage a too large dependency on the supplier. Philips, for example, wishes suppliers to be dependent on Philips for less than 30 per cent of their turnover.

JIT and supplier selection

In the context of supplier selection, suppliers located close to the customer organization are in an advantageous position. Toyota, for example, demands that their main suppliers have production plants within a radius of 30 kilometres! Business is based on open calculations, and agreements about the supplier's quality and delivery performance are reached in advance. If there are no suppliers in the immediate vicinity, then the company will try to do business with suppliers who are concentrated in particular geographical areas. In that way transport can be combined and the associated costs reduced.

Suppliers are required to deliver with zero defects, so that incoming inspection can be omitted. The reduction of incoming inspections is a gradual process of increasing quality and reliability, which takes time. The right products must be delivered at the right quantities at exactly the right moment. Quality and 'on time' are the two main criteria on which suppliers are assessed when applying JIT-purchasing and the following classification of suppliers is often used:

on time delivery	A = excellent	B = good	C = inadequate
quality delivery	1 = excellent	2 = good	3 = inadequate

These scores are a simple way to rate the supplier's performance. A C1 supplier, for example, provides high quality, but does not always deliver on time. At worst this can cause interruptions in the manufacturing process. An A3 supplier, however, delivers on time, but the quality of products is poor. This means that incoming inspection remains a necessity, which is in conflict with the JIT concept.

In discussions with their suppliers, buyers consistently emphasize that, preferably, all suppliers have to get into the A1 category, and remain there. A problem can develop if the buyer occupies a weak negotiating position (*vis-à-vis* the supplier). It will be very hard for a small producer, for example, to persuade large suppliers to provide JIT deliveries. In that situation, the producer should try to find more accommodating suppliers, even if this means a higher purchase price.

In conclusion, it is argued that the implementation of JIT principles automatically leads to more single sourcing, closing long-term contracts and engaging local suppliers. The central issue affecting supplier selection is not so much the purchase prices, but more the magnitude of the total costs, i.e. the costs including the 'waste' that results from poor supplier performance, safety stocks, quality and incoming inspections and (possibly) production standstills. Hence, this kind of supplier relationship should be embedded in agreements based on total cost of ownership (TCO).

SCHEDULING PROBLEMS BETWEEN PURCHASING AND LOGISTICS

This chapter has made clear that production planning and materials planning in most companies are far from simple matters. The large amount of data to be processed, the huge differences in the demand structure of products and the related differences in predictability of expenditure, render these subjects extremely complicated in practice. It is therefore not at all surprising that, in practice, many problems are encountered. Some typical problem situations are discussed below.

■ Lack of well-defined specifications. Specifications are sometimes described ambiguously and bills of materials can be incomplete. In a recent investigation of a manufacturer of food products, it was found that specification sheets were absent or incomplete for 50 per cent of the raw materials that was being purchased. This made it very difficult, if not impossible, to purchase materials at the right quality because it was not clear what the right quality was; each stakeholder in the discussion (production, laboratory, quality control, supplier) appeared to use its own definition. The result was a very high reject rate on incoming raw materials and a lot of useless discussion among the persons involved.

■ Lack of standardization. Needlessly complex specifications are sometimes used where standard products would suffice. These limit the buyer's latitude and lead to an expansion of the article assortment. The result is increasing administrative and logistic complexity and often an excessive dependence on one supplier.

■ Frequent changes in materials planning. Frequent changes in the materials planning due to changes in the production planning disrupt the delivery schedules with suppliers. The consequence is that delivery agreements have to be cancelled or that deliveries have to take place before the agreed delivery dates. This increases the number of rush orders and the cost of non-quality to an unacceptable level.

■ Unreliable planning information. MRP systems must be provided with sound information. Keeping basic but fundamental logistics information up-to-date is an important task. Working with incorrect stock and delivery information causes unnecessary orders to be placed, too frequently, and inside the suppliers' lead times, which generates extra work and raises transportation costs.

■ Insufficient integration of purchasing in materials management. When it is decided to automate the production and logistics systems, purchasing often lags behind. The problems which result often become clear when logistics managers want to add a purchasing control module to their electronic materials planning systems. For then it turns out that descriptions of materials and articles must, for example, be available in four languages, that the units in which purchases are made (e.g. in metres, kilograms) differ from the units which are invoiced (units, volume), etc. Implementation of purchasing systems may then take years instead of months.

Up to now the focus has been on the most important elements of production planning and materials planning. The next section describes the most important elements of the purchasing system.

Elements of the purchasing system

The administrative complexity in purchasing can be very high. In a study conducted among 48 medium-sized industrial companies, it was found that the companies had on average 16 600 different article items or stock keeping units (SKUs), which were obtained from 1155 suppliers. On average 19 980 purchasing requisitions had to be processed, which resulted in 18 900 orders. The deliveries had to be made payable by processing 26,980 purchasing invoices. These numbers show that a solid and efficient administrative organization is a prerequisite for the functioning of any purchasing organization, if it is to focus on its tactical and strategic tasks.

Figure 12.6 shows the most important elements of a purchasing information system. These are now briefly described.

- Requisitioning and ordering. By means of purchasing requisitions the internal users within the company express their requirements regarding goods or services to be purchased. These requisitions can be generated directly by the materials planning system, but they can also be generated manually. This is often the case when it concerns non-recurring purchases (for example investment goods). The purchasing requisition lists the article code (SKU-number), provides a general description of the item, the quantities required, the desired delivery date plus the data necessary for finance and administration (budget number, account number, etc.)

- Product and supplier database. The data on the purchasing requisition are then transferred by purchasing to a purchase order document. Here, specific supplier and product data are added, such as the price per unit and the address where the order should be delivered. In case of a frame agreement the purchase order also mentions the contract number. All purchase orders are given a unique purchase order number, which should be used by suppliers in future correspondence and documents. The purchase order is the basis for delivery. Without it, a supplier should not deliver. Some manufacturers require their suppliers to confirm their orders prior to delivery by means of an order confirmation.

- Order follow-up. Subsequently the order must be monitored (order follow-up or expediting). Delivery of the goods by the supplier in accordance with the agreement must be checked. To ensure effective monitoring, the buyer uses numerous exception reports. One of the most important of these is the delivery overdue list, which lists the purchase orders that should be delivered by a certain date but which have not yet been delivered. Another important list here is the incoming inspection report, which lists the purchase orders which at delivery have been rejected by quality control. Of course, in these cases the buyer will need to take immediate corrective action (this activity is referred to as 'trouble shooting'). Some advanced purchasing systems allow the buyer to assign a code to purchase orders, strategic materials and unreliable suppliers. This code is used

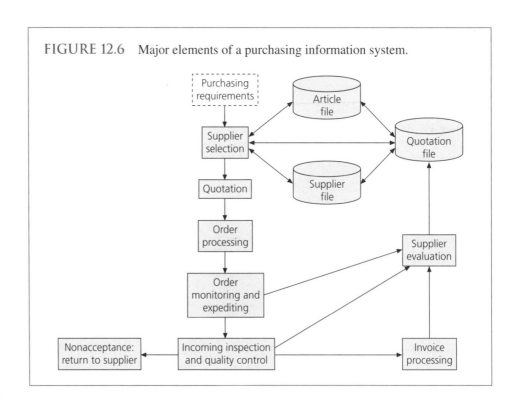

FIGURE 12.6   Major elements of a purchasing information system.

for generating several signalling-reports, through which the buyer can take preventive action: these suppliers usually are requested through fax or e-mail to confirm and restate that they will meet the required delivery dates (this enables a differentiated approach to order-expediting as described in Chapter 3). In case of delivery of complex investment goods it may be necessary to visit the supplier several times during production and assembly. This type of expediting is referred to as field-expediting and is common in the defence and aircraft industries.

- Delivery. Normally, the supplier will deliver the goods which have been ordered at the right time and at the right quantity. At delivery the supplier will produce a delivery document (freight bill), which needs to be signed by personnel of incoming inspection. They will check the delivered goods against the electronic order copy. Both quantity and quality are inspected. When approved, a copy of the delivery document is sent to finance and administration. At the same time the goods are released and shipped to warehousing or the user. When the shipment by the supplier does not match the original order, a complaint form is filled in. Complaints may relate to quality, delivered quantity or packaging. These data are again put into the system. They form the basis of any vendor rating system, which records the performance of a supplier in a given period. Complaint reports are sent to purchasing who will discuss the problems with the supplier to prevent them being repeated in the future. When handled by purchasing, the form will be sent back to the quality control department, which will authorize the report and file it.

- Invoice handling and payment. Some time after delivery the supplier will send an invoice. Normally, the invoice will be sent to finance and administration who will match it with the original order and the delivery document. When matching is possible, the invoice will be paid to the supplier according to the agreed payment terms. Sometimes matching is not possible. In that case the invoice is sent for approval to purchasing, who will investigate why the invoice does not match with the order. After the differences are cleared, the invoice will be sent to finance and administration for final handling.

In recent years various computer systems have become available to buyers and purchasing managers which can support the activities described above. Examples are: SAP, Baan Triton, JD Edwards, MAPICS, and MFG-PRO. These systems have been found appropriate for supporting purchasing transactional processes. However, in many cases these systems are still are not capable of producing the required purchasing management information. Most systems have difficulty in providing overviews of turnover figures ranked by product, supplier, purchaser, country or currency. Furthermore, they lack facilities to support advanced vendor rating. A final aspect is that they do not provide sufficient opportunities to provide management reports on the performance of the purchasing department. Obviously, in this area there is still a lot of work to be done by the large enterprise resource planning (ERP) systems providers.

In many small- and medium-sized companies automation in purchasing is limited to the administrative processing of the purchasing requisitions. Many purchasing systems are isolated and not linked to materials planning systems. This implies that the ordering data must be entered manually into the purchasing system, increasing the risk of mistakes. It also makes the work of buyers very laborious and time-consuming. Therefore, introducing advanced purchasing systems into an organization is a prerequisite for improving both its efficiency and professionalism.

SUMMARY

In this chapter the relationship between purchasing, materials planning and logistics has been discussed. The cooperation between these functions should result in an efficient and uninterrupted flow of products. This requires an integrated approach to managing materials planning processes. Apart from materials management and physical distribution, we have described the role and importance of logistics and supply chain management. Logistics management aims at optimizing the total flow of goods, from customer demands to the supplier. Supply chain management looks at how to optimize materials processes throughout the whole supply chain. These are no simple matters, since in reality customer demands seldomly fit exactly to the capabilities of the firm. Therefore many advanced materials planning methods have been developed, the most important being materials requirements planning and manufacturing resources planning. Both systems are basically forecast-driven and require the use of advanced computer-supported planning systems. Apart from forecast-based planning systems, companies may use order-based planning systems. JIT scheduling is a third type of planning system. Basically, it is forecast-based; however, it is aimed at continuously reducing cycle-times and lead times, so that planning horizons may be shortened. Suppliers play a vital role in implementing JIT. They need to be challenged constantly to look for ways to improve their operational processes. In the end this may result in a situation where suppliers are requested to fully integrate their activities with those of their customers. This principle has been referred to as JIT II.

This chapter has also presented five different structures or ground forms which may underlie a company's production and logistics activities. A central element in the discussion has been the order penetration point. Downstream from this point all activities are customer order driven; upstream of this point activities are forecast-based. Understanding this principle is necessary to understand how purchasing processes may vary in an organization.

Managing suppliers as described in this chapter requires lots of very detailed logistics data and management information. Therefore, the most important elements of a purchasing information system have been discussed. The conclusion is that most available ERP systems are capable of supporting the operational, transactional purchasing activities. However, they do not sufficiently support the need to generate management information and reports.

ASSIGNMENTS

12.1 Supply chain management is about managing the materials flows, information flows and financial flows throughout the supply chain. Discuss how Li&Fung in the introductory Case Study of this chapter keep control of each of these flows.

12.2 What would you consider to be the main difference between supply chain management and value chain management?

12.3 Supply chain management assumes that the companies involved in the supply chain are willing to work closely together and are willing to develop partnership relationships. How valid is this assumption in your opinion? Under what circumstances are companies willing to develop partnership relationships?

12.2 Some critics argue that the supply chain concept is a too narrow view of the reality that can be observed in many industries today. Rather, they favor a network approach since they feel this reflects much better the interdependencies that may exist between customers and suppliers in several sectors. What is meant by this statement? When optimizing supplier relationships, what view do you favor? Discuss.

12.5 What measures could you mention that can be used to optimize the logistics flows between a manufacturer and a supplier? What can both parties do to take costs out of the supply chain? Investigate and discuss.

LEARNING OBJECTIVES

After studying this chapter you should understand the following:

- The structure of the purchasing function within organizations.
- The underlying factors that determine the role, position and organizational structure of purchasing.
- The major tasks, responsibilities and competences of purchasing and how to organize these.
- How to get organized for purchasing in single-unit companies.
- How to get organized for purchasing in multi-unit companies.
- Which criteria to use in deciding on centralized versus decentralized purchasing.

CASE STUDY   ORGANIZING FOR PURCHASING AT HERSHEY FOODS CORPORATION

Over recent years, Hershey Foods Corporation has reengineered its purchasing operations in a major effort to get full value from the supply base. The results? A centralized purchasing group that has moved away from transaction processing towards strategic supply management and a supply base that is deeply integrated into Hershey's operations and business strategy. Keys to Hershey's supply strategy were:

- Centralization – and consolidation – of purchasing, which had been operating with individual purchasing departments at each operating business unit and at the corporate level.
- Major consolidation of the supply base, in order to maximize Hershey's leverage and develop closer supplier relationships.
- Shifting purchasing resources towards strategic supply activities and away from transaction processing, while simultaneously educating the

Hershey organization to the reasons behind the shift.

- Vertical integration of key suppliers into Hershey's operations, which includes open sharing of process and business information and, in some cases, supplier units that are 'dedicated' to Hershey's business.

Frank Cerminara, vice-president of procurement, says it was a simple decision to change purchasing's basic structure at Hershey. 'Four years ago we decided to centralize it all: commodities, packaging, capital purchases, and services,' he says with reference to the purchasing function.

Until that point, Hershey Foods, headquartered in Hershey, Philadelphia, USA, had many small purchasing departments including its several commodity groups at the corporate level as well as in divisions. Between Hershey's core confectionery business and its pasta and grocery division, the number of groups or departments sourcing raw materials and MRO was too large to be effective.

All the core competencies and skills were consolidated into one group of procurement professionals. The team that emerged included Cerminara at the helm, two commodities directors, a capital and services director, and a packaging director. The intention was to leverage the volume of Hershey Foods' buy to cut costs.

Although centralization was a major initiative of Cerminara's efforts, purchasing at Hershey now works closely with all individual business units in a variety of activities, including new-product development.

'Procurement is on every operating division staff – sales, marketing, manufacturing, and other supplier chain operations,' Cerminara says. 'We get involved at the concept stage (of new product development) in order to find the right suppliers.' For instance, procurement reps may work on new-product development teams that also include research and development, food technologists, engineering, manufacturing, and marketing personnel.

Cerminara emphasizes that commodity managers focus on strategy rather than number of contracts. 'We wanted the cocoa bean buyers, for instance, to spend less time working on transactions and more time tracking the market,' he says.

For this effort to succeed, procurement enlisted support from all its units, which took some time. Cerminara notes that any time there is consolidation, 'there's a certain amount of anxiety that goes along with it.' To alleviate concerns, the procurement group embarked on an education process. 'There's no formula; we just looked for opportunities to communicate directly with plant managers and others at Hershey plants who had been involved with sourcing,' says Cerminara. He and other members of the procurement team visited some plants, called others, and spoke to plant managers at one point when the managers were in town for a conference. 'We addressed them to tell them why we were changing,' he says.

For long-term savings, procurement established cross-functional teams to work with suppliers. With certain suppliers, five to seven Hershey representatives sit down regularly with counterparts from a supplier and 'they don't negotiate, they look to take cost out of the system,' says Cerminara.

To ensure that the teams find solutions that are acceptable to Hershey, Cerminara says that packaging director Thomas Bowman 'coaches' the team to set goals and achieve them. The results have been solutions such as labels that lower costs for Hershey, improved manufacturing efficiencies, and added value to the supplier's product

Source: Murphy (1998)

INTRODUCTION

As this Case Study shows, changing customer demands forced Hershey to turn around its purchasing organization. Key decision making on strategic commodities was centralized, whereas at the same time cross-functional cooperation on new product development across the disciplines involved was fostered. The more strategic role of purchasing within Hersheys led to some drastic changes in the way buyers were required to operate. They needed to move away from their operational and transactional tasks into more strategic and policymaking tasks. In order to be able to perform these tasks effectively, higher demands were imposed onto them in terms of communication with the business units and plant managers.

This chapter discusses the major changes which companies are experiencing today in restructuring their purchasing and supply organizations. Our discussion focuses on purchasing organisations within manufacturing companies.

Also discussed is how to get organized for purchasing and supply management. In particular, the question of how to define primary purchasing tasks, responsibilities and competences in relationships with other departments will be addressed. Furthermore, this chapter will describe how to organize for purchasing and supply management in a single and multi-plant environment. In this respect the relationship between purchasing and engineering on the one hand, and logistics management on the other, is discussed. Next, some time is spent on the issue of centralization/decentralization in purchasing and supply management, and the issue of purchasing coordination. Finally, the profiles of some important jobs in purchasing and supply management are presented.

PURCHASING ORGANIZATION STRUCTURE

The location and structure of purchasing is very much dependent on business character-istics and situational factors. For example, the buying of raw materials in chemical indus-tries is often executed by a small group of specialists, which reports directly to the board of directors. Some very large companies, such as Dow Chemicals, have created a separate department or even a separate business unit for this purpose. In small and medium-sized enterprises, however, this could be the exclusive responsibility of the general manager. The same pattern can be seen for the buying of investment goods. As shown in Chapter 2, small companies may buy these goods with only marginal interference from the purchasing department.

However, in large companies (such as AKZO Nobel or Procter & Gamble), these types of buying decisions are prepared by a corporate purchasing department. It is not uncommon to find the purchasing of raw materials, commodities and production-related materials on the one hand, and technical equipment and spare parts on the other, organized completely separately (this traditionally was the case in the aircraft and chemical industry). The organ-ization of purchasing, therefore, is highly dependent on the characteristics of the company and the characteristics of the products bought.

The survey conducted by Fearon and Leenders (1995) in the US and Canada provided some relevant data on how purchasing is organized. This survey was based on an in-depth analysis of international purchasing practices at 302 large multinational industrial and service companies. The results of this survey were compared with a similar survey which was conducted in 1988 (see Table 13.1). The survey showed that a substantial amount of

TABLE 13.1 Centralized versus decentralized purchasing

	1995 Study						1988 Study	
	<10 $billion		>10 $billion		Total			
Organization structure	$	%	$	%	$	%	$	%
Centralized, in which all, or almost all, purchasing is done at one central location for the entire firm	61	24	8	18	69	23	83	28
Centralized/decentralized, in which some purchasing is done at the corporate headquarters and purchasing also is done at major operating divisions/plants	161	62	35	80	196	65	175	59
Decentralized, in which purchasing is done on a division/plant basis	36	14	1	2	37	12	38	13
TOTAL	258	100	44	100	302	100	296	100

Source: adapted from Fearon and Leenders (1995) pp.15–16.

organizational restructuring had taken place. A more detailed analysis of the data showed that only 45 per cent of the companies which reported a centralized purchasing structure in 1988 were still centralized; 48 per cent of this group had moved towards a hybrid centralized/decentralized structure. Of those who reported having a centralized/decentralized structure, 78 per cent reported to still have the same structure. However, 72 per cent of the companies who reported having a fully decentralized structure in 1998, moved towards a more coordinated purchasing structure. It is fair to conclude, based on these figures, that purchasing activities in international companies among business units have become more and more coordinated.

Table 13.2 shows what purchasing techniques, approaches and activities are used. The table also shows to what extent respondents expected that the use of these subjects would increase in the near future. At the time the research was done respondents expected that use of cross-functional teams and teams involving suppliers would increase most. On the whole, participative approaches were expected to increase in the future according to these data.

TABLE 13.2 Use of various purchasing techniques, approaches, activities, and expected use over next 12 months

	Number of firms responding	Percentage of firms using technique/approach/activity					Percentage of firms predicting increase over the next 12 months
		None %	Slight %	Mod-erate %	Sub-stantial %	Extens-ive %	Increase %
Purchasing councils (purchasing managers only)	305	17	22	30	20	11	26
Supplier councils (primarily key suppliers)	305	27	30	30	10	3	38
Commodity teams (purchasing personnel only)	303	11	23	25	25	16	35
Cross-functional teams	307	3	11	30	37	19	54
Teams involving supplier(s)	306	9	27	39	20	5	58
Teams involving customer(s)	304	21	30	28	15	6	43
Teams involving both supplier(s) and customer(s)	304	33	35	20	10	2	43
Co-location of purchasing personnel with users/ specifiers	303	28	23	26	16	7	27
Consortium buying (pooling with other firms)	306	65	25	7	2	0	33

Source: Fearon and Leenders (1995) p. 46.

FACTORS INFLUENCING THE LOCATION OF PURCHASING IN THE ORGANIZATION

The organizational location of purchasing is very much dependent on the view management holds towards the purchasing function. When management considers the purchasing function mainly as an operational activity, this will result in the purchasing department having a relatively low position in the organizational hierarchy. If management considers purchasing to be an important competitive factor, however, and of strategic importance to the organization, then the purchasing manager might very well be reporting to or even be part of the board of directors. Management's view of purchasing is, to a large extent, related to the following factors:

- Purchasing's share in the end-product's cost-price. The higher the purchasing content, the more strategic the purchasing function is considered by management.
- The financial position of the company. In times of severe financial losses, management will become more demanding on its purchasing operations and purchasing related costs, resulting in a greater accountability being requested.
- The extent to which the company is dependent on the suppliers' market. Supply markets with high concentration ratios usually get more attention from management.

The implementation of materials requirements planning or just-in-time principles leads to a greater need for integrating purchasing and supply management with logistics management. As a result the purchasing manager in these companies will often report to the logistics manager.

In technically oriented companies, however, which are confronted with rapid changes in product and/or process technology, the purchasing manager may report to the production manager. Table 13.3 shows how some of these factors may influence the reporting relationships of purchasing managers.

TABLE 13.3 Factors influencing purchasing's reporting relationships

	Purchasing reports to			
	General management	Production management	Logistics management	Financial management
Purchasing turnover ratio				
High	X			X
Low		X	X	
Technical complexity				
High		X	X	
Low	X			X
Logistics complexity				
High		X	X	
Low	X			X
Strategic impact				
High	X			X
Low		X	X	

LEVELS OF TASKS, RESPONSIBILITIES AND AUTHORITY

With regard to the allocation of purchasing tasks, responsibilities and authority, three different levels may be differentiated:

- strategic
- tactical
- operational.

Strategic level

The strategic level covers those purchase decisions that influence the market position of the company in the long run. These decisions primarily reside under the responsibility of top management. Examples of purchase decisions at this level are:

- The development and issuing of operational guidelines, procedures and task descriptions, which provide authority to the purchasing department.
- The development and implementation of auditing and review programs in order to monitor and improve purchasing operations and performance.
- Decisions to outsource activities, which currently have been executed by the company to outside suppliers.
- Establishing long-term contracts and contacts with certified and/or preferred suppliers (for example long-term purchasing agreements, licence agreements, partnership agreements, co-design agreements).
- Decisions related to adopting a supplier strategy based on multi- versus single-sourcing.
- Major investment decisions (in buildings, equipment, computers).
- Decisions with regard to backward integration, i.e. decisions to participate financially in supplier organizations in order to safeguard the future supply of critical materials.
- Decisions related to policies concerning transfer-pricing and intercompany supplies.
- Decisions related to policies on reciprocal arrangements, countertrade and barter-deals.

This list illustrates the long-term, strategic impact that purchasing and supply decisions may have on the company's competitive position.

Tactical level

The tactical level encompasses the involvement of the purchasing function affecting product, process and supplier selection. Examples of purchasing decisions at this level are:

- Agreement on corporate and/or annual supplier agreements.
- Preparing and developing value analysis programs, programs aimed at design-review and product standardization.
- Adopting and conducting certification programs (including audits) for suppliers in order to improve the quality of incoming goods and materials.
- Selection and contracting of suppliers in general, and programs aimed at supply-base reduction, in particular.

TABLE 13.4 Relationship between the three managerial levels of purchasing and some management positions

| | Managerial level | | | | |
Task	Top management	Logistics management	Purchasing management	Senior buyer	Buying assistant/ materials planner
Strategic level	x	x	x		
Tactical level		x	x	x	
Operations level				x	x

Decisions on these issues often have a medium-term impact (one to three years). They are cross-functional in the sense that dealing with them effectively requires the coordination and cooperation of other disciplines within the company, including engineering, manufacturing, logistics, quality assurance. Earlier, in Chapter 1, these activities were referred to as 'initial purchasing'.

Operational level

The operational level addresses all activities related to the ordering and expediting function. This level of activities incorporates the ordering of materials, monitoring the deliveries and settling quality disputes on incoming materials. More specifically, the operational activities of the purchasing function include:

- The ordering process (release of orders corresponding to already concluded agreements with suppliers).
- All expediting activities related to released orders.
- Troubleshooting: solving daily problems on quality, supply and payment in the relationship with the supplier.
- The monitoring and evaluation of supplier performance.

Table 13.4 presents the relationships between the three defined task-levels and a number of purchasing activities.

ORGANIZATIONAL STRUCTURES WITHIN PURCHASING

This section describes some alternative structures on which to organize the purchasing function within companies. For this purpose the discussion differentiates between multi-unit companies and single-unit companies.

Structure of purchasing in multi-unit companies

For the organization of purchasing in multi-unit companies a number of alternatives are available:

- decentralized purchasing structure
- centralized purchasing structure

- line-management organization
- pooling structure
- cross-functional sourcing teams.

Decentralized purchasing structure This structure can be found in companies with a business-unit structure. A major characteristic is that every business-unit manager is responsible for his own financial results (see Figure 13.1).[1] Hence, the management of the business unit is fully responsible for all its purchasing activities. One of the disadvantages of this structure is that different business units, belonging to the same corporation, may negotiate with the same supplier for the same products, and as a result arrive at different purchase conditions. When supplier capacity is tight, business units can operate as real competitors to each other, who are fighting for the same supplier capacity..

This structure is particularly attractive to conglomerates that have a business-unit structure, where each business-unit purchases products that are unique and markedly different from those of the other units. In this case bundling of common purchasing requirements would provide only limited advantages and/or savings.

Centralized purchasing structure In this situation at the corporate level, a central purchasing department can be found where corporate contracting specialists operate at the strategic and tactical level (see Figure 13.2). Decisions on product specifications are made centrally (often in close cooperation with a central engineering or R&D organization), and the same goes for supplier selection decisions; contracts with suppliers are prepared and negotiated centrally. These contracts are often multi-year agreements with pre-selected suppliers, stating the general and specific purchase conditions. The operational purchase activities are conducted by the operating companies.

General Motors Europe and Volkswagen may serve as examples of companies which have centralized their strategic and tactical purchasing operations to a high degree. Other examples are Xerox and the Ford Motor Company. The main advantage of this structure is that, through coordination of purchasing, better conditions (both in terms of prices and

FIGURE 13.1   Decentralized purchasing organization structure (example).

1 The term 'business unit' is used here as equivalent to operating unit or operating company. With this term the author refers to a situation where the unit management is profit-responsible and operates with a large degree of autonomy.

FIGURE 13.2   Centralized purchasing organizational structure (example).

costs and in terms of service and quality) from suppliers can be achieved. Another advantage is that it will facilitate efforts towards product and supplier standardization.

The disadvantages are also obvious: the management of the individual business unit has only limited responsibility for decisions on purchasing. Often the problem is that the business-unit managers are convinced that they are able to reach better conditions on their own, and will act individually; in this way they will gradually undermine the position of the corporate purchasing department.

This structure is appropriate in cases where several business units buy the same products, which at the same time are of strategic importance to them.

Centralized/decentralized purchasing organization[2] In some major manufacturing companies a corporate purchasing department exists at a corporate level, while individual business units also conduct strategic and tactical purchasing activities. In this case a corporate purchasing department usually deals with the design of procedures and guidelines for purchasing. Furthermore, it may conduct audits when requested to do so by the management of the business units (see Figure 13.3).

Often, the central department also conducts detailed supply market studies on strategic commodities, the results of which are made available to the purchasing departments of the business units through periodical brochures, bulletins and/or Intranet. Furthermore, this corporate purchasing department may serve as a vehicle to facilitate and/or solve coordination issues between divisions or business units. However, no tactical purchase activities are conducted here. These all reside within the divisional purchasing organizations or the purchasing organizations at the business units. Finally, the corporate purchasing department in this structure may be responsible for human resource management in purchasing and supply.

From this description it follows that this type of structure is in general limited to very large international companies, for example the Electrolux Group AB in Sweden. General Electric Company and Raytheon Company in the US used to have a line-staff organization, but changed their structure some years ago.

Figure 13.4 lists what activities may be conducted by a corporate purchasing staff in a centralized/decentralized structure.

---

2 Sometimes referred to as a hybrid structure or line-staff structure.

Pooling structure As explained earlier, a pooling structure represents a combination of the previous three organizational structures. The terms 'pooling' and 'coordination' are used interchangeably. Both concepts relate to 'efforts aimed at combining common materials requirements among two or more operating units with the objective to improve the leverage of the company in order to reduce overall materials costs and/or to improve the service obtained from outside suppliers'. However, a lot of variety still exists in practice – depending on the type of commodity, pooling may be forced upon the business units

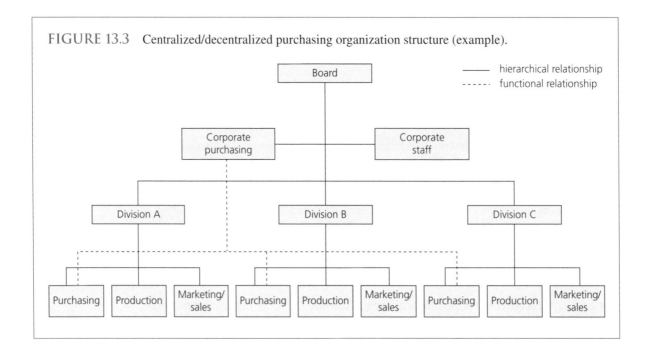

FIGURE 13.3   Centralized/decentralized purchasing organization structure (example).

FIGURE 13.4   Corporate headquarters, role and activities.

- Contracts for common requirements
- Purchasing of headquarters requirements
- Establishes policies and procedures
- Develops supply systems (EDI, purchasing cards)
- Participates in system-wide purchasing/supply personnel decisions/actions
- Develops and/or provides training
- Collects and provides purchasing information
- Evaluates/audits unit/divisional purchasing performance
- Performs special studies and reports
- Interfaces with government
- Interfaces with industry/professional groups/associations
- Provides input to and supports services for special corporate initiatives in areas such as quality, cost, timeliness, productivity, customer satisfaction
- Measures supplier satisfaction
- Participates in interplant purchases and/or goods or services transfers …

Source: adapted from Fearon and Leenders (1995), p. 45

or may have a more voluntary character. In order to illustrate the major characteristics of this structure, some examples of pooling structures are described below.

- *Voluntary coordination.* In this case a considerable exchange of information takes place between the purchasing departments of the operating companies. Based on this data every business unit is free to decide whether to take part in a (corporate) contract or to operate individually. Contracts are prepared by purchasing coordination committees (or commodity teams), in which the largest users are represented.

- *Lead buyership.* In this case the business unit that has the greatest volume for a specific type of commodity is made responsible for negotiating a corporate agreement with the supplier involved. This business unit collects all relevant data from all other units and negotiates with the supplier. Each individual business unit periodically releases orders directly to the supplier referring to the appropriate contract conditions.

- *Lead design concept.* The guiding principle underlying this form of pooling is co-design – the operating unit or division, which is responsible for the design of the specific product or component (the 'lead-house') is also responsible for contracting all materials and components from suppliers. An example would be a division of a major automotive company responsible for developing a new fuel-injection system. After approval of the new product, the system is offered to the other divisions which may incorporate it in their new models. Materials and components, however, are obtained from suppliers which have been approved and contracted by the 'lead-house' division. This practice is also apparent at some electronics manufacturers with regard to the design of new semiconductors. Usually supplier relationships are rather intense. Suppliers are involved in discussions on development and design at an early stage, so that the assembler may benefit optimally from the supplier's technical knowledge.

Pooling may occur at different levels of aggregation:

- at article level
- at supplier level
- at business-unit level
- at division level; and
- at regional level.

As mentioned earlier purchasing organizational structures are influenced by a large number of variables, which makes manufacturing companies difficult to compare. Most companies, however, will have mixed patterns of organization based on the basic structures presented here.

Cross-functional sourcing teams This organizational form is relatively new within purchasing. It can be best described by an example from IBM. As a result of enormous financial loss in 1992, the purchasing function at IBM was reorganized. IBM's new purchasing structure provides a consolidation of needs on components for the whole organization with one single contact point (the commodity team) for the supplier. Contracting is done centrally on corporate level. However, in all cases the operational purchasing activities are decentralized.

Purchasing components and other production-related goods is organized through divisional global procurement executives (see Figure 13.5). These managers are responsible for purchasing, sourcing and supplier policy for a certain group of components. They report to the chief purchasing officer (CPO) and to their own business-unit manager. The business-unit managers meet the CPO during various corporate business councils where purchasing and supplier issues are discussed and decisions are being made. The CPO

FIGURE 13.5   IBM's commodity team structure.

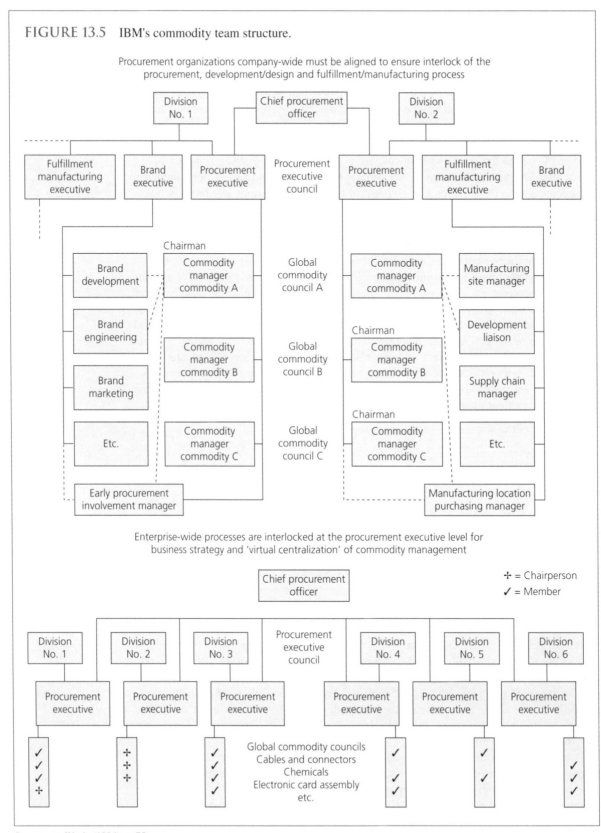

Source: van Weele (1996), p. 75

communicates with every business-unit manager separately in order to match the corporate purchasing strategy with the needs of the individual divisions and business units. This guarantees a thorough integration of the purchasing and supplier policy in the organization. This way IBM uses its enormous purchasing power in combination with maximum flexibility.

Corporate commodity plans are submitted to the CPO and, next, to the procurement executive council. They are prepared by cross-functional commodity teams. These teams consist of professionals in product development, R&D, marketing, production, distribution and finance, together with purchasing professionals. The leader of this team is a commodity manager, who is not necessarily a purchaser. The structure of the team is virtual because most professionals may work all over the world. They communicate through e-mail, fax and video conferencing. These commodity teams have the authority to select suppliers and contract them for a specific commodity.

For purchasing of production-related materials IBM pursues global uniform purchasing procedures. Supplier selection and choice should follow a uniform pattern. They focus more and more on selecting and contracting main suppliers who offer products and services at a world-class level and who have global presence. This leads to lower prices and cost levels, higher quality, shorter delivery cycles and therefore lower stocks. This approach results in fewer suppliers and a growing mutual involvement because the purchasing turnover is spread between less suppliers. Therefore more attention can be given to the relationship with an individual supplier in the value chain and a relationship based on continuous performance improvement can be developed.

Key factors to realizing and improving a global sourcing process are: strong leadership, active involvement of management, aggressive supplier management, corporate commodity plans, cross-functional teams and standardization of logistics and delivery processes.

Centralized versus decentralized purchasing: some criteria to consider The question as to what extent to centralize or decentralize purchasing cannot be easily answered. Most companies balance between the two extremes: at one moment of time they will have a centralized purchasing organization, whereas some years later they may opt for a more decentralized purchasing organization. In recent years many automotive companies have decided to centralize their purchasing operations. The same goes for some major office equipment manufacturers, such as Xerox, while other companies, e.g. KLM, have changed from a functional to a divisional structure. As a result the central purchasing department was split up into five decentralized purchasing departments within each of the divisions and business units that were formed.

The following factors or criteria are commonly used when deciding to opt for centralization or decentralization in purchasing.

- Commonality of purchase requirements. The greater the commonality of the purchased products required by the business units, the more benefits can be obtained from a centralized or coordinated approach. This is why the buying of raw materials and packaging materials in large companies is often concentrated at one (corporate) location.

- Geographic location. When business units are situated in different countries and/or regions this may hamper coordination efforts considerably. In practice there appear to be significant differences in trading and management practices between Europe and the United States. Even within a European context significant cultural differences exist and some large companies have changed their coordination strategy from a global to a regional approach.

- Supply market structure. Sometimes the company is confronted in some of its supply markets with one or a limited number of very large supplier organizations. In such a situation the power balance is definitely to the advantage of the supplier and it makes sense to adopt a coordinated purchasing approach in order to arrange for a better negotiating position *vis-à-vis* these powerful trading partners.

■ Savings potential. Prices of some types of raw materials are very sensitive to volume: in such circumstances buying higher volumes may immediately lead to cost savings. This is true both for standard commodities and high-tech components.

■ Expertise required. Sometimes very specific expertise is required for effective buying, as in the purchase of high-tech semiconductors and microchips; prices are also strongly related to the laws of supply and demand. As a result most manufacturers of electronics goods have centralized the buying of these products. The same goes for the buying of software and hardware.

■ Price fluctuations. If materials (e.g. fruit juices, wheat, coffee) prices are highly sensitive to the political and economic climate, a centralized purchasing approach is favored.

■ Customer demands. Sometimes a customer will dictate to the manufacturer which products it has to purchase. This is typical for the aircraft industries. These conditions are agreed upon with the business unit that is responsible for manufacturing the product. This practice will clearly obstruct any efforts aimed at purchasing coordination.

In practice these considerations appear to be decisive when deciding on buying products centrally or otherwise.

In summarizing this section, the advantages and disadvantages of decentralization are shown in Figure 13.6 – for centralization, the reverse of the arguments may be used.

Over the past years, the topic of how to foster purchasing synergies in a corporate environment has received much attention. Recent research reveals that the way in which corporations should leverage their purchasing and supplier strategies is dependent on two factors, i.e. purchasing maturity and corporate cohesion. Differences in how companies deal with purchasing coordination may be explained by these two variables (see Memo 13.1).

Purchasing organization in single-unit companies

In a single-unit organization the issue of centralized versus decentralized purchasing relates to the question of to what extent purchases need to be made through the purchas-

---

FIGURE 13.6   Some advantages and disadvantages related to decentralized purchasing.

Advantages	Disadvantages
• Direct responsibility for profit centres	• Dispersed purchasing power, lack of economies of scale
• Stronger customer orientation towards internal user	• No uniform attitude towards suppliers
• Less bureaucratic purchasing procedures	• Scattered market research
• Less need for internal coordination	• Limited possibilities for building up specific expertise on purchasing and materials
• Direct communication with suppliers	• Probably different commercial purchase conditions for different business units

ing department. This refers directly to what authority should be assigned to the purchasing department and, in general, depends on the following variables.

- Management's view towards purchasing. This clearly affects the tasks, responsibilities and authority assigned to the purchasing department (see Chapter 5).

- Information technology. This directly affects the possibilities for coordination of all materials-related activities within the company. Generally, implementation of MRP systems will alter the traditional ways of working within purchasing. In general, it will require better discipline and more systematic communication from purchasing operations. As a result purchasing procedures need to be changed and adapted and changes within the materials organization may even be necessary. Information systems also enable better management information and reports. As a result of a greater transparency of purchasing operations, its reporting relationships may need to be reviewed.

- Personal relationships. As in any organizational issue, personal relationships often play an overriding role in discussions on how to structure reporting relationships. If the purchasing manager is to report to the logistics manager, it is important that the latter shows some affinity with the purchasing job. Otherwise, conflicts may occur.

MEMO 13.1 CREATING CORPORATE ADVANTAGE IN PURCHASING

The results from the survey suggest that corporate purchasing initiatives should be congruent with the overall level of corporate coherence and the level of maturity of the purchasing function. Corporate coherence is related to the extent to which the different parts of the corporation operate and are managed as one entity. Major differences across business units in management style, vision, strategy, culture and structure, reflect a low corporate coherence. When differences in culture and structure exist across business units, the integration of the purchasing function will be a significant challenge. Purchasing maturity is related (amongst other factors) to the level of professionalism in the purchasing function as expressed in status of the function, role and organizational status of the purchasing departments, availability of purchasing information systems, quality of the people involved in purchasing, and the level of collaboration with suppliers. Our research suggests that when the purchasing function is highly mature, companies will use a different and more advanced approach to manage corporate purchasing synergy, than in the situation where one is dealing with low purchasing maturity (see Figure 13.7). In cases where both purchasing maturity and corporate coherence are low, decentralized purchasing is most likely to be found. In such a situation central coordination efforts will be hardly sustainable. In this situation, we expect little homogeneity in specifications across business units. However, there are opportunities to realize purchasing synergy through exchanging information of supply markets, suppliers and prices, by using voluntary working groups. In cases where both constructs are high, a centre-led structure has good chances of success. In such a structure cross-functional/cross-business teams conduct coordination activities with active support of the business units, whilst strongly managed by a corporate purchasing staff. If both parameters have a medium value, a hybrid structure, with both central purchasing and voluntary purchasing coordination activities is most likely to be found. Federal (or local-led) purchasing consists of a small corporate purchasing staff supporting a number of autonomous decentralized purchasing units in their voluntary efforts to exploit potential synergies. The central purchasing model represents a situation in which most strategic commodities are contracted from a corporate purchasing department. The latter appears to be only feasible in organizations where purchasing at the operating company level is hardly developed and corporate coherence is high.

In our view, top managers do not add value by choosing a certain approach to create corporate advantage in purchasing as such. They add value by creating a fit between the approach used to create corporate advantage in purchasing, and the level of corporate coherence and purchasing maturity. In practice, this is not very

▶

often the case. Our research revealed a number of initiatives that were not aimed at creating long-term corporate advantage, but at short-term cost reductions. In many of those cases external consultants were hired to drive corporate purchasing cost reduction initiatives. Often, however, after the consultants had left, the companies gradually returned to their former and less cooperative ways of working, not using the momentum to establish formal organizational mechanisms, or other measures, to create sustainable corporate advantage in purchasing. In our view, this is related to the fact that the approach used by the consultants was not congruent with the level of corporate coherence and purchasing maturity of these companies.

Source: Rozemeijer and van Weele (2003), pp. 10–11.

FIGURE 13.7   Corporate purchasing organizational approaches.

- Total cost approach. A better understanding of some important logistics parameters, such as inventory turnover, supplier delivery reliability, the supplier reject rate, etc. will diminish the relevance of purchase prices only. As a result purchasing decisions will become more cost oriented instead of price oriented, which has been the tradition in many companies. Knowledge of these additional 'performance indicators' often leads to a less autonomously operating purchasing department and to a better integration with the logistics function.

Based on these variables purchasing's reporting relationships may take different forms, as differentiated in the structures given below.[3]

- The fully integrated logistics structure. Here, purchasing reports directly to the logistics manager at the same level as production planning and physical distribution (see Figure 13.8).
- The partially integrated logistics structure. In this structure purchasing, production planning and physical distribution report to the logistics manager in various ways. Figure 13.9 shows three possible configurations.

---

3 This discussion has been based upon the contribution by Miller and Gilmour (1979).

In the preceding chapters, some important changes have been discussed which affect the role and position of the purchasing organization. These changes can be divided into external and internal changes. External changes are related to changes outside the company. They are not to be influenced by the company. Internal changes are related to changes inside the company. In most cases they result from rethinking the value chain, i.e. the company's primary processes and its relationships with suppliers.

It will be clear that all of these changes influence the tasks, responsibilities and authority of the purchasing function. And, hence, they will affect and change the structure of the purchasing organization (see Figure 13.10).

Consequences for purchasing professionals

The developments described above will also lead to significant changes in the necessary skills and abilities required by the purchasing department. In most large companies the following positions can be found.

- Corporate procurement officer (CPO). Most large organizations today have a senior executive who is responsible for the management and coordination of key purchasing and supply processes throughout the organization. In most cases this executive reports to the board of executives or is a member of this board. Depending on the company structure the specific tasks of the CPO and his authority may differ.

- Corporate buyers. These are generally focused on very specialized tasks. It is their job to negotiate for large volumes of products and components (in the case of raw materials), large investment projects and services (e.g. in the case of manufacturing equipment and computer hardware and software). Their counterparts are often account managers who are highly educated and experienced. For this reason corporate buyers preferably have a similar educational background, often at university level. They are responsible for developing corporate sourcing strategies for key commodities, which are prepared with the product specialists who reside in different parts of the corporation.

- Purchasing engineers. These buyers, often working at a decentralized level, normally have a shorter planning horizon and a more operational task. As they have to meet and

FIGURE 13.8 Example of a fully integrated logistics structure.

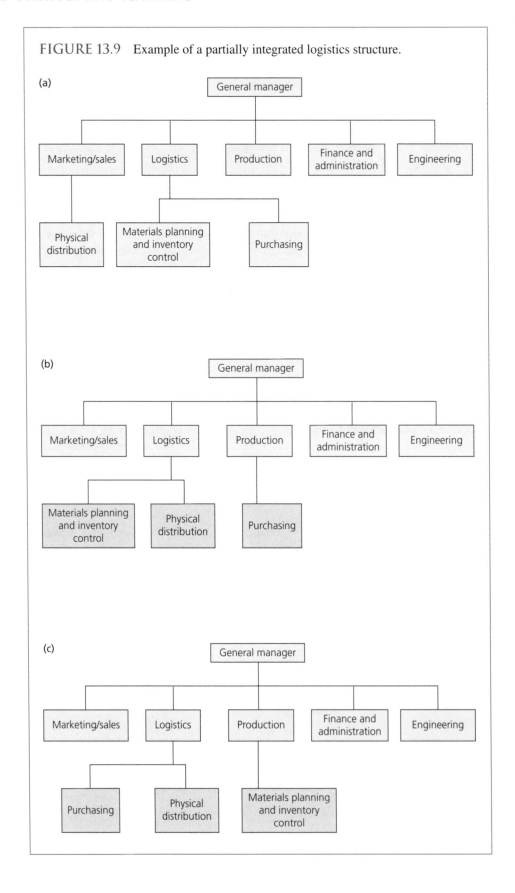

FIGURE 13.9   Example of a partially integrated logistics structure.

converse frequently with engineers and other technical specialists they require an adequate technical background, combined with commercial skills. In fact, purchasing engineers are the liaison between the engineering and purchasing departments in new product development programs. Most of their time is spent on discussing specifications, both internally and externally, conducting supply market research, selection of suppliers, and preparing and conducting contract negotiations with suppliers. As soon as the product has been introduced to the market, their product-, supplier- and contract files are passed on to the category buyer.

- Project buyers. The tasks of the project buyers are somewhat similar to those of the purchasing engineer. However, the purchasing engineer deals with production materials, whereas the project purchaser deals primarily with investment goods. For this job a technical background at university level is required. Since these decisions always require a team approach, project buyers should possess effective communication and presentation skills.

- Materials planners. Materials planners are responsible for materials planning and ordering. In companies with a high degree of computerization within the materials area, both tasks are often combined in one function. Here, the materials planners focus on calling

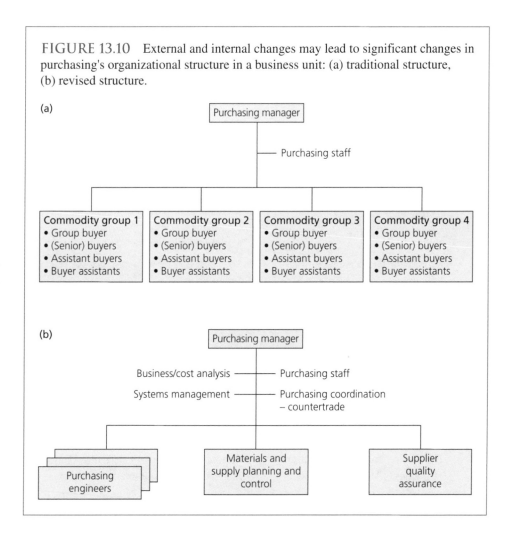

FIGURE 13.10 External and internal changes may lead to significant changes in purchasing's organizational structure in a business unit: (a) traditional structure, (b) revised structure.

off the materials required against the annual agreements. Furthermore they monitor and control suppliers on their quality and delivery performance. For this job a secondary educational level will be sufficient. Most important here are personal abilities, such as stress-resistance, service orientation and the ability to organize the work effectively. Additionally, this job provides a good opportunity for future buyers to become acquainted with the work.

■ Maintenance, repair, operate buyers. For an MRO buyer a general, polytechnic education will suffice. With regard to the purchasing of spare parts, the delivery of these items in general will be covered in the original contract for the investment good. The MRO assortment is generally very large and it is the task of the MRO buyer to manage these assortments effectively, rather than striving to optimize the price performance for each individual item. Therefore, a good understanding of logistics management and techniques (of inventory management and order management specifically), catalog solutions and e-procurement applications would be basic to this type of buyer.

Table 13.5 summarizes the most important skills and abilities of the functions which have been described above. Memo 13.2 describes how the purchasing job has changed over time and how buyers are spending their time today.

TABLE 13.5 Buyer profiles and their most important responsibilities and skills

Function	Responsibilities	Skills required
Corporate buyer	Strategic commodities	Specialist commercial skills Long-term planning horizon Communication skills Broad business orientation
Purchasing engineer	New materials and components New suppliers	All-round technical background Medium-term planning horizon Commercial skills Communication skills
Project buyer	Equipment and services	Specialist project management skills 'Team player'
MRO buyer	MRO supplies	Generalist Efficient order handling Assortment manager Service oriented Commercial skills
Materials planner	Materials and order planning Order handling Vendor rating	All-round 'common sense' Stress-resistant Service oriented Problem-solving skills
Corporate purchasing officer	Developing corporate purchasing strategies, systems, reporting	Superior management skills providing leadership to procurement processes Communication skills

MEMO 13.2   HOW BUYERS ARE CHANGING

Today's purchasing professional is a little older, has been on the job slightly longer, and is responsible for spending a lot more dollars than a comparable buying professional of 10 years ago. Today's purchasing professional is much more likely to be a woman than 10 years ago – or even five years ago. He/she is more likely to have chosen purchasing as a career than in the past. His/her dollar volume responsibility is twice as high as it was in 1997 and three times higher than in 1992. Paperwork and transaction processing continues to be the bane of many of these procurement professionals – despite quantum improvements being made in automating the buying process. He or she is negotiating more long-term agreements with selected suppliers. Looking out on a global market scape, today's purchasing professional is negotiating outsourcing agreements with suppliers around the world. And a vast majority of these buying executives continue to pare away at costs and the size of their supply bases.

These are some of the findings of *Purchasing* magazine's latest survey of procurement officers and supply chain executives. A close examination of this latest picture of the purchasing executive shows a professional who regularly handles huge sums of money, takes part in corporate-wide profitability decisions, is responsible for the performance of a number of non-purchasing functions, works closely with top management, and is constantly on the lookout for new approaches and techniques to cut costs and improve supply chain efficiency.

What follows is a best effort summary and anatomy of the purchasing professional in 2003.

■ Ten years ago men dominated the purchasing profession – holding down 82 per cent of all the jobs. Today, male dominance is still considerable, but falling. Just over 68 per cent of the jobs in purchasing are now held by men.

■ Today 67.4 per cent of all purchasing executives boast a four-year college degree. This compares with 61.2 per cent in 1992. In addition, nearly 13 per cent of all purchasing executives are working for degrees or advanced degrees.

■ Business is the degree of preference with 61 per cent of all degrees held by purchasing executives. Liberal arts degrees are in second place with 17 per cent, followed by science/engineering (15 per cent) and other (mostly assorted technical specialties) at 5 per cent.

■ Certification has grown slowly since it came on the scene in 1987. Today 21 per cent of purchasing executives polled hold either CPM or CPIM (American Inventory Control Society) certification.

■ The average respondent to this survey has been in purchasing 9.8 years.

■ What is the total value of the purchases the individual purchasing professional controls/supervises? Answers to this question vary a great amount – from less than $1 million to $526 million. The average purchasing responsibility is $31.3 million. In 1992 it was a little more than $11 million.

■ More than 81 per cent of purchasing professionals say they are responsible for maintaining inventory levels. This is up from 77 per cent five years ago. Inventory is a shared responsibility for 40 per cent of the respondents – mainly with a sales manager or plant manager. And for 37 per cent of those purchasing officers with inventory responsibility, it's an unshared responsibility.

■ Fifty-six per cent of respondents say they have systems for rating supplier performance. Of the companies with performance measurement systems, 32 per cent are formal systems.

■ Among those purchasing executives involved in product development a rough estimate of time devoted to these activities was 14 per cent.

■ Purchasing departments across the land have experienced serious downsizing efforts in the past two years (82.1 per cent). Much of the downsizing can be traced to the introduction of dedicated e-sourcing tools in

▶

purchasing. Also playing a major role is the introduction of supply chain management techniques to purchasing organizations and increased attention to staffing structures.

■ A large plurality of respondents (31 per cent) feel as Ralph Richardson, manager of purchasing and stores at EPB, Chattanooga, does that there is great satisfaction in 'negotiating long-term deals with suppliers' and potential suppliers. Other areas of job satisfaction listed by survey participants include maximizing sourcing development, reducing costs and problem solving.

Source: J. Morgan, 'How buyers are changing: profile of a purchasing professional', *Purchasing*, 14 August, 2003, pp. 33–36.

SUMMARY

In this chapter issues related to purchasing organization have been discussed. Purchasing structures appear to vary to a great extent among companies. This is due to the different views which top managers hold towards purchasing and supply. Apart from this some company-specific characteristics may define purchasing's reporting relationships. Among these, purchasing's share in the end products' costs, the financial position of the company and the company's dependency on the supplier market are the most important.

When analysing the scope, tasks, responsibilities and authority of the purchasing department, we differentiated between the strategic level, the tactical level and the operational level. When redesigning purchasing structures managers should make sure that each of the task levels is given sufficient attention. The outcome of such a process will probably be different for multi-unit companies and single-unit companies. In a multi-unit environment it should be decided to what extent the purchasing function should be decentralized. In this respect five types of organizational structures have been discussed: the centralized structure, the decentralized structure, the line-management organization, the pooling structure and cross-functional sourcing teams. The last two are the most complicated ones; however, their popularity is growing rapidly. Pooling structures may have different forms. These may be structured based upon voluntary coordination, the lead buyer concept and the lead design concept. The decision whether to centralize or decentralize and what coordination form would be the best, depends on a limited number of parameters. Here, we discussed purchasing maturity and corporate cohesion as important factors. It is fair to conclude that there is no single best way to get organized for purchasing in a corporate, multi-unit environment.

Purchasing structures appear to be highly volatile: a period of centralized purchasing is often followed by a change to the other way around. Due to increasing international competition and the maturing of many end-user markets, the present trend is towards coordination and more participative, process approaches. Many companies try to reap the benefits of coordinated purchasing of common materials requirements, whilst preserving the advantage of entrepreneurship, residing low in the organization.

When designing purchasing structures in a single-unit environment a number of parameters need to be considered. As computerization in the materials-related functions progresses, purchasing activities become more integrated with logistics management. In this respect various options are open to managers. They may choose a totally integrated organizational model or decide on a partially integrated model.

Major organizational changes are reflected in future profiles of purchasing positions. For this reason we discussed the profile of the chief procurement officer, the corporate buyer, the purchasing engineer, the project buyer, the materials planner and the MRO buyer. From this discussion it became clear that the purchasing and supply arena provides significant challenges to those with an engineering and MBA background.

ASSIGNMENTS

13.1 When discussing the opportunity to foster synergies in the area of purchasing, some top managers stated that 'purchasing in our company is too important to leave it only to buyers!'. Would you agree with this? How would you see the buyer's role in creating corporate, leveraged purchasing strategies?

13.2 In this chapter it was argued that most large companies have opted for a hybrid structure to organize their purchasing activities. What is meant by this? Why would companies choose such a structure?

13.3 When applying for a new job in a medium-sized company, a prospective purchasing manager was asked to whom he would prefer to report: (1) the financial manager, (2) the production manager, (3) the logistics manager. Each of these managers reports at the same hierarchical level. What would you consider to be the most important advantages and disadvantages of each option? What option would you prefer?

13.4 Some complaints that can be heard from CPOs is that their carefully negotiated corporate agreements are barely used by the operating companies. These contracts suffer from a high degree of 'maverick buying'. What could be the reason for this phenomenon?

13.5 How would you explain the growing popularity of cross-functional teams when coordinating purchasing at the corporate level? What would you consider to be the critical success factors of such teams?

13.6 Cross-functional teams prepare corporate sourcing plans for strategic commodities. What would such a commodity plan look like? What elements need to be taken into account in such a plan?

CASE STUDY THE INTRODUCTION OF A QUALITY PROGRAM BY AN INDUSTRIAL COMPONENTS MANUFACTURER

The strategy of a large manufacturer of industrial components is to become a quality leader in his business area. According to management's view, quality improvement is the only way to survive in the company's highly competitive environment. Management is aware of the direct relationship between product quality and process quality and that high quality components can only be manufactured if the manufacturing processes are controlled accurately. In this case it was decided to adopt the ISO 9001 standards and a quality manager was appointed to help the organization make the necessary transitions.

The task of the quality manager is, more specifically, to support the company's departments in developing their own quality programs. Furthermore, he has to ensure that the targets, as agreed by the departmental managers, are realized.

The purchasing department is actively involved in the company's quality program and, like his colleagues, the purchasing manager has developed a quality program for his department. However, as time goes by, he meets with little enthusiasm from his buyers to support the plan.

Gradually he gets the impression that they regard implementation of the plan to be the responsibility of the quality manager. Furthermore, the purchasing manager discovers, through complaints from production, that the buyers remain primarily interested in price, rather than quality. When discussing this matter with the quality manager it emerges that targets concerning quality improvement have been translated insufficiently into individual targets. It is not clear to the quality manager how each individual buyer should contribute to the overall quality objectives of the company. On the other hand, objectives with regard to price reduction are readily available and specified in a fair degree of detail. Every month individual buyers are assessed on their budget results at which time actual prices are compared with budgeted prices. Variance reports are prepared on each purchaser's activity and discussed in the purchasing team's monthly meeting. The purchasing manager eventually sees that the buyers respond to what they are inspected on, not on what they are expected to do. He thinks about ways in which to change this situation . . . but what parameters should be used?

INTRODUCTION

This Case Study illustrates the fact that measuring and evaluating purchasing performance is a fuzzy issue, yet it is one of major concern for many companies. The question of how to measure and evaluate purchasing performance is not easily answered. A major problem is that to date no single, practical approach that produces consistent results in different types of companies has been found. It is highly uncertain whether such a yardstick or method of universal application could be developed. This chapter will explain why. The consequence is that managers typically need to rely on their own insight and experience when establishing procedures and systems to monitor the effectiveness and efficiency of their purchasing organizations.

This chapter develops a consistent approach to the subject. Specific questions to be addressed are:

- Why should purchasing performance be measured and evaluated? What are the major benefits to be derived from such an activity?
- What problems are involved in assessing purchasing performance?
- What should be measured and evaluated?
- What measures and techniques exist in order to perform such an evaluation?
- How could an evaluation system be implemented?
- How to benchmark purchasing processes?

FACTORS INFLUENCING PURCHASING PERFORMANCE MEASUREMENT

One of the most important factors that influences the way in which purchasing results are measured, is how management looks upon the role and the importance of the purchasing function. In general, management may hold one of the following views towards purchasing:

- Operational, administrative activity. In this case management evaluates purchasing operations primarily on parameters such as order backlog, purchasing administrative lead time, number of orders issued, number of requests for quotations issued, adherence to existing procedures, etc.
- Commercial activity. In this situation management is aware of the savings potential which purchasing may represent. Targets are agreed upon with the purchasing department on price and/or cost reduction. Purchasing should issue competitive bids to suppliers in order to keep them sharp. Parameters being used here are the total savings

reported by purchasing (per product group and per buyer), number of quotations issued, variance reports, inflation reports, etc.

■ Part of integrated logistics. Management becomes aware that price hunting has its drawbacks and may lead to sub-optimization. Putting too much pressure on prices may seduce buyers to buy 'penny wise and pound foolish'. Demands on lower prices appear always to be met by suppliers to the detriment of quality and delivery reliability. At this stage management introduces targets to buyers on quality improvement, lead time reduction and improving supplier delivery reliability.

■ Strategic business area. Here, purchasing is actively involved in deciding the company's core business and reinforces the company's competitive position. It is actively engaged in make-or-buy studies. Local suppliers are put to the test of international competition. Management evaluates purchasing on a number of aspects including the number of changes (often reduction) in its supply base, the number of new (international) suppliers being contacted (and contracted), and its contribution to the bottom line in terms of savings realized.

Depending on the prevailing view, the position of the purchasing department within the organizational structure will differ, and the measures used for purchasing performance measurement and evaluation will differ significantly. As shown in Figure 14.1, when purchasing is seen as an operational function, performance measures are largely quantitative and administrative in character. On the other hand, when purchasing is considered to be a strategic business area, performance measures are more qualitative and judgmental. In this case, a complex framework of procedures and guidelines typically are used to monitor progress against specific plans to improve purchasing effectiveness.

Which factors determine the prevailing purchasing mode? Firms that consider purchasing as a strategic business area are frequently forced to do so by external factors, such

FIGURE 14.1   How management may look at purchasing.

Alternative viewpoints	Hierarchical position of purchasing	Performance measures
Purchasing as an operational administrative function	Low in organization	Number of orders, order backlog, purchasing administration lead time, authorization, procedures, etc.
Purchasing as a commercial function	Reporting to management	Savings, price reduction, ROI-measures, inflation reports, variance reports
Purchasing as a part of integrated logistics management	Purchasing integrated with other materials-related functions	Savings, cost-reduction, supplier delivery reliability, reject-rates, lead time reduction
Purchasing as a strategic business function	Purchasing represented in top management	'Should cost' analysis, early supplier involvement, make-or-buy, supply base reduction

Source: adapted from Van Weele (1984a), p. 17

as strong pressure on prices and margins, loss of market share, the need for drastic cost reduction on incoming materials, and severe price fluctuations in the supply market. These issues often force managers to focus attention on the need for high-level purchasing performance. In addition, internal factors may also affect or change the view that management holds towards purchasing. Among these are things such as management style, the extent to which supply chain management has been implemented within the company, the degree to which modern quality concepts have been introduced and applied, the degree of computerization in the materials area, etc.

In summary it can be said that the way purchasing activities are measured and judged will differ for every company considered; this makes it almost impossible to develop one uniform yardstick, methodology or system for performance measurement in purchasing.

WHY MEASURE PURCHASING PERFORMANCE?

What benefits can be derived from a systematic performance evaluation? Many purchasing managers were asked this question during one of our surveys and their answers are summarized in the following statements.

- Purchasing performance evaluation can lead to better decision making since it identifies variances from planned results; these variances can be analyzed to determine their causes and action can be taken to prevent their occurrence in the future.

- It may lead to better communication with other departments: e.g. analysing the number of invoices that cannot be matched with a purchasing order, leads to better arrangements in payment procedures and improves mutual understanding between the purchasing department and administration.

- It makes things visible: regular reporting of actual versus planned results enables a buyer to verify whether his or her expectations have been realized. This provides constructive feedback to the buyer and it also provides information to management about individual and group effectiveness, and hence contributes to the recognition of the purchasing department.

- It may contribute to better motivation: properly designed, an evaluation system can meet the personal and motivational needs of the buyer. It can be used effectively for constructive goal setting, and motivational and personal development programs in purchasing.

Collectively, these comments indicate that purchasing performance evaluation should result in a higher added value of the purchasing department to the firm. This added value might take the form of cost reductions, lower material prices, fewer rejects of incoming goods, better sourcing decisions, etc.

Purchasing performance should be evaluated regularly for two reasons. First, performance evaluation should be conducted to rate the individual buyer. In this sense, measurement is used primarily to serve the purposes of functional and individual performance assessment. Second, systematic performance assessment should serve the purpose of self-appraisal. In this sense, improvement of purchasing activities can be achieved most effectively by enabling each buyer to assess the results of his or her own purchasing activities. Hence, the evaluation activity is directed towards support of the individual buyer in doing a better professional job.

PROBLEMS IN MEASURING AND EVALUATING PURCHASING PERFORMANCE

Some academics have concluded that the purchasing department is one of the more difficult departments to evaluate. From the author's own experience we would say that, certainly in comparison with other business areas, this is not necessarily true: things have progressed over the past decade. Advanced business software packages (ERP-solutions) have improved possibilities to trace and track purchasing information considerably. However, there are some major problems that make it difficult to evaluate purchasing performance. These are summarized below.

- Lack of definition. Although frequently used in practice as well as in theory, terms like purchasing performance, purchasing effectiveness, and purchasing efficiency have not been precisely defined; some authors even use these concepts interchangeably.
- Lack of formal objectives and performance standards. As some authors have indicated, the objectives of the purchasing function often are not clearly defined; likewise, most purchasing departments operate without the guidance of well-defined performance standards.
- Problems of accurate measurement. Purchasing is not an isolated function; purchasing performance is a result of many activities which, due to their intangible character, are difficult to evaluate. In general, direct input-output relationships are difficult to identify; this seriously limits the possibility of measuring and evaluating purchasing activities in an accurate and comprehensive way. Memo 14.1 illustrates this problem.
- Difference in scope of purchasing. As was argued in the second section of this chapter, purchasing tasks and responsibilities differ greatly from one company to another. This precludes the development of broadly based, uniform benchmarking and evaluation systems.

These four problems seriously limit an objective and accurate assessment of the purchasing function.

WHAT SHOULD BE MEASURED?

In order to decide what should be measured, it is necessary first to define purchasing performance. For the purpose of this chapter, purchasing performance is considered to be the result of two elements: purchasing effectiveness and purchasing efficiency.

Purchasing effectiveness is defined as the extent to which, by choosing a certain course of action, a previously established goal or standard is being met. It is important to recognize that effectiveness essentially refers to the relationship between actual and planned performance of any human activity. Purchasing effectiveness relates to the degree to which

MEMO 14.1   ACCURATE MEASURING OF PURCHASING PERFORMANCE

A large, multinational company was looking for a young, ambitious purchasing manager. The candidate, when given the job, was required to accept the assignment to reduce purchasing costs by 5 per cent within one year. When asked if he felt uncomfortable with this target, the appointee said 'Not at all; management still has to decide how it is going to measure my performance.'

previously established goals and objectives have been met. A strategy or activity is either effective or not: a goal is reached or not. However, the goal can be expressed in terms of aspiration levels; the strategy or action that realizes a higher level may then be considered as more effective than another.

Purchasing efficiency is defined as the relationship between planned and actual sacrifices made in order to be able to realize a goal previously agreed upon. Purchasing efficiency is related to the resources which are required to realize the previously established goals and objectives and their related activities. Essentially it refers to the relationship between planned and actual costs.

Purchasing performance thus can be considered as the extent to which the purchasing function is able to realize its predetermined goals at the sacrifice of a minimum of the company's resources, i.e. costs.

The given definition is very important. It assumes that any evaluation of purchasing activities would include both measures related to effectiveness and to efficiency.

Effectiveness thus is related to the goals and objectives of the purchasing function. The classical statement summarizing the overall objectives of the purchasing function is that it should obtain the right material, in the right quantity, from the right source, for delivery at the right time and right place, with the right service and at the right price. Next, purchasing should contribute to product and process innovation and reduce the company's overall supply risk. Purchasing efficiency relates, as has been said before, to the resources which are required in order to meet the objectives which have been set for the purchasing function. Therefore efficiency relates to the purchasing organization.

Four dimensions are suggested on which measurement and evaluation of purchasing activities can be based:

- a price/cost dimension
- a product/quality dimension
- a logistics dimension
- an organizational dimension.

The relationship between these dimensions is illustrated by Figure 14.2 and discussed in detail in the following sections.

Purchasing price/cost dimension

This dimension refers to the relationship between standard and actual prices paid for materials and services. Here, a distinction is made between:

- Price/cost control, which refers to the continuous monitoring and evaluation of prices and price increases as they are announced by suppliers. Examples of parameters and measures to be used are ROI measures, materials budgets, price inflation reports, variance reports, etc. The main objective here is to monitor purchasing prices in order to control them and to prevent them getting out of hand.

- Price/cost reduction, which relates to the continuous monitoring and evaluation of activities initiated to reduce costs in a structured way associated with purchased materials and services. Cost reduction may be the result of searches for new suppliers or substitute materials, value analysis and/or coordination of purchasing requirements among business units. The main objective here is to monitor those activities which have been initiated to structurally reduce materials costs.

Budgets are important instruments for performance planning and monitoring with regard to the price/cost dimension. A description of purchasing budgets is given in Memo 14.2.

FIGURE 14.2   Key areas of purchasing performance measurement.

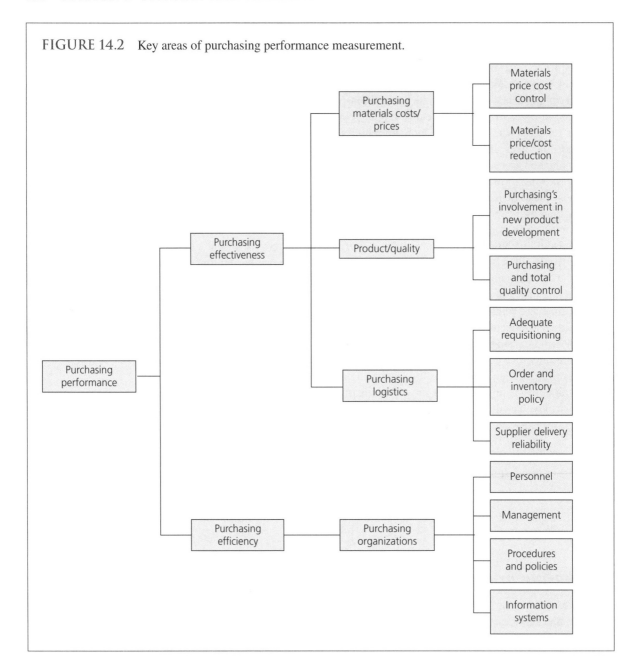

Purchasing product/quality dimension

Purchasing's responsibility with regard to the quality of purchased materials should not, as was seen earlier, be defined too narrowly. Here, we differentiate between purchasing's role in new product development and purchasing's role in total quality control ensuring that products are delivered by suppliers in conformance to the organization's specifications and requirements:

■ Purchasing's involvement in new product development. This relates to purchasing's contribution to product innovation. It is important that the organization's new product plans in terms of target cost and time to market are being met by all disciplines involved, including purchasing and suppliers. Measures to be used here are the number of man hours spent by purchasing on innovation projects, the number of engineering hours spent by suppliers, and the project's overall lead time. Specific measures are the number of technical change orders (indicating the number of engineering changes that have to be communicated to suppliers) and the initial sampling reject rate (i.e. the number of times a sample needs to be presented by the supplier to have it approved by engineering). Measures on these activities will indicate why new product development projects may get out of hand both in terms of costs and time-to-market.

- Purchasing's contribution to total quality control. After product specifications have been released by engineering it is purchasing's job to ensure that goods ordered are delivered according to the company's specifications. Here, parameters are being used such as reject rates on incoming goods, line reject rates, number of approved suppliers, number of certified suppliers, number of reject reports handled, etc. These measures indicate to what extent the company is able to secure a flawless incoming materials flow from suppliers.

Purchasing logistics dimension

A third key performance area is purchasing's role to contribute to an efficient incoming flow of purchased materials and services. This area includes the following major activities:

MEMO 14.2   BUDGETS IN PURCHASING MANAGEMENT

In order to control purchasing costs many companies use budgets. These can be divided into budgets aimed at controlling materials costs and budgets aimed at keeping control of purchasing departmental costs. With regard to the former the following types of budget are used.

- *Purchasing materials budget.* These reflect, often per product item, the volume which is expected for the next planning period (usually a year) and the expected price level for that specific product. The volume estimate is to be derived from the production plan. The estimate for the price to be paid has to come from the buyer. Often the final estimate is decided after a thorough discussion with the senior buyer and/or the purchasing manager in order to make sure that price targets are set at a challenging level.

  However, the price targets are sometimes set by manufacturing management. Many manufacturing companies nowadays are being confronted with severe cost cutting; this means that they need to plan for specific cost reductions (say 8 per cent). When purchasing contributes to (say) 60 per cent of the overall cost price this implies that purchasing materials cost needs to be reduced by 4.8 per cent. This target, then, is imposed upon the purchasing department. Every buyer in that situation should submit plans and targets per product in order to meet the overall goals of the purchasing department.

  Performance against budget is closely monitored through periodic variance reports which indicate, at buyer level, deviations from the plan for specific products. Variance reports are therefore an important factor when it comes to evaluating the performance of the buyer. Some companies have refined their reporting procedures by eliminating the effect on prices caused by external factors (such as fluctuations in currency rates, inflation), which are then reported separately.

- *Tooling budget.* This budget indicates the expected expenditure related to specific tooling (for example casting molds), required by the supplier to manufacture the product. Large companies often want to pay for any specific tooling, so as to maintain legal ownership of this equipment. In some companies buyers must indicate what tooling budget they require, and for what product or supplier; these budgets may not be overrun.

  The purchasing departmental budget is most often used since it is easily determined. This usually shows what costs are related to salaries and wages, social security, automation and systems, travel and development and training; here, variances are also monitored regularly.

- Control of the timely and accurate handling of materials requisitions. Measures used here are average purchasing administrative lead time, number of orders issued, order backlog. Important measures to improve performance in this area are electronic ordering systems, introducing e-commerce solutions to internal customers and suppliers, and EDI.
- Control of timely delivery by suppliers. Measures which can be used here are supplier delivery reliability, materials shortages, over/under delivery, number of JIT-deliveries. These measures indicate the level of control over the incoming materials flow.
- Control of quantities delivered. In some cases, purchasing has the responsibility for determination and control of cost effective inventory levels. Measures used here are inventory turnover ratio, number of over/under deliveries, average order size, pipeline inventory, etc.

Supplier evaluation and vendor rating are techniques used to monitor and improve supplierperformance in terms of quality and delivery reliability. Many of the performance indicators which have been mentioned here will be part of the company's supplier rating system.

Purchasing's organizational dimension

This dimension includes the major resources that are used to achieve the goals and objectives of the purchasing function, namely:

- Purchasing staff. This relates to background, level, training and development and motivation of purchasing personnel.
- Purchasing management. This refers to the way the purchasing department is being managed. It encompasses the quality and availability of purchasing strategies, action plans, reporting procedures. It relates also to management style and communications structure.
- Purchasing procedures and guidelines. This refers to the availability of procedures and working instructions for purchasing staff and suppliers in order to make sure that work is done in the most efficient manner.
- Purchasing information systems. This subject relates to the efforts made to improve the information systems, which are required to support purchasing staff and other employees in their daily activities, and to generate necessary management information on purchasing activities and performance.

Table 14.1 provides an overview of the key areas of purchasing performance evaluation and some examples of performance parameters which can be used per key area. A comprehensive assessment of any purchasing organization should focus on each of these areas, individually and collectively. Hence, it follows that a comprehensive performance measurement system in purchasing should monitor effectiveness as well as efficiency and therefore should include, preferably, measures of each key-performance area.

Interrelationships exist among all four dimensions. For example, if purchasing pushes too hard for lower prices, this action may ultimately affect material quality. The reverse may also be true: the requirement of a zero-defects quality level may ultimately result in higher material prices. However, the result may be a lower total materials cost or lower total cost of ownership.

Finally, each of the four dimensions can be measured and evaluated at different levels of aggregation, such as:

- line-item level
- individual supplier level
- level of the individual buyer;

TABLE 14.1 Examples of purchasing performance indicators

Area	Measurement aimed at	Continuous/ incidental	Examples
Purchased materials prices and costs	Purchased materials cost control	C	Materials budgets, variance reports, price inflation, reports, purchasing turnover
	Purchased materials cost reduction	C	Purchasing cost saving and avoidances, impact on return and investment
Product/quality of purchased materials	Early purchasing involvement in design and development	I	Time spent by purchasing on design and engineering projects, initial sampling reject rate (%)
	Incoming inspection quality control and assurance	C	Reject rate (%), line reject rate (%), quality costs per supplier
Purchasing logistics and supply	Monitoring requisitioning	I/C	Purchasing administrative lead times, order backlog (per buyer)
	Delivery reliability (quality and quantity)		Rush orders, delivery reliability index per supplier, materials shortages, inventory turnover ratio, just-in-time deliveries
Purchasing staff and organization	Training and motivation of purchasing staff	I	Time and workload analysis of purchasing department, purchasing budget, purchasing and supply audit
	Purchasing management quality		
	Purchasing systems and procedures		
	Purchasing research		

Source: van Weele (1991).

- departmental level;
- overall company level.

It is therefore clear that performance measurement systems in purchasing will show a large degree of variation in that measures are tailored to the specific needs of the company.

PURCHASING AUDIT AS A MANAGEMENT TOOL

Through a purchasing audit, management may assess the extent to which goals and objectives of the purchasing department are balanced with its resources. The latter relate to the elements of the organizational dimension. The purchasing audit is a form of action research, the effectiveness of which depends on the expertise with which it is conducted. More important, however, are the actions which are derived from it at a later stage. The audit must therefore be conducted in such a way that people do not feel threatened, and in a way which builds trust and generates professionalism.

Audits can be preventive or corrective in nature. Preventive audits can be compared with periodical check-ups – with the aid of a limited number of standard checks, the department is checked to see whether it meets the expectations of its most important stakeholders. Corrective audits focus on acute problems apparent in the functioning of the department – the situation can be sufficiently grave that immediate treatment is imperative. Based on a quick scan, the (internal) auditor determines the treatment, which is then carried out rigorously. This is known in management consulting as turn-around management. After such an operation, the purchasing organization will often go through a substantial metamorphosis. Purchasing management and personnel are reorganized, new managers are recruited, the product assortment and supply base are reorganized and so on. Audits for turn-around situations should be conducted by experts.

Figure 14.3 shows the points of reference which must be included in a purchasing audit. This figure shows that final purchasing performance is affected by several factors:

- The requirements that the corporate system lays down for the purchasing function. Purchasing policy must be tuned to overall company policy; changes in the business system will affect purchasing objectives or the required performance of the department.

- Changes in the company's supply chain. The purchasing function must react optimally to the requirements of its internal customers. Changes in the supply chain manifest

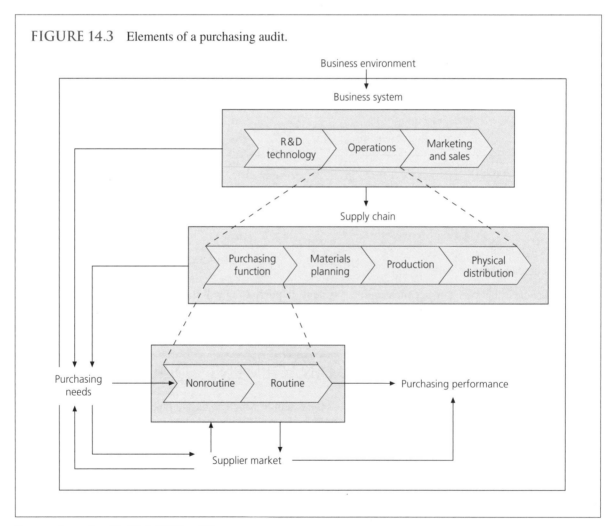

FIGURE 14.3   Elements of a purchasing audit.

Source: redraawn from Van Weele (1991), p. 131

themselves in changing materials requirements. The purchasing department will have to react to these changes or anticipate them flexibly.

■ The opportunities provided by the supplier market to fulfill the materials requirements, as defined. Changes in the supplier's technology and/or organization or in the supplier market can strongly affect materials availability and prices (suppliers determine, to a large extent, internal customer satisfaction).

The purchasing audit will have to map the major requirements that the stakeholders assign to the purchasing department, as well as the changes which occur in these requirements. This implies that the audit must pay attention to the quality of the interfaces between purchasing and other departments. Regarding the internal performance of the purchasing department, a distinction can be made between non-routine purchasing activities (purchasing engineering, purchasing market research, supplier selection, etc.) and routine purchasing activities (e.g. order processing, expediting, supplier rating, etc.).

The starting point is the intake interview, in which the auditor clarifies the goals and structure of the audit. This is done in a meeting with the purchasing manager and his superior. The auditor explains what can be expected of the audit as well as the methods to be used. Ideally this is followed by an introduction to the purchasing department, during which the purchasing manager explains the functioning of his department. The rest of the organization is informed about the audit and the auditors will set to work. First of all they will gather factual information concerning the purchasing department, with the aid of a structured checklist. Figure 14.4 shows several subjects on which data could be gathered. A selection is then made of the key personnel to be interviewed; confidentiality towards the respondents must be guaranteed, a factor that frequently constitutes a reason for using external consultants in this kind of research. Figure 14.5 shows some questions which may serve as terms of reference for the investigation.

Based on the information gathered the auditor will prepare a report, the initial findings of which are first checked with the purchasing manager. This provides the opportunity to find out to what extent the results are recognized. Also at this stage some ideas about improvement measures can be exchanged. A meeting with top management will then follow, after which a final report is drawn up containing recommendations in the form of a policy plan or action program. An important part of the final report is taken up by the

---

FIGURE 14.4   Examples of key data relating to the purchasing function.

• *Commercial data:* sales turnover, cost of materials, ratio of materials cost to sales turnover

• *Personnel and organization*: total number of employees, number of purchasing employees (classified according to educational level, functioning level, years of experience), ratio of purchasing employees to total employees

• *Purchasing's place in the organization* (organizational diagram)

• *Reporting relationships*: top management, materials management, etc.

• *Job description:* primary tasks, authority and responsibilities of the purchasing department

• *Purchasing data:* number of articles (production related, non-production related), number of suppliers, number of purchasing requisitions, number of requests for quotations, number of orders, number of purchasing invoices, Pareto analyses of purchasing turnover according to article, order quantities, supplier, country of origin, etc. Purchasing department budget, divided according to nature of costs

• *Relationships with other departments*

• *Action plans:* in the areas of cost reduction, quality improvement, automation, etc.

• *Purchasing procedures and systems*

documentation of performance indicators, which will serve in the future as a means to monitor progress.

ESTABLISHING A PURCHASING PERFORMANCE EVALUATION SYSTEM

Different methods can be used to arrive at proper performance measures and norms and standards in purchasing. The more common methods of establishing performance standards are as follows:

■ Subjective by management. Objectives and targets are defined and imposed on purchasing by management.

FIGURE 14.5 Aspects to be considered in a purchasing audit.

Goals and objectives

Goal orientation

• What are the purchasing department's goals?

• What are the purchasing department's responsibilities?

• To what extent are the purchasing department's tasks stated in objective and verifiable terms?

Client orientation

• Does the purchasing department communicate efficiently with its internal customers?

• Is there adequate reaction to the requirements and wants of the internal customers?

• Is the purchasing department sufficiently aware of new internal developments and changes in the supplier market?

Risk

• What are the major risks with regard to price behavior of high-value items and availability of critical materials?

• Is purchasing sufficiently aware of these risks and what measures have been taken in order to cope with them?

• In general, is continuity of supply and purchasing operations sufficiently guaranteed?

Resources

Results and resources

• To what extent does purchasing meet its tasks and objectives?

• Is the purchasing department adequately equipped in terms of people and systems to be able to meet expectations?

• What measures are taken in order to improve on results on the one hand and systems and human resources on the other?

Flexibility

• Does purchasing adequately react to changing materials requirements and internal customer needs?

• Is purchasing sufficiently interested in pursuing new technology?

• What important changes have taken place in the service and organization of the purchasing department?

Management

• Is teamwork within the purchasing department sufficiently developed?

• Is the purchasing department a well-respected partner for discussion of internal customer problems?

• What measures have been taken in order to keep the quality of human resources up to date?

- Expert opinion. Targets for purchasing performance are provided by experts, who have broad experience with purchasing issues.

- Time series analysis. Past performance is extrapolated to the near future. Targets for purchasing performance are based on historical data, assuming that trends which have appeared in the past will continue in future years.

- Intercompany and interindustry comparison (benchmarking). As has been argued this cannot be done without understanding the specific background of the purchasing organizations which serve as a terms of reference for the comparison. However, benchmarking in purchasing has become more and more popular and accepted (see Memo 14.3).

MEMO 14.3 BENCHMARKING IN PURCHASING

More and more companies are interested in comparing their purchasing performance against those of their competitors or those companies who are considered to be best-in-class. Through benchmarking initiatives one tries to assess the effectiveness and efficiency of purchasing organizations. An example is Philips Electronics who during the early 1990s conducted a benchmarking study into the purchasing and supply strategies of some leading-edge companies such as Motorola, BMW and Marks & Spencer. In particular Philips wanted to get a thorough insight into how these companies acted in the areas of:

- global purchasing market research;
- supplier management;
- purchasing coordination among business units;
- negotiation and contract management;
- managing the supply process in the relationship with suppliers;
- purchasing and supplier involvement in new product development;
- collaboration with marketing and services.

Through this study Philips gained a thorough understanding of the strategic role of purchasing and supply management. As a result every divisional manager was summoned to develop a purchasing action plan to bring Philips into the league of leading-edge companies. It is fair to conclude that this study has generated significant awareness on the role that purchasing and supply management should have within the company.

CAPS (Center for Advanced Purchasing Studies) in the USA periodically reports on a score of purchasing performance indicators per industry. Every year questionnaires are sent to the purchasing managers of large, multinational companies, covering a large number of subjects. Items which are investigated and reported are, among others:

- total purchasing dollars spent as a percentage of corporate sales;
- purchasing operating expense as a percentage of total purchasing dollars spent;
- total purchasing headcount as a percentage of total company headcount;
- total purchasing department purchase dollars per purchasing employee;
- average purchasing spent per supplier;
- percentage of active suppliers that account for x per cent of total dollars spent;
- percentage of company purchase dollars spent with small suppliers;
- percentage of total purchase dollars processed through EDI;
- percentage of total goods purchases handled by the purchasing department.

This type of research may provide some insight into whether the purchasing function is moving in the right direction. Comparison with companies on just one aspect is less useful. However, comparing all aspects provides a picture of the relative position of the company in the area of purchasing among competitors.

The most common method is to keep track of specific measures over time – standards and norms may be derived from analysis of trends, i.e. by extrapolating historical data. The initial steps involved in the development of a systematic performance measurement system are typically those noted below:

- First, after careful analysis, management must determine which targets and objectives, as well as activities, are most important and justify the effort of evaluation.

- Next, it is necessary to determine the frequency and format for data reporting, as well as which personnel will assume these responsibilities.

- Once the preceding decisions have been made, it is necessary to develop a systematic procedure for collecting a great deal of historical and statistical data that may be used in the evaluation program.

- The next step in the process typically involves analysis of the data. Managers must look for interrelationships between various types of data and also attempt to establish relationships between means and ends. At the same time, the manager must differentiate between purchasing effectiveness and purchasing efficiency.

- Following the analytical stage, various measures are developed, implemented, and subsequently refined. A danger to avoid at this stage is the possibility that the measures may become too complex and too numerous. Simplicity is the key.

- The final step in the operating process is timely reporting of the results to those who should use them, along with appropriate follow-up.

The entire process is self-reinforcing. After standards and plans are initially developed and implemented, results are reviewed and used for further refinement of measures and standards. Hence, the process of data collection, analysis, and program refinement continues in a cycle characterized by increasing precision and sophistication.

SUMMARY

Performance measurement in purchasing cannot be considered in isolation. Rather, it is part of the purchasing management process. Planning and control go hand in hand. If the purchasing function lacks a clear vision, when purchasing strategies and action plans are ill-developed and management reporting is absent, systematic performance measurement and evaluation will be difficult if not impossible.

This chapter has shown that the degree of sophistication in measuring purchasing performance differs among companies. A major factor influencing the parameters used to assess purchasing is the view which management holds towards purchasing. When purchasing is considered primarily as an administrative function, this will be reflected in administrative parameters that are used. If purchasing is regarded as a strategic business function, which is deeply rooted in the overall business strategy and processes, this will result in extensive management reporting.

Purchasing performance measurement is important since it may lead to a greater recognition by all other business functions. When applied effectively, it may lead to better communication with other disciplines, better decision making, a higher motivation of staff involved and a greater transparency of the company's dealings with suppliers.

Objective performance measurement is, however, in many cases a difficult matter since it is hampered by poor definitions and poor planning. Moreover, information systems may not support the data gathering and reporting structures required.

When measuring purchasing performance, it is suggested to focus both on purchasing effectiveness and efficiency. Purchasing effectiveness is covered by three key areas, i.e. purchasing materials costs and prices, new product development and total quality control, and purchasing logistics. Purchasing efficiency is related towards the resources which are needed to realize predetermined targets and plans. Therefore it encompasses the purchasing organization, i.e. purchasing staff, management, procedures and guidelines and information systems. For each of these key areas a number of tools, monitoring reports and performance indicators can be selected, which enable a holistic view of how purchasing has performed. Actual performance needs to be compared with standards. These may be derived from various sources, such as time-based series analyzes or future plans and budgets.

The purchasing audit can be used to thoroughly analyze the purchasing organization. Conducting such an audit in general meets with resistance from the organization, which is why it needs to be carefully prepared and introduced to the organization.

Apart from the purchasing audit, managers may also turn to benchmarking as a tool to assess their position. Comparing performance with that of other companies requires, however, a thorough understanding of the way in which the data concerned has been gathered. Therefore, benchmarking in purchasing should be applied with care and caution.

ASSIGNMENTS

14.1 The general manager of a manufacturing firm uses the ratio of purchasing departmental costs as a percentage of purchasing turnover to assess the performance of his purchasing staff. Would you consider this a valid procedure? Discuss the pros and cons.

14.2 What parameters would you use when benchmarking the performance of your purchasing department against that of other companies? Explain.

14.3 How would you measure cost savings realized by the purchasing department?

14.4 What are the major differences between purchasing performance measurement and vendor rating?

14.5 Some financial managers today use the balanced score card as a tool to measure organizational performance. A financial manager of a medium-sized manufacturing firm is interested in developing a specific balanced score card for a purchasing department and for an individual buyer. He has requested you to support him in this. What would your balanced score cards look like?

PRACTICE

CASE STUDY   DESIGNING AND BUILDING A NEW HEADQUARTERS

The management of an international company is considering building a new headquarters. As this is a major project, management approaches several architects and, based on the submitted provisional designs, a choice is made. Only then does the real work start, beginning with the basic specifications. The structural design is prepared meticulously: the foundation of the building is specified in detail, the strength of the structure is calculated based on the various types of materials that are going to be used. Once the basic design is complete, quotations are solicited from a few selected contractors.

Naturally, management will have indicated the available budget at an early stage. Based on empirical data and price information, the design department prepares a cost estimate of the project.

At this stage, without detailed specifications being available, the estimate is only approximate. As the design is elaborated, it becomes possible to estimate the costs at a more detailed level. However, the final price will depend to a large extent on the buoyancy of the construction industry. If there is a need for work, the sum contracted for will be related directly to the estimated costs. If the contractors' order books are filled, however, the price will be influenced considerably by the supply and demand situation. An intimate knowledge of the local market, an insight into the order positions of individual contractors, and an idea of the expected building costs, are therefore of crucial importance in preparing for the negotiations with the contractor.

INTRODUCTION

As has been seen earlier, materials make up a large part of the cost price of industrial end products, and decisions relating to the purchasing price determine the cost price of the end product to a high degree. The importance of purchasing as a function increases if rises in materials prices cannot be automatically passed on to the customer. Price is therefore one of the most important elements in the purchasing decision.

Industrial salesmen will always attempt to hide their prices and cost structures as much as possible. It is in their interest that the pricing method remains obscure to the buyer. However, it is the buyer's task to unveil his suppliers' pricing methods and cost structures and, if this cannot be done directly, he should try more indirect methods. The buyer must constantly and systematically gather information that will yield some insight into the seller's pricing methods and his cost structures.

Cost-analysis techniques provide tools to check whether price increases announced by the supplier are justified. Insight into the cost price, and comparison of this cost price with those of the supplier's competitors, may help the buyer decide whether or not to agree to the suppliers' request. The buyer often works with several suppliers, so he can compare the most effective manufacturing techniques, track down inefficiencies in the production process of a specific supplier, provide the latter with suggestions for improvement, and therefore get better prices. In dealing with suppliers, the following questions should be asked:

- Does a particular supplier belong to the 'best-in-class' companies?
- What is the supplier's ratio of direct to indirect costs?
- What is the supplier's cost breakdown in terms of overheads, labor and materials?
- Does the supplier experience learning curve effects in his production?
- What are the costs of non-quality for this particular supplier?

The answers will indicate whether a particular supplier is among the most advanced and respected companies in a particular industry.

Pricing and cost-price information are of course insufficient to answer all of these questions. It is also essential that the buyer knows how to use financial–economic analysis techniques. From annual reports and additional financial information, a complete picture of the supplier's financial situation can be built up. This chapter will discuss several costing methods and in this context will also address the learning curve, particularly from the buyer's perspective. It will also touch upon a few analytical techniques used in the area of financial auditing.

HOW IS THE PURCHASE PRICE DETERMINED?

Basically, the price ultimately paid for materials and services is the result of environmental factors – both internal and external. Figure 15.1 shows the relationship between these factors.

Internal factors can bring about a change in the materials before the finished product is placed on the market. These factors may be logistical, technical or organizational in character; examples are changes in delivery time, quality, or product specifications.

External factors are those factors that change the availability of a product in a given market and they can be divided into economic, socio-political, and technological developments. Examples are changes in general economic conditions, changes in the structure of the supply market, legislation, product technology, etc. External factors in general influence internal factors, although the reverse never occurs. The price of a product can be influenced by external factors in two ways (see Figure 15.2): directly, due to changes in the cost structure of a particular product or, indirectly, due to changes in market structure and shifts in supply/demand relationships.

If the change in cost factors is identified by the symbol $f(c)$, and the change in market factors by the symbol $f(m)$, with f as a weighting factor, then the formula is:

$$\Sigma\,(f(c) + f(m)) = 100\%\text{ of the price}$$

According to this formula, a change in the price paid is to be considered as the sum of the changes in the cost factors and/or changes in the market factors. Changes in cost factors can stem from:

$f(c1)$: change in labor costs
$f(c2)$: change in materials costs
$f(c3)$: change in energy costs
$f(c4)$: labor productivity
$f(cn)$: etc.

Changes in the market structure can stem from:

$f(m1)$: change in demand
$f(m2)$: change in supply

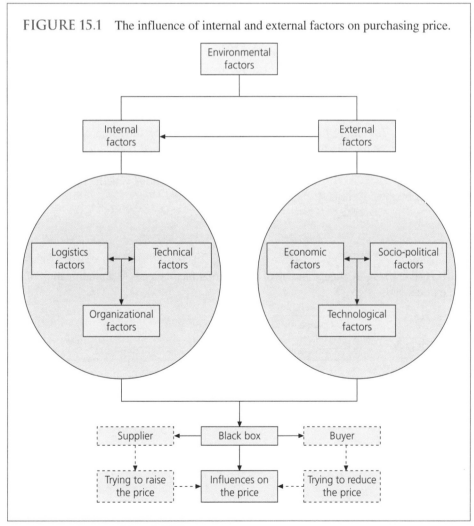

FIGURE 15.1   The influence of internal and external factors on purchasing price.

Source: redrawn from van Eck *et al.* (1982)

f (m3): change in supply side inventory
f (m4): change in supply side capacity utilization
f (mn): etc.

Some products react almost entirely to changes in cost factors, others to changes in market factors. Still others react to changes in both cost and market factors; see Memo 15.1.

The classification described here agrees to some extent with the concepts discussed by Corey (1978), who considers prices to be based essentially on three different models:

- Cost-based pricing. In this case the supplier's offering price is derived directly from his cost price; what most systems boil down to is that a particular profit margin is added to all costs, including the costs of sales (mark-up pricing).

- Market-based pricing. The price of the product is determined on the market, and is generated exclusively by market circumstances such as demand, supply, stock positions, the economic situation and political factors.

MEMO 15.1   VARIATIONS IN DETERMINING PURCHASE PRICE

For plastic components, Σf(c) is nearly 100. In other words, the price modification can be attributed almost exclusively to a change in the cost factors. For example, an increase in labor costs will cause the price of these components to increase in proportion with the share of labor costs in the product's price.

For copper, Σf(m) is almost 100, but only in the short term. In other words, the price paid for copper is almost completely determined by the market situation, and cannot be influenced by the individual buyer. For instance, if economic activity declines, market circumstances will change and the price will fall. Clearly, the purchase price for derivative products is strongly related to the market price for the raw material.

For petrochemical raw materials, the sum of the cost factors is about the same as the sum of the market factors, i.e Σf(c) = Σf(m). In other words, the ultimate market price is determined both by cost elements and by general market conditions. Relative to time, the price level will tend to move, both upward and downward, at a given distance from the predictable cost line. In this case, the purchase price is neither determined entirely by the market price nor by the cost price.

FIGURE 15.2   A change in one of the external factors leads to a modification of the price paid.

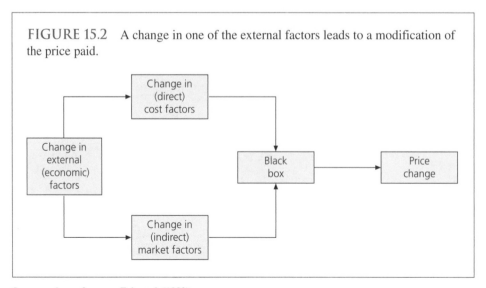

Source: redrawn from van Eck *et al.* (1982)

- Competitive bidding. The price of the product is influenced by market factors as well as cost factors. This situation is the most common.

Raw materials and semi-manufactured products are traded mainly in a relatively free market in large quantities. The purchase price paid at a given moment strongly depends on market conditions at a given point in time.

As far as technical components are concerned, one must differentiate between components made to the supplier's specification (standard), and those made to the customer's specification (non-standard). In the latter case, the buyer will know precisely the cost of the material to be purchased; in the first case, the buyer can only obtain a rough indication of the product's cost by means of market research. For this reason, prices for non-standard components are typically determined on the basis of competitive bids or negotiation. What has just been said about non-standard components also applies, for the most part, to finished products.

MRO products comprise such a heterogeneous group of materials that no general statement can be made about the methodology utilized in setting prices. Their prices are determined neither by market circumstances alone, nor on the basis of cost factors only.

The most heterogeneous group, however, is that consisting of the various services provided by external companies. The price for services can usually be based on cost, assuming that the activities to be performed have been specified with precision and that the hours and hourly rates have been previously agreed upon. For cases such as software design and implementation, however, the price typically is based on market factors. In this case, the cost structure is so difficult to determine and the demand so large, that usually the price quoted by the firm must be paid.

Table 15.1 reflects the relationship between the pricing methods and the various purchasing product groups.

TABLE 15.1 Relationship between various purchase product groups and methods of price setting

		Method of 'price setting'			
	Primarily based on cost factors	Based both on market and cost factors			Primarily based on market factors
Purchase product group		With the emphasis on cost factors	50/50	With the emphasis on market factors	
Raw materials				X	X
Semi-manufactured goods			X	X	
Components					
Standard		X	X	X	
Non-standard	X	X	X		
Finished products	X	X	X		
MRO		X	X	X	
Services	X	X	X	X	X

Source: van Eck, de Weerd and van Weele (1982).

PRICING METHODS

Fixing the selling price is no simple matter. The supplier has to take into account many factors, a few of which are listed below:

- The expected demand for his product – if demand is high, the supplier will normally set the price a little higher than when demand is low. In addition he will not be willing to make price concessions.

- The number of competitors in the market – the monopolist's situation is, of course, ideal. Buyers have to go to him for a specific product. He therefore has a high degree of freedom in determining the selling price. This situation is rare in practice and, as a rule, suppliers will look to their competitors' prices when setting their own prices.

- The expected development of the cost price per product unit – large-scale production makes low prices possible. If the supplier expects his production volume to increase in the future, he will take this into account. He will anticipate his cost development based on potential learning-curve effects (see next section).

- The customer's order volume – suppliers are often willing to make price concessions in exchange for the promise of 'more business' in the future. This principle is often recognized in pricing methods, usually by awarding extra discounts for larger purchased quantities. Many suppliers employ a sliding scale to indicate which price and/or discount applies to which quantities.

- The importance of the customer to the supplier – from a commercial point of view the supplier's position may be strengthened by good references. For this reason he will be eager to do business with certain large, well-reputed companies. In order to gain access to this type of customer, suppliers often charge 'special prices'. However, after some time has passed they will try to re-establish the price at 'normal' levels.

- The value of the product to the customer -some products (for example spare parts for manufacturing equipment) have a value to the customer that bears no relationship to their manufacturing cost. In some circumstances supply of spare parts is critical for continuity of production. It is not uncommon for suppliers to charge prices for critical spare parts which are a multiple of the original cost price.

All of these factors affect the selling or purchasing price. In practice the following pricing methods can be distinguished (Kotler, 1984, pp. 515–22):

- Cost-plus pricing. The most common way of setting a price is by adding a fixed percentage mark-up to the cost price. If the cost price of a product is €100, and a mark-up of 50 per cent is used, then the selling price will be €150. This method of pricing does not take competitors' prices into account, nor does it acknowledge developments in the demand for the product. Nevertheless, this method is frequently used in practice because of its simplicity. Another important reason is that it is often difficult for the seller to estimate the demand for the product. But he does know the cost price, so why not take this as a starting point for his sales price?

- Target-profit pricing. In this situation the price is determined based on the amount of profit that should be realised. Based on the fixed and variable costs and the expected selling price, the required sales volume is calculated. This is done in two steps: first, the break-even volume is determined through a break-even analysis; then, based on the profit that is to be made, the required extra volume is determined; finally, a check is made as to whether this required sales volume can be realized at the estimated price. If this is not the case, then the calculation is repeated based on a lower price. In this situation, it is essential that the buyer finds out the potential total volume of sales of the product involved, as well as the supplier's sales target. If the sales representative has realized his goal, chances are that he will probably honor extra pressure on the price in negotiations. He will be less willing to do so if he hasn't made his profit and sales targets yet.

■ Pricing based on the buyer-perceived value. A general rule in marketing is that you do not base your selling price on the cost price of the product, but rather on what the market can bear. In this reasoning the price that the buyer is willing to pay is related primarily to the value he attaches to the product. This pricing method is often used for consumer products (well-known branded articles), and also for industrial products; as explained earlier, the price of spare parts for production machinery are often not directly related to the costs of the product; they are usually related to what they are worth to the buyer in particular emergency situations.

■ Pricing based on competitors' prices. Some oligopolistic markets are characterized by price leadership. Smaller companies follow the market leader's pricing behavior, often at some distance. Fuel prices in many European countries are examples of this pricing method.

■ Tender-based pricing. One special variety of the method discussed above is public tender (also known as the tender system). This method is common in public procurement and some industries, such as the construction and defence industries. Based on a request for quotation from the principal, contractors are invited to submit bids for a specific job. These bids are handed over in a sealed envelope to the principal by all bidders simultaneously (sealed bidding). The job is awarded to the contractor who submits the lowest bid.

One special characteristic of pricing policies for industrial products is the discount policy which is applied. Some authors differentiate between the following discount practices:

■ Cash discount. This discount usually depends on the industry (e.g. 2 per cent discount with 10 days payment). The advantages are, among other things, acceleration of payments, advantages for quick payers and reduction of the amounts of accounts receivable.

■ Quantity discounts. Small orders often require the same amount of work, in terms of production and administrative and physical processing, as large orders. This means that small orders have a higher cost per product. To stimulate larger quantity orders, many suppliers use quantity discounts in which the advantage for the buyer is that he can realize a lower price per unit. However, this price advantage must be considered against the extra costs as a result of longer storage and the risk of obsolescence.

■ Bonus agreement. This discount is linked to the amounts purchased from a specific supplier for a specific period (usually one year). The supplier often employs a sliding scale, in which the bonus percentage increases in proportion to the turnover. The advantage of this procedure for the supplier is that it reinforces customer loyalty. Bonuses are paid to the buyer at the end of the year based upon the order volume that actually has been made.

■ Geographical discount. This discount is given to customers who are located close to the supplier's factory or distribution centre, making the transportation costs much lower than average: part of the cost benefit is passed on to the buyer.

■ Seasonal discount. This discount is applied to improve manufacturing capacity utilization in periods when sales decline. If the buyer orders out of the season, he gets a lower price. By means of the winter discount system, bicycle manufacturers, for example, stimulate dealers to place their orders in the winter (when consumer sales are rather low due to weather conditions), after which delivery takes place in spring. In this way manufacturing volume is spread evenly throughout the year.

■ Promotional discount. This discount is provided to temporarily stimulate the sale of a product, or, if it concerns a new product, to lower the entry barrier (special offer discount).

It is not easy for the buyer to track down the pricing method used by the supplier, and the discount policy makes this matter even more difficult. To get a grip on the prices used by the supplier, a distinction should be made – in line with what has been discussed before – between the cost price analysis and the pricing method. The following list can help the buyer gain some insight into the supplier's cost structure:

■ materials costs – to be itemized according to the major components;

■ direct labor costs – information about labor costs can often be obtained by consulting the collective labor agreements for that particular industry;

■ transportation costs;

■ indirect costs – these can often be divided into general management, overheads and sales costs.

As a general rule, the higher the share of the fixed costs in the cost price of the end product, the greater the price elasticity; by enlarging the order volume, the buyer achieves a decrease in the fixed costs per unit, and this should result in lower prices.

Products whose prices are mainly determined by variable costs are affected by price variances. In this situation, a price increase at the supplier's purchasing side must be closely monitored to prevent the supplier issuing unwarranted price increases.

THE LEARNING CURVE

The learning curve is an important instrument in the development of purchasing strategies. The learning curve was originally developed in the American aircraft industry. It was discovered that the cost price per airplane decreased at a fixed percentage as experience, i.e. the cumulative production volume of a particular type of aircraft, increased. This decrease of costs per unit had nothing to do with effects of scale; the result was to be attributed to the learning effect. The learning effect in general results from the following factors:

■ reduced supervision as experience with production of a particular product grows;

■ increased profits, from improved efficiency through streamlining the production process;

■ reduced defects and line reject rates during the production process;

■ increased batch size (as a rule), which means that less time is spent on resetting machines; the result is reduced production down-time;

■ improved production equipment (after a while);

■ improved process control: reduced loss of time as a result of emergency measures;

■ reduced engineering changes (initially required to deal with unforeseen manufacturing problems).

The basic principle of the learning curve is that 'each time the cumulative production volume of a particular item doubles, the average time required to produce that item is approximately × % of the initially required time'. An 80 per cent learning curve means that if the cumulative number of produced goods is doubled, only 80 per cent of the original amount of hours is needed to produce one unit (see Table 15.2).

These data can also be reproduced graphically; regular graph paper yields a curve (see Figure 15.3), while log–log paper produces a straight line (see Figure 15.4).

TABLE 15.2 Learning effect results in cost price reduction (example)

Cumulative amount produced	Required time in hours per unit
1000	20.0
2000	16.0
4000	12.8
8000	10.24
1 6000	8.2

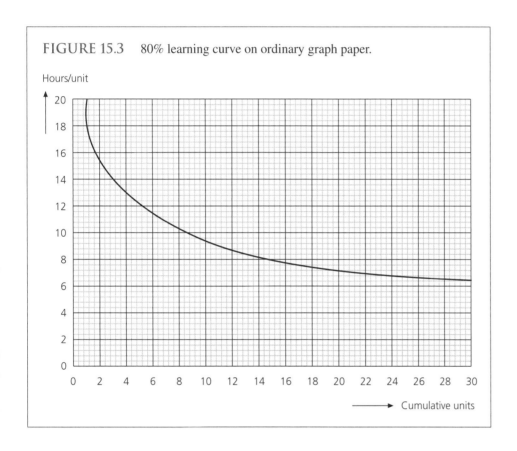

FIGURE 15.3   80% learning curve on ordinary graph paper.

This knowledge is clearly of vital importance to the buyer. Anticipating the supplier's learning experience, he can negotiate price reductions in the future. The learning curve is preferably used in the following situations:

- when it concerns customized components, manufactured by a supplier at the customer's specification;

- when large amounts of money are involved (so that the costs which must be incurred to apply the technology in question can be recovered);

- when the buyer cannot request competitive quotations because, for example, a considerable investment has to be made in molds and specific production tooling, which leads the buyer to single sourcing;

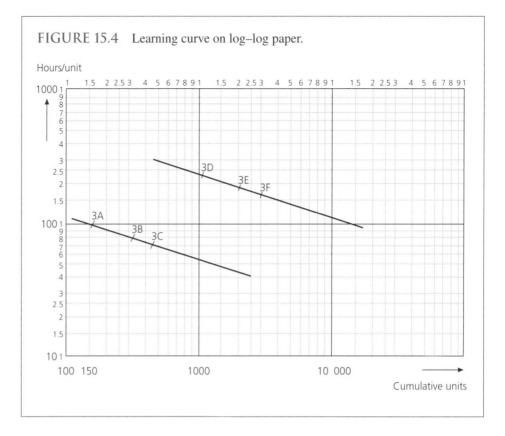

FIGURE 15.4   Learning curve on log–log paper.

- when direct labor costs make up an important part of the cost price of the product to be produced.

SUPPLIER ASSESSMENT

Levels of assessment

The growing role of suppliers in the company's business chain increases the need for objective assessment of supplier performance. In many cases it is not sufficient that the supplier is able to meet the materials and service requirements of today. The buyer also wants to determine whether a supplier is sufficiently equipped to live up to the company's longer-term requirements and needs. This requires knowledge of the strong and weak points in the supplier's performance. Furthermore, it is necessary to know whether the supplier can guarantee sustained continuity of supply. The systematic gathering of supplier performance data enables the buyer to negotiate strict agreements about improving reject rates, reducing total lead time and contributing to cost reduction.

Supplier assessment may take place at four different levels of abstraction:

- Product level. This level focuses on establishing and improving the supplier's product quality; incoming inspections and quality inspections are conducted, which result in establishing the degree of quality conformance of incoming materials.

- Process level. Here it is not the product which is the subject of inspection, it is the production process that is closely investigated. The underlying idea is that the quality of the product strongly relates to the supplier's manufacturing process. If this process is under control through consistent application of quality procedures, this will result in a product which conforms to the expressed quality standards and specifications. In this approach the state of the supplier's machinery and the quality control system are subjected to in-depth auditing.

- Quality assurance system level. Quality assurance means checking the way in which procedures regarding quality inspection are developed, kept up-to-date/maintained and refined. In other words, not only the procedures and guidelines are investigated, but the entire quality organization is the subject of investigation by the customer.

- Company level. This is the highest level of investigation. In this approach auditors not only focus on quality aspects; they also take financial aspects into consideration. And finally, they want to get an idea of the quality of the management. In this way the customer tries to establish how competitive that particular supplier will be in the near future.

Most supplier evaluation is limited to the first two levels.

Assessment methods

The methods used to assess supplier performance may vary from company to company; two types may be differentiated. Subjective methods are used when companies evaluate suppliers through personal judgements, for example by combining various departments' experiences with the supplier; objective methods attempt to quantify the supplier's performance. In general the following tools and techniques can be used for supplier assessment:

- Spreadsheets. These are used to systematically compare and assess quotations obtained from the suppliers. The most important criteria for evaluation are listed on one axis, the supplier quotations on the other. This gives a matrix with fields that can be filled in. Applying this very simple, but often extremely illuminating method, is made easier when the suppliers have drawn up their quotations in a similar way. For this reason buyers are advised to use well-structured requests for quotations, which provide clear guidelines to suppliers on how to submit their quotations.

- Personal assessment. This method is used for those suppliers with whom close business relationships exist. Various specialists, who have experience with this supplier (e.g. quality control, engineering, manufacturing, production planning, purchasing) are asked to 'rate' him according to a previously agreed checklist.

- Vendor rating. This is limited to quantitative data only. It entails measuring the aspects of price, quality and delivery reliability per supplier. The supplier's price history is investigated and compared with the development of his competitors. Quality is measured in terms of the rejection percentage or the number of production-line stops as a result of faulty materials. Delivery reliability is measured by means of registration of the number of late (or early) deliveries. This may appear simple, but such systems are very difficult to establish, due to the enormous amounts of administrative data which need to be extracted from internal company records. To do this economically, an integrated computerized materials planning system should be in place.

- Supplier audit. This method requires that the supplier is periodically visited by specialists from the customer. They subject his production process and quality organization to a thorough investigation. Faults and weaknesses are reported and discussed with the supplier. Measures for improvement are negotiated and established. During a subsequent visit it is checked to see to what extent progress against targets has been made.

■ Cost modelling. This is a very detailed approach. Specialists at the buying company estimate by means of a shadow calculation, based upon the production technology used by the supplier, what the supplier's actual cost price should be. A detailed analysis is made of the supplier's direct and indirect costs: materials consumption, materials prices, storage costs, waste, personnel costs, costs of supervising, overheads, etc. Usually this analysis leads to some interesting insights, which then can be discussed with the supplier. Based upon this information, some professional buyers go one step further and conduct a should-cost analysis. Based upon what they consider to be the most advanced state-of-the-art production technology and structure it is calculated what the supplier's cost price of a particular component really should be. The difference between the two then becomes, of course, the subject of discussion between buyer and supplier. There is an intensive exchange of ideas on how the should-cost position might be achieved. These discussions frequently result in the supplier having to invest in the existing manufacturing equipment. To compensate, the client is often prepared to offer long-term purchasing contracts.

The use of cost-models and should-cost techniques usually deepens the relationship between both parties. These cannot, however, be implemented overnight since the supplier needs to develop trust in the other party. The supplier should be convinced that the buyer is not after a next round of cutting into his margin but that both parties equally will benefit from the efficiency improvements gained. The issue of developing trust in buyer–seller relationships actually takes a lot of time!

Memo 15.2 illustrates how to proceed when developing a cost model for purchasing.

Laseter (1998, p. 51) provides an interesting framework that may help buyers identify the most important cost drivers for their commodities (see Table 15.3).

The techniques mentioned above cannot be applied in all circumstances. Naturally, the costs and the benefits must be weighed. The last two methods are extremely labor intensive and will only be used with 'strategic' suppliers and products. Application of all

---

MEMO 15.2 DEVELOPING COST MODELS FOR PURCHASING

Cost models should provide a clear picture of the total cost of ownership of a purchased component. Since these models require a lot of analysis and many data, these still are not widely used. As experience shows, only some leading-edge companies are applying this technique. However, its popularity will increase steadily for years to come.

In developing cost models a few principles can be used. First it is important to build cost models not only on cost elements (such as labor, materials) but also around the actual cost drivers. Capturing the cost drivers produces a model that answers the question 'what if?' instead of 'what is?' (Laseter, 1998, p. 37). Examples are production lot sizes, set-up times, labor rates.

Cost models should expose at least three elements: materials purchase prices, the actual acquisition costs that the company incurs in buying the materials, and the cost of use. Taking copying equipment as an example, it is seen that the purchase price of this type of equipment in general only represents a small part of the total usage cost. Building a cost model for copying machines would then require a detailed breakdown of (a) the actual supplier cost price of the equipment, (b) the company's acquisition costs and (c) the cost related to accessories, maintenance and other services, costs and supply of spare parts, etc. Building a cost model for an aluminum die casted product would require a breakdown of the following cost elements: tooling, quality, logistics, purchasing administration, scrap, supplier inventory, supplier overheads, supplier indirect and direct labor, energy consumption and materials costs. In each of these cases these cost elements should be related to the actual cost drivers.

methods requires cooperation between specialists in the areas of engineering, manufacturing, calculation, quality control and purchasing.

The first three methods, being less time consuming, are more broadly applicable. Table 15.4 indicates the major differences between supplier auditing and vendor rating. Vendor rating will be used to judge existing suppliers. It has a more quantitative focus than auditing techniques.

Financial assessment

The financial assessment of suppliers is carried out on the basis of annual financial reports which can be obtained from the supplier. In most European countries legislation requires companies to file a summary of their financial reports at the local Chamber of Commerce where the supplier is registered. Dun & Bradstreet, Graydon and other information brokers provide on the world wide web detailed electronic databases nowadays from which up-to-date financial and other information can be obtained (see for example www.dnb.com). Based on these financial reports the supplier's financial performance can be evaluated.

TABLE 15.3 Identifying cost drivers

Category	Description	Examples
Design	Costs attributable to product design trade-offs	Materials specifications Product line complexity
Facility	Costs related to the size of the facility, equipment and process technology employed	Facility scale Degree of vertical integration Use of automation
Geography	Costs associated with the location of the facility relative to the customer	Location related wage rate difference Transportation costs to customer
Operations	Costs that differentiate a well run facility from a poorly run facility	Labor productivity Facility utilization Rejection rates

Source: Laseter (1998), p. 51.

TABLE 15.4 Major differences between supplier auditing and vendor rating

Aspect	Supplier auditing	Vendor rating
Orientation	Focus on future	Based on historical data
Application	New and current suppliers	Current suppliers
Nature	Mainly qualitative	Mainly quantitative
Scope	Broad, many aspects	Limited, few aspects
Work	Time consuming	Standard data
Data processing	Subjective, manually	Factual, computerized
Relation with suppliers	Cooperation required	Based on internal administrative data

When conducting this analysis, one should keep in mind that this analysis is based on historical data. However, quite often it is possible, using financial forecasting techniques, to judge the potential future opportunities and threats based on these data. This makes financial analysis an interesting instrument to the buyer. A financial analysis can only be carried out if one has access to the supplier's annual reports. The results give a first impression of the quality of the supplier's management. Such an analysis enables the buyer to visit the supplier well-prepared, and to ask pointed questions.

A financial analysis provides insight into the development of the quality of the supplier's results. If information is available about other companies (either directly, or indirectly in the shape of the industrial statistics of the Central Statistical Office), comparison with competitors becomes possible. This knowledge can be used in discussions with the supplier to achieve improvements in his organization.

SUMMARY

Pricing and cost structures of suppliers are always interrelated, but the effect they have on one another is not always clear. Pricing policies of industrial products and services are subjected to both external market factors and internal cost factors. The prices of goods and services can be based on market factors, on cost factors, or on a combination of both. The latter situation is the most common.

The supplier will take numerous additional (frequently political or strategic) factors into account when deciding on his pricing policy. The supplier's pricing policy is in most cases already obscure, and it may even be aggravated by the discount and bonus system he uses.

It is crucial for buyers to be able to lift the veil that covers the supplier's pricing policy. The buyer can achieve this by closely monitoring the developments in the supply and demand situation on the purchasing market. He can also monitor the individual supplier's financial performance and can make an analysis of the supplier's cost price, either with or without specialist assistance. Experience shows that the basis for negotiations becomes considerably more professional as a result of this knowledge. It furthermore facilitates reaching agreements on product and process improvements.

Finally, the buyer should monitor developments in the supplier's performance. Price behavior, quality and delivery performance should be closely monitored. This information justifies the development of computerized vendor rating systems. It should be noted, however, that vendor rating can only be applied to existing suppliers who deliver goods on a more or less regular basis. For new suppliers and suppliers delivering critical items on a project basis other techniques must be used.

ASSIGNMENTS

15.1 This chapter discusses a number of methods in the field of supplier assessment. In addition to objective and quantitative methods, such assessments can also be made in a more subjective manner. The objective of supplier assessment is to determine the extent to which a particular supplier will be able to meet his delivery obligations, both now and in the future. Name a few issues which may indicate that a supplier's performance is deteriorating, and which can be observed by the buyer during a visit to the supplier.

15.2 A supplier of components announces that he has to raise his prices by 10 per cent, because he has lost a major customer. He states he is now forced to spread his overheads across a smaller production volume. What costing method does this supplier use? What do you think of that? Assuming that this supplier is important to you, how would you deal with the supplier's request? What steps would you take?

15.3 In this chapter vendor rating was named as one of the methods that can be used to measure supplier performance. Delivery reliability and quality performance of the supplier are two aspects of vendor rating. How can a supplier's delivery reliability and quality performance be measured in a practical way? What criteria are used? Name some examples.

15.4 Last year you purchased 100 units of product X from a supplier at €50 each. You estimate that you will purchase 300 units of this product from the same supplier this year. You are now preparing for the price discussion with the supplier. What price are you willing to pay, assuming that an 80 per cent learning curve applies to this product?

15.5 Name examples of products where the price is set by means of cost-based pricing, market-based pricing and competitive bidding. What are the consequences of this distinction for the purchasing policy, or for the buyer's attitude during negotiations with the supplier? Which arguments will the buyer use in each of these cases to obtain the lowest possible purchase price?

CASE STUDY   NEGOTIATING A CAR PURCHASE

Two gentlemen enter a car dealer's showroom. After looking for some time at several of the cars on display they approach the salesman. They tell him they are interested in a particular type of car. However, their willingness to do business depends on the price they will get for the car they want to trade in. The salesman goes outside to inspect their car.

The salesman decides to take it for a test drive and leaves both customers at the dealer's site. There is some heavy consultation between the two gentlemen during the salesman's absence. A little later, the salesman comes back. They all go inside and settle around the table.

The discussion proceeds laboriously. The salesman asks what price the two gentlemen had in mind for their used car, but they don't want to tell him. The salesman has to take the lead. After some dis-

cussion and calculation, he writes down a figure on a piece of paper, folds it, and hands it over. A few seconds later, both customers know the price offered. One of the gentlemen acts as spokesman. His reaction is one of incredulity: such a price for their car is impossible; a pure swindle! Other dealers offered much more! The discussion turns hostile. The prospective buyers stand up, then sits down again. At one point the customer who has done all the talking so far tells his colleague: 'Come on, John, this isn't going anywhere. Let's go!' He makes ready to leave. The other customer remains seated. In a confidential tone of voice he resumes the discussion with the salesman, and tells him that his colleague is a bit excited, but he has his reasons. If the salesman will improve his offer, then maybe he can talk some sense into his colleague . . .

INTRODUCTION

Negotiations as described in the Case Study occur daily. Execution of the purchasing function without negotiation is unthinkable. Experiences with buyers show that at least 20 per cent of their time is taken up by preparations for and the actual negotiations with suppliers. Knowledge of the negotiating process and negotiating skills are necessary for the buyer to be able to offer resistance to the frequently well-trained salesman.

When thinking of negotiating, we usually picture the commercial process that occurs in every buy-and-sell transaction. However, the subject can be viewed in a much broader sense, for, aside from negotiations with suppliers, the buyer often also has to negotiate within his own organization. An effective buyer must be able to maintain good contacts with his internal users. He must be able to judge the feasibility of certain ideas. He must also be able to make product designers change their minds if they have overlooked an alternative that is better for the organization. This chapter addresses the general principles that underlie negotiating processes. In doing so we have adopted an European view on the subject. The chapter starts by describing the major differences between negotiations for industrial purposes and negotiations for retail buying. Next, the various stages that can be distinguished in a negotiating process are discussed. Finally, the various tactics that can be used in negotiations are addressed. All of these subjects will be investigated from the buyer's perspective.

CHARACTERISTICS OF NEGOTIATIONS FOR INDUSTRIAL PURCHASES

Very little attention is given to the basic differences between industrial buying and retail buying, both in the relevant literature and in training courses. However, it is important to appreciate these differences, because they strongly affect the nature of the negotiations, as shown below.

- The purchasing policy of a trading company is closely related to its sales policy, because the purchase price directly influences the saleability and profitability of the product. This is much less so in industrial companies. In comparison with a trading company, the purchasing share in the cost price of the end product is lower. Therefore, the prices of purchased products have a less direct impact on the sales price of end products.

- Retail buyers generally have more freedom in decision making than industrial buyers. The latter are limited by production planning, technical specifications (small tolerances), call-off schedules, etc. This makes them less autonomous than their colleagues in the retail sector.

- The buyer of industrial goods usually has a longer term, more intense relationship with his suppliers than his colleagues in the retail company. This is particularly so when it involves products which are manufactured to customer design. The retail buyer often buys products which were developed by the supplier. This means that it is easier for him to change suppliers than it is for the industrial buyer.[1] For the industrial buyer, a change of supplier is often preceded by a long screening process with regard to technical and delivery reliability.

---

1 Of course, the retail buyer may also face some situations in which he is very dependent on a supplier, i.e. in the case of suppliers of strong A-brands.

- Price is often less important for the industrial buyer than good quality, delivery reliability and service. Although these aspects are also important in retail buying, the purchase price is even more important, since it decides what margin the buyer is going to make on the product.

All of this means that the retail buyer will usually be able to take a more independent attitude towards a supplier than the industrial buyer. He is reasonably autonomous in his work, and has to deal with fewer people in his own organization. This is reflected in his attitude towards the supplier. Negotiations in retail will generally be 'harder' and more focused on price than industrial purchasing negotiations. This means that a number of the negotiating techniques used in trade negotiations are less suited to industrial purchasing negotiations.

RECOGNIZING NEGOTIATING SITUATIONS

One of the most important elements in negotiation, irrespective of whether it takes place in a commercial or a non-commercial context, is being able to recognize when the situation is a negotiating situation. If your neighbor comes over on a sunny afternoon to ask you if he can borrow your lawn mower, many of you will answer his question with a 'yes' or a 'no'. The experienced negotiator immediately spots an opportunity in his neighbor's request. Maybe you also want your neighbor to do something for you. Then the request is a good opportunity to make a counter request. For example you noticed earlier that day that there is almost no fuel left in the machine and you ask your neighbor to fill it up. Or perhaps you will agree to his request on the condition that your neighbor also mows your lawn.

The essence of this type of situation is that somebody else asks for or wants something you are basically willing to provide. A request can be transformed into a negotiating situation when you discover that this person can also be of use to you. Negotiating situations are aimed at bringing together the parties through concessions in such a way that both parties can look back on the negotiations with satisfaction.

In the example of the lawn mower, the negotiating situation emerges spontaneously. In a business context often negotiating situations emerge long before the first contact with the other party takes place.

It is important to observe that negotiations concern more elements than price alone. Negotiations concern all elements that are important in reaching the agreement; this observation is of special significance for industrial products. Experience with purchasing departments in many companies shows that issues like quality and delivery reliability, as well as after-sales services are frequently more important elements in the purchasing decision than price and terms of payment.

Negotiations are focused on arriving at a good deal for both parties. If one of the negotiating parties is so powerful that they can impose their will on the other, there is no negotiating situation. In this context negotiating would be defined as 'a process, aimed at solving problems experienced by two or more parties, in such a way that the interests of all parties involved are served.'

From the definition it may be concluded that good negotiating requires a cooperative attitude, characterized by receptivity to the other party's interests. Furthermore, willingness to reach an agreement that is beneficial to both parties is indispensable.

FACTORS WHICH CAN WEAKEN THE NEGOTIATING POSITION

If a person does not have a clear picture of his target, the negotiating process will be affected. This occurs frequently in situations between industrial buyers and sellers. It is well known that, in general, salesmen have a more solid training than buyers. As a result of the numbers of suppliers the buyer has to deal with, and the size of his purchasing portfolio, he is frequently unable to prepare for all negotiations sufficiently. An insufficient knowledge about the subject of the negotiations can easily lead to being snowed under by detailed information provided by the other party. Buyers have identified many aspects which may weaken their negotiating position (see Memo 16.1). These issues can be summarized in three main points which must be predetermined for every negotiation:

- Goals and objectives. Is it clear what the negotiations should accomplish? What is the minimum result that must be achieved and what are the maximum concessions one is willing to make?
- Authority. What authority does the negotiator have to make a deal? Does he/she have the necessary support from higher management levels?
- Expertise and knowledge. Do the people who are going to conduct the negotiation have the required expertise and knowledge? Are they experts on the subject? Do they actually know the business?

These items are essential prerequisites to entering into any negotiation.

MEMO 16.1 FACTORS WHICH MAY WEAKEN THE BUYER'S NEGOTIATING POSITION

- Lack of preparation time.
- Lack of knowledge with regard to market developments, the market position of the supplier, and own company's relative position.
- Lack of knowledge of the supplier's cost structure.
- Insufficient information on the supplier's organization (authority).
- Too little listening and too much talk on the buyer's side.
- Insufficient command of foreign languages.
- None or very few alternative sources available.
- Few valid arguments to support the buyer's point of view.
- A negotiating partner on the buying team speaks out of turn.
- Insufficient authority to close an agreement.
- The supplier uses arguments that were not anticipated.
- Lack of experience with a supplier.

PREPARING FOR NEGOTIATIONS

Planning and preparing for negotiations starts long before the actual negotiation takes place. It is important to find out at an early stage what the other party's view of the negotiations will be: what exactly are they hoping to achieve? In exceptional cases a supplier doesn't want to sell at all, but keeps the discussion going to collect basic information about changing usage patterns and/or competitors. What interests are possibly shared, and what are the expected potential subjects of opposing interests (conflict)? To get some idea, a useful tactic can be to ask what subjects the other party wants on the agenda (this in itself can prompt preliminary negotiations – consider the disarmament negotiations between the Americans and the Soviets in Geneva in the late 1980s).

It is important to find out as much as possible about the other party. If it is a new supplier, examination of annual reports and bank references is a prerequisite. If it is an existing supplier, it is wise to analyze the past deliveries – have there been problems in the past with this supplier? (e.g. low delivery reliability, quality defects, unexpected price increases, etc.). There is no harm in trying to quantify the scope of these problems. Furthermore, it is also important to know who will represent the supplier in the negotiations. Are they people you know? If not, then the authority of the negotiating partners must be investigated. How far does their power of decision go? Do they have the authority to conclude an agreement? At first sight this may seem too detailed an approach; however, the buyer must take into account that sales people have an eye for detail and come very well prepared.

It is important, having gathered the necessary information, to have an idea of possible points of agreement between you and the other party. If there are few, you might reconsider the wisdom of negotiating.

PLANNING NEGOTIATIONS

When the homework has been done, planning of the negotiations can begin. Clayton (1984) proposes a ten-step approach.

1 Establish the objectives of the negotiation for yourself. What exactly do you want to accomplish by means of the transaction with the supplier? What is it you want him to do? What are you willing to do in return? Make a distinction between the short-term benefits you want to achieve, and the long-term benefits you see. Sometimes it is necessary that you tone down your short-term expectation a little for the benefit of the long-term interests. Take the manufacturers of copying equipment, who, for example, are often willing to give something off the sales price, only to compensate for this reduction at a later stage through higher service rates, spare parts and supplies.

2 Gather facts that can have a big impact on the negotiations. If a supplier wants to come and talk about a price increase, it is worthwhile finding out how this increase relates to his competitors. Alternatively, a supplier might be willing to moderate the announced price increase if we are willing to consider larger purchases in the near future. These are examples of what we call objective facts which can influence the negotiation. However, there are also subjective facts that can affect the course of the negotiation. It is important to know what the other party thinks of us. Will they be influenced by possible bad experiences they have had with our company in the past? Do the negotiators on both sides get along on a personal level? It is worthwhile keeping a file of major negotiations with suppliers?

3 Assess the power position of each of the parties. A power position in a negotiation can be derived from various aspects (see Figure 16.1). It is important to realize that power is a relative concept. It also depends on how the position (power) is perceived by the other party (think of the poker game in which the player's power position is often based on bluff). It is important, therefore, to determine the foundation of the other party's power position, and whether this is a reason for concern. In price negotiations sales people sometimes hide behind the price list or the company's guidelines. Do you accept this type of argument or don't you?

4 Determine the points of common interest. In many negotiations most of the time is spent on issues one cannot agree on. If these are the only issues that receive attention, it will be very difficult to reach an agreement. It is more important to establish, in advance, the points of agreement. Focusing attention here leads to a more positive atmosphere. The question of 'how do we solve our conflicts?' then becomes 'how can we turn the points of common interest into the largest possible mutual advantage?'. Keep the negotiating atmosphere as positive and open as possible.

5 Make a list of questions. A systematic approach is important in negotiations. Resist the temptation to respond immediately to details or new information presented by the other party. If this new information sheds a completely different light on matters, it is better to discontinue the negotiations and redo your homework. So draw up a list of questions and stick to it.

6 Define your tasks. Both parties will probably make concessions during the process of negotiation. It is unrealistic to expect the other party to do it all (and this doesn't fit in the negotiating concept presented here). You can plan your concessions in advance. To be able to do this, it is important that you establish what for you would be the best possible result (what do you think is the feasible maximum result the other party would agree to, given the circumstances?). What for you would be the most likely result (what do you think is realistically feasible, and would that result be acceptable to you?). What for you would be the worst possible result (what is the minimum you would settle for, if there is no other possibility?)

FIGURE 16.1   Aspects of a power position – factors which may lead to a better power position in negotiations.

Competition
Letting the supplier know he's not the only option

Written word
Often applied by suppliers 'according to our list the price is . . .', or 'in view of your order we regret the maximum discount is . . .'

Trust
The other party will be more willing to make concessions if they trust you

Knowledge
Insight (about products, markets, alternatives) enhances your negotiating position and prevents surprises

Time
Time constraints will put negotiations under pressure and may lead to unexpected concessions

Money
The person who pays has the initial lead

Negotiating power
The person who is more skilled in negotiating and/or has prepared his work more thoroughly, clearly has the advantage

FIGURE 16.2   Composition of a purchasing negotiating team.

Buyer	Price/cost analysis	Calculator
Captain of the team interprets the contract, assesses supplier performance, closes the contract	Analyses costs, projects economic trends, determines acceptability of rates, screens cost structures	Reviews designs, judges manufacturing processes, assesses labor costs, determines value of function

Strategy

Team approach focused on use of combined knowledge and skills

7   Decide on the composition and division of roles in your negotiating team. The composition of the team will depend on the subject of the negotiations. Who are the best people to use? Do you need help from outside the purchasing department? (This will often be the case in major negotiations.) Who will be the spokesperson for your company? Who will take notes? Who watches the other party's reactions? It may be helpful to assemble a special, cross-functional team for strategic negotiations (see Figure 16.2).

8   Plan your concessions. What will be your opening bid? When will you make it? Never make a concession without asking for something in return; but also, never ask for a concession without offering something in return. Discuss with your team members which concessions you are willing to make, and which concessions you absolutely will not make under any circumstance. You can do the same for the opposition: what concessions do you think they are willing to make and what is absolutely unrealistic to expect?

9   Agree upon the negotiating tactic you will follow. This subject is discussed in the next section.

10   Indicate how you think you will conclude the negotiations. What working agreements do you think you can reach with the other party? Is it necessary to schedule the next discussion? Summarize the results and agreements for the other party, to prevent misunderstandings.

These ten steps are essential in every significant negotiation process. It is obvious that effective negotiating requires appropriate preparation in order to arrive at a satisfactory outcome.

TACTICS IN PURCHASING NEGOTIATIONS

Determining the tactics to adopt during purchasing negotiations is an important aspect of the preparation. The literature which covers negotiating tactics (Karass, 1970, 1977, 1979) identifies the following approaches:

- Take-it-or-leave-it. One party wants to impose its terms on the other party, without making concessions. This tactic is contrary to the author's idea of negotiating and is less suitable in an industrial setting. Nevertheless, it is sometimes used by buyers who are aware of their power position *vis-à-vis* the supplier, and is intended to lower the other party's aspiration level.

- Bogey. In this tactic the buyer approaches the supplier in a very friendly way and comments on his proposal positively. However, the buyer lets the supplier know that, if there is to be any business, the proposal 'will have to be slightly adjusted in view of the very specific situation'. With this tactic the negotiating atmosphere remains open and the supplier can utilize all his talents to develop a better deal.

- Chinese crunch. In this situation it is declared that an agreement with the supplier is possible, as soon as he solves just one little problem. Obviously, this little problem is interpreted differently by the seller! This tactic is intended to effectively sink the agreement, which was as good as settled in the seller's mind, just before a deal is struck; for example, there is an agreement about the price, but the buyer then informs the seller that transportation is the latter's responsibility. Practice shows that sales people are ready to make considerable concessions in this stage of the negotiating process.

- Auction, also referred to as Dutch or Chinese auction. In this situation the buyer makes the supplier explain why they should do business together. If the buyer also applies this tactic to the other candidates, a lot will be learned about the competition. Information is obtained without too much effort. It is, of course, desirable to check the accuracy of the information.

- Good guy–bad guy. This was very popular among the Germans during World War II. A prisoner was first interrogated by a tough officer. When he had almost lost courage, a second, much friendlier, officer would appear. He would reprimand his colleague and subsequently draw out the prisoner. This tactic is frequently employed by used-car dealers. The purpose of this tactic is to dim the other party's expectations about the outcome of the negotiations.

Several other tactics are feasible based on different considerations. For example, does one take the initiative in the negotiation, or leave this to the other party? Does one build in a recess or is this not desirable? In the context of this book, the discussion of the tactical components of purchasing negotiations can only be limited.

STAGES IN PURCHASING NEGOTIATIONS

If the preparations have been concluded and agreement is reached about the tactic to be used, the negotiations can be started. In practice, negotiation processes follow a certain pattern and, in general, four stages can be discerned in the course of the negotiation process.

- Exploration. During this first stage both parties try to get acquainted. Next they try to discover their mutual interests and intentions. They also try to assess the importance of the negotiations for the other party. This is done by exchanging information: everybody listens, both parties explain or ask for clarification of particular statements, and they continually check whether they understand each other. It is important to listen closely to the other party, and not make a first offer. Furthermore, one should not respond specifically to questions from the other party. The objective of this stage is to establish the context of the negotiations.

- Reflection. This stage consists of digesting the information received from the other party. Does this information necessitate a revision of your objectives? Did you overlook certain things in your preparations? Were your assumptions about the other party's willingness to reach an agreement correct, or do they now turn out to be wrong? Receiving new information can cause you to request a short break so you can consult with your partner.

- Negotiation. In this phase true negotiation takes place. Concessions are made on both sides. It is important to check how the other party responds to concessions made by you (through both verbal and non-verbal reactions). Don't jump to conclusions during this stage; avoid insulting remarks and, most importantly, don't concede more than your planning allowed for.

- Closing. Repeat and summarize the agreements that have been made. Is the other party satisfied with the results? Take your time to round off the negotiations well, so there is no possibility of misunderstandings about the results that have been achieved.

This list can be helpful to buyers. It is important to be aware of the stage the negotiations are at, all of the time. Practice shows time and time again that the first stage is the most time-consuming. This leaves less time for the actual negotiations and the closing part and one common result is misunderstandings about who is supposed to do what. Both parties will then dispute (parts of) the agreements afterwards.

Negotiating is a difficult job, because it can involve so many different subjects. This work furthermore requires a certain disposition, namely a willingness to cooperate to reach an agreement that will benefit both parties.

TRUST, PURCHASING ETHICS AND RULES OF CONDUCT

During the past decade many debates in business have occurred on the issue of trust in business-to-business relationships. As companies become more dependent on each other, trust becomes more important. Some academics have advocated that future competition will not be among individual companies any more, rather competition will occur between integrated supply chains. Supply chain integration, however, will require a long-term orientation towards the relationship, a willingness to mutually share information and active collaboration among the parties involved. As research evidence has shown, partnership in business-to-business relationships is still ill-developed. In a research project conducted in the 1990s by the Center of Advanced Purchasing Studies (CAPS) in the US, it was found that real partnerships among over 300 companies investigated were less than one per cent of the total number of supplier relationships. We therefore conclude that trust is a topic that usually meets with a lot of interest, both in academia as well as among business practitioners; however, apparently it is extremely difficult in practice to build trustful relationships. Of course, the question is: why is this the case? And why this interest for trust in business-to-business relationships?

The answer may come from insights that were developed originally at Motorola some years ago (see Bhote, 1989). Motorola considers trust to be the result from two factors: trustworthiness, i.e. the situation in which trust is granted to you by other parties, and competence. Obviously, trust cannot be asked for by a person or requested; it is the other party who decides whether it is willing to grant trust to you or not. In order to make the other party willing to do so companies need to work both on competence and trustworthiness (see Figure 16.3). Building competence is about developing people's skills, experience and creativity. Companies that have skilled staff available, who have great expertise in what they do, generate more confidence and trust at their clients than companies that do not have competent staff. Having a skilled labor force is a necessary but not a sufficient condition for building trust in business-to-business relationships as is shown. In order to be able to generate trustworthiness, companies also need to have strict ethical principles and procedures. Trust can only be generated if company staff act in a consistent and reliable manner. Sales staff should be able to live up to their word; if sales staff are replaced, customers should be able to trust that agreements made are met by the new person. The same is true for changes at management level. These observations apply both for the organization of the seller and buyer. Trustworthiness, as we see it, primarily stems from ethical and consistent organizational behavior. Traditionally, most companies have made great efforts and continue to do so in improving the skills and competences of their labor force. This may be one explanation why topics such as 'competence management' and 'knowledge management' have generated so much interest over the past decade. However, only very few companies have explicit policies and corporate programs on 'business integrity and ethics'. The fact that a few large multinational companies have got into deep financial problems due to unethical behavior may change this picture in the future.

It is in the interest of the company that purchasing negotiations achieve the best possible results by using means and tactics that are proper and responsible in terms of ethics. A buyer is exposed to many temptations. These vary from Christmas presents which are sent to his/her home address at the end of the year, to vacations, which are offered disguised as a business trip to an overseas office. In sales practice lots of activities are undertaken to put the customer in the most positive frame of mind about a possible purchase. The question of course is what can and what cannot be accepted from the supplier. In business, this question is not easily answered. Questions can also be raised on the side of the buyer as to how far one should go in a relationship with a supplier. In this context the following questions may occur:

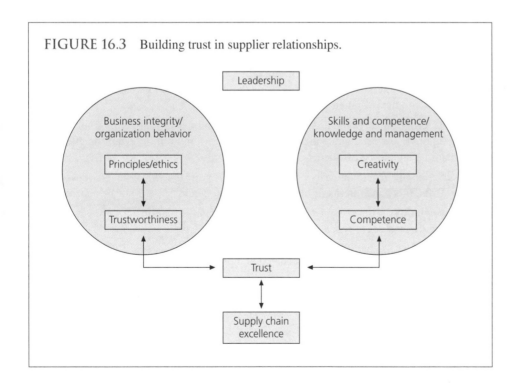

FIGURE 16.3   Building trust in supplier relationships.

- How should confidential supplier price information be handled?
- How to deal with quotations: should we only use quotations if we are seriously considering requesting a firm bid from a supplier, or do we also use them to check our current supplier's prices?
- What is the maximum share we as customers want to have in the supplier's turnover, in order to prevent excessive dependency on us?

MEMO 16.2   THE ETHICAL CODE OF IFPMM

1 *Precepts*. Members shall not use their authority or office for personal gain and shall seek to uphold and enhance the standing of the Purchasing and Materials Management profession and the Federation by:

- Maintaining an unimpeachable standard of integrity in all their business relationships both inside and outside the organizations in which they are employed.
- Fostering the highest standards of professional competence amongst those for whom they are responsible.
- Optimizing the use of resources for which they are responsible so as to provide the maximum benefit to their employers.
- Complying with the letter and the spirit of:
  - The laws of the country in which they practise.
  - The Federation's 'Principles and Standards of Purchasing Practice' and any other such guidance on professional practice as may be issued by the Federation from time to time.
  - Contractual obligations.
- Rejecting and denouncing any business practice that is improper.

2 *Guidance*. In applying these precepts, members should follow the guidance set out below:

- Declaration of interest. Any personal interest which may impinge or might reasonably be deemed by others to impinge on a member's impartiality in any matter relevant to their duties should be declared to their employer.
- Confidentiality and accuracy of information. The confidentiality of information received in the course of duty must be respected and should not be used for personal gain; information given in the course of duty should be true and fair and not designed to mislead.
- Competition. While considering the advantages to the member's employer of maintaining a continuing relationship with a supplier, any arrangement which might, in the long term, prevent the effective operation of fair competition, should be avoided.
- Business gifts. To preserve the image and integrity of both the member and the employer, business gifts should be discouraged. Gifts, other than items of very small intrinsic value, should not be accepted.
- Hospitality. Moderate hospitality is an accepted courtesy of a business relationship. However, the recipients should not allow themselves to reach a position whereby they might be or might be deemed by others to have been influenced in making a business decision as a consequence of accepting such hospitality. The frequency and scale of hospitality accepted should not be significantly greater than a recipient's employer, through the recipient's expense account, would be likely to provide in return.
- When in doubt of what is acceptable in terms of gifts or hospitality, the offer should be declined or advice sought from the member's superior.

Source: International Federation of Purchasing and Materials Management.

- Do we always strive to have at least two suppliers (dual sourcing) or are single sources allowed in particular circumstances?

- How far do we go in negotiations with suppliers? Are we willing to buy at prices we know for a fact aren't sufficient to cover the supplier's cost price?

To increase uniformity in behavior towards the business community, a number of large companies have become explicit on their policies with regard to 'business integrity' explaining their company's business values and regulations on matters such as conflict of interest. As a part of these policies they have urged their purchasing managers to draw up and subscribe to several rules of conduct for their dealings with suppliers. Rules of conduct have also been drawn up by the International Federation of Purchasing and Materials Management (IFPMM), see Memo 16.2, which may serve as a guide to purchasing managers that want to set up specific policies on this topic for their company.

We may safely conclude that companies need to overcome these ethical issues if they want to be able to build constructive relationships with their suppliers.

SUMMARY

Negotiating is an important aspect of the buyer's activities. It takes up a large part of his time. Every negotiation is an interactive process between two or more parties. Negotiating demands a cooperative attitude, and a receptivity to the other party's interests. Before starting negotiations with a supplier, it is important to determine:

- the goals and objectives of the negotiations (preferably formulated in terms of different aspiration levels);

- what authority the negotiators have to conclude an agreement with the supplier's representatives (and vice versa);

- what information is required to negotiate effectively.

A sound preparation is half the job! This chapter has presented a ten-step method that may help buyers to prepare for effective and professional negotiations; of course it is not necessary to go through each step in every negotiation. One important aspect of the preparations is deciding on the negotiating tactics. Purchasing practice shows a wide variety of methods and techniques. As practice has shown, every negotiation evolves around a relatively fixed four-stage pattern: exploration, reflection, negotiation and the closing stage. As we have seen throughout this book building constructive relationships with suppliers is a prime responsibility of any buyer and purchasing manager. As companies become more dependent on their suppliers, supply chain integration is a challenge to them. Supply chain integration can only be built upon constructive, long term supplier relationships. To be able to do so requires a fair degree of trust among the parties involved. Developing trust in business-to-business relationships requires competent and experienced staff. Next it requires consistency and reliability in the way the company staff and managers operate and behave towards outside parties and the way in which commitments that have been agreed upon are met. This explains why issues such as 'business integrity' and 'purchasing ethics' have met with great interest over the past years. We hypothesize that this topic will even gain more relevance in the near future. For purchasing professionals this will imply that they need to work according to the highest professional and ethical standards that have been laid down in explicit procedures and guidelines. The ethical code of the International Federation of Purchasing and Materials Management can serve as a guideline here.

ASSIGNMENTS

16.1 You are the buyer in a machine factory. Management is considering the purchase of a CNC milling machine, representing an investment of more than €350 000. You have selected one supplier from a number of potential suppliers, with whom you have had an explorative discussion. A second discussion is scheduled for next week about the terms and conditions of a possible order. What issues would you pay attention to in preparing for the discussion with the supplier? Present an overview.

16.2 The preparations of negotiations should mention the location of the negotiations. One can basically choose between the buyer's office, the supplier's office and neutral territory. List the advantages and disadvantages of each of these locations.

16.3 Under what circumstances would you feel that the following should be allowed in purchasing: (1) accepting gifts from a supplier; (2) accepting invitations for a dinner; (3) engaging in a personal friendship with a supplier sales representative; (4) extending the deadline for a competitive bid to one of your suppliers; (5) giving the 'right of first refusal' to your current supplier?

16.4 In a discussion about trust in business-to-business relations a senior purchasing executive stated that 'Trust is against the nature of any business man'. Discuss what he meant by this statement. Would you agree with this point of view?

16.5 What do you think are the major differences between negotiations with European suppliers and negotiations with suppliers from the Far East?

LEARNING OBJECTIVES

After studying this chapter you should understand the following:

- The main characteristics and importance of purchasing and supply in trade and retail companies.
- The most important developments going on in the purchasing policies of trade and retail companies.
- The way in which the purchasing function can be organized in trade and retail companies.
- The profile of the trade and retail buyer.

CASE STUDY   EFFICIENT CONSUMER RESPONSE IN RETAIL

Ahold is one of the leading supermarket chains in Europe and the United States. With sales of over 66 billion euros, it operates more than 9000 stores in 28 countries on four continents. Apart from retail Ahold wants to increase its 'share-of-stomach' in the countries where it operates through building up a strong position in foodservice. One of its major supermarket chains in The Netherlands is Albert Heijn. This operating company is leading-edge in applying new concepts in retail and supply chain management.

Modern retail thinking within Albert Heijn centres on the term ECR: efficient consumer response. ECR means that the consumer is the trigger for the logistics process within the food chain. Cash register scanning (using barcode-technology) immediately shows how much of a particular product has been sold on a particular day. If the stock drops beneath a certain level, then an order is automatically generated for the supplier. The supplier is expected to restock within a certain, previously agreed time period (often limited to a couple of hours), either through direct delivery to the shop (fresh products) or to the distribution centre of the retailer.

In the view of Albert Heijn, ECR is a situation in which the manufacturer/supplier is no longer paid for the products that have been delivered. Preferably, payment is based on the volume that actually has been sold within a given period. In essence the manufacturer/supplier becomes the logistics manager and distributor to the retailer. The supplier performs most of the logistics tasks. Based upon actual sales information, the manufacturer is supposed to determine the volume which is to be replenished the next day. In case full truckloads are preferred by the manufacturer (for reasons of transport economies), the surplus volume can be stocked in the distribution centre; however, the square metres that are being used for this purpose are to be paid for by the manufacturer. Replenishment generally takes place on the basis of the principle of cross docking. Deliveries to the distribution center are cross-loaded to waiting trucks, which transport the goods directly to the stores, instead of leaving them to be stored at the distribution center).

Retail buyers (now often referred to as category managers) increasingly focus on refining retail concepts and improving category management. In this way the traditional retail buyer in many supermarket chains has evolved rapidly into a sophisticated retail entrepreneur. Customer loyalty cards form the basis for in-depth studies about consumer behavior. Using customer loyalty programs, retailers try to attract and retain customers with tailor-made offers. Using intricate logistics systems, the logistics goods flow can be tracked and traced. As a result, store personnel can check on the status of orders and deliveries independently. Order processing and payment take place electronically using EDI or some other electronic purchasing solution. Advanced shelf allocation systems (e.g. SpaceMan) allow for detailed yield analyzes per article, per article group, or per supplier.

In order to make sure manufacturers meet world market standards, Ahold started the World Wide Retail Exchange (WWRE) in 1998 aimed at facilitating global sourcing. Through internet-enabled reverse auctions suppliers are challenged to provide their best offer to the Ahold companies. Web supported transaction processing allows the company to drastically reduce transaction costs and speed up the process of ordering, shipment, delivery and payment. Next, the WWRE is used to monitor tracing and tracking of products, inventories and goods flows within Ahold's global and supply networks.

INTRODUCTION

Welcome to the world of retail! As this Case Study demonstrates buying for retail is much more than just buying products. Due to the narrow margins, retail buyers have to take cost out of their supply chains where they can. This is one reason why retail buyers have adopted advanced supply chain management concepts and techniques. Through intricate and realtime logistics systems they are able to trace and track their materials flows from minute to minute. Of course, their activities are based upon sound category management. Based upon a thorough analysis of consumer buying patterns product assortments are constantly adapted and changed. Since retail buyers usually deal with large and powerful manufacturers of branded products, they have adopted new methods and tools in order to stimulate competition among them. Electronic auctions and marketplaces belong nowadays to the standard toolbox of retail buying.

The purchasing function in trade and retail companies is much closer to sales. Although the term 'buying' is more used in retail companies, the terms 'buying' and 'purchasing' are used interchangeably in this chapter. As will be seen, the sales, purchasing and logistics functions over the years have become highly integrated in these companies. In retail, buyers are responsible for decisions related to running a whole product assortment. Sales and purchasing decisions are weighed against each other so that an optimal financial return can be achieved. It goes without saying that in order to be able to do this, buyers in trade companies need to have a broad business orientation, in which price is only one of the elements of the decision-making process.

Trade and retail companies in most European countries account for a considerable share of the total number of transactions. The purchasing-to-sales content is rather high, since these companies do not add significant value to their products. A purchasing-to-sales ratio of more than 80 per cent is not uncommon. This means that functions such as purchasing, logistics and sales are core activities. Buying for trade companies means 'bottom line' thinking. Margins on products (especially in the retail business) are usually very small. This means that the buyer must take into consideration all the costs that are made in the trajectory from manufacturer to end-customer. Effective cost control is a prerequisite for the continued existence of trade companies. Costs related to materials handling, transportation and storage cannot be ignored. This concept is at the root of the development of strategic cost management techniques (such as direct product cost and direct product profitability) and shelf or display simulation systems, which will be explained in this chapter. These information systems are today important management tools for the modern retail buyer.

This chapter describes the role and importance of the purchasing function in trade and retail companies. In doing so the issue of how to organize for purchasing in these kinds of company will be addressed. Major developments and changes taking place in the sourcing and supply management strategies of retailers and their relationships with suppliers are also discussed; however, definitions of some important concepts are outlined first.

DEFINITIONS

Trade companies are characterized by the absence of a production process. There is no transformation in the technical sense. At most there are some packaging or 'bulk-breaking' activities. The value added in trade and retail companies, when compared with manufacturing companies, is therefore rather low. The mere existence of the trade company is based primarily on the exchange of value, i.e. products between different parties in the market. Essentially the trade function can be described as 'bridging time, place, quantity, assortment and knowledge'. The products that are sold must travel the road from manufacturer to final consumer. The primary process of the trade company takes care of this. The purchasing function, together with (inbound) logistics, is of major importance. In addition, outbound logistics (physical distribution) is a major activity in trade companies. Due to the lack of a production function, the time which elapses between the purchase and the actual sale is very short. This is one reason why in some retail companies buying and selling are integrated into one function, since buying decisions may to a large extent determine the sales potential for a specific product (and *vice versa*). Where this occurs, this integrated commercial function is often referred to as category management.

Trade companies can be divided into two different levels: the wholesale level and the retail level. Companies that operate on the wholesale level deliver their products to other companies. Their customers are the retail, industrial and service companies, which in their turn may deliver directly to the final consumer (see Figure 17.1).

FIGURE 17.1 Wholesale and trade in the business chain.

Wholesale companies differ from retailers in several ways. As a rule they spend less effort on promotion, shop layout and selection of location since their contacts are mostly other industrial companies or retailers, rather than final consumers. Furthermore, wholesalers often make large transactions with a limited number of retail companies. The retailer, however, derives his income primarily from small purchases from a large number of consumers.

ROLE AND IMPORTANCE OF PURCHASING IN TRADE AND RETAIL COMPANIES

Trade companies fulfill the function of intermediary between producer and end user. They are able to execute several activities more efficiently than the manufacturers. Their added value, and therefore the rationale for their existence, lies in the following activities:

- Sales and promotion. Trade companies can reach many small customers at relatively low costs. Through their marketing and advertising activities, which are often considerable, they can create a brand image that is experienced as more positive than the image of the (for the consumer, often distant) producer.

- Purchasing and building up a product assortment. Trade companies select products and build up an assortment based on the needs of a specific target group. In this way they make the market offer transparent and more easily accessible for the customer.

- Bulk breaking. By buying products in large quantities and then selling them in smaller units, the trade companies reduce costs for the producer and improve the accessibility of his products for the public.

- Storage. By maintaining stocks they reduce the costs for both manufacturer and end user. At the same time they realize a high degree of availability for the end user.

- Transportation. There is also an added value factor of trade companies in the fact that they take over the transportation function from the manufacturer. As a result of a higher loading level they are often able to execute this function more efficiently.

- Carrying the risk. Some products are perishable or carry a high risk in terms of pilferage, damage and obsolescence. Trade companies take over part of these risks from the producer.

- Market information. Thanks to the continuous advances of information technology (e.g. customer loyalty cards), many trade companies have an excellent picture of the characteristics of their target groups and of the sales opportunities and problems with regard to the assortment they carry. This aspect is becoming more and more important in their relationship with producers who can use this information to improve existing or develop new products.

- Management and marketing services. Intensive interaction between trade and manufacturers results increasingly in new ideas and concepts in the area of shop layout, shelf layout, displays and the improvement of inventory management systems. Quite often trade companies take the initiative here.

Trade companies may handle an extensive range of products. In the wholesale business these products can vary from raw materials for numerous manufacturing companies and bulk food products for the catering industry, to office supplies for government institutions. With regard to the retail trade, various types of stores can be distinguished in the area of consumer products, such as:

- specialty store

- department store

- supermarket

- convenience store

- combination store, superstore and hypermarket

- service business.

The wide variety of enterprises in the trade sector, and their widely different modes of operation, make it impossible to generalize on their purchasing policies and the 'ideal' structure of the purchasing organization. The scope of this book necessitates a decision on this issue, so for the remainder of this chapter the focus will be on the purchasing function in retail organizations.

MAIN DIFFERENCES WITH INDUSTRIAL COMPANIES

In comparing trade purchasing with buying for industrial companies, several differences may be recognized.

- Bottom-line thinking. The primary reason for buying in trade companies is to sell at a profitable margin. No matter what, it must be possible to sell that which is bought. Business policy is primarily aimed at improving turnover and margin, and at reducing working capital. The main objective is to realize the largest possible difference between sales price and total cost (net margin). Logistics policy is aimed at keeping products constantly in motion in order to avoid stock situations which would take up unnecessary working capital. Sales, margin and logistics cost information are, therefore, basic information to sound purchasing decision making. Recently, some major retailers have shifted their orientation from margin to economic value added (EVA). Here, the objective is to generate a maximum return on investment (in line with our DuPont-analysis discussion in Chapter 1). Apart from revenue and cost issues, the issue of how to reduce the company's cash-needs through smart logistics solutions is a prime concern for buyers who operate under this concept.

- Broad assortment. Trade companies generally have a very broad product assortment. Carrying more than 25 000 items is no exception for a medium-sized trade company. Orders, prices, qualities, materials flows and supplier conditions must be monitored for all these articles, in addition to the sales information. Managing these product groups, i.e. assortments, efficienctly again poses great demands in terms of the management information system.

- Buying against supplier specifications. Trade companies frequently buy what the market offers. A large part of the assortment consists of standard products. This can be quite different from industrial companies where many components may be manufactured to customer specification. At first sight this could mean that a trade company is usually able to change suppliers quickly and easily. However, this is not true for branded products. Manufacturers of strong brands (e.g. some fast moving consumer goods) usually enjoy a strong negotiating position. Due to their marketing and advertising policies they often have been able to build strong consumer preference and loyalty, which is the reason why retailers cannot eliminate them from their assortments.

- Short feedback loop. Because the moments of buying and selling are closer together in a trade company, the sales results become visible more quickly. This means that fast feedback to buyers (and suppliers) is possible. Products can be eliminated from the assortment quickly if it becomes clear that they are less well received by the target group than expected. Such fast feedback loops are much less common in industrial companies.

Although retail buying is more commercial in nature, there are similarities in the purchasing decision-making process between retail and industrial companies. Essentially the purchasing process model, as explained earlier in this book, may also be helpful here to explain the logic of the retail buying process. More or less the same logic applies to the stages of supplier selection, contract negotiation and management, ordering, expediting and evaluation. However, as well as the similarities, some major distinctions must be emphasized. Retail buyers definitely need to give more attention to marketing and sales aspects of the products they buy than their counterparts in industry. Thus the buying cycle in retail companies starts with estimating demand for an item and determining a concise product assortment policy and distribution strategy. Next, given the high ordering frequency, ordering and expediting are often organized as separate activities within the retail company. While purchasing and product management are centralized, ordering is decentralized as much as possible, using sophisticated computerized logistics, ordering and inventory control system.

More and more often the retail buyer is responsible not only for straight buying, but his/her prime concern is category or commodity management. Retail buyers participate in cross-functional category teams in order to generate maximum return. These teams are responsible for managing all aspects of the category: assortment policy, product policy, purchasing and supplier management, distribution policy and effective and efficient order fulfillment by the supplier.

STRUCTURE AND ORGANIZATION OF THE PURCHASING PROCESS

As has been seen, the purchasing, sales and marketing functions are closely interrelated in trade companies. This is especially true in the case of products with short life cycles, such as perishables, which usually have a shelf-life of some hours or days, and fashionable clothing, in particular leisure goods, where the shelf-life is a couple of weeks or months. Some perishables (such as vegetables, fresh fruit) may even find their final destination on the same day that they were purchased by the retailer. As a result the effectiveness of purchasing decision-making is easy to assess. In the words of the purchasing manager of a retail chain store: 'We know on Friday whether Monday's purchases were good or not.'

The following stages in the buying–selling cycle can be distinguished:

- Estimating the demand for a particular item. In this stage the sales opportunities of the product concerned are estimated based on either market research or 'market intuition'. These sales opportunities are translated into sales forecasts and budgets for the coming period, preferably detailed at a monthly or weekly level. This information provides the basis for the next stage.

- Determining product assortment policy and distribution strategy. The next step is to determine the product's assortment policy. Important decisions here are to decide how deep (number of product items per product line) and how broad (number of product lines per product group) the assortment needs to be. With regard to the distribution policy, important elements are to decide which products will be kept in stock, for which products consigned stocks will be used, which products are to be delivered through the company's own distribution centre, and which products are to be delivered directly from the manufacturer to the store or even to the customer.

■ Selection of the most suitable supplier. Based on the information indicated above, a list of potential suppliers can be drawn up. In general the circle of (potential) suppliers is limited. Quite often the ideas for new products are presented to the retail buyer by the manufacturers. In this situation the buyer will have to judge whether the new product fits into the assortment policy, or whether the latter must be adjusted. If the buyer has personally developed a viable product idea, he or she will have to start looking for a supplier. The procedure that can be followed in this case is identical to the procedure described in Chapter 3. That risks are also run by retailers during this stage of the purchasing process is demonstrated in Memo 17.1.

■ Contractual agreements. When the most suitable supplier has been selected, a contract is drawn up. This contract records all rights and obligations of both parties, as well as terms and conditions related to, among other things, price, method of packing, order size, payment, delivery and quality. Other important factors are product safety and environmental issues. Especially when the trade company has its own brand (private label), making specific arrangements on these topics in a contract can prevent many problems. In the food industry some products are bought on committed volumes: based on a thorough forecast the buyer is obliged to purchase a certain volume of the product

---

MEMO 17.1   PROBLEMS SURROUNDING THE PURCHASE OF NEW SOFT DRINK BOTTLES

Soft drinks suppliers in the Benelux countries have standardized their arrangements about bottles (contents and material), crates, deposits and prices. One of the results of this agreement has been that one manufacturer can take in the bottles of another. The following case concerns plastic soft drink bottles.

A large retail organization in food products wanted to expand its assortment with a low-cost soft drink, and intended to sell it under a private label. The retail buyer asked for quotations from several bottling companies with the result that all suppliers quoted almost the same price. The buyer, however, also requested a supplier in another European country to prepare a bid. This supplier was an affiliate of a large conglomerate located in Southern Europe. Negotiations were started and it soon turned out that this supplier could provide the required quantities at a much more favorable price. However, the bottles were different from those normally used in the Benelux countries. The crates were also different and were covered with the Southern European company's name. Another problem was the deposit. The retailer had to invest a considerable sum of money in deposits, the money being returned by the bottling company only when the bottles and crates had been received. Before signing the contract, the retailer had requested a bank guarantee from the Southern European company's bank. This guarantee did not arrive in time, and the buyer decided to go ahead without waiting for the bank guarantee.

Sale of the company's new soft drink, under its own private label, started. The turnover was high. However, a year after signing the contract, the retailer learned that the bottling company had become bankrupt. This was a setback, because at least €750 000 worth of crates and bottles were in the pipeline from distribution centres to consumers. These crates differed from the other crates on the market, so the retail organization had no way of reusing them. None of the money could be recovered through the lawyers or the trustee of the southern European firm.

The problem was later solved when a new supplier of soft drinks proved willing to fill the empty bottles and sell them to the Middle East.

and the seller is obliged to supply. This is often the case with so-called harvest products (canned and pickled products), where the buyer wants to secure a particular quantity. Other products often have no firm agreements about quantities. The buyer only provides an estimate of the amounts to be purchased, based on historical information and sales forecasts. Based on this information the parties try to arrive at a price. In general, negotiations between retailers and suppliers have become more complex over the years, as more and more requirements, in addition to quality and price, are being put forward (see Memo 17.2).

■ Ordering. The ordering process is kept as simple as possible in view of the philosophy that the stores should focus primarily on selling products. Because the retail outlets often have limited space for storage and materials handling, frequent delivery is required, which is why most retail companies have developed sophisticated ordering techniques: with the aid of a pen that reads the bar codes of the various products (order entry) and a portable computer, orders are placed directly at the distribution centres, which subsequently make the delivery. In most retail companies nowadays, all products are scanned at the cash register; at that moment the product is reduced from the store

---

MEMO 17.2   MORE SUBSTANTIAL NEGOTIATIONS IN RETAIL TRADE

At present, negotiations between buyers for supermarket chains and their suppliers are very tough, not only because of the buyers' increased power, but also due to the pressure on their profits. The suppliers have to prove themselves repeatedly, and the outcome of negotiations is less predictable than it used to be.

Typical characteristics of modern discussions about terms and conditions include the following:

Element of marketing mix   *Topics*

Product mix
- assortment portfolio-analysis (performance in terms of turnover and DPP)
- market research data (concerning consumer behavior, brand performance, competition)
- exclusivity in sales and new products
- arrangements on returnable items (slow movers, new product introductions, seasonal products)
- shelf filling packaging (in order to use shelf space to the maximum)
- uniform article codes (to optimize product scanning)

Price mix
- price and delivery conditions (a classic area of negotiation)
- recommended selling prices (in order to provide retailer with terms of reference)
- pre-pricing of products (to reduce handling in stores)

Presentation mix
- detailed shelf layouts and displays
- cost saving materials and packaging (ready for sale packaging and displays, etc.)
- optimal use of transport packaging (in line with shelf systems)

Personnel mix
- effective use of supplier sales staff for in-store activities, commercial advice and training
- rack jobbing for difficult and labor intensive categories (improved operations)
- training and development (providing knowledge to sales personnel and other staff)

Promotion mix
- incentives for in-store personnel (turnover and display contests)

inventory. When the store inventory has been reduced beyond a certain minimum level, a order signal is automatically triggered to the distribution center. The distribution centers are responsible for maintaining their stocks at the desired level. Their ordering systems are directly coupled to the receiving orders systems of the suppliers, often through EDI. Invoicing takes place at the central level. For some products, such as fresh foods, central order handling is not suitable. These products, then, are ordered by the retail outlets straight from the supplier, who also directly delivers the order.

■ Advanced information systems have enabled 'automatic replenishment'. Based upon cash-register scanning, retailers now know what has been sold on a specific day. This information is transferred to suppliers through electronic linkages, and they are requested to ship exactly these volumes of products to the retailer's distribution centre during the night. Early in the morning the stores are replenished with the requested volumes. This practice is often referred to as 'quick response logistics'. In fact, suppliers are able to monitor on a daily basis what has been sold by their customers. Through these advanced information systems, logistics (planning) tasks are increasingly shifted to the food-manufacturers and their suppliers.

■ Expediting and evaluation. As has been discussed, the ordered goods are delivered by the supplier either directly to the retail outlets, or to the distribution centres. Monitoring the delivered quantity and quality and time of delivery takes place where the goods are delivered. The delivered quantities are also entered into the inventory control system. Some large retailers have sophisticated vendor rating systems in place in order to monitor and improve the overall supplier performance.

Based on this description the following additional observations are worth making:

■ The process, as described here, illustrates that the function of the retail buyer has evolved gradually from straight buying to commodity or category management, where cross-functional category teams are responsible for managing all aspects of a category in order to generate a maximum return for the retail company. Ordering and purchasing are often separate activities within the retail company. Purchasing and category management are conducted centrally within the organization, whereas ordering is carried out, as much as possible, decentrally (by the stores and the distribution centers). Decentralized ordering has become possible thanks to sophisticated, computerized ordering and inventory control systems. Where automatic replenishment has been implemented, planning tasks are shifted to the supplier who is kept fully responsible for the timely delivery of products in the exact quantity needed.

■ Given the scope and importance of the purchasing function it makes sense to have it report high in the organizational hierarchy. As a rule, the purchasing director reports directly to general management. With regard to the organization of purchasing it is possible to differentiate between a functional purchasing structure and a cross-functional structure.

  – In a functional purchasing structure the purchasing department predominantly acts as a separate organizational entity, which operates more or less autonomously from physical distribution and sales and store management. Based on sales forecasts retail buyers prepare their category plans.

  – In the cross-functional structure the buying function, styling, visual merchandising and physical distribution (apart from store operations) operate in one organizational entity. As has been mentioned before, this often is referred to as 'category management'. Category managers are responsible for assortment policy, product policy, purchasing and supplier management, and distribution policy. Store operations mostly reside outside their area of responsibility.

DEVELOPMENTS IN TRADE AND RETAIL COMPANIES

The purchasing function in trade companies is subject to significant changes, some of which are now described.

- Changing consumer behavior. Changes in consumer behavior have a major impact on the retailer's product-market strategies. It is the retail buyer's job to identify these changes in time and to translate them into new product concepts and design new shelf displays and shop layouts. The following are typical of changes that confront retail organizations in European countries:

  - aging population, ongoing individualization, more men shopping;

  - increasing income gap between population groups, more one- and two-person households (in large urban areas);

  - growing number of earning couples (two incomes, no children);

  - increased integration of ethnic minorities, exposure to other cultures through tourism, adopting other cultural consumption patterns;

  - increased concern for the environment, manifested in the demand for biodegradable containers and packaging;

  - increased attention to healthier living, expressed in a strong growth of the number of health food and diet products.

  This means that the commodity manager or retail-buyer must constantly tailor his/her product assortment to ever more specific, and often smaller, target groups. This results in a wider variety of products and an increased complexity with regard to managing the incoming and outgoing goods flow.

- Concentration. In retail and food manufacturing particularly, globalization of competition and concentration through mergers and acquisitions are characteristic developments. For manufacturers this concentration means that there will be more mono-production, which makes it possible to achieve better economies of scale. It is expected that there will be fewer and fewer suppliers of food products in the near future and, as a result, retail companies will be dealing primarily with a few very large manufacturers. The trend towards globalization of business and economies of scale will also affect the scale of retail businesses. As a result many large retailers have become very active in mergers and acquisitions over the past decade.

- International cooperation. Due to the concentration of power on the suppliers' side, many trade companies are diligently searching for possibilities with which to counterbalance this development. Internationalization is an option seen by many. It can be difficult to realize internationalization of retail organizations. In Europe, for example, the market often turns out to be culturally determined or dependent on the country. There is only a limited number of products that can be sold internationally with the same marketing formula. Packaging is also culturally related; e.g. the French consumers will not accept canned soup. On packaging, the product labels should always be stated in the language of the country in question. These realities limit the possibilities of achieving further economies of scale. International purchasing combinations have great difficulty getting off the ground. The Dutch Ahold group of companies has entered into collaboration with six other large retailers in Sweden, France, Great Britain, Finland and Denmark. By buying products jointly, price advantages are being realized. This does not function optimally, however, because there are few 'europroducts' and because large suppliers like Unilever, Coca-Cola and Nestlé prefer, for obvious reasons, to sell their products to each country separately.

- Private labels. More and more retail companies have embraced private labels or company brands. Private labels support retailer identity and their quality image. By purchasing products, giving them a company label and taking over the promotion, the retailer will have the advantage of a higher margin. Carrying their own private label implies that product liability lies with the retailer. As the product carries the trade company's brand, this company presents itself as the producer of the product. The buyer must be aware of this and should include it in the contract with the supplier. In case of any problems about the quality of the product, or customer complaints, the retailer then may be able to recover the costs from the producer.

- Space management. Since shelf-space is limited, the extensive product lines offered by manufacturers force the retail-buyer to make a selection. In this context computerized space-management systems may support him. They enable the simulation of several display layouts (for a different number of facings) based on detailed cost information, to decide on the most profitable layout. Important concepts underlying space management systems, are direct product cost (DPC), and direct product profitability (DPP). DPC relates to all costs that can be allocated directly to the product, including the costs of materials handling, taking in return packaging, pricing, etc. The retail buyer tries to trace these costs in detail: he compares these to the sales price, and is then able to determine the direct profit margin per product (DPP).

- 'Green' issues. Ecological considerations are growing in importance. This started initially with the replacement of artificial flavorings and odors by natural products. At present the emphasis is on biodegradable packing materials, PVC-less packaging and a minimum of blister packs. There are some problems, such as the soft drink bottle, that should be solved by the industry in question so that standardization can be achieved (see Memo 17.1). International suppliers bring extra problems, for instance manufacturers of toothpaste have been obliged to eliminate their carton boxes, which they used as packaging for their end products, due to environmental legislation. Recently, the government in Germany decided to put a refund on tins and cans to discourage the use of one-way packaging in the drink industry.

- Information. Information technology is an important tool for the retail buyer. Some developments in information technology have an immediate impact on the consumer. They are manifest in, for instance, electronic banking, barcoding and teleshopping. There are also developments that are far less visible to the consumer.

These developments generally relate to the retail trade, wholesale trade and manufacturing companies. Let's see what is happening to the sourcing and supply chain strategies of these companies.

SOURCING AND SUPPLY CHAIN STRATEGY TRENDS

Supply chain management is at the heart of successful modern retailing. Wal-Mart is widely recognized for their landmark performance in this area. Their philosophy on 'everyday low prices' is founded on the belief that taking cost out of the supply chain is the only way to remain competitive. The idea is that a more efficient supply chain allows them to pass on cost economies to the final consumer, who given the price difference compared to competitors, would therefore be seduced to buy from Wal-Mart. Here, we will discuss some important concepts on which modern supply chain management in retail is based. We will consecutively look at vendor managed inventory (VMI), efficient consumer response (ECR), collaborative planning, forecasting and replenishment (CPFR), electronic marketplaces, and radio frequency identification detection (RFID).

Vendor managed inventory (VMI)

Vendor managed inventory popularly known as VMI is now a widely practiced initiative in the retail industry. Also known as continuous replenishment or supplier-managed inventory, it was popularized in the late 1980s by Wal-Mart and Procter & Gamble. Successful VMI initiatives have been trumpeted by other companies in the United States, including Campbell Soup, Kraft Foods, and Johnson & Johnson and by some European firms. Vendor managed inventory is a continuous replenishment program that uses the exchange of information between the retailer and the supplier to allow the supplier to manage and replenish products at the store or warehouse level. In this program, the retailer supplies the vendor with the information necessary to maintain just enough products to meet customer demand. This enables the supplier to better plan and anticipate the amount of products it needs to produce or supply. Through the use of electronic transfer of information VMI gives visibility across the supply chain pipeline. With information available at a more detailed level it allows the manufacturer to be more customer-specific in planning. With the ability of supply chain applications to manage inventories at retailer locations, VMI concepts are being used at both the distribution centre-level and the store-level of retail companies.

Using VMI in the fulfillment process the activities of forecasting, scheduling, requisitioning and ordering are typically performed by the supplier and not by the retailer. Electronic data interchange (EDI) is an integral part of VMI process and takes a vital role in the process of data communication. The retailer sends the sales and inventory data to the vendor via EDI and the supplier creates the purchase orders based on the established inventory levels and fill rates. In the VMI process, the retailer is free of forecasting and creating the orders as the vendor generates the orders. The vendor is responsible for creating and maintaining the stock plan for the retailer. The vendor sends the shipment notices before shipping the product to the retailer's store/warehouse. Soon after this, the vendor sends the invoice to the retailer. Upon receiving the product, the retailer does the invoice matching and handles payment through their account payable systems.

Trading partners who focus on changing business relationships definitely maximize their bottom lines by using VMI. Those who have implemented VMI have seen the following benefits:

- eliminated repetitive purchasing activities, resulting in a considerable reduction in receiving costs;
- lowered cost of processing claims;
- reduced inventory;
- increased inventory turns;
- solidified customer–vendor relationship.

Benefits of implementing VMI also include reduced shipping costs and lead times, elimination of human errors and improved service levels. Perhaps the most important benefit of engaging in a strategic VMI alliance is the opportunity to build a strong and lasting relationship between the vendor and the customer, which in the long run can bring rich rewards to both. Another attractive feature of VMI is changing the retailer focus from buying to selling. Under VMI, manufacturers, retailers and distributors can focus on the same issue – how to sell more products to the end consumer more efficiently.

VMI has its disadvantages when not properly implemented. Some possible drawbacks of VMI might include: EDI problems, employee acceptance, trust among supply chain partners. EDI sometimes creates a challenge due to the many different standards in use. This makes it difficult to communicate and translate information between companies. If manufacturers are to assume stock keeping responsibility, they must be able to communicate in real time with their retail partners in a uniform way. With VMI, all employees involved in the process must fully understand and accept this new way of doing business. All employees who are involved must be willing participants.

VMI can also fail when setting up rules for how the relationship should work. For example, the supplier and the customer must agree on how to deal with overstocks, ordering errors and obsolete stock. Finally, both parties must understand that this is a learning process that takes time. Equally important as time is trust. Many retailers and consumer goods firms are naturally reluctant to share information in advance, fearing that the information will somehow fall into the hands of competitors or they will lose control in some way.

VMI represents a powerful tool to take cost out of the supply chain. Developed in the early 1980s this approach to inventory and order fulfillment is still used by many companies and also acts as an underlying concept for more recent trends, such as ECR and CPFR, which share the same idea of supply chain integration through information sharing and employ the same technological principles.

Efficient consumer response (ECR)

ECR is a grocery industry supply chain management strategy aimed at eliminating inefficiencies, and excessive or non-value-added costs within the supply chain, thus delivering better value to grocery consumers. It is designed to re-engineer the grocery supply chain away from a 'push system' in which manufacturers 'push' products into stores, towards a 'pull system' in which products are 'pulled' down the supply chain into the store by consumer-demand information captured at the point of sale. ECR came into existence in the US as a direct response by the grocery industry to threats from alternative store formats/types.

The ultimate goal of ECR is to produce a responsive, consumer-driven system which allows distributors and suppliers to work together in order to maximize consumer satisfaction and minimize cost. The technologies, which are primarily electronic commerce (e-commerce) components, are used to automate these efficient business processes, as well as to enhance the communication and relationships between companies. ECR is thus an application of e-commerce within the grocery supply chain.

One of the most celebrated examples of an ECR in the UK is that achieved by Tesco and Birds Eye Walls (BEW) (McKinnon, 1996). This resulted in delivery lead times dropping from seven days in 1986 to two days in 1993. Over this period both firms dramatically reduced their inventory levels: Tesco's stock of BEW products fell by 71 per cent and BEW's stocks by 50 per cent. There are similar examples of ECR success in other countries such as Albert Heijn and Heineken in the Netherlands, and Wal-Mart and Proctor and Gamble in the US.

ECR attempts to eliminate inefficiencies within the grocery industry supply chain by introducing strategic initiatives in four areas:

- Efficient store assortment. This initiative is aimed at optimizing the productivity of inventory and shelf management at the consumer interface – the store level.
- Efficient product introduction. The objective of this initiative is to maximize the effectiveness of new product development and introduction activities, in order to reduce costs and failure rates in introducing new products.

■ Efficient promotion. This initiative aims at maximizing the total system efficiency of trade and consumer promotions. This can be achieved by introducing better alternative trade and consumer promotions, such as pay for performance and every day low price policy.

■ Efficient product replenishment. The objective of this initiative is to optimize time and cost in the replenishment system by the provision of the right product to the right place at the right time in the right quantity and in the most efficient manner possible.

These strategies are supported by two programs and five enabling technologies as shown in Figure 17.2.

Programs that companies need to have in place are:

■ Category management. Category management supports the first three initiatives of ECR discussed above. It can be defined as 'an interactive business process whereby retailers and manufacturers work together in mutual cooperation to manage categories as strategic business units within each store'. A category is a group of products which can be

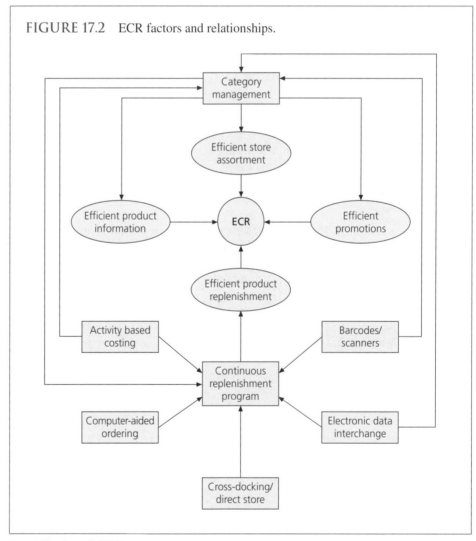

FIGURE 17.2 ECR factors and relationships.

Source: Kurnia *et al.* (2002)

substituted for one another by a consumer and examples include cereals, bakery, household products, body care and so on. The types of categories to be included in a store have to be determined correctly to meet consumer demand and at the same time, to maximize profit. Category management employs EDI, barcodes and scanners to accurately capture information on customer demand for each category and to share the information between trading partners.

■ Continuous replenishment program (CRP). This program supports the efficient product replenishment initiative. CRP is defined as 'the practice of partnering among distribution channel members that changes the traditional replenishment process from distributor-generated purchase order to one based on actual or forecast consumer demand'. CRP transfers responsibility for inventory replenishment from retailers/ distributors to suppliers and, thus, the approach is also known as 'vendor-managed inventory' (see above). With CRP, orders are transmitted electronically and are made more frequently and in smaller quantities. CRP is also supported by the category management program which forms the shelf management strategy to track the inventory and demand for each individual category.

Category management and continuous replenishment need to be supported by some critical technologies and concepts:

■ Barcodes/scanners. The use of barcodes and scanners is a fundamental element for ECR implementation in the grocery industry as it allows accurate and faster information capture to be obtained, which in turn can be shared with trading partners.

■ Electronic data interchange. Electronic data interchange can be defined as 'an inter-organisational exchange of business documentation in a structured, machine-processable form'. Besides purchase orders and invoices, another common business document exchanged electronically in the grocery industry is the advance shipping notice (ASN), the EDI message which precedes the arrival of pallets at their destination.

■ Computer-aided ordering. Computer aided ordering is 'a retail-based system that automatically generates orders for replenishment when the inventory level drops below a pre-determined reorder level'. The system keeps track of the inventory levels of all items in the store and makes necessary adjustments when sales or replenishments occur.

■ Cross-docking/direct store delivery. Cross-docking or 'flow-through distribution' is 'a direct flow of merchandise/ product from receiving to shipping, thus eliminating additional handling and storage steps in the distribution cycle'. The idea of cross-docking is analogous to 'direct store delivery', in which manufacturers deliver products directly to the retailer, bypassing the wholesaler to eliminate warehouse handling.

■ Activity-based costing. Activity-based costing (ABC) is a costing tool which works on the principle that activities (as opposed to product volumes or labor in traditional accounting) are what really affect costs. ABC offers a better understanding of how profits are generated, as it increases the visibility of costs in a particular environment. It can be used to gain top management commitment and leadership to support the implementation of ECR and its key elements.

The main obstacle to ECR is not technical but managerial, with many managers reluctant to transform their traditional, often adversarial, trading relationships into the open partnership that ECR requires. The ideal state envisioned by ECR cannot be reached through individual self-interested activity of the participants. ECR adoption requires cooperation and trust between trading partners, which is unlikely to happen unless costs, benefits and risks of ECR implementation can be mutually shared.

Collaborative planning, forecasting and replenishment (CPFR)

Another concept that is based on joint decision making through information deployment is collaborative planning, forecasting and replenishment (CPFR). This concept allows co-operation across the supply chain, using a set of processes and technology models. Its goal is to provide dynamic information sharing that integrates both 'demand' and 'supply' side processes (thus linking manufacturers, retailers and carriers), and effectively planning, forecasting, and replenishing customer needs through the total supply chain.

This concept was introduced in 1996, and has been embraced by several retailers such as Target, Best Buy, Wal-Mart, Tesco as well as some of the world's largest consumer goods suppliers (Procter & Gamble, Henkel, Colgate-Palmolive, Johnson & Johnson). It has been reported that the concept take-up is rather slow and not too many companies have employed it (Nannery, 2002; Sliwa, 2002).

The essence of CPFR is in utilizing technology/information capabilities to support trading partner interaction and joint decision making. A great deal of time and effort is needed up-front to negotiate specific items such as goals and objectives, frequency of updates to the plan, exception criteria, and key measures. The result is a published document defining relevant issues that have been jointly developed and agreed to.

Foote and Krishnamurthi (2001) provide a case example of CPFR employment between Wal-Mart and Warner-Lambert. The company started its journey towards complete supply chain collaboration by integration of their own data from all the stores and warehouses into one single data warehouse. This was triggered by their need to obtain detailed information at a store level to be able to meet the needs of customers who come to a specific Wal-Mart store. The next step was establishing CPFR with their key suppliers.

The forecasting process begins with a data warehouse, which is designed for CPFR. The retail link system extracts the data relevant to Warner-Lambert products sales. The data are then sorted in a CPFR server. Wal-Mart buying agents use a spreadsheet (CPFR workbench) to make a preliminary forecast. A copy of this forecast appears on Warner-Lambert's CPFR server, so Warner-Lambert's planners can add comments and suggest revisions, which are then viewed by Wal-Mart's planners. After a few iterations, an agreed-upon forecast is made for each product. This is used as a guide for production planning at Warner-Lambert (using SAP applications) and the inventory management at Wal-Mart. The communication between Wal-Mart and Warner-Lambert is done electronically.

IT tools that are used for CPFR come from a very broad area. They rank from tailor-made applications from large IT vendors to simple tools based on a combination of non-proprietary processes and technology models. In general these models should be: (1) open, yet allowing secure communications; (2) flexible across the industry; (3) extensible to all supply chain processes; (4) support a broad set of requirements (new data types, inter-operability with different databases, etc.).

According to McCarthy and Golicic (2002) there are several barriers for CPFR implementation. These mainly relate to the provision of adequate technology and software, difficulties of real-time coordination of information exchange, substantial investment of time and personnel for set-up, the process intensive nature of maintaining the efforts across several suppliers and products, lack of scalability from the pilot stage, and the required synchronous changes in corporate culture for both firms in the collaborative relationship.

The advantages of CPFR are many, yet the authors who are publishing in this field hold differing views on their importance. According to McCarthy (2002) the advantages can be summarized as follows: increased responsiveness, product availability assurance, optimized inventory and associated costs, increased revenues and earnings. Other researchers claim that the main opportunities for retailers are reducing inventory levels and associated costs, increasing inventory turns, reducing or eliminating out-of-stocks, maximizing the profitability of the product mix and purchasing at the lowest cost, saving on invoice processing, resolving exceptions, and transaction costs. For example, in the apparel industry, Sara Lee and Wal-Mart have reported a reduction of inventories through CPFR by 12 per cent while increasing service levels by 2.7 per cent for 23 branded underwear items. Procter & Gamble anticipates saving over 1.5 billion dollars using the streamlined CPFR initiative by 2005. Most participants see improved relationships with their trading partners as the main advantage of CPFR.

One of the biggest impediments to mass adoption of CPFR seems to be the issue of trust. Many retailers, competitive by nature, continue to be reluctant to perform the kind of data sharing that CPFR requires as they fear that giving away too much forecast and/or inventory data will damage their negotiating position. Furthermore, the fact that technology for many-to-many CPFR has not yet been developed prevents widespread adoption. Collaborative replenishment requires constant sharing of point-of-sales data and is especially difficult to gauge during a promotion.

E-marketplaces and supply chain management

A widespread application in retail is business-to-business electronic marketplaces (e-marketplaces). A distinction can be made between open exchanges (accessible for everyone) and private exchanges. Some of the open exchanges are founded by retailers and could therefore be viewed as retailer oriented: Worldwide Retail Exchange (WWRE) and GlobalNetExchange. Also, some giant retailers develop their own private marketplaces for safety reasons and because in this way the retailers are able to tie their suppliers closer to the company (not all companies have access to their suppliers). Two examples of retailers who have developed their own private marketplace are Tesco (Tesco Information Exchange) and Sainsbury's (Sainsbury's Information Direct).

An e-marketplace using a shared internet-based structure can provide companies with a platform for:

- Core commerce transactions which can automate and streamline the entire requisition-to-payment process online (including procurement, customer management and selling).

- A collaborative network for production design, supply chain planning, optimization and fulfillment processing.

- Industry-wide product information that is aggregated into a common classification and catalog structure.

- An environment in which sourcing, negotiations and other trading processes such as auctions can take place real-time (online).

- An online community for publishing and exchanging industry news, information and events.

These functions allow the traditional supply chain process to reduce costs and increase speed to respond to supply and demand needs. It can reduce purchasing costs and achieve higher volume contract terms with preferred suppliers by accumulating purchasing across divisions and companies. It also provides a single point of contact, minimizes off-contract buying and lowers selection cost through multiple suppliers.

In general, e-marketplaces in retail seem to contribute to greater efficiency in the supply chain (Eng, 2003). The perceived contributions of e-marketplaces to supply chain management are: unit cost reduction, increased efficiency, and streamlined operations. The main process which contributed to these advantages was the electronic auction.

While the e-marketplace may provide many benefits for supply chain management, firms must not overlook the time-consuming process of relationship development.

Companies always have to weigh the costs and benefits associated with the implementation of the e-marketplace system.

E-marketplaces offer companies a real-time web-based solution that can be used to increase efficiency of sourcing, buying and negotiating. They can streamline the supply chain, reduce non-value adding costs and speed up the response time to supply and demand needs. Of course, before the advantage can be obtained some barriers have to be overcome. Companies must have a sufficient amount of trust before they share 'valuable and confident' information with outside parties. Also, technologically, it is very important to be able to guarantee the security of the system, which is fairly difficult when it concerns a web-application. These are the two main barriers to adoption/use of e-marketplaces. Some other obstacles that have to be challenged are employee acceptance and (initial) costs of entering and using the system.

Radio frequency identification (RFID)

The next step into total cooperation between partners in the retail industry is creating an open global network that can identify anything, anywhere, automatically. This dream-like solution is currently under development by Auto-ID Center (foundation of several universities including MIT, University of Cambridge, and Keio University). It is attracting attention and sponsorship from industries including among others: Ahold, Coca-Cola, Accenture, Sun, Gillette, Home Depot, Johnson & Johnson, Kraft, Lowes, Metro, Pepsico, Pfizer, Procter & Gamble, Sara Lee, Target, Tesco, Unilever, UPS, Wal-Mart).

The Auto-ID Center is designing, building, testing and deploying a global infrastructure – a layer on top of the Internet – that will make it possible for computers to identify any object, anywhere in the world, instantly. This network will not just provide the means to feed reliable, accurate, real-time information into existing business applications; it will

---

MEMO 17.3 ELECTRONIC MARKETPLACES IN RETAIL: THE TESCO INFORMATION EXCHANGE

One of the best examples of a private marketplace is the Tesco Information Exchange (TIE). It is a collaboration between Tesco and Global eXchange Services (GXS). More than 450 suppliers of Tesco are currently using this system. Via a web-browser, TIE allows suppliers to view daily electronic points of sale (EPOS) data, which enables them to respond more quickly to variations in customer demand and ensure that the optimal stock is available on Tesco shelves at all times. Notoriously complex, the promotional process requires significant interaction between retailer and supplier. The Promotion Management feature of TIE enables Tesco and its suppliers to jointly plan, execute, track and evaluate promotions by sharing common data through a structured online process. Other features that TIE provides to Tesco's suppliers are:

- collecting real time sales data and making them available for suppliers;
- enabling trading partners to track service levels performance at different points in the supply chain;
- handling new product introduction;
- putting store directories and manuals online.

A lot of advantages are obtained by using this system. It enhances customer satisfaction, improves product availability, reduces waste, streamlines the business process, reduces 33 per cent of the lost sales on promotions and reduces 30 per cent of the promotion overhead and waste!

Source: 'Promotions management extranet helps to ring up sales', www.gxs.com/downloads/cs tesco2.pdf usher in a whole new era of innovation and opportunity. It seeks to give companies near-perfect supply chain visibility. Companies will be able to know exactly where every item in their supply chain is at any time. The system, if widely adopted, could eliminate human error from data collection, reduce inventories, keep product in-stock, reduce loss and waste, free up staff to perform more value-added functions, and improve safety and security. The possibilities seem limitless.

The technology is radio frequency identification (RFID). RFID is a generic term for technologies that use radio waves to automatically identify individual items. There are several methods of identifying objects using RFID, but the most common is to store a serial number that identifies a product, and perhaps other information, on a microchip that is attached to an antenna. The antenna enables the chip to transmit the identification information to a reader. The reader converts the radio waves returned from the RFID tag into a form that can be passed on to computers.

Although the described network might seem a bit like science fiction, it receives considerable support from large companies. Wal-Mart has already demanded that their top suppliers ship products with Auto-ID tags, and Tesco has opened an RFID-enabled warehouse for high volume items. Business researchers have also started giving this development appropriate attention, arguing already about its commercial profitability. It can be concluded that this field will continue to attract attention in the coming years, and is likely to be recommended as a possible direction for future research.

These four major developments show how the landscape of the traditional retail buyer has changed and will continue to change in the near future. Electronic payment systems and customer loyalty cards, which are providing insight into purchasing frequency, composition of the consumer's daily shopping basket, and the customer's address, are at the heart of the retailers' planning and logistics systems. These systems will allow them to carefully optimize their supply chain operations. Scanning gives the retail buyers an immediate insight into the actual sales in their stores and the stock situation in the distribution centres. Space management enables them to simulate display layouts, based on detailed cost information, so that the optimal return can be realized. The concepts that have been described here show that the future competition in retail will no longer be among individual companies. Rather it will be among clusters of companies, with the retail firm at the heart, surrounded by a limited number of large manufacturers who are highly integrated through intricate information and logistics networks which are tied to the retailers operations. As research evidence shows the development towards this kind of highly integrated supply network is long and troublesome due to the fact that interfirm collaboration requires trust between the partners, a long-term commitment and a balanced sharing of risks and rewards from the relationship. These are conditions which in practice are seldom met.

SUMMARY

This chapter shows that the purchasing function plays a very important role in trade companies. We have discussed this role for both wholesale and retail companies. The basic difference between these two trades is in the type of customer: the wholesaler sells to other companies and institutions, whereas the retailer sells to the final consumer. Trade companies fulfill the role of intermediary between manufacturer and end user. The buyer's basic task is to translate customer demands into a suitable offer of products and services and make the product offerings available to them in the most cost-effective way.

Several differences exist in the area of purchasing when retail companies are compared with industrial companies. In retail companies purchasing policy is much more integrated with sales and marketing policy, and company policy is primarily focused on improving turnover and margin whilst reducing working capital. As a result of fierce competition most retailers and wholesalers over the years have adopted a strong bottom line orientation. Thanks to modern information technology, important progress has been made in terms of integrated logistics, distribution, transportation and store operations.

The buying–selling cycle usually begins with an estimate of the demand for a particular item. Based on this estimate the assortment and the distribution strategy will be determined. Then the investigation of what to contract for, and whom to contract with, can be started. At the same time preparations can be made for renegotiating contracts with existing suppliers. In most retail companies the initial purchasing activities are coordinated centrally. Ordering, expediting and evaluation often take place decentrally in the stores and the distribution centres. Thanks to computerized order entry systems, the number of administrative actions can be kept to a minimum.

Retail today is a truly international business. Both the retail market and the market for fast-moving consumer goods are characterized by a high degree of concentration. In order to improve their negotiating position retailers increasingly turn to private labels. Space management systems allow them to have detailed insight into direct cost and direct profitability of the products that are sold to them by manufacturers. These data are used in the relationship with suppliers to challenge them to continuously improve their logistics and quality performance. Advanced information systems are at the heart of the modern retail organization, allowing the application of new logistics concepts and tools such as vendor managed inventory, efficient consumer response, collaborative planning, forecasting and replenishment and electronic marketplaces. Implementing these concepts and using these tools in practice, however, requires that all partners commit to these initiatives for a long period of time and share the same vision and beliefs. The more advanced the concepts, the higher the commitment and requirements in terms of trust and cultural fit. It is here where most concepts suffer from the lack of willingness to share information and gains and risks resulting from the relationship.

ASSIGNMENTS

17.1 The critique often made to retail buyers is that they are too price- and margin-oriented. Rather, they should look into total cost of ownership in their dealings with suppliers. How would you explain such critique? What tools would you suggest retail buyers could use to negotiate more effectively on the basis of total cost of ownership?

17.2 ECR is sometimes referred to as a concept in which suppliers are not paid any more for the products that they have delivered. Explain. What are the necessary conditions that should be present to make ECR work in a relationship with a supplier?

17.3 What are the main differences between retail buying and category management? What tasks does a category manager fulfill?

17.4 What does it take for a retailer and a manufacturer to implement vendor managed inventory (VMI)? Discuss the implications for strategy, organization, processes, information systems and communication between both parties.

17.5 What functionality do electronic marketplaces offer to retail buyers? Answer this question by comparing at least three such marketplaces. To what extent are they successful? Why?

After studying this chapter you should understand the following:

- Trends and developments in the service industry.
- The role and position of purchasing in a facilities environment.
- Key success variables for purchasing in a facilities environment.
- Measures aimed at improving the effectiveness of purchasing in a facilities environment.
- How to classify services that are contracted by organizations.
- How to improve buying of services.

CASE STUDY   PURCHASING POLICY IN A LARGE INSURANCE COMPANY

Four years ago the management of a large European insurance company decided to drastically change its purchasing operations. As these activities were scattered throughout the company, internal control on purchasing spend was suffering. Since managers did not give much attention to purchasing decisions, most employees had a large degree of freedom in dealing with suppliers. In some cases, it appeared that this freedom was used for personal advantage. Apart from fringe benefits (such as fairly large gifts at Christmas and luxury study trips paid for by suppliers) a few employees appeared to have received fairly large amounts of money in their personal bank accounts as a reward for the business that they awarded to some suppliers. Since the credibility of the company was at stake and company morale was affected, the board of management had to take immediate action. The staff concerned were fired and management started

to consider how best to prevent these problems in the future. The ensuing discussion resulted in the decision to centralize all purchasing activities into a single department. A purchasing manager was appointed from outside the company and was given a free hand to form this department. The assignment was simple: see to it that all purchases were made through the department. All departmental managers within the organization were informed about this decision by sending them copies of the new purchasing charter, signed by the president of the board. The purchasing manager and his colleagues set to work.

Three years later the purchasing manager assessed his position. After careful analysis it appeared that only 25 per cent of the total purchasing spend of the company went through purchasing! This was a disappointment – according to the purchasing manager it should have been much higher! However, during the previous three years he had found achieving credibility for his department was an extremely difficult matter. Most budget holders and other managers responsible for purchasing decisions seemed not to be very cost conscious; neither were they disciplined in the way they arrived at their decisions. Most had pursued their existing relationships with suppliers, without involving or even consulting the purchasing department! At best the purchasing department was asked to deal with administrative matters, after supplier selection had been made. This seemed particularly true for all kinds of services that were bought. The large ICT organization, for example, contracted annually for large sums of money with various IT specialists. The marketing organization negotiated agreements with advertising agencies in their own manner and appeared very sensitive to interference from the purchasing department. Car leasing agreements were dealt

with by finance and administration, given the financial nature of this type of contract. And the HRM departments made their own deals on temporary labor and training. The board itself seemed not to be aware of the money that was spent on accountants, fiscal and legal specialists and management consultants; these professional services were in almost every case decided upon on a very personal basis by one of the board members.

The situation was very unsatisfactory to the purchasing manager since he felt that this company context prevented him from doing a professional job. He decided that top management should now be informed of the problem – departmental managers should adhere more strictly to company policies and procedures, and the board should see to it that they actually did! He planned to write a detailed memorandum to point out the responsibilities of top management in this matter . .

INTRODUCTION

E arlier chapters have demonstrated that purchasing, as a management discipline in industrial companies, has developed strongly over the last few years. Due to increased international competition, industrial companies have given first priority to issues such as cost reduction, quality improvement and cycle time reduction in their relationships with suppliers. At the same time many top managers have focused on reinforcing their company's core activities. Non-core activities have increasingly been outsourced to specialized suppliers. The purchasing department has played an important role in initiating and implementing these management policies.

Companies in the service sector have lagged behind in this development. Here, purchasing activities traditionally have an operational character and are limited to placing orders, expediting and invoice checking. The situation in most companies is reflected by the Case Study above: purchasing operations are scattered throughout the organization through the absence of a professional purchasing department.

However, this picture is gradually changing. As in the Case Study, many service companies face the problem of how to improve purchasing professionalism. Managers often try to translate successful purchasing practices, as applied in the industrial sector, to their own organization. However, this is not without problems. This chapter discusses some of these problems which, for the most part, stem from the fundamental differences between the purchasing function in the industrial sector and in the service sector. First, however, it is necessary to be aware of the most important trends and developments within the service sector in Western economies. It is also important is to understand how the trend towards facilities management affects, or will affect, purchasing operations in service organizations. Next, the key success factors underlying successful purchasing in service companies will be discussed. Building on these, measures which may lead to more effective purchasing operations in service companies are described. Given the importance of services to this kind of companies, the chapter discusses the role and nature of buying services. Of course, services are defined and classified. Our description will reveal that in buying services personal relationships and trust play an important role. This explains why the user is always heavily involved in the purchasing process. In dealing with the specific characteristics related to the buying process for services, we will elaborate on the purchasing process model. It appears that in buying services special attention must be given to the specification of the performance that needs to be delivered by the supplier, and the supplier selection process.

TRENDS AND DEVELOPMENTS IN THE SERVICE SECTOR

The importance of the service industry has increased over the last two decades in most Western economies. In the European Union, the value created by the service sector as a percentage of the gross domestic product (GDP), increased from 47 per cent in 1960 to 68 per cent in 1995. In the United States the increase was even larger over the same time period: from 47 to 72 per cent. Another indication that the service industry is growing in importance is the number of people employed in this sector. Statistics indicate that in most developed economies, services account for around 65 per cent of employment.[1]

Several factors explain the rapid growth of service companies in Western economies. In their book on service marketing, Rust *et al.* (1996)[2] mention several reasons. One of the most important reasons is the reallocation of manufacturing companies from Western countries to developing countries with lower labor rates. Another reason for the service industry growth is the introduction of new technologies in the last decade such as information and telecommunication technologies (ICT). ICT has created a whole new industry and is a key factor for the restructuring that many traditional Western economies experience today. This new industry, which includes the development, production and implementation of these technologies, is a typical service-related industry. Leasing has also contributed to the increase of the service industry as many companies have switched from owning production facilities to leasing them. The most important reason explaining the growth of the service sector, however, is the fact that companies nowadays have focused much more on their core competencies. Hence, non-core competencies are outsourced to specialized suppliers. As a result, companies have become much more interconnected and interdependent on their supply networks and on the service performance of the suppliers they work with.

Table 18.1 provides some figures related to the importance of the service industry for some Western economies.

As a result of the growing importance of services during the last decades, the management and marketing of services have received considerable interest (see e.g. Grönroos, 2000). However, the buying of services has only recently emerged as an area of interest, both to practitioners and managers. Purchasing professionals have found that in addressing services there is only little that can be derived from industrial buying practices. They find out that getting involved in this type of organizational buying process is an extremely sensitive and political activity; internal customers and specialists usually are not willing to let purchasing staff interfere in their relationships with suppliers that have been built up carefully over time. Later in this chapter we will explain why this is the case and what buyers can do to support their internal customers in buying services more professionally.

---

1 See Grönroos, C. (2000) *Service Management and Marketing*, Chichester: Wiley, 394 pp.
2 See Rust, R.T., Zahorik, A.J. and Keiningham, T.L. (1996) *Service Marketing*, New York: HarperCollins, 508 pp.

TABLE 18.1 Civil employment in services as a share of total civilian employment for a selection of OECD countries in percentages of total employment.

Country	1987	1997
France	62.2	69.9
Germany [3]	55.4	60.2
Japan	57.9	61.6
The Netherlands	68.3	74.1
Sweden	66.3	71.3
United Kingdom	64.8	71.3
United States	69.9	73.4
G7	63.9	68.2
EU-15	59.0	65.2

Source: OECD (1999) as quoted by Axelsson and Wynstra, 2002, p. 5.

PURCHASING AND FACILITIES MANAGEMENT

The most important characteristic of service companies is the absence of a physical transformation, i.e. a manufacturing process. Also, a clear and well-defined relationship between input, throughput and output is frequently absent.

Looking at the cost structure of service companies it is clear that the larger part of costs is related to labor. As a result, contrary to industrial and retail organizations, the purchasing-to-sales turnover ratio is comparatively low. This may run from less than 10 per cent for an accounting firm, to 20–25 per cent for a large banking organization, or even 50 per cent for an international airline company. This implies that although impressive amounts of money may be at stake here, purchasing savings only have a limited effect on the return on assets (RONA) of service companies. When discussing competitive strategy, top management in service organizations will understandably spend most of their time on value-added and people-related issues and activities. In general they will spend little time and effort on the support activities, among which is purchasing.

However, although the relative purchasing spend may be rather low, the products and services on which the company's money is spent show a large diversity. This is illustrated by Figure 18.1. Using Porter's value chain concept it is clear that almost all purchasing activities are aimed at the other support activities (see Chapter 1). Purchasing for the primary process is almost absent, since service companies by definition do not have a production process in which inputs are physically transformed to outputs. This is an important difference from industrial companies, where buying for primary activities represents the bulk of purchasing expenditure. It explains why managers in service companies reveal so little interest in the purchasing operations of their company – they consider it primarily as a support activity.

The competitive scene for the service sector is gradually changing from a traditional, local national arena to a truly international arena. As a result, service companies strive to improve their services to the end user whilst reducing operational costs. In some cases service companies have tried to establish international networks through mergers and acquisitions and joint ventures with overseas companies, as can be observed for example

3 Former Federal Republic of Germany only.

in the airline industry. As a result, an increasing concentration can be perceived in the service industry. Large companies are becoming larger and more powerful through mergers and acquisitions. This development has affected purchasing operations in several ways:

■ Increased outsourcing of support activities. Focus on core activities often leads to the decision to put non-core activities to the market test. This was the prime reason for contracting out transportation and distribution by a major international bank. As a result the bank personnel involved were hired by the transportation company on a five-year fixed contract. Other activities which are often outsourced as a result of this exercise are:

– security
– catering
– cleaning services
– mail-room activities
– maintenance activities
– print and photocopying
– garden and greenkeeping services.

FIGURE 18.1 Major categories of non product-related expenditure.

Buildings, installation and infrastructure

- Real estate
- Restructuring and renewal
- Maintenance
- Technical installations
- Security systems
- Office furniture
- System walls
- Kitchens and canteens
- Temporary buildings

Housekeeping

- Energy
- Catering
- Cleaning and sanitary services
- Greenkeeping
- Removal services
- Security
- Garbage removal
- Clothing
- Technical support materials

Temporary labor

- Hiring of temporary personnel
- Interim managers
- Consultants
- IT programers, analysts and project managers

Services

- Transport services
- Cars and transport vehicles
- Travel
- Accommodation
- Training and education
- Search and recruitment services
- Market research
- Marketing and promotion
- Media
- Events
- Factoring
- Professional services

IT and telematics

- Mainframes, hard- and software
- Midrange systems
- PCs
- Peripherals
- Data communication networks
- Telephone switching equipment
- Infrastructure
- IT projects
- Outsourcing
- Information services

Office supplies and printing

- Copying
- Office equipment
- Office supplies
- Paper
- Packaging materials
- Printing
- Representation
- Books and subscriptions

Source: adapted from Rietveld (1995), pp. 138–40

■ Integration of support activities in a facility management organization. In order to reduce costs and to improve the quality level of support activities, more companies have adopted a facilities management concept (see Memo 18.1) in which these activities are brought under one managerial responsibility. This development is not without relevance for purchasing: first, it often implies that the purchasing manager is to report to the facilities manager; second, it can lead to more purchases going through the purchasing organization, because this organizational concept facilitates the cooperation between purchasing and the other support areas.

■ Increased scale of operations. As a result of the growth which some service companies have experienced, opportunities to form a specialized purchasing department have increased. This is especially true for companies which have merged with other organizations. These mergers often result in an impressive non-product-related purchasing spend which, because of the amount of money involved, warrants treatment by professional buyers. This has encouraged companies to set up a professional purchasing department.

It may be concluded that some service companies nowadays are actively pursuing opportunities to improve their competitive edge. As a result they are looking for ways to reduce labor and operational costs, while improving the quality of their services to the customer. These efforts have consequences for purchasing. The trend towards outsourcing means that service companies have a lot to gain from a professional purchasing organization, which can take care of defining purchasing requirements, supplier selection, contract negotiation and control. By adopting a facilities management concept support activities are much better integrated and managed, providing purchasing departments with the chance to work more closely with 'big spenders' within the service organization. Finally, since the scale of operations of many service organizations has increased through mergers and acquisitions, opportunities for a more professional approach to purchasing have improved considerably.

Given the nature of service companies and their comparatively low purchasing-to-sales ratio, cost considerations are not prime to internal customers, i.e. departments. They often feel it is more important for suppliers to deliver on time and in the right quantity, rather than to pursue the lowest purchasing price. Given the specialized nature of most investment buying (information technology, software, construction) the user and the budgetholder

MEMO 18.1 FACILITIES MANAGEMENT

Facilities relate to all the physical conditions that enable an organization to conduct its primary activities. This includes the buildings, general installations, equipment, and their related services, but excludes human resources and all manufacturing equipment. Facilities management can therefore be described as 'the management (planning, execution and control) and the realization of housing and accommodation, the services related to these, and other means in order to enable the organization to realize its mission'. It includes activities such as building and technical maintenance, security, catering, travel, reception, transportation and distribution, warehousing and inventory. Traditionally one would find these activities scattered throughout the organization. Within a facilities management concept these activities are brought under one organizational responsibility. Adoption of the concept often leads to a more professional view on each of these activities. Most large companies are aware of the amount of money related to these activities. Moreover, the management of these activities consumes a lot of management's time and energy. The task of facilities managers is to provide their services at a competitive cost and quality level. When these conditions cannot be met, a decision to contract out this activity to outside suppliers is likely. The trend towards facilities management explains, among other things, the rapid growth of some of these industries (catering, transportation, courier services, security, etc.).

play a dominant role in decision making (developing specifications, supplier selection, negotiation), leaving administrative matters, at best, to the purchasing department. This situation develops when purchasing does not possess sufficient knowledge in the appropriate specialist areas to enable it to act as a valuable partner to the internal customers. As a result, strong relationships can develop between internal users and suppliers, which are very difficult to change. The purchasing department therefore concentrates on what is left, the general, routine and low-cost items, which are ordered through fixed order routines from traditional sources of supply.

These considerations suggest that in most service companies an impressive potential for improvement in purchasing probably exists. Indeed, as experience with several of these companies has shown, a professional approach to purchasing can result in savings of between 5 and 20 per cent! At the same time, however, it will be clear that improving purchasing professionalism is a far from simple matter. Because of the relatively low purchasing spend, top management will often fail to provide support to purchasing procedures, and buyers will achieve recognition only by providing a superior service to their internal departments. Purchasing managers operating in a service company should therefore be service driven rather than cost driven.

TOWARDS MORE EFFECTIVE PURCHASING IN A FACILITIES ENVIRONMENT

It has been shown that some major differences exist between buying for production purposes and buying for support activities. In particular, effective purchasing in a facilities environment requires that buyers are sympathetic to the needs and requirements of their internal customers. In practice, however, a gap exists between how internal customers perceive the role of the purchasing department, and how this department sees its role. This is illustrated in Figure 18.2.

Most managers of other departments will point to the following success factors for their purchasing department:

- easy access, both by telephone and personally;
- fast reaction to questions and problems;
- prompt delivery of goods ordered;
- short delivery times;
- consistent quality of goods delivered;
- immediate feedback in case of unforeseen order changes.

Provided that buyers are able to meet these requirements, users are willing to allow purchasing to take a more pro-active role in the purchasing process. The purchasing department will emphasize, however, other aspects in the relationship with the internal customer, such as low price, savings, good contracts, alternative sources of supply and clear specifications. It is clear that when the expectations of both the purchasing department and the internal users differ with regard to the role of the purchasing department, this may lead to significant boundary problems and friction between the parties involved. In those cases most internal departments will prefer to deal with the purchasing process themselves, simply to avoid these problems

When improving purchasing professionalism, a prime concern, therefore, should be how to improve the customer orientation of the purchasing department. In order to do this the following approach may be useful.

FIGURE 18.2 Differences in expectation of purchasing's role in a facilities environment.

1 Analyze and document internal product/customer combinations step-by-step. Here the idea is first to find out the total purchasing expenditure per department (often to be gathered from budget and accounting information) and per product group or purchasing segment. This sounds simple but is often a time-consuming matter, since many organizations do not keep account of these data in a systematic way. Next, it should be assessed what part of the expenditure is contracted through the purchasing department. In this way the internal market share of the purchasing department, both for specific departments and product groups, can be established (see Table 18.2).

2 Assess internal customer satisfaction. Next, each relevant department should be visited to find out how they experience the service provided by the purchasing department. The attitude here is: 'You are OK, but how are we?' This is easier said than done, since when this investigation is conducted by employees of the purchasing department they will immediately explain or defend themselves against every criticism they encounter. At least one additional objective interviewer is therefore essential in this kind of investigation, the purpose of which is to find out what bottlenecks exist in the relationship between other departments and purchasing. These need to be documented and thoroughly analyzed. Next, ideas should be developed on how to solve these bottlenecks.

3 Target setting. Based on the information gathered in the previous step, targets now can be set with regard to increasing the market share of the purchasing department in each of the cells. It often appears that although tremendous potential for improvement does exist in some cells (for example PCs for the internal computer department) a target cannot be set because of a lack of experience and specialist knowledge within the purchasing department in this area. It should then be decided whether to build up expertise first, in order to increase market share in this area. This step should result in a detailed action plan for the purchasing department, indicating:

(a) in what customer/product combinations the purchasing department will maintain or reinforce position, i.e. market share;

(b) the actions which will be necessary to make this happen;

(c) the results which can be expected from these actions (in terms of savings, lead time reduction, less suppliers, etc).

4 Cross functional buying teams and organizational structure. The analysis so far often provides sufficient information on what competences are required in order to handle the different commodities. As has been argued earlier, a cross-functional team approach is crucial for success. Specialists from user departments who work with suppliers and buyers should be put together in cross-functional buying teams in order to develop sourcing and commodity plans. These teams could be supervised by the purchasing manager; they should, however, report to the line management or management team. Apart from a team structure, an appropriate organization structure should be decided upon for the purchasing department. This subject will be covered in the next section.

5 Develop supply-market strategies. Each buying team should develop its own supply strategies and commodity plans. A valuable aid here is the purchasing portfolio matrix (see Chapter 8). By depicting each product/supplier combination graphically, each team can decide on the preferred supply strategy. Each team probably will come up with different strategies, depending on the position of a certain commodity in the portfolio. This

TABLE 18.2 Customer product group matrix (example)

Internal department → ↓ Product group	Computer department	Technical maintenance	Distribution department	Etc.	Total volume
Computer hardware/software	A ___ B ___ C ___ D ___	Etc.			
Computer supplies	Etc.				
Office equipment					
Office furniture					
Office supplies					
Temporary labor					
Services					
Etc.					
Total volume					

Notes: A = Total purchasing volume; B = Purchasing expenditure through purchasing department; C = Market share purchasing department; D = Expected future total purchasing volume (↗ → ↘)

step should result in a detailed action plan for each product group, which is presented to purchasing and senior management for approval.

6 Implementation. At this stage the plans which have been developed need to be executed. This requires close and careful monitoring by purchasing and general management. Results are to be measured in terms of:

(a) market share per customer/product combination as a measure of how satisfactorily the purchasing department performs in the eyes of internal customers;

(b) operational measures such as:

- savings generated as a result of the actions conducted towards suppliers;

- purchasing customer satisfaction expressed by some form of index based upon a standardized survey, to be conducted periodically;

- purchasing administrative lead time expressing the responsiveness of purchasing to internal customer needs;

(c) progress against other targets, as described in the purchasing action plan.

Figure 18.3 provides some practical suggestions with regard to actions which can be taken in order to improve overall purchasing effectiveness and efficiency.

This approach need not apply to service companies only. Facilities, i.e. non-production buying, is increasingly being acknowledged as an area where substantial savings can be captured. For this reason many large companies have initiated corporate programs in this

---

FIGURE 18.3 Some suggestions for improving purchasing effectiveness and efficiency.

Improvement measures with regard to the purchasing–customer interface

- Joint efforts aimed at reducing the number of products through standardization
- Joint efforts at supplier reduction ('doing more with less') through:
  - establishing well-defined procedures for supplier selection
  - introducing 'prime vendorship'
  - introducing tender boards, buying committees, or cross-functional benefits teams for important purchasing decisions (large investments and service contracts)
- Improve on accessibility and customer orientation through:
  - improving telephone facilities
  - effective help desk
  - improving social skills through training
  - brochures on how purchasing operates
  - improving purchasing systems and procedures

Internal measures to improve the purchasing operations

- Improving product and market knowledge
- Improving purchasing techniques and skills
- Differentiating between routine and non-routine activities; in the case of routine buying delegate order handling (if possible and useful) to internal customer
- Simplifying orders systems by using:
  - blanket order agreements
  - systems contracting
  - electronic purchasing and electronic commerce
  - simplifying authorization procedures
  - simplifying invoice checking and approval procedures

area, including Philips Electronics, which started an initiative in 1996 with the aim of reducing 12 per cent on purchasing expenditure in this area (see Memo 18.2).

In discussing the optimal structure for a purchasing department within a service company the question is posed as to what principle to use. Several options in general exist:

- Customer characteristics. The purchasing departmental structure reflects the different departments it works for (one group for department A, one group for department B, etc.)

- Product characteristics. Buying groups are formed around products with common characteristics.

- Service characteristics. Buying groups are formed around services provided by the purchasing department: for instance a contracting group, an ordering group, a project-buying group.

- Supply market characteristics. Buying groups are formed around groups of suppliers.

The basic dilemma is how to secure an effective internal customer orientation in combination with knowledge of products and supply markets. Although all four options may be considered, the structure most often encountered is that based on product characteristics. Interface problems with internal customers are solved by assigning one of the buying group leaders as the account manager for a specific customer department. On a daily basis the employees of a customer department can deal with any of the buying personnel. However, policy matters and specific problems are discussed with the account manager. He/she acts as an intermediary between the customer and the purchasing department. The interface with the supply market is often much more easy to manage, given the high correlation between product characteristics and suppliers. Most suppliers sell products within a limited number of product groups and hence often deal with only one buying

MEMO 18.2 NON PRODUCT-RELATED PURCHASING AT PHILIPS

In 1995 the board of management of Philips Electronics ordered a worldwide purchasing benchmark survey to be carried out by an international consulting firm. This firm concluded that, through aggressive program-driven action, the total annual savings in non product-related (NPR) purchasing for Philips could be in excess of 1.2 billion dollars! For this reason a focused cost saving program was launched under the name OCOO (other cost of organization) (see Figure 18.4). OCOO is a Philips' global NPR program focused on a short-term substantial and sustainable reduction of NPR costs. The idea behind it is that every dollar not spent in NPR purchasing will add to Philips' bottom line for the full 100 per cent.

OCOO is a business owned and funded program that rests on a self-reinforcing approach. A business targeting process aimed at reducing costs in the following areas:

- accommodation;
- personnel-related costs;
- sales-related costs;
- distribution;
- automation and communication;
- office-related costs;
- professional services;
- production- and development-related costs.

Source: based upon internal company brochures and press information.

FIGURE 18.4   Brochure OCOO Program Philips Electronics.

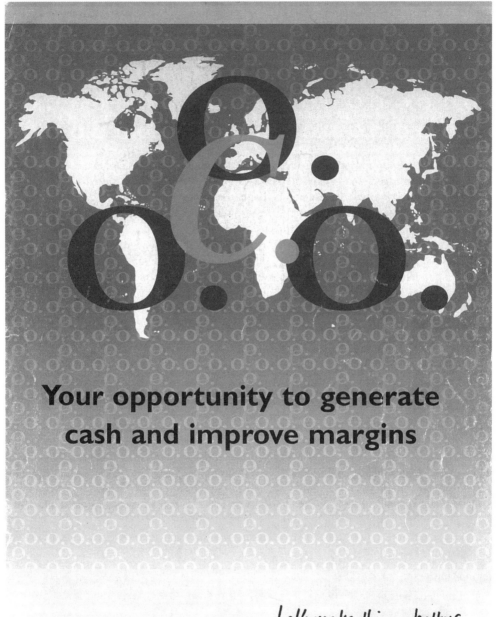

group. Figure 18.5 provides an illustration of a purchasing department within a large international bank. Here the buying groups are formed around commodities, i.e. product groups. However, routine operations are separated from these groups by means of a special help desk and order group. This group focuses on answering routine questions from internal customers and placing small orders directly. Large orders are transmitted to the appropriate buying groups. Office and computer supplies have been covered by annual agreements with a limited number of suppliers; internal users directly place call-off orders with these suppliers for the materials they need. All products, and the terms and conditions, are available through an attractive electronic catalog, which is developed and kept up to date by the 'systems, research and catalog-group'. In this way the organization is able to free up considerable time, traditionally spent on administrative matters by the professional buyers, while at the same time reducing order cycle time for the internal users.

Since services play a major role in any facilities environment the remainder of this chapter is devoted to this issue. Apart from providing a proper definition we will discuss how the purchasing process for services can be improved.

BUYING SERVICES: DEFINITIONS AND TYPOLOGY

In literature, many definitions of services can be found. A useful definition is provided by Grönroos (2000) who defines a service as:

a process consisting of a series of more or less intangible activities, that normally (but not necessarily always) take place in interactions between the customer and service employees, and/or physical resources or goods and/or systems of the service provider, which are provided as solutions to the customer problems.

Some elements of this definition need explanation.

First, services can be offered in combination with the provision of tangible goods. Examples are investments goods that are delivered by the suppliers in combination with a service contract for technical maintenance. Next, apparently, services are supplied in response to some kind of need or problem which is experienced by the customer. In some

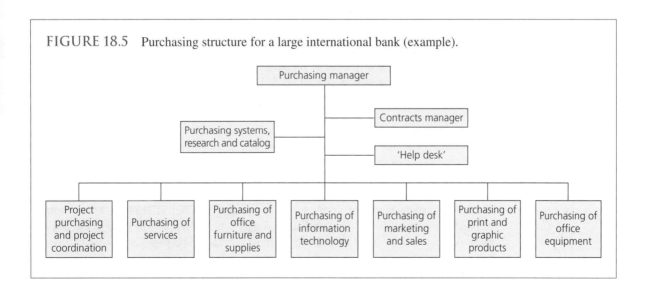

FIGURE 18.5   Purchasing structure for a large international bank (example).

cases the problem may be clear and well defined, as is the case with a car driver who needs immediate repair for his flat tire. However, in other cases the problem and solution to be provided may be fuzzy and need to be defined properly before a contract and workplan can be prepared. An example may be the financial manager who wants an accounting firm to conduct an annual financial audit for his company. Here, the boundaries between the customer and the auditing firm need to be explained: what information is available at the customer, what part of the auditing process can be prepared internally by the customer itself, how detailed does the audit need to be, when is the annual report to be published, etc. In this case it may be necessary to conduct a short investigation before the accounting firm is able to provide a proposal to the customer. Third, an important element of the definition is that a service takes place in interaction between customer and service employees. Hence, exchanges on services concern essentially exchanges between people.

In order for this exchange to take place the customer's staff and the supplier's staff need to meet, to get acquainted and a relationship between them needs to develop before they can engage in a formal agreement with the supplier. For the service provider to perform, the customer needs to provide him with proper information and instructions. In developing the relationship, many aspects play a role: perceptions about expertise and knowledge, economic aspects, technical aspects; also personal aspects, such as emotions, feelings and preferences. This is one reason why it is so difficult for any buyer to interfere in a relationship which has been established between company staff and supplier staff. When a relationship between key company staff has developed, it seems logical that they do not appreciate the interference by any newcomer in what they perceive as their process and relationship.

Since they relate to human exchange of knowledge and expertise, services are intangible. Services relate to the performance of a predefined activity that is executed in cooperation with the customer. It may be difficult to separate what is considered to be the supplier's responsibility and the customer's responsibility and contribution. Anticipating potential boundary conflicts that may occur, usually takes time and effort to discuss. Services are intangible: they cannot be made on stock, and availability of capacity is therefore an issue that should be secured in the discussions with the supplier. Capabilities and resources should be available at the right time and at the right level of expertise in order to meet the customer's service requirements. This is not easy in situations where customer demand cannot be forecasted in advance. An example would be a service level agreement where the customer stipulates that the supplier will be on site within two hours after an unplanned machine breakdown has been reported. The customer in that case not only pays for the hours actually spent on the job, but also for the reserve capacity that the suppliers needs to keep in place in order to be able to respond quickly to unforeseeable service calls.

Compared to goods or products, services have some important differences. Table 18.3 points out the differences between goods and services.

The differences between goods and services mentioned above, have important implications for managing the procurement of services. These issues are discussed later in this chapter.

As Table 18.3 shows, value offerings as supplied by suppliers may range from fully tangible products to services that have no tangible element at all. In fact one can speak of a spectrum or continuum where value offerings can be placed depending on the degree to which they are based upon product- and service characteristics. Most value propositions nowadays have elements of both. As we have seen, product offerings are increasingly embedded in some kind of service that is provided by the supplier to support the use and maintenance of the product after the moment of purchase. It is therefore useful to propose a typology of services before we discuss the specific purchasing elements related to each type of service offering.

When categorizing services, the purchasing portfolio approach may be used as a terms of reference.[4] Based upon this approach we might differentiate between:

- strategic services, e.g. software, telecommunications, marketing and advertising, information technology services;
- leverage service, e.g. cleaning, catering, temporary labor;
- routine services, e.g. courier services, greenkeeping;
- bottleneck services, e.g. specialist technical and maintenance services.

For each of these services the four basic supplier strategies that were explained earlier in this book can be pursued. However, this typology does not reflect the specifics related to the actual use and the organizational environment in which services are used.

Axelsson and Wynstra (2002) refer to a service typology that has been suggested by the OECD (1999). Here, a differentiation is made between:

- Facility services. Cleaning, catering, security and real estate maintenance are examples of facility services.
- Financial services. This category of business services contains banking, finance, salary administration, insurance.
- Information and communication technology services. All services regarding ICT issues such as hardware implementation, customization and maintenance, telecommunication services, software development and implementation.
- Business organization services. Management consultancy, environmental consultancy, risk management, public relations, accounting and auditing, legal services.
- Research and development and technical services. Technical maintenance, repairs and assistance, development and engineering.
- Transportation and distribution services. Warehousing, value added logistics, transportation services.

TABLE 18.3 Goods and services: differences

Pure services offerings	Combined product-service offerings	Pure products offerings
Intangible		Tangible
Heterogeneous		Homogeneous
Production, distribution and consumption are simultaneous processes		Production and distribution are separate from consumption
More difficult to demonstrate (not available)		Can be demonstrated before the purchase
Cannot be transported		Cannot be transported
An activity or a process		An item
Core value produced in the interaction between buyer and seller		Core value produced in facility
Customers participate in production process		Customers do not usually participate in production process
Cannot be stored		Storable
Ownership is not passed		Ownership is passed

---

4 See Chapter 8.

- Human resource development services. Training, education and recruiting.
- Marketing services. Sales, reselling, advertising, agents.

This typology basically reflects the functional environment in which the service supposedly is being consumed. It can be used to hypothesize how the DMU (decision making unit) is build up, i.e. what kind of specialists within the company will be involved in the organizational buying process.

Looking at the different kinds of services and the ways in which these can be classified, we conclude that the Kraljic matrix is appropriate for defining what purchasing strategies will be most appropriate. The typology that has been suggested by the OECD may help to orchestrate the purchasing process within the organization since it provides some clues on who needs to be involved in the buying process.

Before dealing explicitly with the purchasing of business services we will take a closer look at the marketing of these services. This subject has been dealt with extensively and lessons can be learnt for the purchasing of services.

WHAT CAN WE LEARN FROM THE WAY SERVICES ARE BEING SOLD?

As we have concluded, service companies by definition are not able to produce their actual service offerings beforehand. In fact, only the service concepts and preparations for the service process can be made in advance of the actual consumption by the customer.

Services are special because compared to the exchange of products, there is a lot more contact and interaction between the buying and selling company. For the selling company this can be beneficial because customers in general like to be treated individually. The intensive interaction enables the seller to constantly obtain information about the customer's needs and perceptions, which enables him to tailor his value offering more in line with these. Apart from the formal full-time marketers and sales engineers, a service company in fact has a much larger sales staff. We refer here to all those service employees who work on a regular basis with their counterparts of the customer organization. What emerges is a multi-level communication pattern among the companies involved which requires careful planning and orchestration from both sides. Because service firms have a lot more ways to communicate with their customer, we may conclude that they have a lot more chances to tailor their service offering to the final customer. However, if these contact- and communication patterns are not properly managed, this may work out negatively for the service provider. This aspect, therefore, should be a prime concern for any manager who is interested in making the buying process for services more professional.

Given the human interaction patterns in services, the final user within the customer firm is very important for a supplier. In fact, the service firm is not able to provide a valid service proposition without direct contact with the end user. The user is of the same opinion on this matter. This may explain the difficulties purchasing managers and buyers are experiencing when trying to get their department involved in the purchasing process for services.

This conclusion is in line with the research that has been conducted by Wetzels, Ruyter and Lemmink (1999). These researchers have presented a useful framework to better understand business service relationships. They state that in addition to service quality, market and relationship characteristics may determine the level of commitment and trust in a relationship. These researchers not only stress the importance of service quality and the supply market characteristics relating to the buyer–supplier relationship, they also demonstrate that relationship characteristics are at least as important. As they see it, the formal transactions between account managers and buyers reflect informal and inter-personal agreements. As research has shown, in business service markets personal contact between supplier and customer is seen as the most important source of information.

When investigating these personal contacts, a distinction should be made between affective and calculative commitment. The first refers to the extent to which customers like to maintain the relationship with the supplier and is based on general positive feeling toward the partner. Calculative commitment refers to a firm's motivation to continue the relationship because it cannot easily replace its current partner and because it cannot obtain the same resources and outcomes outside the current partner. This part of commit-ment is based on balancing the costs and benefits of the relationship.

Wetzels *et al.* conclude that the service employee in business-to-business services plays a vital role and because of the complexity of relationships, all three variables of the frame-work play a role of some importance: the decision to remain in a certain relationship will be based on affective as well as cognitive motivations.

PURCHASING SERVICES: SERVICE LEVEL AGREEMENTS

Purchasing process related to services

The differences between products and services are reflected in some specific characteris-tics related to the purchasing process of services:

- Pre-qualification of service provider of prime importance. As we have seen, a service does not yet exist when the customer contracts for it. Services cannot be tested or inspected beforehand to ensure they conform to the specification of the buyer. Buying companies, therefore, should thoroughly check the references, or earlier experiences with the service provider, or check experiences that other customers have had with the same supplier. Since the result of buying a service is rather difficult to see in advance, the preliminary assessment and pre-qualification will strongly focus on the organiza-tion, processes, expertise and capabilities of the service provider, rather than on his or her product.

- Secure supplier capacity and capabilities. Because services can only be produced at the same moment as they are consumed, it is important to secure supplier capacity in terms of manpower, equipment and other resources beforehand to ensure delivery at the moment the service is needed. Of course, the same is true for the internal capabilities and resources that should become available to the service provider.

- Check upon key personnel. Providing services requires effective and efficient inter-action between employees of the service provider and his customer. The quality of the services to be provided are directly related to the expertise, experience and quality of the service provider's employees. For the buyer this means that, when pre-qualifying service providers, he/she should check the qualifications of key personnel. The more knowledge intensive the service, the more important this check will be.

- Availability of working space and other working conditions. In cases where services will be delivered within the company's physical environment, sufficient working space or office space needs to be arranged to host the technical staff of the service provider. In some cases it will be necessary to provide access to the company's internal informa-tion and administrative systems with proper security measures.

- Defining and managing expectations beforehand. Since both the customer and supplier are involved in the 'production process' of the service, it should be agreed who will be responsible for what part of the result. When the quality of the services is not according to the buyer's expectations, he will probably blame the supplier whereas it's quite possible that the lack of communication and instructions from the customer in fact caused the quality problems. Therefore, it is necessary to clearly define expectations of *both* parties at the outset. Detailed project planning, with a clear outline of the different milestones to be reached, is often part of the contractual arrangement.

- Contractual arrangements. In the case of buying goods, it is relatively easy to ascertain when a contract comes into existence and when it is fulfilled. When the supplied goods are as agreed on, payment can be made according to the contract. But in the case of services, this can be less clear cut. When is the service delivered according to the customer's expectations? What if an architect delivers several designs which meet the customer's criteria but do not meet the customer's aesthetic tastes? In such a case a contract may not give a solution unless it contains clauses that can deal with this situation. For services it is almost impossible to include clauses that can deal with all possible misunderstandings.

- Performance-based contract. When contracting for services a performance-based contract should be preferred over a 'best effort' agreement. Rather that making the effort of the provider the core of the agreement, it is preferable to focus on the performance or result that should be derived from these efforts. This requires a thorough discussion of what needs to be delivered in terms of outcome.

Professional buyers are aware of the differences that exist between buying products and buying services. Compared to buying products they feel it is more difficult to determine the total costs that are related to buying a specific service. It is also much more difficult to decide on clear specifications and scope of work. The fact that a service provider has done well on one occasion and location does not necessarily mean he will also perform well in another situation. In comparing supplier offerings, the objective comparison of the service providers is a difficult task. One of the problems related to buying services, as buyers see it, is to forecast future supplier performance based on past performance. Another problem reported by buyers was to have trust in a continuous, reliable performance level (Graw and Maples, 1994). This discussion illustrates why purchasing services in organizations is such a highly sensitive and political matter. In the next section we discuss what buyers can do to arrive at a proper description of the scope of work and to make appropriate arrangements with the selected supplier.

Service level agreements

In order to have a clear understanding of what is expected from the service supplier, a clear specification of services is needed. Here, many buyers increasingly try to make arrangements through service level agreements (SLAs). A service level agreement is a performance-based agreement. The results or the performance to be delivered by the suppliers are stated in quantitative terms, usually in the form of a limited number of key performance indicators (KPIs). Where the supplier meets the agreed service levels, he will receive full payment. When he is unable to meet these targeted service levels, he will be paid less. Of course, when arranging for this type of agreement the buyer and supplier should agree on the precise definition of the key performance indicators. The buyer should be able to report regularly on the supplier's performance. These reports should then be discussed to see where both parties could make improvements to realize a better result. An advantage of using an SLA in the relationship with a service provider is that both parties need to become very specific about the results that should be gained from the provider's services. Furthermore, both parties should be explicit about who within the customer company is going to benefit from the service and in what way (lower cost, faster response, less process interruptions, etc.). Apart from the results, the SLA will outline the resources that will be used by both the buyer and the supplier to be able to fulfill the service requirements. In doing so, the service level agreement helps both parties to be explicit about the expectations both parties have from the relationship.

Preparing a detailed service level agreement usually takes a lot of time and effort. In some case, circumstances may be such that this time and effort is not available. In general, services may be specified in one of the following ways (Axelsson and Wynstra, 2002):

- Specifying inputs that are going to be used by the service provider. Here the agreement focuses on describing the resources that will be used by the provider to deliver the service required. An example would be an HRM manager looking for temporary labor for seasonal work. Usually the temporary labor agency will send him a few *curricula vitaes* (CVs) of people that are available, from which the HRM manager can make his choice. No agreements on the actual performance to be delivered by the people involved are made.

- Specifying the throughput or process that needs to be in place in order to provide the service required. Here the buyer meets with the supplier and, based upon a general works description, agrees with the supplier on the range of activities that will be performed. This is common in contracting for construction projects where both parties (apart from price) agree on a detailed project schedule which provides a fair estimate of the number of manhours and materials that will be used for the project, the time-planning and milestones for the project and the payment schedules.

- Specifying the output or results that need to be obtained by the customer through the supplier's service activities. Here the buyer provides a description of the final result to be gained from the supplier's intervention. The functionality of the service is stressed rather than the activity itself. An example would be a service contract for a technical installation. The contract may outline the maximum allowable unplanned downtime of the machine (usually a percentage of total operating time); the contractor is responsible for setting up a preventive maintenance schedule in such a way that this percentage is being met. Although the buyer will show interest in this maintenance schedule, he will only measure the supplier's performance based upon the monthly report of the indicators that have been agreed upon. The functionality of the service is stressed (keeping the machine running) rather than the activity itself (inspect the machine twice a week takes two manhours). SLAs are an example of this method of specifying services.

Apart from these three methods, Axelsson and Wynstra (2002) mention a fourth method which specifies services in such a way that outcome, rather than output, is defined. In this method the value rather than the functionality of the service is stressed. This value can be measured in financial terms. For example: the maintenance provider is not measured on a percentage of unplanned downtime but in terms of value of extra production that was possible due to the lower unplanned downtime that actually happened. The service provider is paid a percentage of the extra value that accrued for the customer thanks to his outstanding maintenance service (and pays a penalty in case he did not meet the agreed service level). Another example is a specialist purchasing consultant who is able to realize significant purchasing savings for a customer; rather than getting paid for the hours he spent, he may agree to receive a percentage of the savings that accrued because of his work.

As we have seen, buying services differs from buying products in many ways. First, arriving at a proper description of what the outcome of the service needs to be, requires a

FIGURE 18.6   Contracting for services: some suggestions.

- Specify performance or outcome to be delivered from service rather than activities to be conducted
- Describe when and where the service needs to be provided
- Describe who will benefit from the service and in what way
- Check supplier reputation, expertise and qualifications
- Ask for CVs of key personnel and secure their availability during the service period
- Analyze supplier service process and quality system: assess and discuss weaknesses and threats and major risks
- Invite service provider to present business case based upon work description
- Assess 'cultural fit' between buying company and service provider
- Pursue performance-based contract, i.e. service level agreement which outlines:
  – key performance indicators
  – detailed workplan and time schedule
- Agree on what financial, human, technical and information resources will be made available by the principal
- Allow for detailed inspection and quality procedures
- Discuss and agree on dispute resolution procedure
- Agree on performance-based payment schedules
- Describe communication structure and make working arrangements

lot of effort and time. Next, selecting the right supplier is often a difficult matter. Since the quality of services is determined to a large extent by the effectiveness of the relationship with the internal customer, experiences with a supplier may differ from time to time and location to location. Although references may be, and should be, checked beforehand, this information is no guarantee that the supplier will perform satisfactorily. Finally, in making arrangements with service suppliers buyers should avoid 'best-effort' contracts. Rather, they should go for service level agreements or similar performance-based contracts.

Figure 18.6 provides some suggestions that buyers may support in contracting effectively for services.

SUMMARY

In this chapter the most important trends and developments within the service sector have been discussed. Service companies represent a growing share of economic activity in most European countries. Purchasing represents, in general, a low share of the service company's overall cost. Purchasing savings therefore have only a limited effect on the company's return on net assets. Moreover, purchasing expenditure is related to a large variety of activities, which are usually scattered throughout the organization. One result is that the purchasing function in service companies is far less visible to management than in industrial companies. This explains why the development of purchasing management in service companies has lagged behind that in industrial enterprises. This picture is gradually changing for three reasons: (1) the tendency nowadays to outsource support activities; (2) the trend towards facilities management that can be observed; and (3) the increased scale of operations of many service organizations. These developments have in general increased the need for a professional purchasing approach. As a result many service companies have built up separate purchasing departments within their organizations.

Developing a professional purchasing approach in service organizations is a far from simple matter. An important reason for this is that top management frequently fails to support and control purchasing procedures. This explains the freedom exercised by departmental managers when purchasing activities are involved. Also, professional handling of some purchasing decisions requires considerable specialist knowledge, which often is not available from within the purchasing department. In these cases the purchasing department has little value to add to its internal customers. From this it was concluded that buyers, in order to be effective, should be primarily service driven, rather than cost driven. Next, in order to be able to structure the buying process a team-based approach was recommended in which the user and product specialists play a major role. A strong customer orientation and cross functional teamwork are prerequisites for the success of any purchasing department in this kind of organization. In order to professionalize purchasing in a facilities environment a six-step approach was presented: (1) analyze and document internal product/customer combinations in order to assess present and future market share; (2) assess internal customer satisfaction in order to discover bottlenecks and problems in the relationship with internal departments; (3) set targets for improving internal service levels; (4) decide on what organizational structure will be most appropriate; (5) develop supply-market strategies for each of the buying groups; (6) implement and monitor progress.

Since buying services is of such importance in a facilities environment we have discussed this topic in this chapter. We concluded that due to the special characteristics of services compared to products, the purchasing process of services poses important challenges to buyers. First, due to the fact that services are delivered in close interaction with the company's specialists, the buyer of services needs to adopt a facilitating rather than a leading role in the buying process. In most cases the internal customer is much more knowledgeable about the service to be acquired than the buyer. Moreover, specifying services takes a lot more time and effort than specifying products. Here, companies may use different approaches. Services may be specified based upon the inputs that they need, the process through which they will be realized and/or the results or outcome to be gained from them. Using service level agreements (SLAs) encourages internal customers to become specific about the expectations and outcome that will result from the relationship with the service provider. Key performance indicators, reflecting the degree to which the service provider was able to meet specific targeted service levels, may help buyers to generate an objective picture of the performance of service providers. This will facilitate communication with the other members of the cross-functional buying team when discussing improvement measures to be made in the relationship with the buyer.

ASSIGNMENTS

18.1 Place yourself in the position of the purchasing manager of the introductory Case Study. What would you do in order to improve the effectiveness of your department? How would you try to gain a better recognition for your department both from other departmental managers and top management?

18.2 How would you assess the degree of customer friendliness of a purchasing department in a service company? What elements would you consider? How would you proceed in order to obtain the necessary information?

18.3 Purchasing departments in many service companies deal with many small orders related to standard materials (MRO materials). Much time and effort can be spent on small orders, which prevents buyers from spending sufficient

▶

time on the large items. What suggestions would you make in order to reduce the number of small orders?

18.4 Why is it so difficult to structure and control procurement processes related to services? Provide the five most important reasons.

18.5 A facilities manager is considering outsourcing the company's internal catering to an outside specialist supplier. If he was to use a service level agreement, what key performance indicators would you suggest in order to monitor the caterer's service performance?

LEARNING OBJECTIVES

After reading this chapter you should be able to:

- Identify the most important differences in purchasing between private enterprises and governmental institutions.
- Understand the relationship between public procurement and the EC Directives on Public Procurement.
- Have an understanding of the basic principles which underlie the EC Directives on Public Procurement.
- Know the workings and contents of the most important EC directives and purchasing procedures.
- Understand the limitations and shortcomings of these directives.

CASE STUDY   TENDER PROCEDURE FOR THE STOREBAELT BRIDGE

Purchasing and tendering are for governmental institutions no simple matters. This can be illustrated by the problems which have arisen around the public tendering of the construction of a major bridge in Denmark some time ago.

The Case Study concerns the tendering process of a bridge with a length over 6 km which was part of an infrastructural project to connect Funen and Seeland spanning the Great Belt in Denmark. The total distance of the project was 17 km. Tendering for this part of the large investment project had to be done according to the EC Directives for Public Procurement. The Danish government had opted for the negotiation procedure with publication in the EC Tender Bulletin. From the construction firms that applied, five combinations of companies (so-called consortia) initially were selected. Finally, the tender was awarded to the European Storebaelt Group (ESG). This consortium of companies was controlled by the Danish government.

However, before the tender was awarded, one of the other consortia submitted a complaint to the European Commission since the tender process had obviously violated the EC Directives.

The scope of work, which was submitted to all consortia, stipulated that all parties would use Danish suppliers for all materials and services. Moreover, Danish employees needed to be contracted for the execution of the assignment. Such arrangements were, according to the plea, in conflict with the principle of non-discrimination as laid down in the EC Treaty and its Directives on Public Procurement.

Another complaint concerned the fact that when conducting the negotiations, the bid by European Storebaelt Group had been used as a reference. This, as was argued, would have been to the detriment of all other consortia which applied. A final complaint was that the bid as submitted by ESG did not meet specifications and evaluation criteria as announced in both the EC Tender Bulletin and the scope of work.

Even before the contract was awarded, the European Commission acknowledged these complaints and informed the Danish government on all matters. A formal complaint procedure was initiated, in which it was demanded that the tender process was terminated. After refusal by the Danish government, the case was submitted to the European Court. At the same time the Commission requested the Court to demand that all activities were postponed by the Danish government until the Court had come to a decision.

When the case was discussed before Court, the Danish government had to admit that the non-discrimination principle had been violated. Only after the Danish government declared that it was willing to pay a penalty to the consortium whose interests were damaged, was the procedure withdrawn. According to several publications in the press the Danish government had to settle for a penalty of over seven million euros.

INTRODUCTION

For many suppliers and construction firms the government represents an interesting party. It is estimated that in Europe the volume of public procurement amounts to about 16.3 per cent of the Union's gross domestic product for the EC member states (figures relate to 2002). The amount of money which is related annually to government procurement within the EC probably exceeds 1.500 billion euros.[1] This huge amount of money is being spent by a large number of governmental institutions on a wide variety of goods, services and projects. It varies from specialized medical equipment for hospitals, to fuel for government-owned cars and trucks, to the construction of large infrastructural works such as roads, railways and bridges.

Hence, it cannot come as a surprise that the EC has initiated some directives which stipulate that the market for government contracts should be open to all potential suppliers and firms, regardless of their nationality. This, because a compartmentalized government procurement market would not fit in a 'Europe without frontiers'. Although the adoption of the directives has been rather slow, they now have become part of the standard procurement practice of the member states. The figures speak for themselves, as reported by the EC. An illustration of the importance of public procurement is the constant rise of the number of tender notices which have been published in the Official Journal: 106 346 invitations to tender were published in 2002, as against 54 731 in 1995, which represents a 15 per cent increase every year.

After a short *tour d'horizon* of the general characteristics of public procurement, this chapter discusses the most important public procurement directives and procedures. Apart from their content, the consequences for the public procurement policy and organization will be discussed. When this chapter refers to 'government' it implicitly includes institutions of the central government (ministries and related bodies), the provincial institutions and municipalities, some public bodies such as water supply and energy, as well as institutions which are financed by the government. It will become clear that public utilities (such as the energy sector, railways, other public transport and telecommunication companies) are also subject to the EC directives.

---

1 See report IP/04/149 i.e. 'Report on the functioning of public procurement markets in the EU: benefits from the application of EU directives and challenges for the future', January 2004.

PURCHASING POLICY OF GOVERNMENTAL INSTITUTIONS

In general, decision making within governmental bodies is far from transparent. This is due to the many stakeholders involved, the often conflicting interests among these, and the many political aspects that need to be considered. This is not only true for large societal issues, such as health care, employment, national security and environmental protection, but also for large governmental procurement projects. It explains why decision making concerning, for instance, buying defence equipment is often troublesome and difficult to manage. Apart from technical aspects, compensation-orders may play a significant role in deciding what manufacturer will get the order. Other examples are large infrastructural projects such as the high speed train from France to The Netherlands or the 'Chunnel' project between France and the UK. As a result of the complexity and duration of the decision-making process these projects usually are executed at higher costs than anticipated and against a much longer lead time.

Political objectives

Governmental purchasing often serves political objectives. At the same time the government needs to spend its financial resources as efficiently as possible. Both objectives do not need to be necessarily complementary. An example will illustrate this. For a municipality, which wants to tender for a new city hall, it may be wise to tender among a large number of construction firms to get the best value for money. However, this may be against their political intent to involve primarily local firms in order to stimulate employment in their region. Social and political objectives often are in conflict with a rational spending of budgets. It means that many purchasing decisions in governmental institutions cannot be made solely on economic grounds. Purchasing management in such organizations, in order to be effective, therefore requires a thorough understanding of their political context.

Budget policy

There are striking differences between governmental institutions and private enterprises in the way they deal with purchasing budgets. Every governmental institution is constrained by the central government's budget policies. These in general point out that the money which is allocated to them in a certain year should also be spent in that year. In many cases it is difficult to build up financial reserves and to shift these to the next year. Postponing procurement projects may lead to a new round of budget decisions for the next year, a situation which many governmental managers want to avoid. Purchasing savings may lead to a similar effect: when a certain department, through smart purchasing, is able to save money, it will be required to return this amount at the end of the year to the local authorities. This explains why many managers in the government consider a purchasing budget as a 'license to spend'. In general, it is wise to spend somewhat more than your budget in order to get more budget for the next year. Another complicating factor is that in many countries investments and exploitation are financed from different budgets. Hence investment decisions are often made without a careful balancing of costs during the exploitation stage. This prevents the adoption of a purchasing approach based upon total cost of ownership (TCO).

Due to the rigid budgeting systems a clear incentive to save money through professional purchasing within the government is missing. This explains the 'spending-fever', which can be observed in many governmental bodies at the end of the financial year! Memo 19.1 illustrates this.

Public accountability

Another important difference with private companies is that governmental institutions are publicly responsible for how they spend their money. Reports on this are in general open to the public community and explain why most institutions are very careful in making decisions. Usually, purchasing procedures are embedded in lots of bureaucracy and require that every superior puts his signature under the intended contract. The extensive authorization procedures make purchasing ordering a tedious, laborious and slow process. It explains why most purchasing organizations within the government are procedure rather than result oriented!

Contract management

In the case of large investment projects it is not uncommon for the contract to be awarded to the contractor at a reasonable sum, while all parties involved already know that the actual costs will exceed the intended budget. Suppliers, of course, in general do not object to such a way of working. In some countries the Minister of Finance has frequently reported about the failing contract management and the lack of consistent purchasing procedures. Most countries still seem to struggle on how to control and monitor governmental purchasing expenditure effectively.

Nationalist approach

Although the Treaty of Rome which formed the basis for the current EC was signed in 1957, and most European countries today should be used to the idea of being part of a truly international economic community, national and often regional interests are favored above EC interests. Many governmental institutions, for a number of reasons, express a clear preference to place contracts with local suppliers. An example of this was the rumor that occurred when the Ministry of Defence in one of the member countries, acting in line with the Directive 93/36/EEC on the award of public supply contracts, decided to place a large order for uniforms at a supplier located in another member country.

MEMO 19.1   HOW TO DEAL WITH PURCHASING SAVINGS IN THE GOVERNMENT

Several years ago one of the EU countries set up a support program for Bangladesh. Within the context of this program a large quantity of supplies, facilities and equipment was purchased. Among the supplies was an order for a certain tonnage of fertilizer. European suppliers were invited to supply prices and it proved possible to buy the intended volume from one of these suppliers. Then, just before the order was awarded, a supplier from Turkey made a bid, which was considerably lower in price. The buyer who was involved decided to place the order at the Turkish supplier. However, at the end of the year he was reprimanded by his superior, since the budget was clearly underspent. Now, his superior was to face some problems since, without doubt, his budget for next year would be cut!

Experiences with governmental procurement projects have proved that a lack of purchasing procedures and a non-professional approach to purchasing may lead to significant cost overruns and overruns of time schedules. The European Commission estimates that its member countries annually would save at least 4 per cent of their purchasing budgets, provided that they apply consistent and objective competitive tender procedures in their dealings with suppliers.

EC DIRECTIVES ON PUBLIC PROCUREMENT

The Directives on Public Procurement, which have been issued by the European Commission, have been designed to structure tender procedures for governmental institutions. In fact these are an essential element of the Treaty of Rome, which was founded with the sole purpose of enabling free trade among its member states. As a consequence the Treaty of Rome embodies initial procurement rules which prohibit any discrimination on grounds of nationality and restriction in the choice of supplies or services. However, these arrangements appeared insufficient to establish a single market in the area of public procurement. Differences between national rules in combination with the lack of obligation to open up contracts to Community-wide competition still enabled local contracting bodies to place their orders at local suppliers. Further legislation was therefore needed to ensure that the basic principles as laid down in the Treaty of Rome were being met.

A first attempt was made in 1976 when the European Council adopted a specific directive on coordinating procedures for the award of supply contracts (see Council Directive 77/62/EEC of 21 December 1976). This directive stipulated that government contracts should be advertised to all suppliers in all member states, it banned the use of discriminatory technical specifications and it stipulated that objective criteria would be used for the selection of suppliers. However, this directive did not lead to the anticipated result. Member states still continued their protectionistic and nationalist approach in awarding contracts to suppliers.

Next, in 1988 a new directive was issued to make up for these deficiencies (see Council Directive 88/295/EEC of 22 March 1988). This directive provided more details on transparency of procedures, the definition of technical specifications and information and tendering conditions but did not bring the results that were expected.

Then more detailed guidelines and directives were considered to be required. These were decided in 1993, when the Directive on Public Supply Contracts was approved. This directive brought together in a single text all the rules that were previously dispersed between a number of different instruments.

The objective of all these actions has been to allow public and semi-public bodies to buy goods and services of a better quality and at a better price in order to contribute concretely to economic growth by stimulating competition (EC Brochure, p. 4). At present, the following directives have been adopted:

- Directive 93/36/EEC coordinating procedures for the award of public supply contracts ('Supplies Directive').

- Directive 93/37/EEC coordinating the procedures for the award of public works contracts ('Works Directive').

- Directive 92/50/EEC relating to the coordination of procedures for the award of public service contracts ('Services Directive').

As we will discuss later in this chapter a special directive was created for the utilities sector ('Utilities Directive' i.e. Directive 93/38/EEC), which applies to entities operating in the water, energy, transport and telecommunication sector. As a result the organizations which operate in this sector do not have to meet the often stringent requirements on public procurement which need to be followed by public institutions. Public utilities need to operate under a more relaxed regime.

The aim of these directives is to provide some general rules that need to be applied when awarding contracts to suppliers. Most directives cover the following rules:

- Rules describing which public institutions need to work according to the directives and what type of contracts are considered.

- The types of award procedures or purchasing procedures that need to be followed in a specific situation.

- Rules on how to deal with technical specifications, whereby preference is given to Community standards. The use of discriminatory specifications is strictly forbidden.

- Advertising rules, describing what public institutions must do to communicate their intended purchases to the international supplier community and what time limits need to be respected in the relationship with suppliers.

- Some common rules on how suppliers need to be selected and the criteria that can be used to award the contract in a specific situation.

These directives need to be translated into the national laws and directives of each member state. When national governments are negligent on this matter, however, suppliers may submit claims with direct reference to the EC Directives. Hence, the directives have direct legislative power.

Of course, it should be clear for whom these directives are relevant. Do these relate to all governmental institutions or are some of these excluded? The same holds for the type of purchases. Need these directives be pursued for all types of purchases under any circumstances or are exceptions in some cases possible? The answers to these questions can be found in the directives themselves. The directives are relevant to all contracting authorities which are part of the state, regional or local authorities and bodies governed by public law. In fact, this description covers the entire government. However, the working of the directives is even broader. They are also relevant for private enterprises, who perform public tasks and/or who conduct activities based upon a concession granted by the government. To give an example: although Shell Oil is a private company, it needs to follow the directive for the utilities sector for its oil exploration activities, which it only can perform thanks to the concessions granted by local governments. Hence, all (sub)contracting activities by Shell for these projects should meet the (somewhat enlightened) requirements of the directives on public procurement. Or to give another example: in the health sector it is common, when a new hospital needs to be built, to contract an engineering firm for turn-key delivery. Such an engineering firm in most cases is also a private enterprise. The directives may be relevant in this case in two ways: first, the engineering firm needs to be selected following the directives on public procurement. Second, when the engineering firm starts its activities, selecting the sub-contractors (for civil engineering, installation, construction) will be subject to these directives. In case of any questions or uncertainties about whether or not an organizational entity will be subject to the EC Directives on Public Procurement the EC has listed per member-state the institutions which need to adhere to these.[2]

What types of contracts are covered? In fact the directives relate to all commercial, public supply contracts. In the terminology of the EC: 'all contracts for pecuniary interest concluded in writing involving the purchase, lease, rental or hire purchase, with or without

---

2 See Annex 1 'List of bodies and categories of bodies governed by public law' of the 'Guide to the Community rules on public supply contracts' of the European Commission.

option to buy, of products and services'. Whether a project would fall under the Directive of Supplies, Works or Services depends on the nature of the activities to be performed. If the estimated contract value relates for the largest part to products, the Directive of Supplies needs to be followed. This is relevant since in most cases projects may represent a combination of both contracting for goods and supplies, and for construction and services. To give an example: when contracting for a new integrated computer network for a public entity, it is important to know in advance what the value of the computer hardware and software will be, as well as the value of the value added services (systems development and design, application engineering, installation services). Usually, the preparation that this takes in many cases leads to the insight that design and development of these systems can be better separated from the delivery of hardware and software. As a result, the assignment may be contracted for in two stages: (a) a tender procedure for the appropriate development and design (following the Services Directive), and (b) a separate tender procedure for delivery of the required equipment (following the Supplies Directive).

The value of the contract under consideration determines whether it should be tendered following the directives or not. Contracts which exceed a threshold value of 200 000 euros should follow the EC Procedures for Public Procurement. For this reason it is important to know how the value of a contract is to be calculated. The directives provide ample guidelines for this. In general the expenditure for the next 12 months within a given product category needs to be considered. This is true for contracts with a duration of a year or less. Of course, in some cases public bodies may engage in long-term contracts with suppliers, without indicating when the contract will end. In those cases the contract value needs to be calculated based on a 48-month period. Of course, in practice, many attempts have been made to bypass the workings of the directives. One of the ways to do this is by splitting one large contract into smaller portions, each of which is lower than the indicated threshold. It will not come as a surprise that this is strictly prohibited, and when discovered can lead to severe penalties.

The directives use different threshold values. This is illustrated in Figure 19.1.

Under normal circumstances the EC Directives for Public Procurement will apply. Of course, small, one-time contracts are excluded from their workings, which is fair. This is

FIGURE 19.1   Standard threshold values under the EC public procurement directives.

EC Public Procurement Directive	Standard threshold values (as per 1st January 2004)
Supplies (93/36/EEC)	
– Central government	€154.014,00
– Other government	€236.945,00
Works (93/37/EEC)	€5.923.624,00
Services (92/50/EEC)	
– Central government	€154.014,00
– Other government	€236.945,00
Utilities (93/38/EEC)	
Telecom	
– Supplies/Services	€600.000,00
– Works	€5.000.000,00
Other utilities	
– Supplies/Services	€473.890,00
– Works	€5.923.624,00

because a contracting procedure following these directives needs to be prepared carefully, which takes time and effort. Therefore, this time investment will only pay off in cases of larger projects and contracts (which may cover 80 per cent of the public entities purchasing budget). Smaller purchases and contracts (often 80 per cent of the transactions, covering only 20 per cent of the budget volume) do not need this type of scrutiny. For these types of purchases the public organization may act much more flexibly and swiftly.

In some cases, which are described exhaustively, the directives may not apply. Such is the case when contracting for very specific purposes, such as research and development (where very special materials are required), for defence (when it concerns weapon systems and ammunition), or when materials are required very urgently due to unforeseen circumstances (in case of a disaster or war).

EC PROCUREMENT PROCEDURES

Depending on the situation, the following purchasing procedures are available for awarding public supply contracts:

- The open procedure. In this case the public entity will submit a tender through a contract notice in the Official Journal of the European Communities and/or the Tender Electronic Daily (an electronic database), on which all interested suppliers may submit their proposals. This obviously may lead to a situation where the contracting authority will receive hundreds of proposals from suppliers, who they do not know. In order to prevent these problems the next procedure may be followed.

- The restricted procedure. This is a procedure, where, of the suppliers who have expressed their interest following publication of the contract notice, only those so invited by the contracting authority may submit tenders. The restricted procedure, thus, consists of two steps: during the first step suppliers are prequalified by some kind of screening procedure. During the second step only the suppliers who passed the screening test are invited to the actual tender. Usually, following this procedure takes a lot of time, which the contracting authority may not have. Therefore, an accelerated form of the restricted procedure has been developed, enabling public organizations to move faster, when required. This may be the case when products are required urgently due to unforeseen circumstances. Under this procedure, as under the open procedure, contracts should be awarded without negotiation based upon previously established contract award criteria. This is not true for the next type of procedure.

- Negotiated procedure. This procedure is one where the contracting authority consults the suppliers of its choice and negotiates with them the terms of the contract, e.g. the technical, administrative and financial conditions. Although this procedure has more degree of freedom for the contracting authority, the procurement officer still needs to adhere to some basic requirements. These are that more than one supplier is being solicited (usually a minimum of five potential bidders) and that all suppliers are treated equally (fair treatment). The directives describe exhaustively when this procedure may be applied. This may be the case, for example, when too few suppliers have responded to an earlier tender, where one of the previous purchasing procedures was followed. The negotiated procedure may be conducted with or without prior notification in the Official Journal.

All directives are very specific about the lead times which need to be adhered to when dealing with suppliers. First, in cases of contracts for supplies exceeding 750 000 euros contracting authorities are obliged to publish an indicative notice in the Official Journal in order to enable suppliers to anticipate on the order. Second, all tenders need to be published in advance through a contract notice (see Figure 19.2). A minimum of 52 days (depending on the directive pertaining to the situation) should be granted to potential suppliers from the date of dispatch of the notice for publication in the Official Journal for preparing their bids. Of course, longer lead times may be required when suppliers need to make a visit and have a discussion before being able to submit a bid. Third, contracting authorities are obliged to respond within six days to questions raised by suppliers on the potential contract. Fourth, contracting authorities need to be very explicit beforehand on (a) the criteria to be used for supplier prequalification and (b) the criteria to be used for awarding the contract. With regard to the latter, two possibilities exist: (i) lowest price or (ii) most advantageous offer. In the last case the public entity should indicate what aspects will be considered and should list these criteria (in descending order of importance) in the documentation which is made available to suppliers. Finally, when the contract is awarded, this decision should be made public as well through the Official Journal by

---

FIGURE 19.2   Example of contract notice (open procedure).

1. Name, address, telegraphic address and telephone, telex and fax numbers of the contracting authority.
2. (a) Award procedure chosen;
   (b) Form of the contract for which tenders are being requested.
3. (a) Place of delivery;
   (b) Nature and quantity of the goods to be supplied. CPA reference number;
   (c) Indication of whether the supplier can tender for part of the goods required.
4. Time-limit for delivery, if any.
5. (a) Name and address of the service from which the contract documents and additional documents may be requested;
   (b) Final date for making such requests;
   (c) Where applicable, the amount and terms of payment of the sum to be paid to obtain such documents.
6. (a) Final date for receipt of tenders;
   (b) Address to which they must be sent;
   (c) Language or languages in which they must be drawn up.
7. (a) Persons authorized to be present at the opening of tenders;
   (b) Date, time and place of such opening.
8. Where applicable, any deposits and guarantees required.
9. Main terms concerning financing and payment and/or references to the provisions in which these are contained.
10. Where applicable, the legal form to be taken by the grouping of suppliers to whom the contract is awarded.
11. Information concerning the supplier's own position, and information and formalities necessary for an appraisal of the minimum economic and technical standards required of the supplier.
12. Period during which the tenderer is bound to keep open his tender.
13. Criteria for the award of the contract. Criteria other than that of the lowest price must be mentioned if they do not appear in the contract documents.
14. Where applicable, prohibition on variants.
15. Other information.
16. Date of publication of the indicative notice in the Official Journal or reference to its non-publication.
17. Date of dispatch of the notice.
18. Date of receipt of the notice by the Publications Office.

Source: Guide to the Community rules on public supply contracts (1999), p. 34

indicating the contract price agreed, the winner of the tender and the price range between the lowest and the highest bidder. The contracting authority is obliged to maintain a contract report on every tender project in order to be able to inform the appropriate official bodies.

The scope of the directives which have been discussed so far on supplies, works and services, excludes contracts awarded by so-called 'utilities' (organizations operating in the water, energy, transport and telecommunications sector). For this sector a separate directive has been developed due to political, industrial and legal considerations. In general this sector is subject to an 'enlightened' regime. First, the threshold values are higher than in the previous directives (400 000 euros in case of supply and services contracts; for the telecommunications sector this value is 600 000 euros). Second, the contracting entities have a free choice between the open, restricted and negotiated procedures.

GOVERNMENT PROCUREMENT AGREEMENT

For buyers working for governmental institutions there are additional guidelines to the EC Directives on Public Procurement that may influence their work. Traditionally, one of the other guidelines they have to reckon with has been GATT (General Agreement on Trade and Tariffs). This agreement stipulated that all institutions belonging to the central government should open up their purchasing contracts to all suppliers of all member states. The GATT agreement has been replaced since 1996 by the Governmental Procurement Agreement (GPA), which was agreed among the EC member states, USA, Japan, Canada, Switzerland, Israel and South Korea and which proves to be more ambitious. The GPA also covers supplies, works and services. Apart from this, it covers contracts awarded by public authorities at regional and local level. Finally, it covers the ports, water, electricity and urban transport sectors. It is expected that this new arrangement will open up government contracts to international bidding worth around 350 billion euros every year.

The GPA is built upon the general principles of national treatment, non-discrimination and transparency and follows the EC Directives closely. Just like these directives the GPA provides a system of threshold values in order to trigger competitive tendering among suppliers. On other aspects the GPA follows the EC Directives closely and therefore is not further elaborated on here.

CONSEQUENCES FOR PROCUREMENT PROFESSIONALS

The previous sections have described how the directives provide public organizations in any member state with objective guidelines on how to proceed in their contractual relationships with suppliers. The purchasing procedures described are congruent with the purchasing process model which was presented in Chapters 1 and 3.

- First of all, they support the idea of preventing customers being locked into supplier relationships by favoring objective and functional product specifications. Any description of specifications which may lead to a captive supplier relationship should be prevented. Therefore the EC favors and stimulates the use of uniform technical standards.

- Second, a large part of the EC Directives is devoted to describing how to arrive at an objective supplier selection. It favors stimulating competition among suppliers by adopting both a uniform supplier prequalification procedure and a contract award procedure.

- Third, the directives favor that contracts with suppliers are conducted in writing, providing in this way an objective basis for the evaluation of the supplier's performance.

- Fourth, when the decision has been made to award the contract, all parties must officially be informed about its outcome. This certainly contributes to a transparency of supplier markets.

In order to facilitate communication between government procurement officers and suppliers, the EC has set up the SIMAP-initiative. SIMAP stimulates electronic data transfer between parties and provides up-to-date information on the EC Public Procurement Directives (see Memo 19.2)

In general, the Directives on Public Procurement have met large resistance, from governmental officials both inside and outside purchasing. Most complaints relate to the lack of flexibility, the level of detail, the time-frames which need to be adhered to, the fact that partnership relationships are not particularly fostered and stimulated through these directives and the degree of administration which is involved in order to provide an adequate tracing and tracking of the different stages of the purchasing process.

It is clear that working with the directives effectively requires thorough planning and preparation. First, the contracting authority needs to have a good understanding of its purchasing order specifications, which in general will require ample discussions among the users, budget holders, accounting people and purchasing professionals. Furthermore, based upon the specification to be used for supplier selection and award of the contract the requirements need to be laid down. Based upon this information, it needs to be decided what purchasing procedure will need to be pursued. It should be realized that, when a purchasing procedure actually has started, no changes whatsoever can be made during the process. In case, in hindsight, changes are deemed necessary in, for instance, the technical specifications, the procedure should be officially stopped. A new procedure might be started based upon the new specification. The same holds when the contracting entity wants to change the criteria to be used for supplier qualification or award of the contract. The idea behind this is 'fair play' i.e. providing every supplier with the same chance to quote for the contract.

MEMO 19.2 FACILITATING ELECTRONIC DATA TRANSFER IN PUBLIC PROCUREMENT

Important changes which are taking place in the field of information and telecommunication technology open new opportunities to improve the efficiency of the whole public procurement process. Therefore the European Commission has launched the project SIMAP (Système d'information pour les marchés publics) (www.simap.eu.int) which brings EU-wide electronic public procurement a lot closer.

SIMAP will create a more open procurement market by collecting, processing and diffusing accurate and up-to date information on tender opportunities and contracts awarded, plus other information already available in the member states such as list of standards, contact points, potential sub-contractors, electronic catalogs, etc. In future developments, SIMAP will provide the means for enabling a paperless procurement process by supporting the creation and electronic exchange of tender documentation, bids, invoices, payments orders and other information exchanged between procurers and suppliers.

Source: European Procurement Brochure (2003).

In conclusion the EC Directives on Public Procurement resemble sound purchasing principles. However, at the same time it should be acknowledged that the political climates and cultures of most governmental institutions do not foster purchasing professionalism. In general the reward system within governmental organizations does not support a purchasing approach based upon 'getting the best value for money' or 'lowest total cost of ownership'. A coherent control system to ascertain that the directives are being followed by the member states is not present. These factors may explain why implementation of these directives in most countries is so troublesome and adoption so slow. According to recent research, transparency rates which indicate the degree of public procurement published as a percentage of estimated total procurement value, differ greatly among EU countries. Greece, Spain and the UK have the highest transparency rates with 46, 24 and 21 per cent; at the other end of the scale are Germany, The Netherlands and Luxembourg with a mere 7.5, 8.9 and 13.3 per cent. The same research showed that application of the EC Directives actually pays off: governmental institutions report price reductions as a result of these directives of around 30 per cent due to cross border competition.[3]

Given these positive results the European Commission decided to review and modernise the Public Procurement Directives and to adapt them to modern administrative needs. For example, by facilitating electronic procurement and, for complex contracts, by introducing more scope for dialog between contracting authorities and tenderers in order to determine contract conditions. Next the threshold amounts will be increased and it will be possible to award contracts not only based upon price but also upon social and environmental criteria. The present directives will be consolidated into one general directive for the procurement of goods, works and services. A special directive is foreseen for procurement by the utilities sector. These two new directives will replace the current four directives and need to be written into national law before 2007 latest.

SUMMARY

Public procurement represents an important area within European economies. On average member states of the EC spend 12 per cent of their gross domestic product on contracts with suppliers. This massive amount of money is spent on a large variety of products, projects and services by an even larger variety of organizations.

Central to the idea of the EC is free competition and free trade among its member states. This has, as seen earlier, considerable consequences for the initial purchasing processes within the governmental institutions and organizations.

This chapter has presented some major differences that exist between purchasing for private enterprise and public procurement. First, purchasing decision making is often intertwined with political objectives and issues. Second, the budget system used by the government does not provide sufficient incentive for budget holders to actively strive for the best value for money. Usually, budgets should be spent in the year they are assigned. Building up financial reserves and shifting these to the next year is difficult. This explains the spending fever that may be observed at the end of each financial year. Third, most countries still favor a nationalist and protectionistic approach when it comes to placing orders with suppliers. In most cases local suppliers, for a variety of reasons, are favored.

The EC Directives try to foster a uniform and consistent approach to purchasing decision making within the EC countries. Basic underlying principles are non-discrimination, fair play, transparency of procedures and open communication to the international supplier

---

3 *Ibid.* IP/04/149, p. 15.

community. For most governmental institutions three directives are most relevant: the Supplies Directive, the Services Directive and the Works Directive. In some cases the directives may also be relevant for semi-governmental and private enterprise. For organizations which operate in the utilities sector, the Utilities Directive will provide guidance in their dealings with suppliers. The latter are more free in their choice of the three basic purchasing procedures: the open procedure, the restricted procedure and the negotiated procedure.

Apart from these directives governmental buyers need to adhere to the arrangements made within the Government Procurement Agreement, which ties in with other countries such as the USA, Canada and Japan.

Although the EC regulations on public procurement reflect sound purchasing theory and practices, it will be difficult to implement them. This is due to their contextual complexity. Apart from a lack of control by the EC itself, various factors explain why implementation of these directives in most countries is so troublesome and adoption so slow.

ASSIGNMENTS

19.1 Why would public entities often favor local suppliers? What political objectives could be served by such behavior? Discuss.

19.2 Describe the basic EC Directives on Public Procurement. List the key elements of each of them. Make use of available electronic EC-databases.

19.3 A municipality within the EC wants to renew its contract for copiers. In order to prevent the contract from surpassing the threshold value it pursues decentralized purchasing: each department needs to take care of its own needs. What is your opinion about this way of working? Discuss.

19.4 When reviewing its car lease contract the police department of a large city thinks about what purchasing procedure to follow. Discuss each purchasing procedure and decide what procedure would be most appropriate.

19.5 Governmental institutions may award contracts based upon two principles: (1) lowest price or (2) most advantageous offer. What criteria might be used to award a contract based upon the latter contract award principle?

BIBLIOGRAPHY

Aljian, G.W. (1984) *Purchasing Handbook*, New York: McGraw-Hill.

Allen, S. and Chandrashekar, A. (2000) 'Outsourcing services: the contract is just the beginning', *Business Horizons* (43) March-April: 25–34.

Anderson, J. and Narus, J. (1998*) Business Market Management, Understanding, Creating and Delivering Value*, New Jersey: Prentice Hall.

Arnold, U. (2000) 'New dimensions of outsourcing: a combination of transaction cost economics and the core competence concept', *European Journal of Purchasing & Supply Management*, 6: 23–29.

Aston, M. (1989) 'Method, trade-offs and DPP', *Focus*, 8(8).

Axelsson, B. and Wynstra, J.Y.F. (2002) *Buying Business Services*, Chichester: Wiley.

Barreyre, P.Y. (1976) 'La fonction approvisionnement dans la strategie de l'entreprise', *Revue Francais de Gestion*, Sept–Oct: 61–67.

Brand, G. (1968) *How British Industry Buys*, London: Hutchinson.

Brandes, H., Lilliecreutz, J. and Brege, S. (1997) 'Outsourcing – success or failure?', *European Journal of Purchasing & Supply Management*, 3(2): 63–75.

Broersma, H. (1991) *Co-makership: Cooperation Between Producer and Supplier*, Groningen: Wolterns Noordhoff (Dutch text).

Business Week (1991) 'The racy Viper is already a winner for Chrysler', *Business Week*, November 4.

Christopher, M. (1992) *Logistics and Supply Chain Management*, London: Pitman.

Clayton, R.F. (1984) Effective Negotiations Seminar, Veldhoven, 1983–1985.

Cooper, M.C. and Ellram, L.M. (1993) 'Characteristics of supply chain management and the implications for purchasing and logistics strategy', *The International Journal of Logistics Management*, 4(2): 13–24.

Corey, E.R. (1978) *Procurement Management: Strategy, Organization and Decisionmaking*, Boston: CBI Publishing Company.

Corsten, D. and Zagler, M. (2000) 'Purchasing consortia and Internet technology', in Erridge, A., Fee. R. and McIlroy, J. (2001) *Best Practice Procurement: Public and Private Sector Perspectives,* ch. 19, pp. 184–96. London: Gower.

Croom, S.R. (2000) 'The strategic contribution of e-commerce to MRO procurement', in Erridge, A., Fee, R. and McIlroy, J. (2001*), Best Practice Procurement: Public and Private Sector Perspectives*, ch. 16, pp. 160–68. London: Gower.

Crosby, P.B. (1984) *Quality without Tears*, New York: McGraw-Hill.

Deckelman, B. (1998) 'Strategic outsourcing: the contractual perspective', May, www.outsourcing-journal.com

Dobler, D., Lee, D. and Burt, D. (1990) *Purchasing and Materials Management*, 5th edn, New York: McGraw-Hill.

DTI (1989) *Getting the Best From Your Suppliers*, London: DTI.

DTI (1994) 'A review of the relationships between vehicle manufacturers and suppliers'. Report of the DTI/SMMT Automotive Components Supplier Initiative Stage Two, p. 28.

Dyer, J. (1996) 'How Chrysler created an American Keiretsu', *Harvard Business Review*, July–August: 42–91.

Eck, A. van and de Weerd, H. (1981) 'Introduction to purchasing market research'(internal paper), Philips Electronics Cy (Dutch text).

Eck, A. van, de Weerd, H. and van Weele, A.J. (1981) 'De beoordeling van de inkoopprijs: een conceptuele benadering', *Bedrijfskunde*, 52(3): 277–88 (Dutch text).

Ellram, L. and Billington, C. (2001) 'Purchasing leverage considerations in the outsourcing decision', *European Journal of Purchasing & Supply Management*, 7: 15–22.

Ellram, L. and Hendrick, Th. (1993) *Strategic Supplier Partnering: an International Study*, PX: Arizona: Center for Advanced Purchasing.

Eng, T.Y. (2003) 'The role of e-marketplaces in supply chain management', *Industrial Marketing Management*, (33): 97–105.

European Commission (1999a) The Rules Governing the Procedure in the Award of Public Procurement Contracts, Brussels.

European Commission, (1999b) Guide to the Community Rules on Public Supply Contracts, Brussels.

Faes, W. and de Rijcke, J.G. (1982) 'Management in het inkoopgebeuren: noodzakelijk en mogelijk', *Economisch en Sociaal Tijdschrift*, (4): 419–41 (Dutch text).

Faes, W. and de Weerd, H. (1983) 'Research is a must for purchasing', *Purchasing and Supply Management*, Sept: 36–40.

Farmer, D.H. (1974) 'Training procurement personnel in negotiating skills', *Journal of Purchasing and Materials Management*, Feb: 00–00.

Fearon, H. (1976) *Purchasing Research: Concepts and Current Practice*, New York: American Management Association.

Fearon, H.E. and Leenders, M.R. (1995) 'Purchasing's organisational role and responsibilities', Center for Advanced Purchasing Studies, Phoenix, Arizona.

Fisher, L. (1970) *Industrial Marketing: an Analytical Approach to Planning and Execution*, 2nd edn, London: Business Books.

Fisher, M.L. (1997) 'What is the right supply chain for your product?', *Harvard Business Review*, March–April: 105–16.

Floor, J.M.G. and Schraders, J.G. (1983) *Account Management en Nieuwe Samenwerkingsvorm tussen Fabrikant en Handel*, Samsom: Alphen a/d Rijn. (Dutch text).

Foote, M. and Krishnamurthi S. (2001) 'Forecasting using data warehousing model: Walmart's experience', *The Journal of Business Forecasting Methods & Systems* (Fall), 20(3): 13.

Ford, D. (1980) 'Development of buyer–seller relationships in industrial markets', *European Journal of Marketing*, 14(5/6): 339–53.

Gartner, Inc. (2003) 'Gartner says outsourcing grows in declining European IT services market', press release 28 April 2003, Egham, UK.

Gilley, K.M. and Rasheed, A. (2000) 'Making more by doing less: an analysis of outsourcing and its effect on firm performance', *Journal of Management*, 26(4): 763–90.

Giunipero, L.C. and Monczka, R.M. (1990) 'Organisational approaches to managing international sourcing', *International Journal of Physical Distribution and Logistics Management*, (4): 3–12.

Graw, L.H. and Maples, D.M. (1994), *Service Purchasing: What Every Buyer Should Know*, New York: Van Nostrand Reinhold.

Greco, J. (1997) 'Outsourcing: the new partnership', *Journal of Business Strategy*, July-August, 48–54.

Grönroos, C. (2000) *Service Management and Marketing*, Chichester:

Hakansson, H. (1982) *International Marketing and Purchasing of Industrial Goods*, New York: John Wiley.

Hakansson, H. and Wootz, B. (1979) 'A framework of industrial buying and selling', *Industrial Marketing Management*, 8: 28–39.

Hakansson, H., Johansson, J. and Wootz, B. (1977) 'Influence tactics in buyer–seller processes', *Industrial Marketing Management*, 5: 319–32.

Hamel, G. and Prahalad, C.K. (1994) *Competing for the Future*, Boston: Harvard Business School Press.

Hammer, M. and Champy, J. (1993) *Reengineering the Corporation*, New York: HarperCollins.

Hart, H.W.V. van der (1984) *Industrial Buying Behaviour in Purchasing Management*, Samsom Bedrijfsin formatie: Alphen a/d Rijn.

Hoekstra, Sj. and Romme, J.H.J.M. (eds) (1985) *Op weg naar integrale logistieke strucuren*, Deventer: Kluwer (Dutch text).

IBM and Crosby, P.B. (1980) First Time Right, IBM.

Ittner, C.D., Larcker, D.F., Nagar, V. and Rajan, M.V. (1999) 'Supplier selection, monitoring practices and firm performance', *Journal of Accounting and Public Policy,* (18): 187–286.

Jurg, P. (1997) 'Contract forms in commercial relationships', in van Weele, A.J. and van der Hart, H.W.C. (eds), *Dynamics in Commercial Relationships*, Utrecht: F&G Publishing (Dutch text).

Kalakota, R. and Robinson, M. (2001), *E-Business 2.0, Roadmap for success*, Reading, MA: Addison Wesley.

Kaplan, S. and Sawhney, M. (2000), 'E-hubs: the new b2b-marketplaces', *Harvard Business Review*, May-June: 107–103.

Karass, C.L. (1970) *The Negotiating Game, How to Get What You Want*, New York: Thomas Y. Crowell Company.

Karass, C.L. (1977) *Give and Take, The Complete Guide to Negotiating Strategies and Tactics*, New York: Thomas Y. Crowell Company.

Karass, C.L. (1979) *How to Fight a Price Increase*, Los Angeles: Karass International.

Keough, M. (1993) 'Buying your way to the top', *McKinsey Quarterly*, 3: 41–62.

Kluge, J.N. (1996) Simply Superior Sourcing, 5th Annual IPSERA Conference, Eindhoven, The Netherlands, April.

Kotler, P. (1997) *Marketing Management: Analysis, Planning, Implementation and Control*, 9th edn, Upper Saddle River: Prentice-Hall.

Kotler, P. and Bloom, P.N. (1984) *Marketing Professional Services*, Englewood Cliffs, NJ: Prentice-Hall.

Kowalski, Th. (1993) Purchasing portfolio management. Keynote presentation at 25th International Purchasing and Supply Management Conference, Management Centre Europe, London.

Kraljic, P. (1983) 'Purchasing must become supply management', *Harvard Business Review*, Sept/Oct: 109–17.

Kudrna, D.A. (1975) *Purchasing Manager's Decision Making Handbook*, Boston: Cahners Books.

Kurnia, S., Swatman, P.M.C. and Schauder, D. (2002) Efficient consumer response: a preliminary comparison of US and European experiences. 11th International Conference on Electronic Commerce, Bled, Slovenia, June 8–10, pp. 126–43.

Lamming, R. (1993) *Beyond Partnership, Strategies for Innovation and Lean Supply*, Hampstead: Prentice-Hall.

Laseter, T.M. (1998) Balanced Sourcing: Cooperation and Competition in Supplier Relationships, SF: Jossey-Bass Publishers.

Leenders, M.R., Fearon, H.E. and England, W.B. (1989) *Purchasing and Materials Management*, Homewood, IL: Dow Jones Irwin.

Lehmann, D.R. and O'Shaughnessy J. (1974) 'Different industrial products', *Journal of Marketing*, April: 36–42.

Lehmann, D.R. and O'Shaughnessy, J. (1984) 'Difference in attitude importance for different industrial products', *Journal of Marketing,* April: 00–00.

Lysons, K. (1996) *Purchasing*, London: Pitman Publishing.

Margretta, J. (1998) 'The power of virtual integration: an interview with Dell Computer's Michael Dell', *Harvard Business Review*, March-April: 73–84.

Margretta, J. (1998a) 'Fast, global and entrepreneurial: supply chain management Hong Kong style', *Harvard Business Review*, September-October.

Marx, William B. (1996) 'Purchasing's new muscle', in *Strategic Purchasing: Sourcing for the Bottom Line*, The Conference Board, pp. 9–10.

Matthijssens, P. and de Rijcke, J. (1982) 'Unieke dimensies van industrie le marketing', *Tijdschrift voor Marketing*, July/August: 3–10.

McCarthy, T.M. and Golicic, S.L. (2002) 'Implementing collaborative forecasting to improve supply chain performance'. *International Journal of Physical Distribution & Logistics Management*, 32(6): 431–54.

McKinnon, F.J. (1996) The development of retail logistics in the UK. Edinburgh: School of Management, Heriot-Watt University.

McQuiston, D.H. (2001) 'A conceptual model for building and maintaining relationships between manufacturers'representatives and their principals. *Industrial Marketing Management*, 30: 165–81.

Michael F. Corbett & Associates Ltd. (2002) Highlights from the 1999 Outsourcing Trends Study. www.firmbuilder.com

Miller, J.G. and Gilmour, P. (1979) 'Materials managers: who needs them?'*Harvard Business Review*, July-August: 143–53.

Moffat, P.K., Bettinger, D.E., Howarth, M.A. and Casavant, A. (1993) 'Quality Assurance', in Fearon, H.E., Dobler, D.W. and Killen, K.H., *The Purchasing Handbook*, ch. 13, pp. 403–36. New York: McGraw-Hill.

Momme, J. and Hvolby, H-H. (2002) An outsourcing framework: action research in the heavy industry sector. *European Journal of Purchasing and Supply Management*, 8: 185–96.

Monczka, R,M. (1999) 'What is so exciting about purchasing?'*Quality Matters*, Philips Electronics, January, 1994, pp. 16–17.

Monczka, R.M. and Trent, R.J. (1991) 'Global sourcing: a development approach', *International Journal of Purchasing and Materials Management*, 27(2): 2–8.

Monczka, R.M. and Trent, R.J. (1992) 'Worldwide sourcing: assessment and execution', *International Journal of Purchasing and Materials Management*, 28(4): 9–19.

Murphy, E.E. (1998) 'At Hershey Foods purchasing restructures to tap full supply value', *Purchasing*, June 4 (www.purchasing.com).

Nannery, M. (2002) 'Dropping the "R" ', *Chain Store Age*, (May) 78(5): 162.

NEVI (2000) Working group outsourcing. CD-ROM.

Ohmae, K. (1994) Competitive advantage in the information age, Northern Telecom, Annual Report.

Peters, T. (1992) *Liberation Management*.

Philips Electronics (1999) 'Purchasing becoming supply chain management', *Quality Matters*, 94: January.

Porter, M.A. (1980) *Competitive Strategy, Techniques for Analyzing Industries and Competitors*, New York: The Free Press..

Porter, M.E. (1985) *Competitive Advantage*, New York: The Free Press.

Quinn, J.B. (1992) *Intelligent Enterprise*, New York: The Free Press.

Quinn, J.B. (1999) 'Strategic outsourcing: leveraging knowledge capabilities', *Sloan Management Review*, Summer: 9–21.

Quinn, J.B. and Hilmer, F.G. (1994) 'Strategic outsourcing', *Sloan Management Review*, 36 (Summer), 43–55.

Rietveld, G. (1995) *Facilitair Inkoop Management*, Schoonhoven: Academic Service (Dutch text).

Robinson, P.J., Faris, Ch. W. and Wind, Y. (1967) *Industrial Buying and Creative Marketing*, Boston: Allyn & Bacon.

Rozemeijer, F.A. and van Weele, A.J. (2003) 'Creating corporate advantage through purchasing: a contingency model', *The Journal of Supply Chain Management*, Winter: 4–13.

Rust, R.T., Zahorik, A.J. and Keiningham, T.L. (1996) *Service Marketing*, New York: HarperCollins.

Schmidt, R.C. (1986) 'Logistiek Management als instrument voor klantgerich opereren', *Tijdschrift financieel management*, (4): 59–66 (Dutch text).

Sheth, J.N. (1973) 'A model of industrial buyer behaviour', *Journal of Marketing*, Oct.: 50–4.

Stekelenborg, R. van (1997) 'Purchasing information systems'(PhD diss.), Eindhoven: Eindhoven University of Technology.

Stevens, G.C. (1989) 'Integrating the supply chain', *International Journal of Physical Distribution and Materials Management*, 19(8), 3–8.

Tarlo Lyons (2001) Outsourcing survey 2001. www.tarlolyons.com

The Conference Board (1996) Strategic Purchasing: Sourcing for the Bottom-line, ???: New York.

The Outsourcing Institute (1998) Top ten outsourcing survey. www.outsourcing.com

The Outsourcing Institute (2000) Effectively managing the outsourcing relation. www.outsourcing.com

The Outsourcing Institute/Dun & Bradstreet (2000) The outsourcing index 2000. www.out-sourcing.com

Treacy, M. and Wiersema, F. (1995) *The Discipline of Market Leaders*, Reading, MA: Addison-Wesley.

Van der Ster, W. (1993) *Marketing and Retail*, 5th edn, Groningen: Wolters Noordhoff (Dutch text).

Van Echtelt, F.E.A. (2004) 'New product development: shifting suppliers into gear'(PhD diss.), Eindhoven Center for Innovation Studies (ECIS) Eindhoven University of Technology.

Van Goor, A. (1998) *Partnership through Supply Chain Logistics*, Samsom: Alphen a/d Rijn (Dutch text).

Vanhorick, J.F. (1986) 'Commodity Markets as a Tool for Buying Raw Materials', *Purchasing Handbook*, Samsom: Alphen a/d Rijn (Dutch text).

Venkatesan, R. (1992) 'Strategic sourcing: to make or not to make', *Harvard Business Review*, Nov-Dec: 98–107.

Vigoros, M. (1998) 'Sourcing info and supplier ratings combined on "Net"', *Purchasing*, (Nov), 5: 00–00.

Vigoros, M. (1999) 'Electronic marketplaces save buyers time and money', *Purchasing*, (Jan), 14: 00–00.

Vollman, Th.E., Berry, W.E. and Whybark, D.C. (1984*), Manufacturing Planning and Control Systems*, Homewood, IL: Dow Jones Irwin.

Von Hippel, E.R. (1978) 'Successful industrial products from customer ideas', *Journal of Marketing*, Jan: 39–49.

Webster, F.E. and Wind, Y. (1972) *Organizational Buying Behaviour*, Englewood Cliffs: NJ: Prentice-Hall.

Weele, A.J. van (1984a) 'Purchasing Performance Measurement and Evaluation', *Journal of Purchasing and Materials Management*, Fall: 16–22.

Weele, A.J. van (1984b) *Purchasing Control, Performance Measurement and Evaluation of the Industrial Purchasing Function*, Groningen: Wolters-Noordhoff.

Weele, A.J. van (1987) 'Perspective on purchasing', *International Management Development Review 1987*, Management Centre Europe, Belgium, Brussels pp. 383–8.

Weele, A.J. van (1990) 'Volvo Car BV, towards "zero-defects" with suppliers (working paper), Eindhoven: Eindhoven University of Technology (Dutch text).

Weele, A.J. van (1990) *Buying Projects*, The Hague: Dutch Association of Purchasing Management (Dutch text).

Weele, A.J. van (1991) 'Purchasing as a service center: the purchasing audit as a management tool', in W.F.G. Mastenbroek (ed.), *Managing Quality in the Service Sector*, Oxford: Blackwell.

Weele, A.J. van (1994) *Inkoop in Strategisch Perspectief: Analyse, Planning en Praktijk*, Samsom Bedrijfsinformatie: Alphen a/d Rijn.

Weele, A.J. van and Gelderman, C. (1998) *Purchasing Management*, Heerlen Open University (Dutch text).

Weele, A.J. van and Rozemeijer F.A. (1998) 'Mirror, mirror on the wall . . . Let suppliers guide you towards improvement', in Capaldo, G. (ed.), *Supply Management*, ch. 16, pp. 337–55, Napoli: Edizione Scientifiche Italiane.

Weele, A.J. van and Rozemeijer, F.A. (1996) 'Revolution in purchasing: building competitive power through pro-active purchasing', *European Journal of Purchasing and Supply Management*, 2(4): 153–60.

Weele, A.J. van and Rozemeijer, F.A. (1996) *Revolution in Purchasing*, Philips Electronics/Eindhoven University of Technology, 142 pp.

Weele, A.J. van and Rozemeijer, F.A. (1996) *Revolution in Purchasing: Building Competitive Power Through Pro-Active Purchasing*, Philips Electronics/Eindhoven University of Technology (limited edition).

Weele, A.J. van and Rozemeijer, F.A. (1998a) Getting organised for purchasing and supply management in the information age: towards the virtual purchasing organisation? Proceedings of the Second Worldwide Research Symposium on Purchasing and Supply Management, London, 1–3 April 1998, pp. 421–31.

Weele, A.J. van and Rozemeijer, F.A. (1999),'Getting organised for purchasing and supply management in the information age: towards the virtual purchasing organisation', in Hahn, D. and Kaufmann, L. *Handbuch Industrielles Beschaffungsmanagement*, Wiesbaden: Gabler.

Weele, A.J. van and Rozemeijer, F.A. (2000) 'The role of power in partnership relationships: an empirical investigation in the current body of knowledge', in Erridge, A. (et al.) *Best Practice Procurement: Public and Private Sector Perspectives*, ch. 10, pp. 90–9. London: Gower.

Weele, A.J. van and van der Horst, H.J. (1992) *Public Procurement in European Perspective*, Deventer: Kluwer Bedrijfswetenschappen (Dutch text).

Weele, A.J. van and van der Vossen, G.J. (1998) 'Purchasing DuPont analysis of some major Dutch companies', Holland Consulting Group, Research report.

Weele, A.J. van and van Hespen, J. (1986) *Professioneel Inkopend Nederland, Deelrapport 1: Inkoopfunktie in Industrie le Ondernemingen*, Deventer: Kluwer (Dutch text).

Weele, A.J. van, Faes, W. and de Rijcke, J.G. (1984) *Developments in Purchasing in the Eighties*, The Hague: Dutch Association of Purchasing Management.

Weele, A.J. van, Rozemeijer, F.A. and Rietveld, G. (1998) Professionalising purchasing: towards a purchasing development model, IPSERA Conference Proceedings 1998, London, pp. 515–23.

Weele, A.J. van. and Veth, A.F.L. (2001) 'Concurreren in het e-Tijdperk: nu of nooit', *Holland Management Review*, March-April: 64–71 (Dutch text).

Wetzels, M.G.M., de Ruyter, J.C. and Lemmink. J.G.A.M. (1999) 'Antecedents and consequences of service quality in business-to-business services', pp. 343–56, in T. Swartz and D. Iacobucci (eds), *Handbook Services Marketing and Management*.

Wijnstra, F.Y.W. (1999) 'Purchasing involvement in new product development' doctorate thesis), Eindhoven: Eindhoven University of Technology.

Wijnstra, F.Y.W. and Ten Pierick, E. (1999) A portfolio-approach for supplier involvement in product development: differentiating lean and rich interfaces, Proceedings of the 8th IPSERA Conference, 28–31 March 1999, Belfast–Dublin, pp. 815–26.

Wijnstra, J.Y.F. (1998) 'Purchasing involvement in new product development' (PhD diss.), Eindhoven Center for Innovation Studies (ECIS), Eindhoven University of Technology.

Wijnstra, J.Y.F. (1998) 'The role of purchasing in product innovation' (PhD thesis), Eindhoven: Eindhoven University of Technology, 285 pp.

Williamson, O.E. (1983) Markets and Hierarchies: Analysis and Antitrust Implications: A Study in the Economics of Internal Organization, London: Collier Macmillan.

Williamson, O.E. (1985) *The Economic Institutions of Capitalism*. New York: Free Press.

Womack, J.P., Jones, D.T. and Roos, D. (1990) *The Machine That Changed the World*, New York: Macmillan.

INDEX

Bold numbers denote figures and *italic* numbers denote tables.